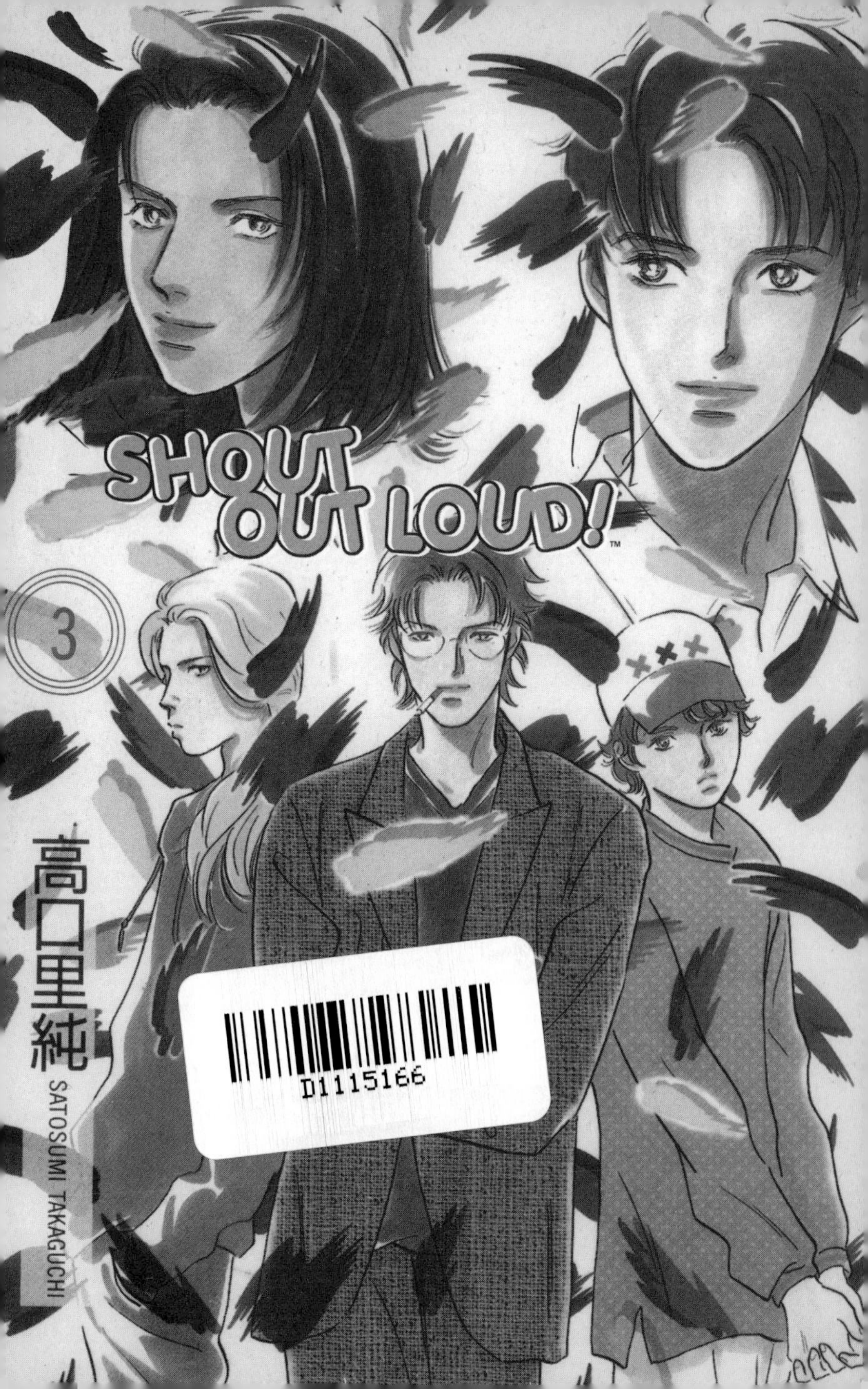
SHOUT OUT LOUD!™
3
高口里純
SATOSUMI TAKAGUCHI

CONTENTS

In order to maintain as much authenticity as possible,
Shout Out Loud retains the original Japanese name order for
all names.
Thus family name comes first, followed by the given name.
The series will also retain honorifics.

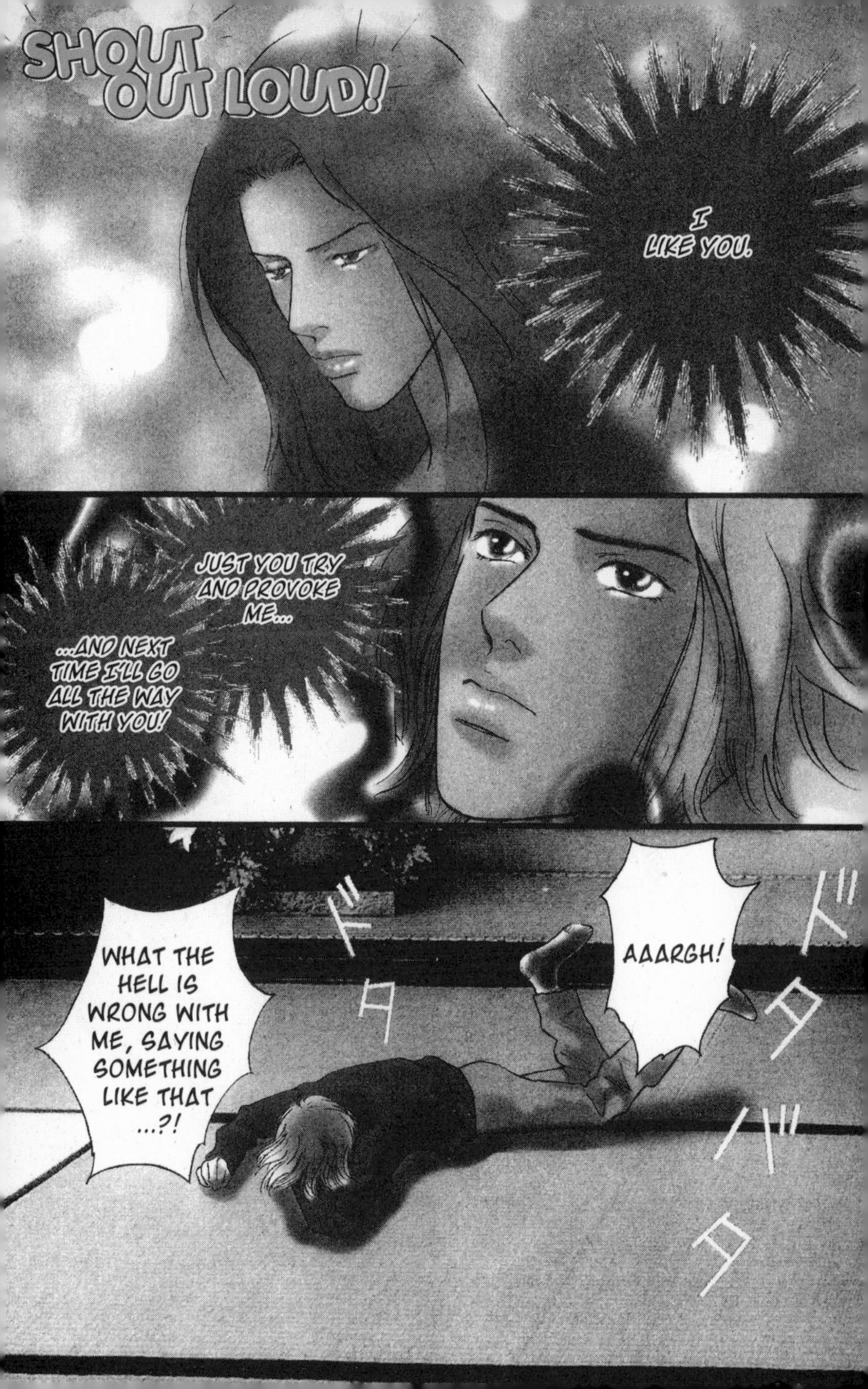
SHOUT OUT LOUD!
I LIKE YOU.
JUST YOU TRY AND PROVOKE ME...
...AND NEXT TIME I'LL GO ALL THE WAY WITH YOU!
AAARGH!
ドタバタ
ドタ
WHAT THE HELL IS WRONG WITH ME, SAYING SOMETHING LIKE THAT ...?!

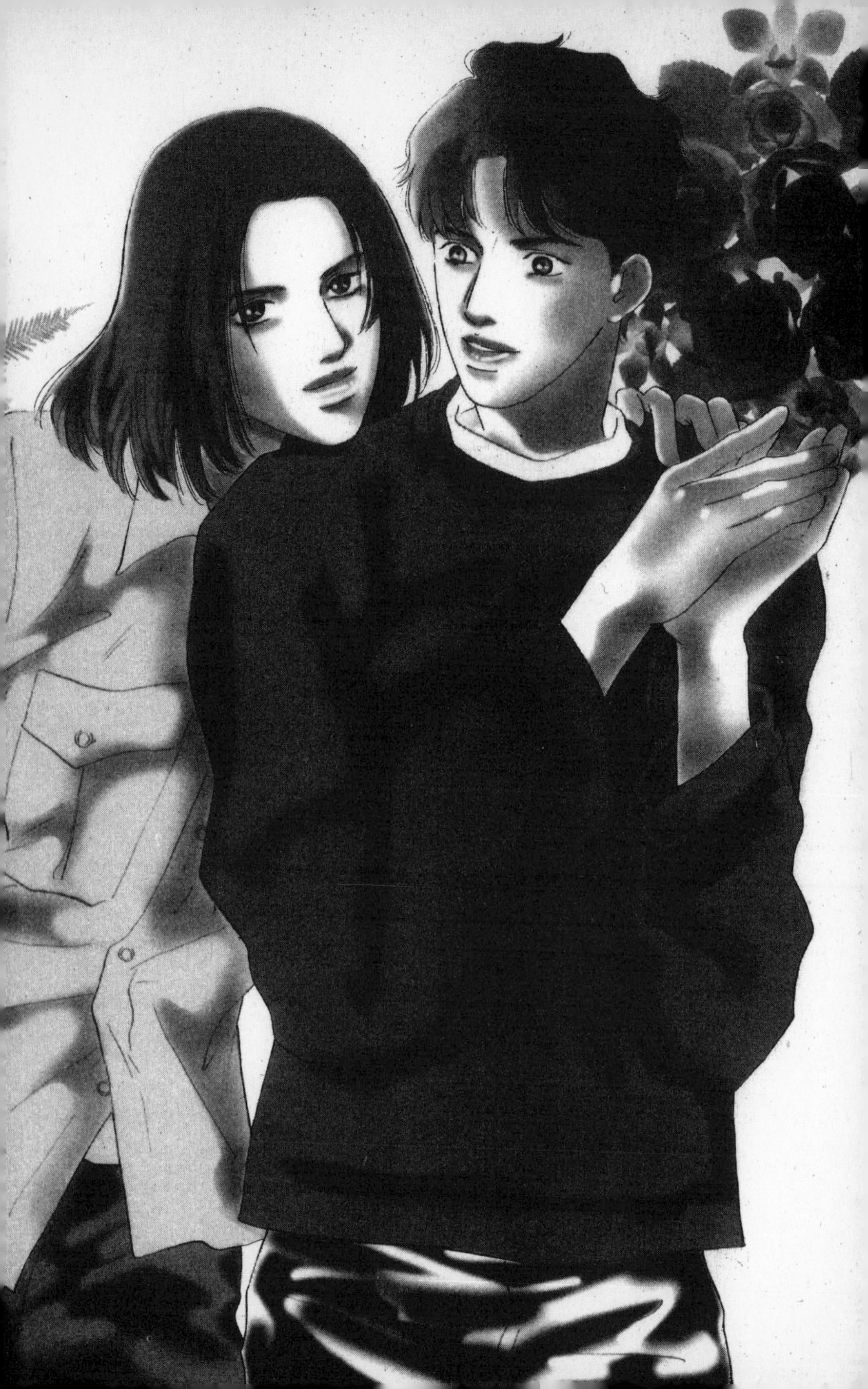

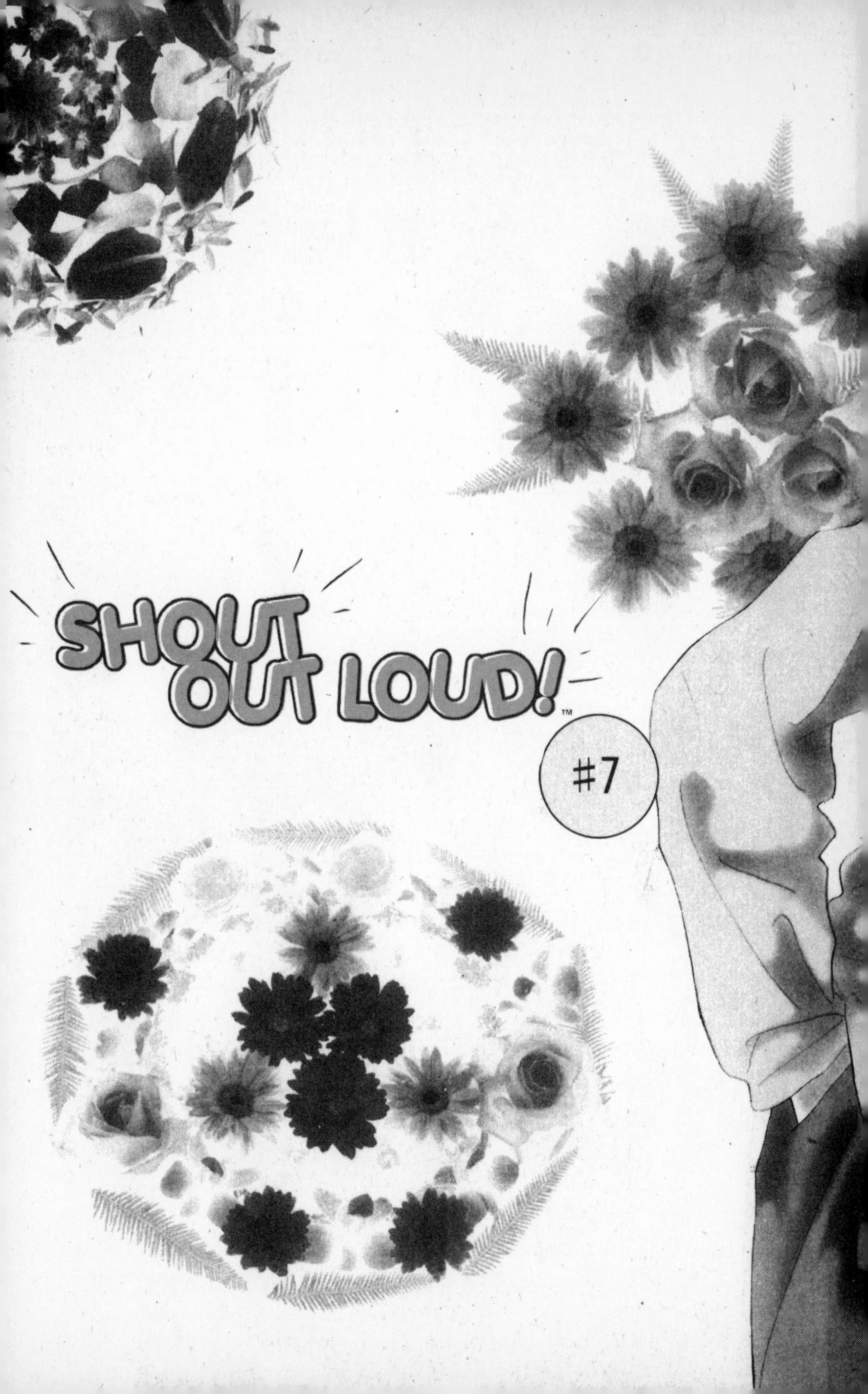
SHOUT OUT LOUD!™
#7

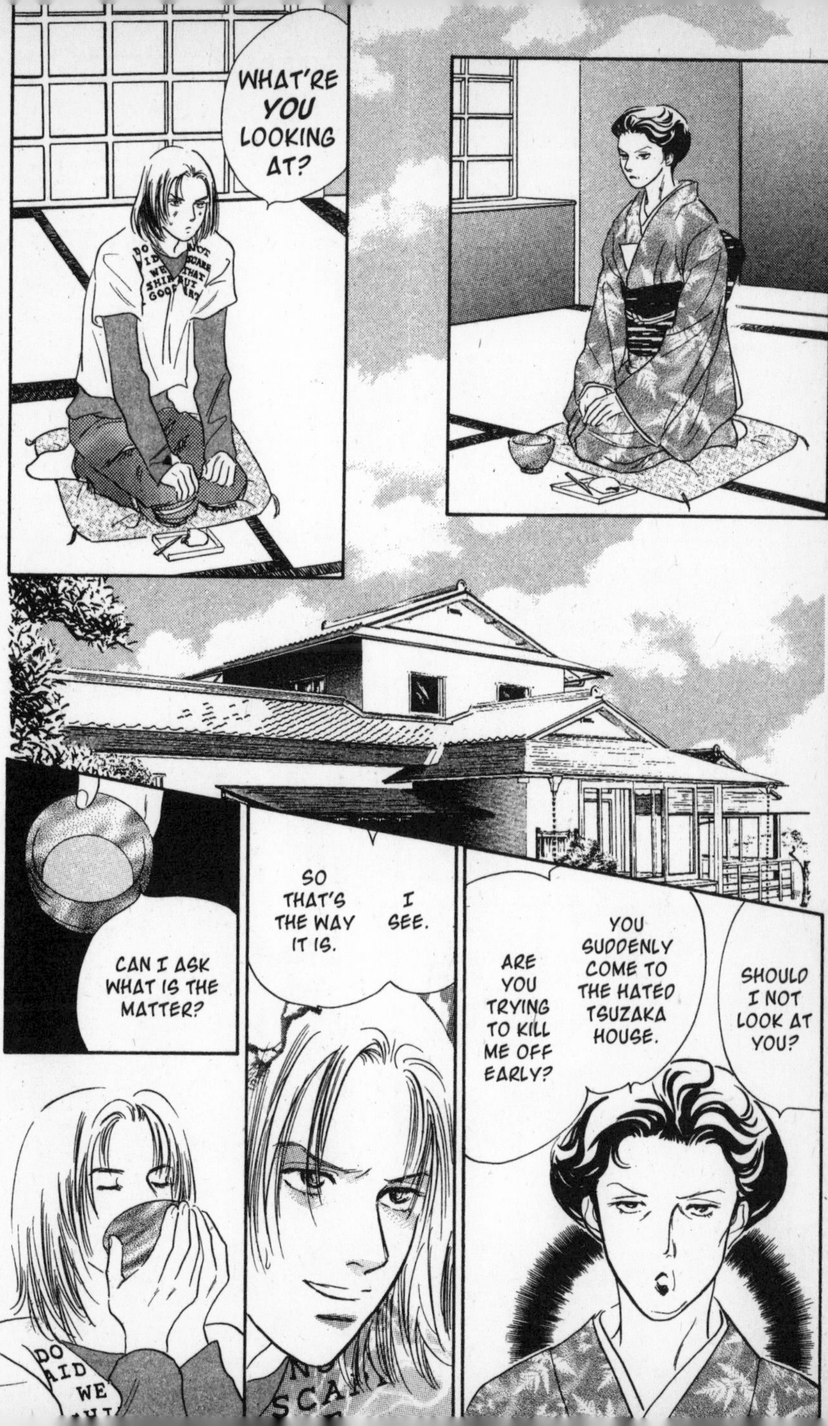
WHAT'RE YOU LOOKING AT?
SHOULD I NOT LOOK AT YOU?
YOU SUDDENLY COME TO THE HATED TSUZAKA HOUSE.
ARE YOU TRYING TO KILL ME OFF EARLY?
I SEE.
SO THAT'S THE WAY IT IS.
CAN I ASK WHAT IS THE MATTER?

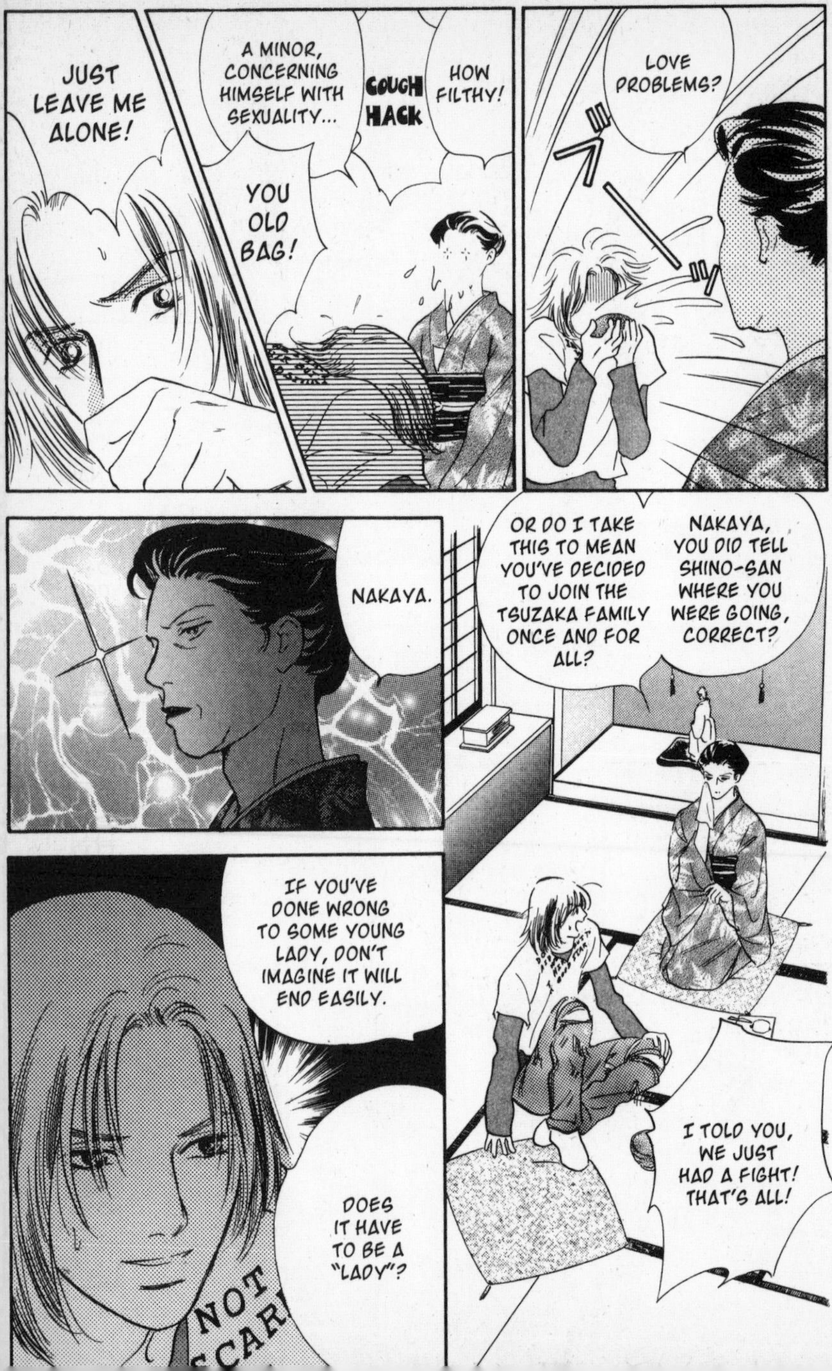
LOVE PROBLEMS?
HOW FILTHY!
COUGH HACK
A MINOR, CONCERNING HIMSELF WITH SEXUALITY...
YOU OLD BAG!
JUST LEAVE ME ALONE!
NAKAYA, YOU DID TELL SHINO-SAN WHERE YOU WERE GOING, CORRECT?
OR DO I TAKE THIS TO MEAN YOU'VE DECIDED TO JOIN THE TSUZAKA FAMILY ONCE AND FOR ALL?
I TOLD YOU, WE JUST HAD A FIGHT! THAT'S ALL!
NAKAYA.
IF YOU'VE DONE WRONG TO SOME YOUNG LADY, DON'T IMAGINE IT WILL END EASILY.
DOES IT HAVE TO BE A "LADY"?
NOT

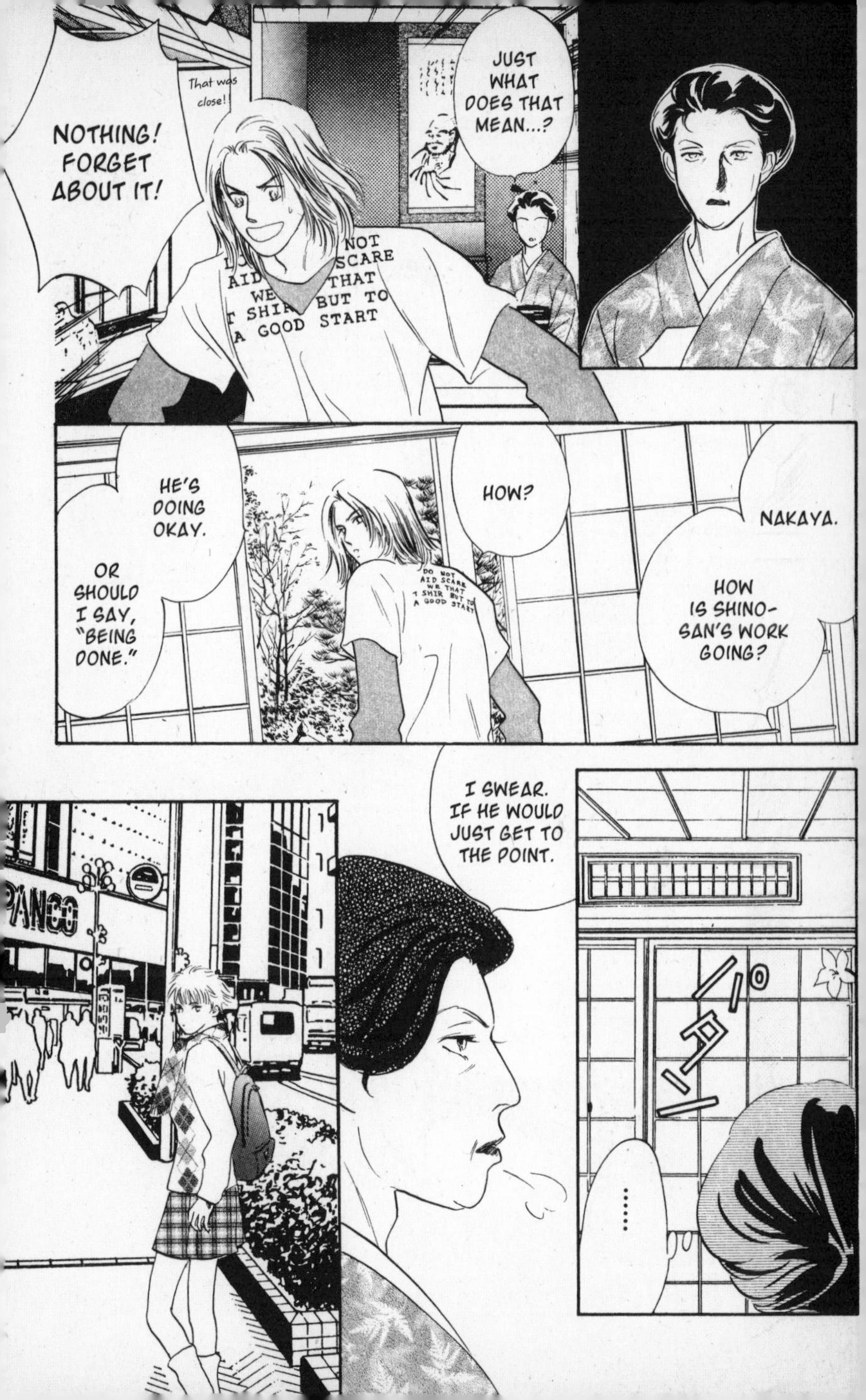
JUST WHAT DOES THAT MEAN...?
That was close!
NOTHING! FORGET ABOUT IT!
NAKAYA.
HOW IS SHINO-SAN'S WORK GOING?
HOW?
HE'S DOING OKAY.
OR SHOULD I SAY, "BEING DONE."
......
I SWEAR. IF HE WOULD JUST GET TO THE POINT.
PANCO

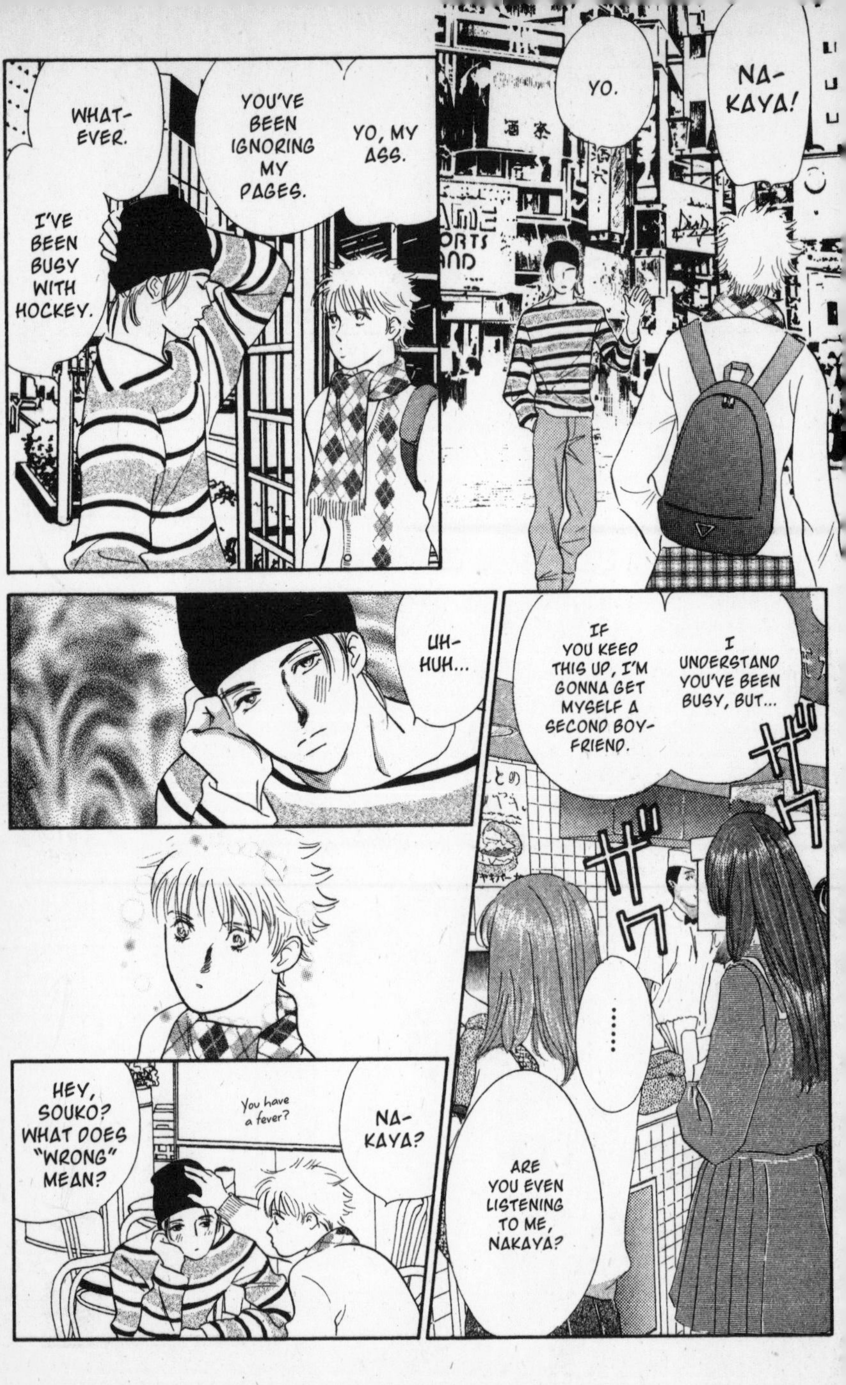
NA-KAYA!
YO.
YO, MY ASS.
YOU'VE BEEN IGNORING MY PAGES.
WHAT-EVER.
I'VE BEEN BUSY WITH HOCKEY.
I UNDERSTAND YOU'VE BEEN BUSY, BUT...
IF YOU KEEP THIS UP, I'M GONNA GET MYSELF A SECOND BOY-FRIEND.
ザワ
ザワ
......
ARE YOU EVEN LISTENING TO ME, NAKAYA?
UH-HUH...
NA-KAYA?
You have a fever?
HEY, SOUKO? WHAT DOES "WRONG" MEAN?

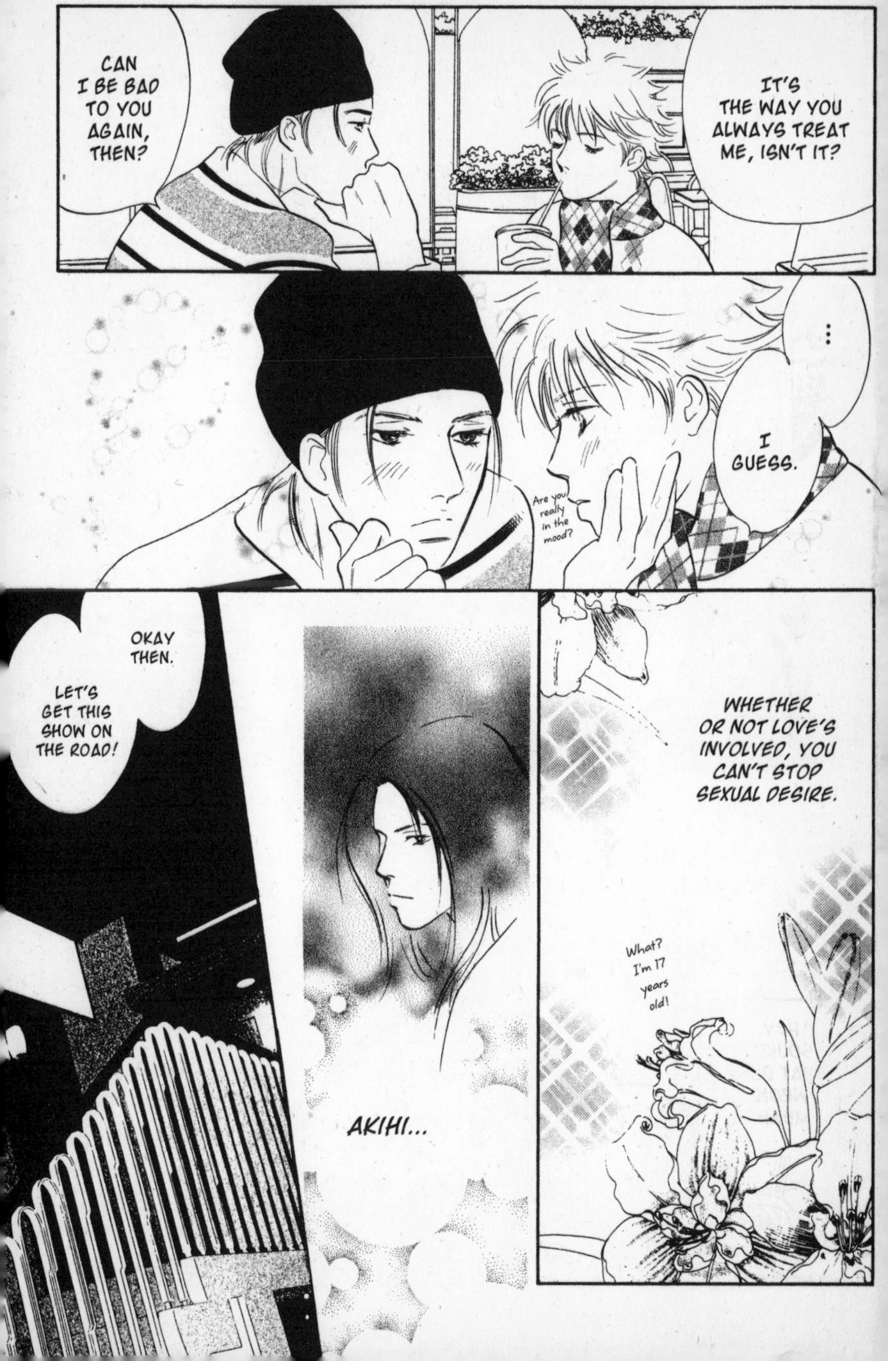
IT'S THE WAY YOU ALWAYS TREAT ME, ISN'T IT?
CAN I BE BAD TO YOU AGAIN, THEN?
...
I GUESS.
Are you really in the mood?
WHETHER OR NOT LOVE'S INVOLVED, YOU CAN'T STOP SEXUAL DESIRE.
What? I'm 17 years old!
AKIHI...
OKAY THEN.
LET'S GET THIS SHOW ON THE ROAD!

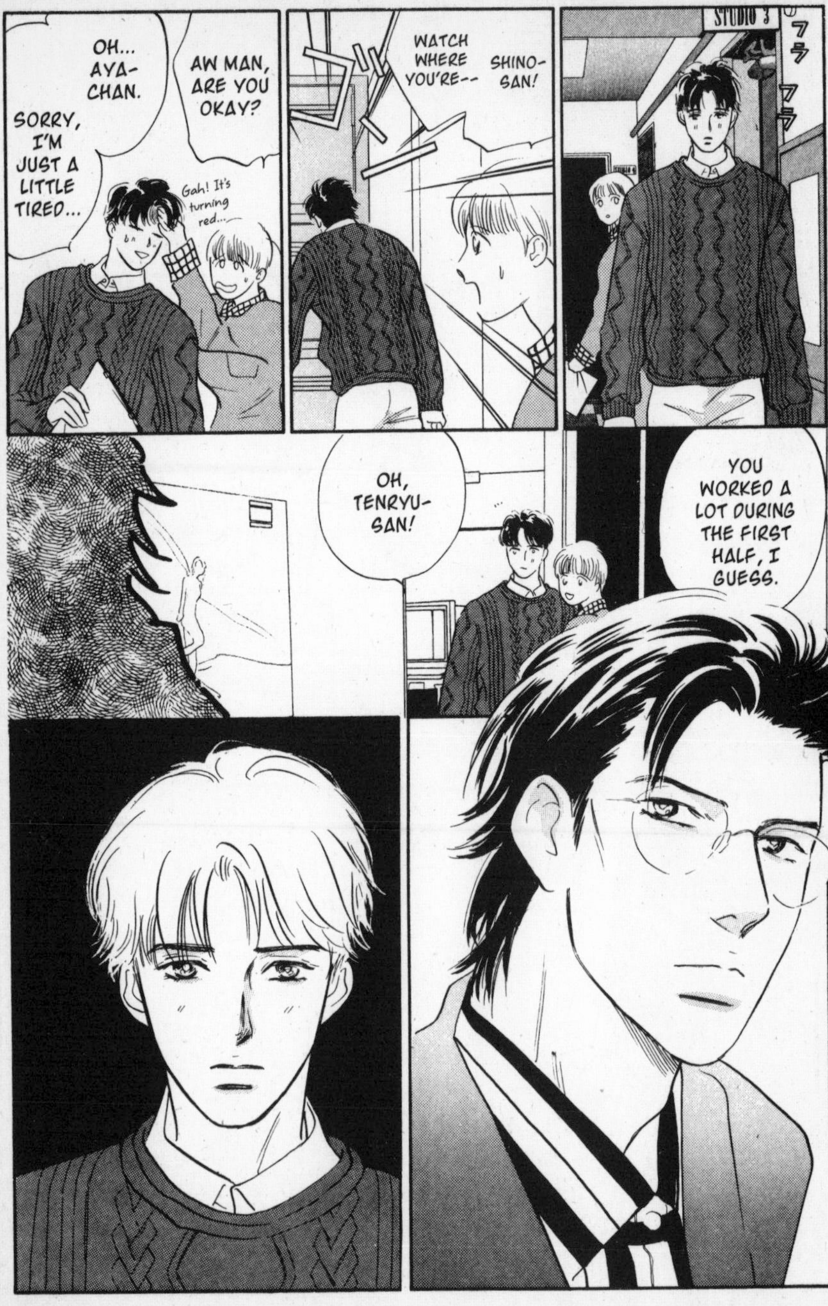
STUDIO 3
フラフラ
SHINO-SAN!
WATCH WHERE YOU'RE--
AW MAN, ARE YOU OKAY?
OH... AYA-CHAN.
SORRY, I'M JUST A LITTLE TIRED...
Gah! It's turning red...
YOU WORKED A LOT DURING THE FIRST HALF, I GUESS.
OH, TENRYU-SAN!
...

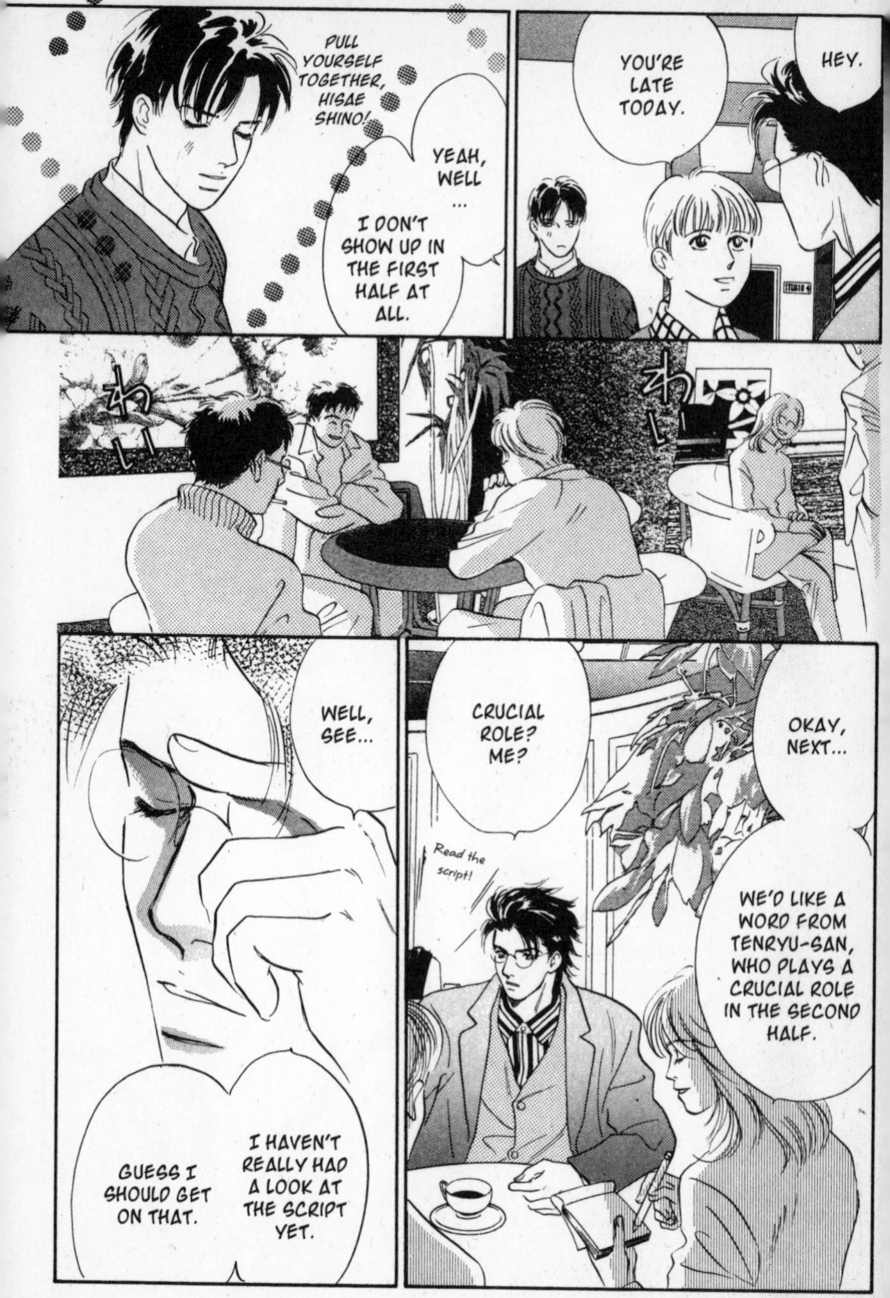
HEY.
YOU'RE LATE TODAY.
YEAH, WELL ...
I DON'T SHOW UP IN THE FIRST HALF AT ALL.
PULL YOURSELF TOGETHER, HISAE SHINO!
わい
わい
OKAY, NEXT...
WE'D LIKE A WORD FROM TENRYU-SAN, WHO PLAYS A CRUCIAL ROLE IN THE SECOND HALF.
CRUCIAL ROLE? ME?
Read the script!
WELL, SEE...
I HAVEN'T REALLY HAD A LOOK AT THE SCRIPT YET.
GUESS I SHOULD GET ON THAT.

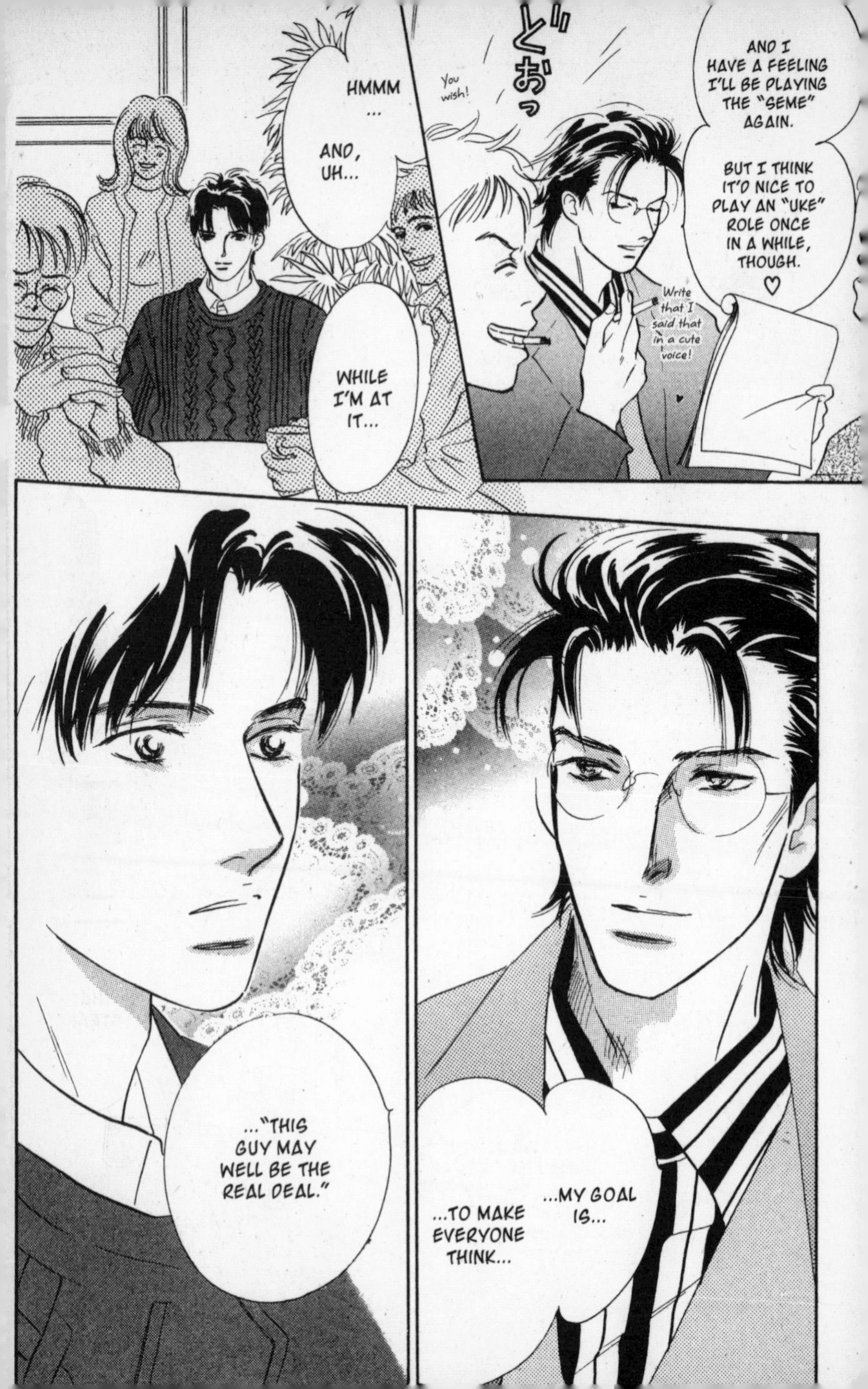
AND I HAVE A FEELING I'LL BE PLAYING THE "SEME" AGAIN.
BUT I THINK IT'D NICE TO PLAY AN "UKE" ROLE ONCE IN A WHILE, THOUGH. ♡
Write that I said that in a cute voice!
どぉっ
You wish!
HMMM ...
AND, UH...
WHILE I'M AT IT...
...MY GOAL IS...
...TO MAKE EVERYONE THINK...
..."THIS GUY MAY WELL BE THE REAL DEAL."

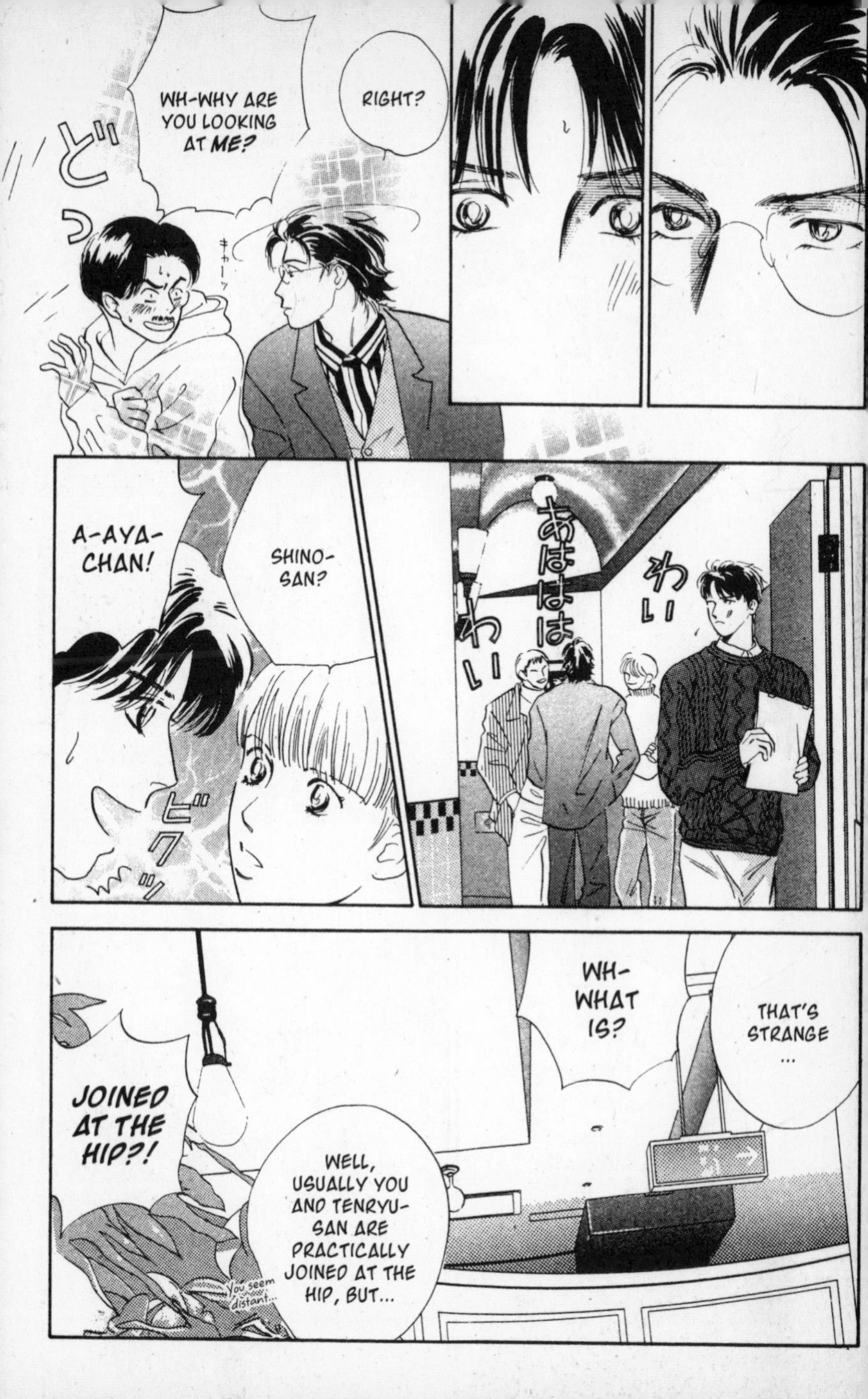
RIGHT?
WH-WHY ARE YOU LOOKING AT ME?
キャーッ
どっ
あははは
わい
わい
SHINO-SAN?
A-AYA-CHAN!
ビクッ
THAT'S STRANGE ...
WH- WHAT IS?
WELL, USUALLY YOU AND TENRYU-SAN ARE PRACTICALLY JOINED AT THE HIP, BUT...
You seem distant...
JOINED AT THE HIP?!

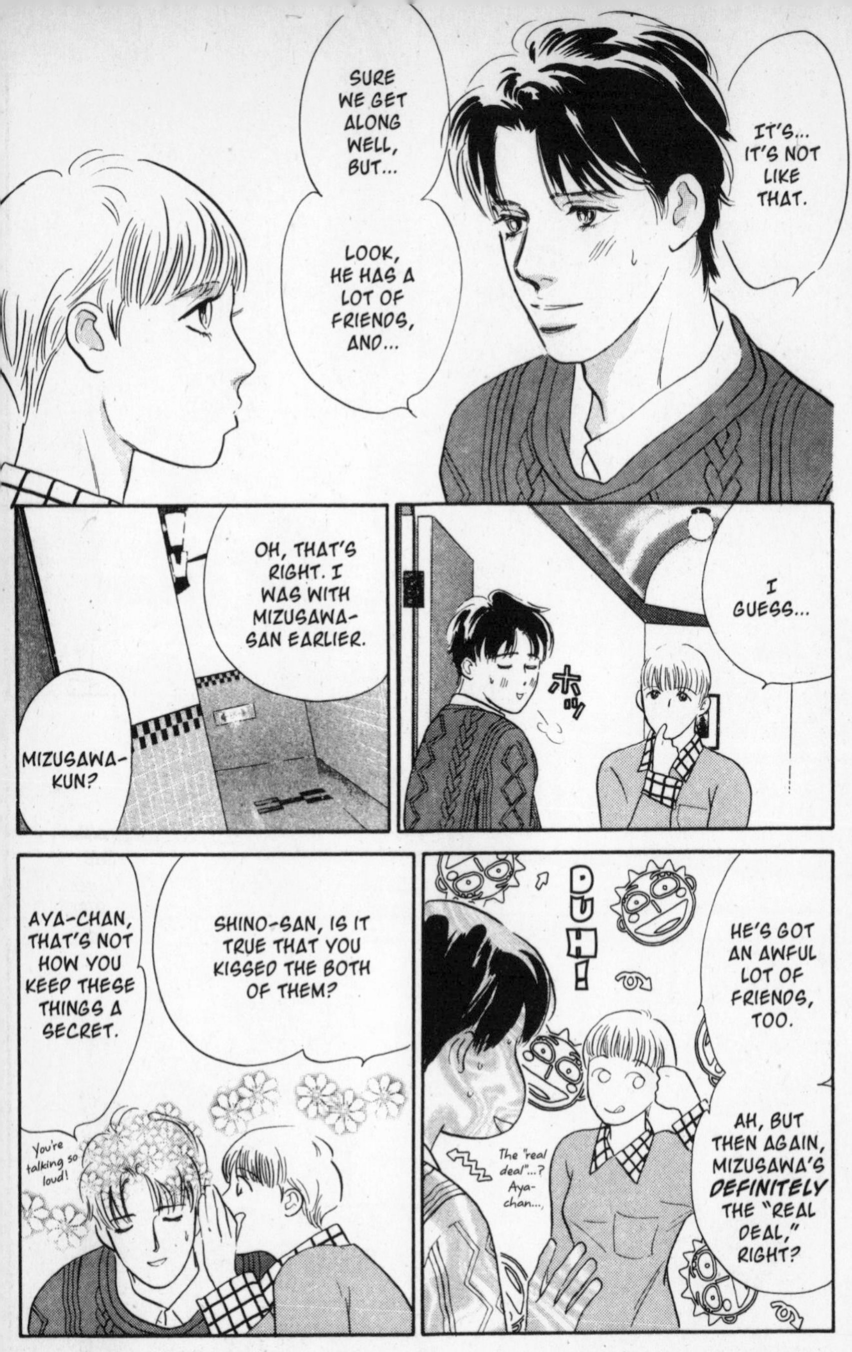
IT'S... IT'S NOT LIKE THAT.
SURE WE GET ALONG WELL, BUT...
LOOK, HE HAS A LOT OF FRIENDS, AND...
I GUESS...
ホッ
OH, THAT'S RIGHT. I WAS WITH MIZUSAWA-SAN EARLIER.
MIZUSAWA-KUN?
DUH!
HE'S GOT AN AWFUL LOT OF FRIENDS, TOO.
AH, BUT THEN AGAIN, MIZUSAWA'S *DEFINITELY* THE "REAL DEAL," RIGHT?
The "real deal"...? Aya-chan...
SHINO-SAN, IS IT TRUE THAT YOU KISSED THE BOTH OF THEM?
AYA-CHAN, THAT'S NOT HOW YOU KEEP THESE THINGS A SECRET.
You're talking so loud!

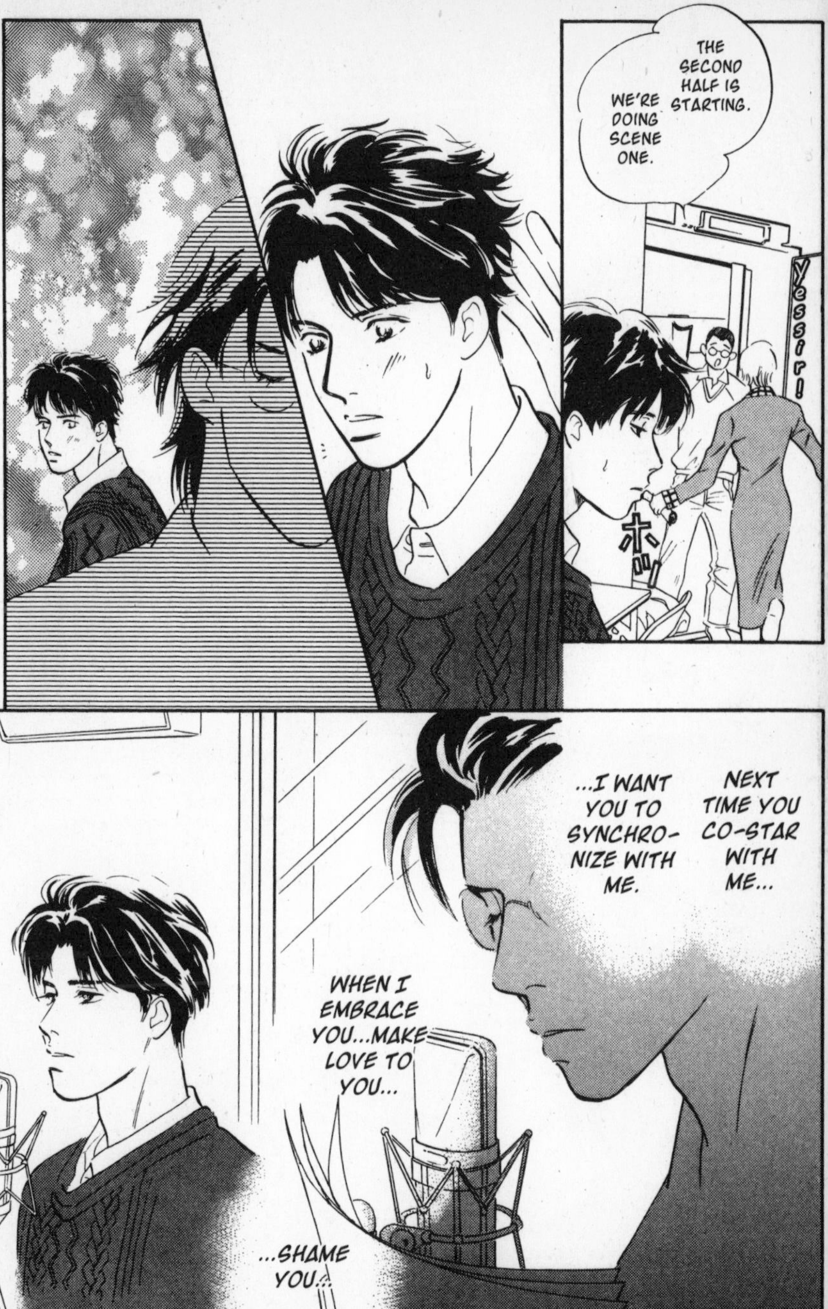

THE SECOND HALF IS STARTING.
WE'RE DOING SCENE ONE.
Yessir!
NEXT TIME YOU CO-STAR WITH ME...
...I WANT YOU TO SYNCHRO-NIZE WITH ME.
WHEN I EMBRACE YOU...MAKE LOVE TO YOU...
...SHAME YOU...

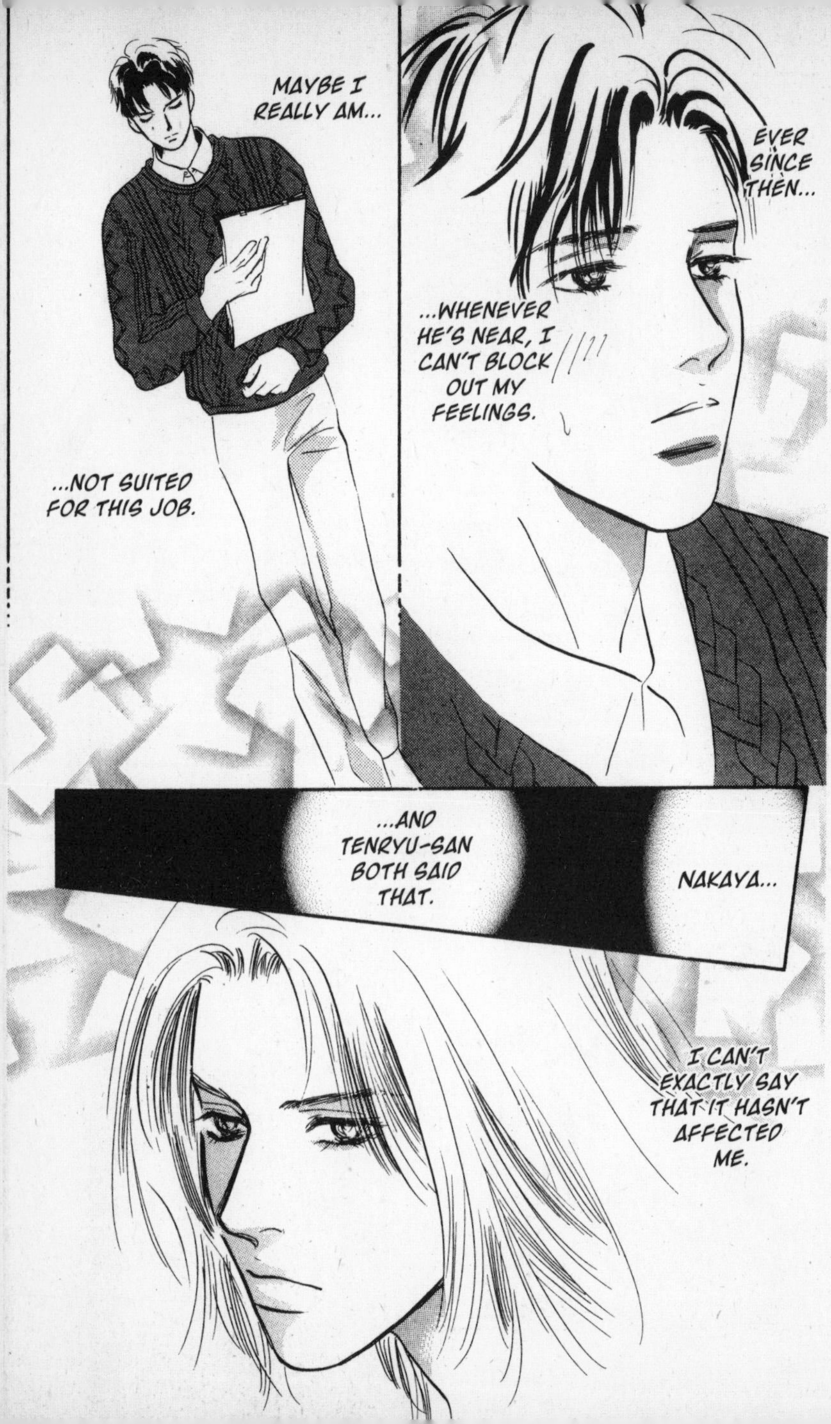
EVER SINCE THEN...
...WHENEVER HE'S NEAR, I CAN'T BLOCK OUT MY FEELINGS.
MAYBE I REALLY AM...
...NOT SUITED FOR THIS JOB.
NAKAYA...
...AND TENRYU-SAN BOTH SAID THAT.
I CAN'T EXACTLY SAY THAT IT HASN'T AFFECTED ME.

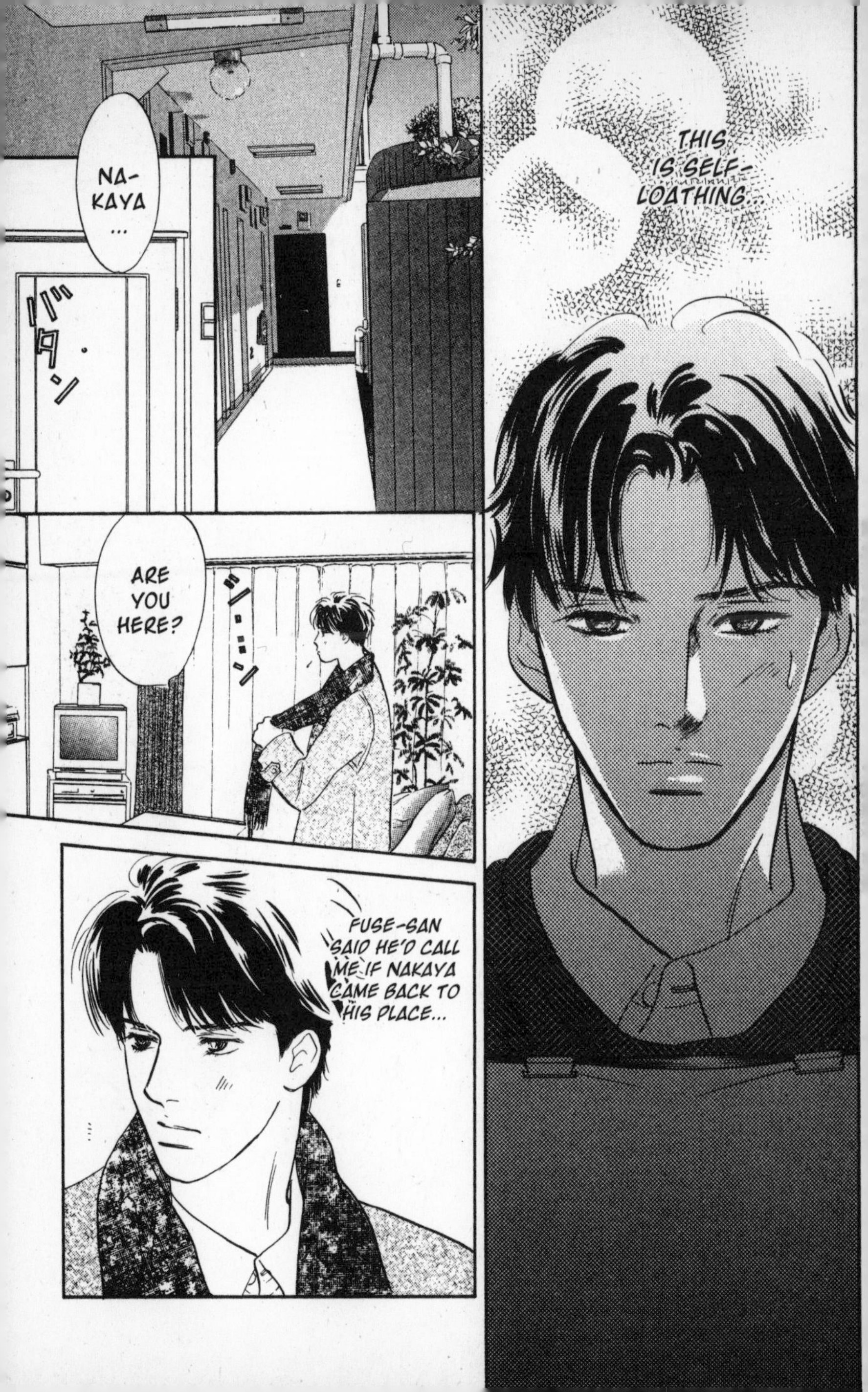
THIS IS SELF-LOATHING...
NA-KAYA...
バタン
ARE YOU HERE?
FUSE-SAN SAID HE'D CALL ME IF NAKAYA CAME BACK TO HIS PLACE...
...

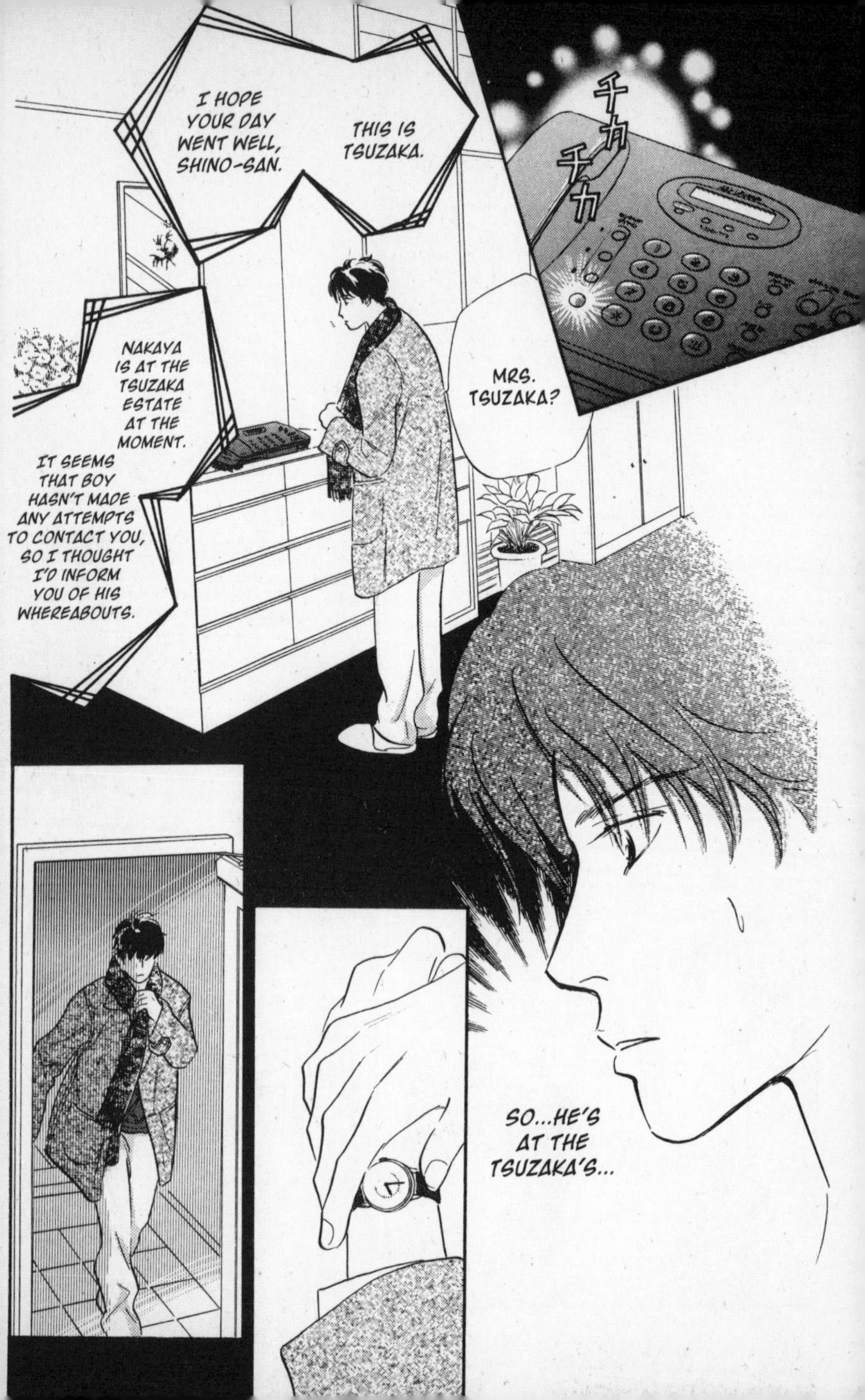
チカ
チカ
THIS IS TSUZAKA.
I HOPE YOUR DAY WENT WELL, SHINO-SAN.
MRS. TSUZAKA?
NAKAYA IS AT THE TSUZAKA ESTATE AT THE MOMENT.
IT SEEMS THAT BOY HASN'T MADE ANY ATTEMPTS TO CONTACT YOU, SO I THOUGHT I'D INFORM YOU OF HIS WHEREABOUTS.
SO...HE'S AT THE TSUZAKA'S...

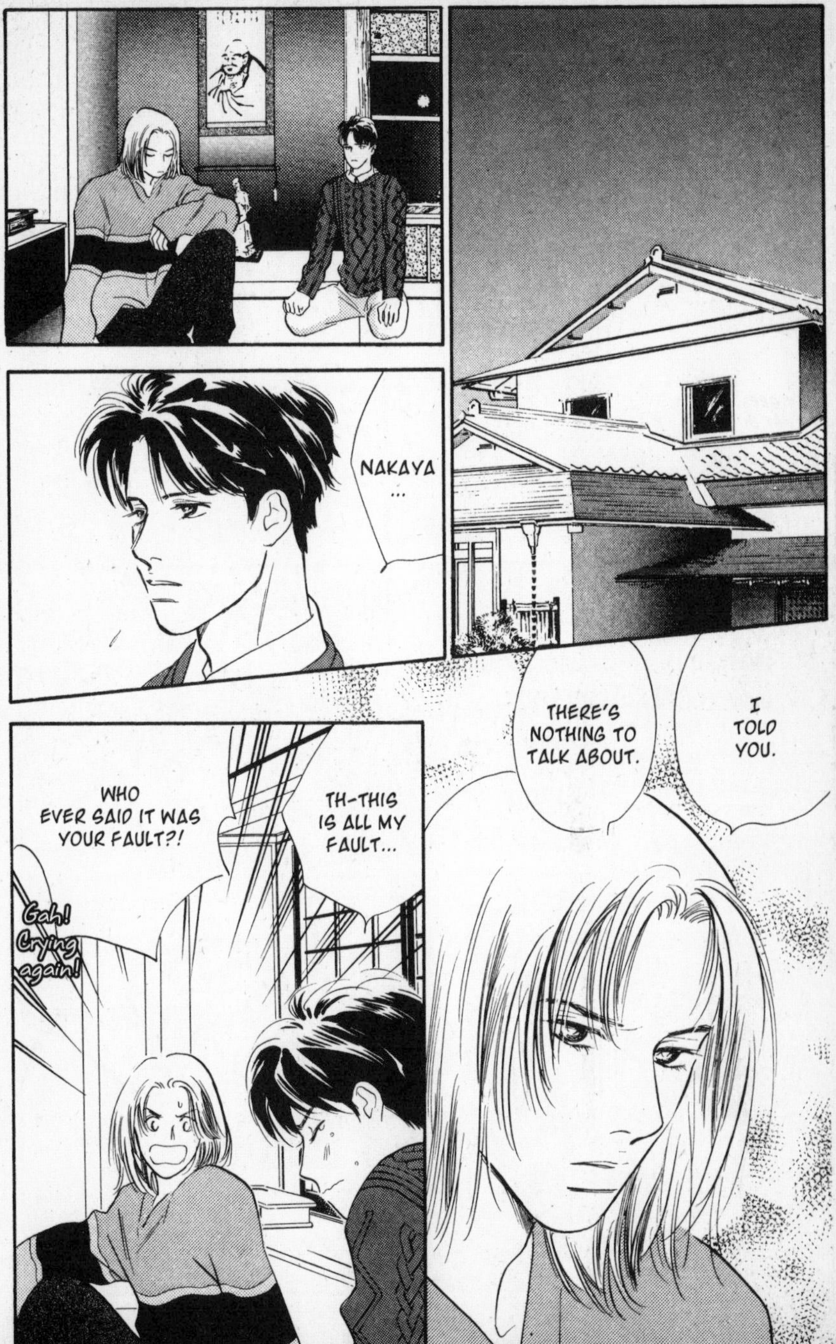
NAKAYA ...
I TOLD YOU.
THERE'S NOTHING TO TALK ABOUT.
TH-THIS IS ALL MY FAULT...
WHO EVER SAID IT WAS YOUR FAULT?!
Gah! Crying again!

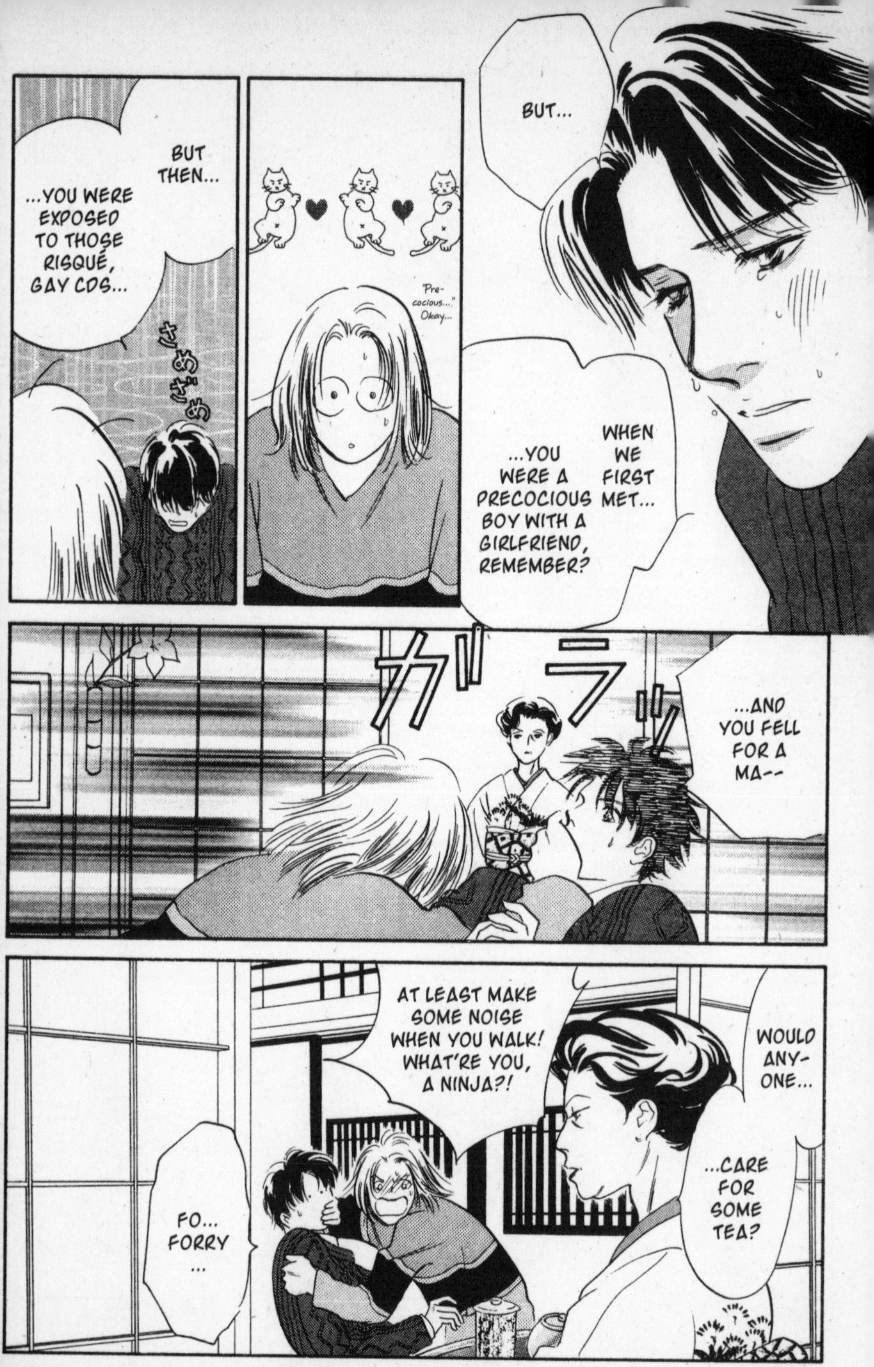
BUT...
WHEN WE FIRST MET...
...YOU WERE A PRECOCIOUS BOY WITH A GIRLFRIEND, REMEMBER?
"Pre-cocious..." Okay...
BUT THEN...
...YOU WERE EXPOSED TO THOSE RISQUÉ, GAY CDS...
さめざめ
...AND YOU FELL FOR A MA--
ガラッ
WOULD ANY-ONE...
...CARE FOR SOME TEA?
AT LEAST MAKE SOME NOISE WHEN YOU WALK! WHAT'RE YOU, A NINJA?!
FO... FORRY ...

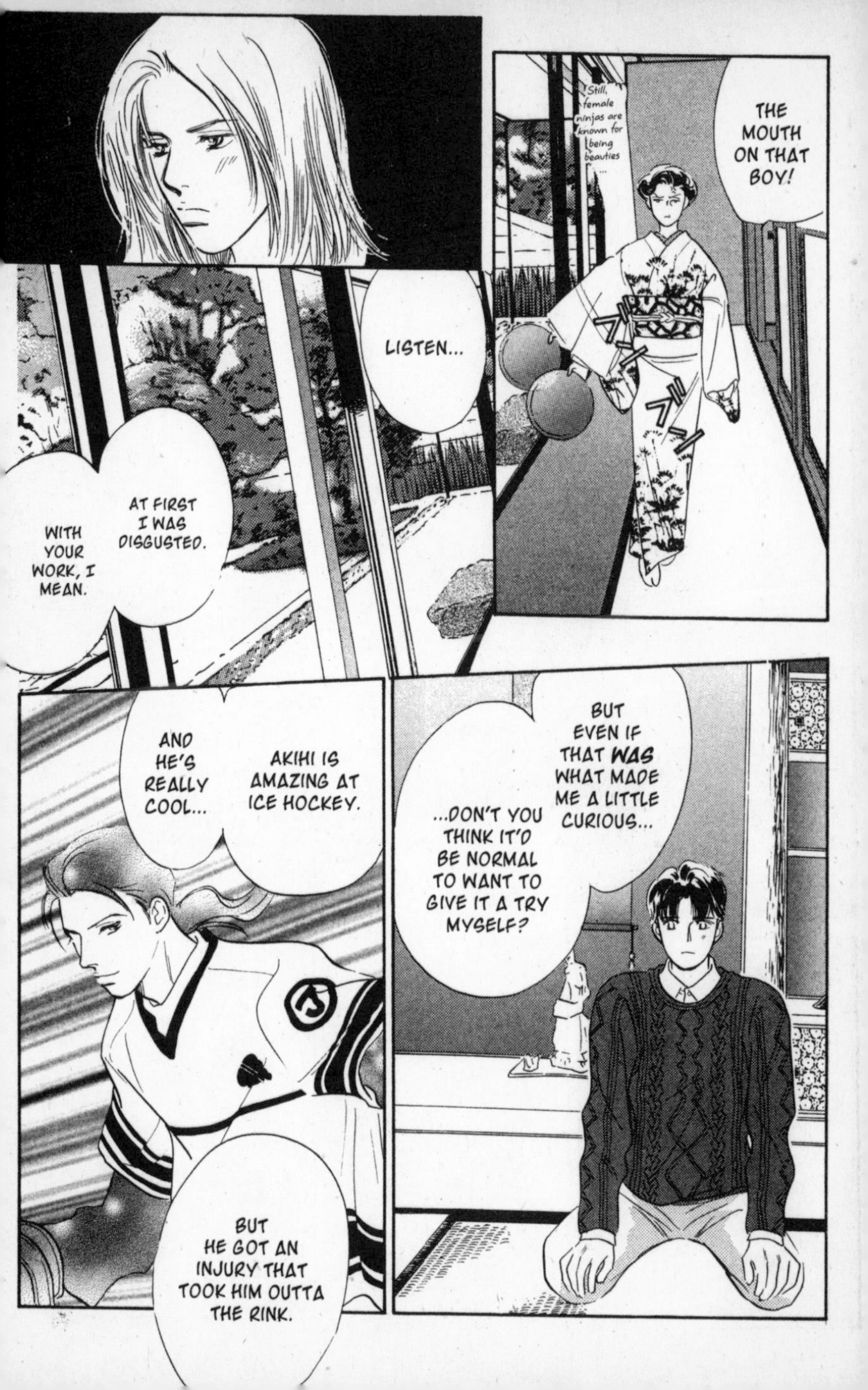
THE MOUTH ON THAT BOY!
Still, female ninjas are known for being beauties ...
LISTEN...
AT FIRST I WAS DISGUSTED.
WITH YOUR WORK, I MEAN.
BUT EVEN IF THAT WAS WHAT MADE ME A LITTLE CURIOUS...
...DON'T YOU THINK IT'D BE NORMAL TO WANT TO GIVE IT A TRY MYSELF?
AKIHI IS AMAZING AT ICE HOCKEY.
AND HE'S REALLY COOL...
BUT HE GOT AN INJURY THAT TOOK HIM OUTTA THE RINK.

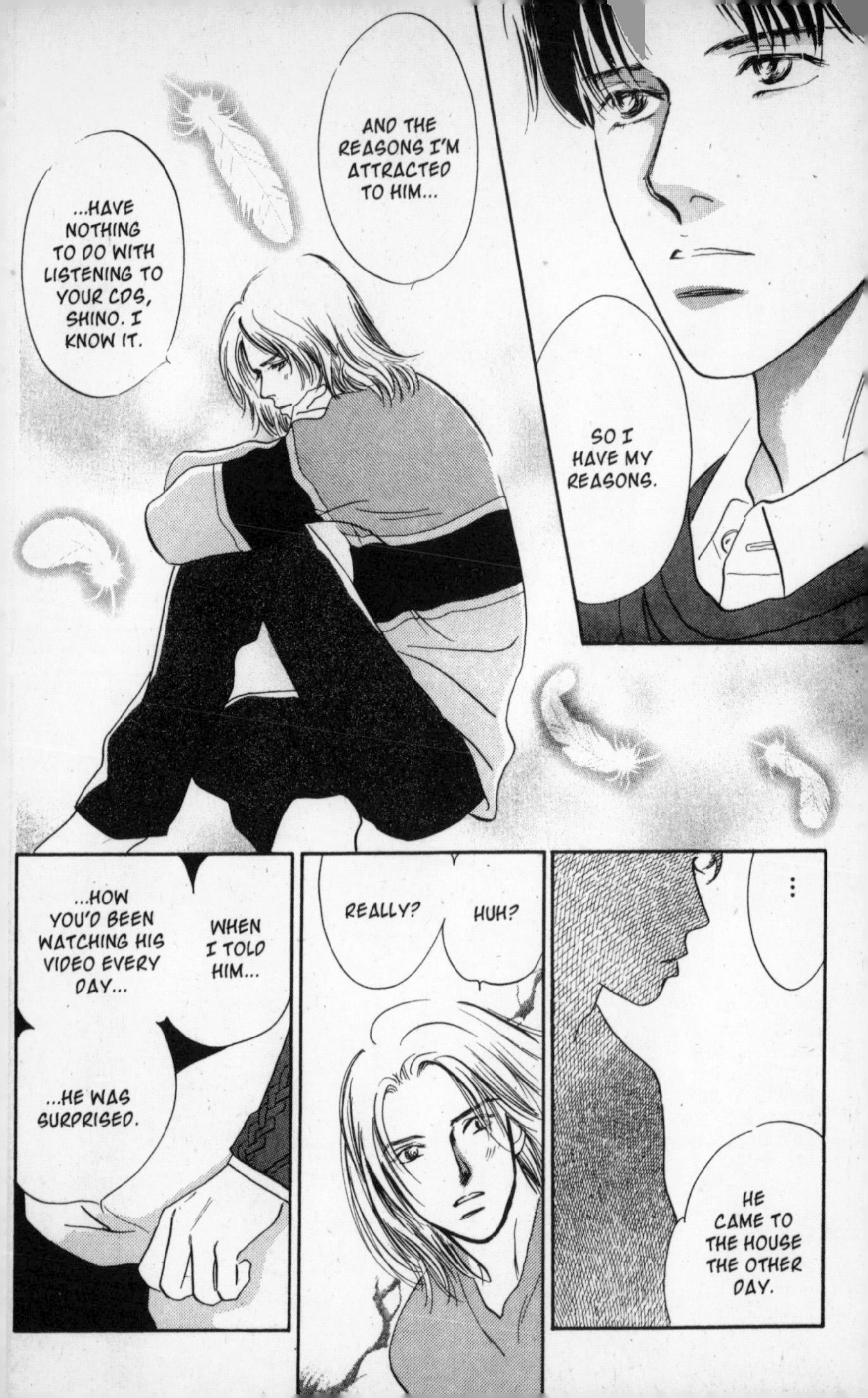
SO I HAVE MY REASONS.
AND THE REASONS I'M ATTRACTED TO HIM...
...HAVE NOTHING TO DO WITH LISTENING TO YOUR CDS, SHINO. I KNOW IT.
...
HE CAME TO THE HOUSE THE OTHER DAY.
HUH?
REALLY?
WHEN I TOLD HIM...
...HOW YOU'D BEEN WATCHING HIS VIDEO EVERY DAY...
...HE WAS SURPRISED.

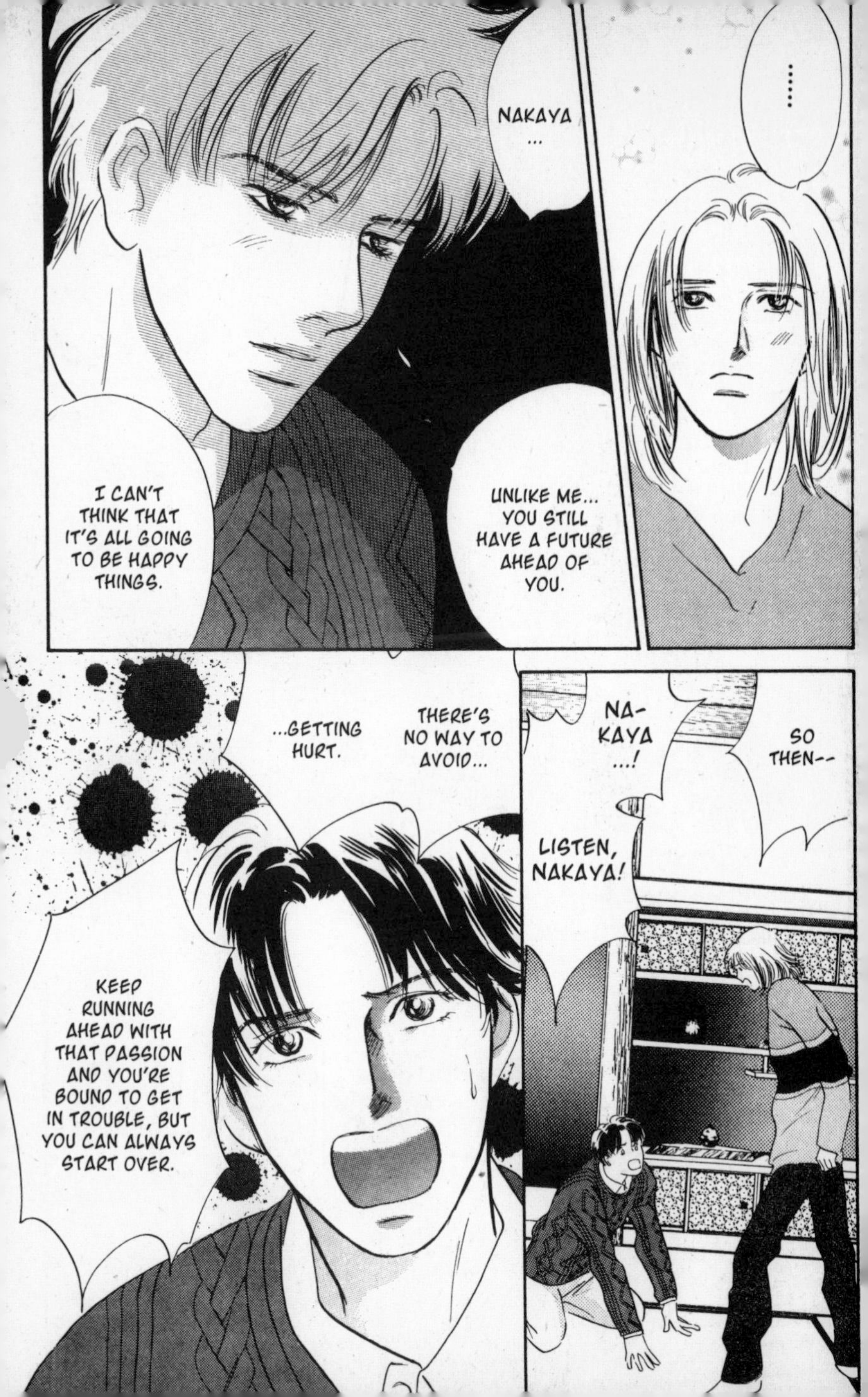
……
NAKAYA ...
UNLIKE ME... YOU STILL HAVE A FUTURE AHEAD OF YOU.
I CAN'T THINK THAT IT'S ALL GOING TO BE HAPPY THINGS.
SO THEN--
NA-KAYA ...!
LISTEN, NAKAYA!
THERE'S NO WAY TO AVOID...
...GETTING HURT.
KEEP RUNNING AHEAD WITH THAT PASSION AND YOU'RE BOUND TO GET IN TROUBLE, BUT YOU CAN ALWAYS START OVER.

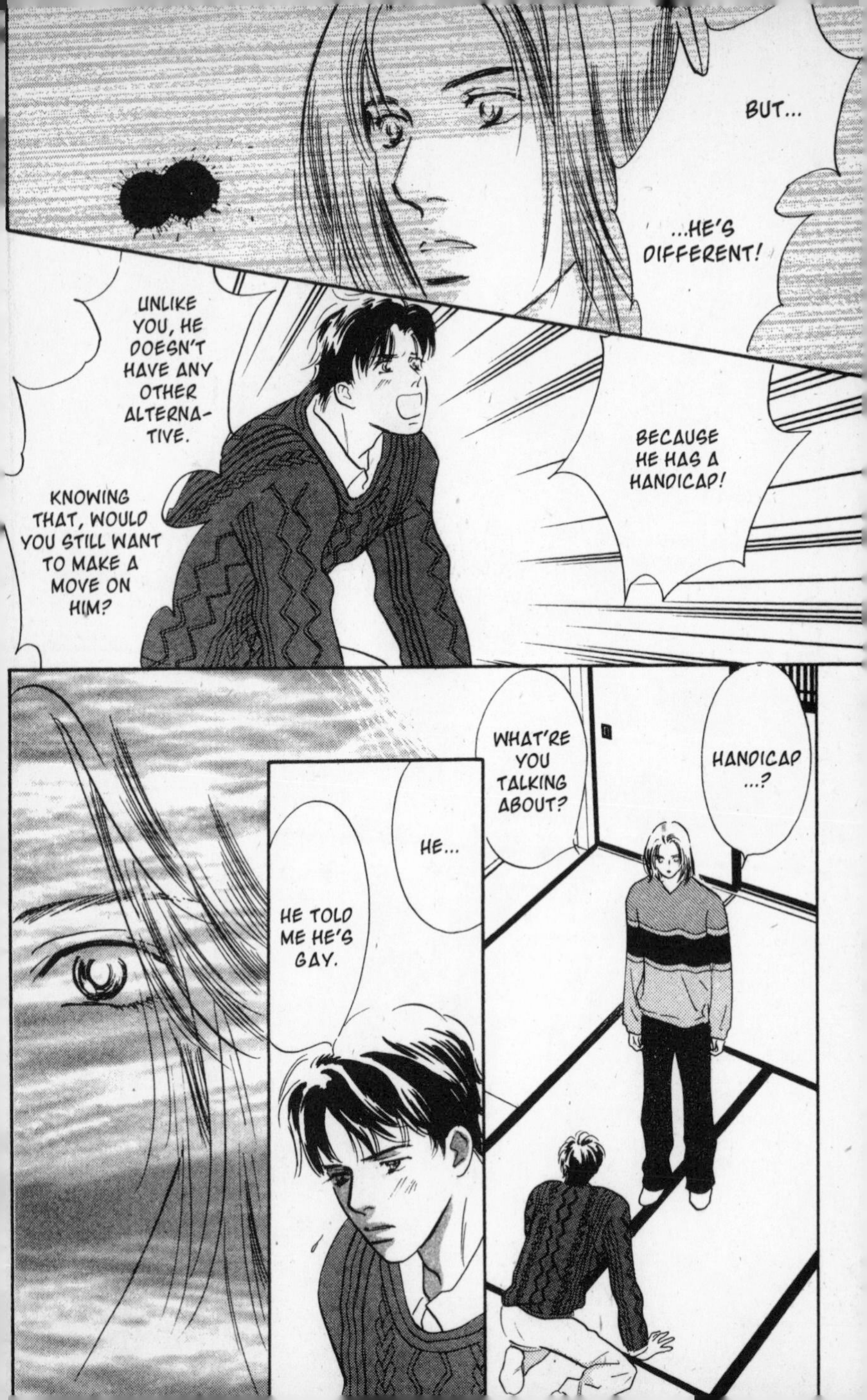
BUT...
...HE'S DIFFERENT!
BECAUSE HE HAS A HANDICAP!
UNLIKE YOU, HE DOESN'T HAVE ANY OTHER ALTERNA-TIVE.
KNOWING THAT, WOULD YOU STILL WANT TO MAKE A MOVE ON HIM?
HANDICAP ...?
WHAT'RE YOU TALKING ABOUT?
HE...
HE TOLD ME HE'S GAY.

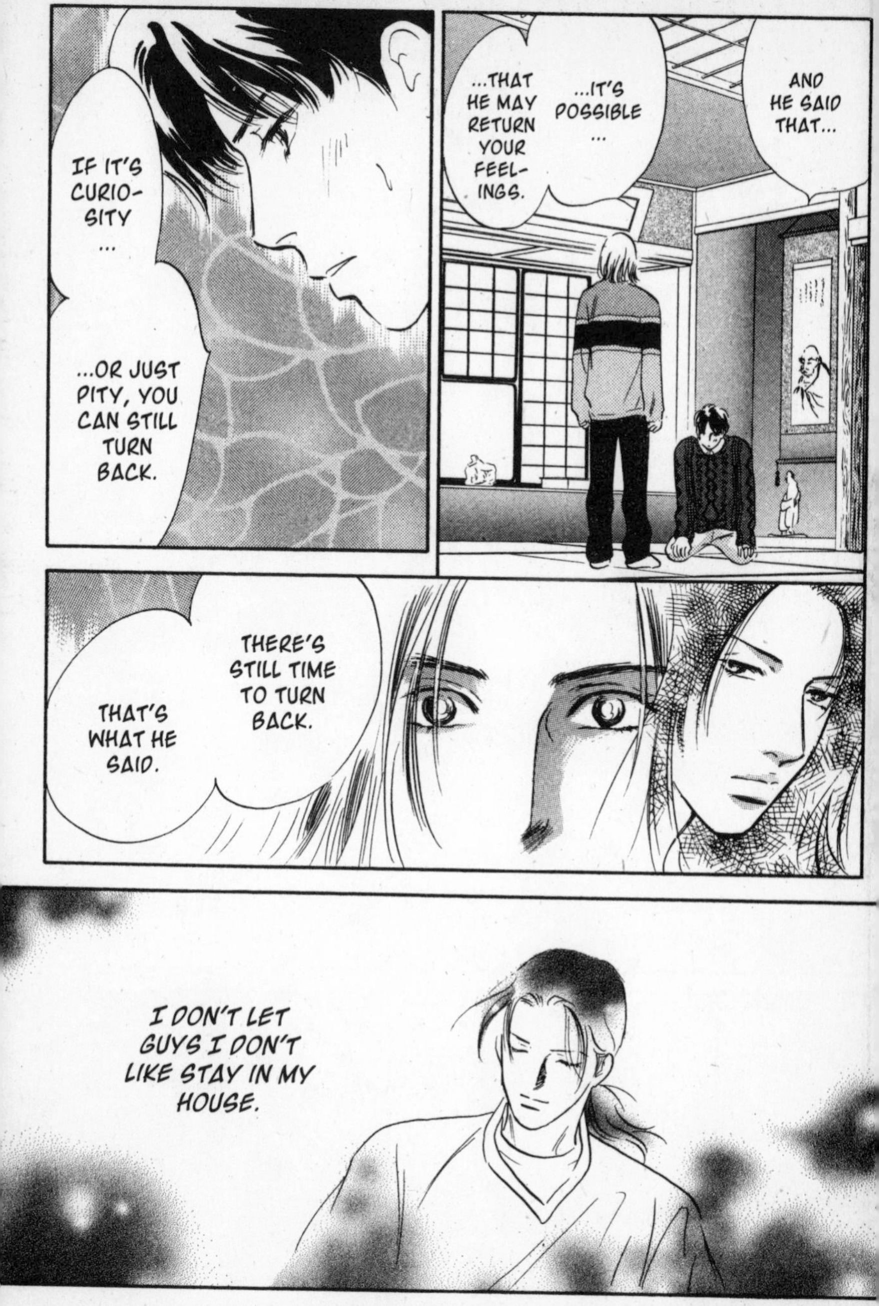
AND HE SAID THAT...
...IT'S POSSIBLE ...
...THAT HE MAY RETURN YOUR FEEL-INGS.
IF IT'S CURIO-SITY ...
...OR JUST PITY, YOU CAN STILL TURN BACK.
THERE'S STILL TIME TO TURN BACK.
THAT'S WHAT HE SAID.
I DON'T LET GUYS I DON'T LIKE STAY IN MY HOUSE.

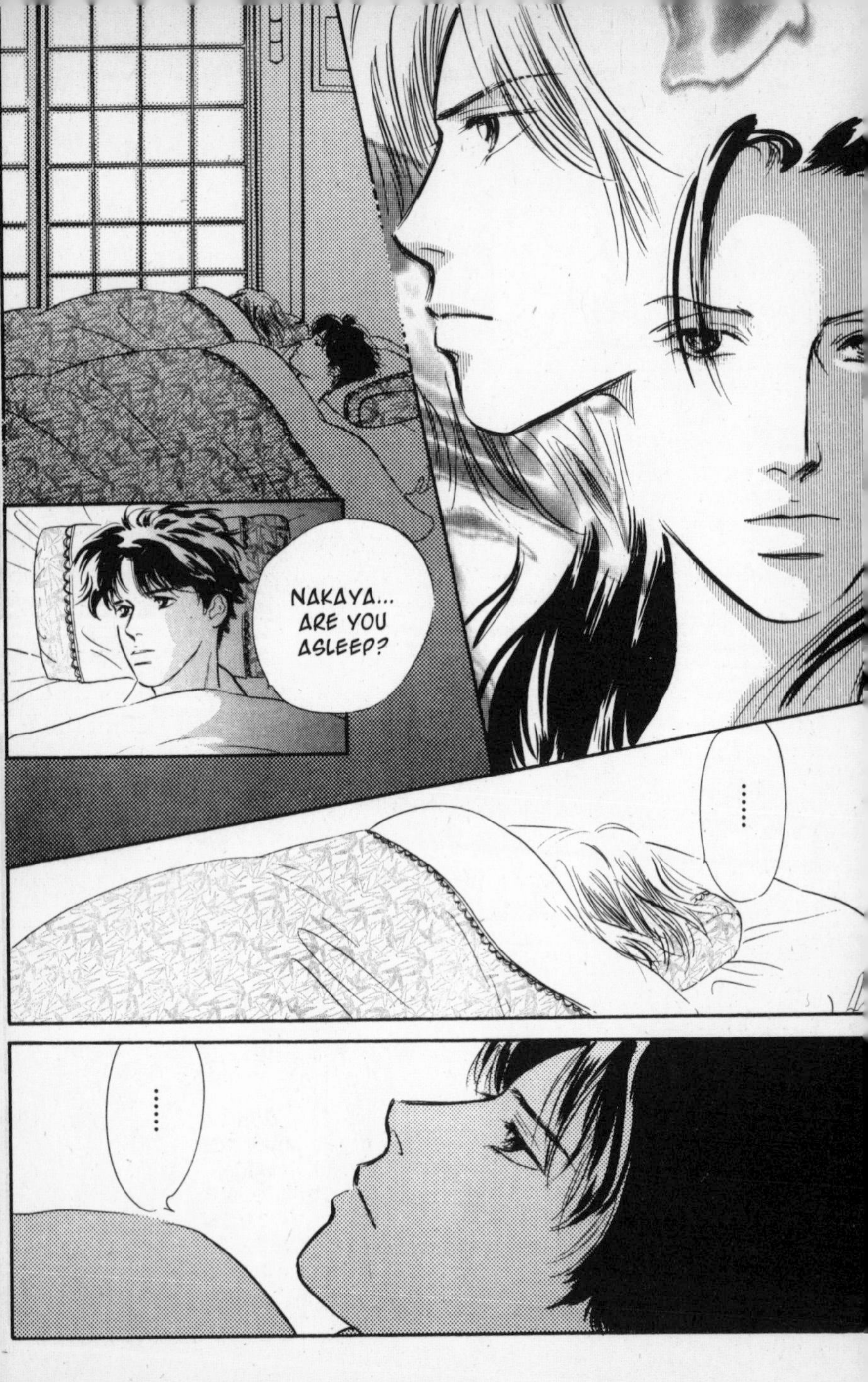
NAKAYA... ARE YOU ASLEEP?
......
......

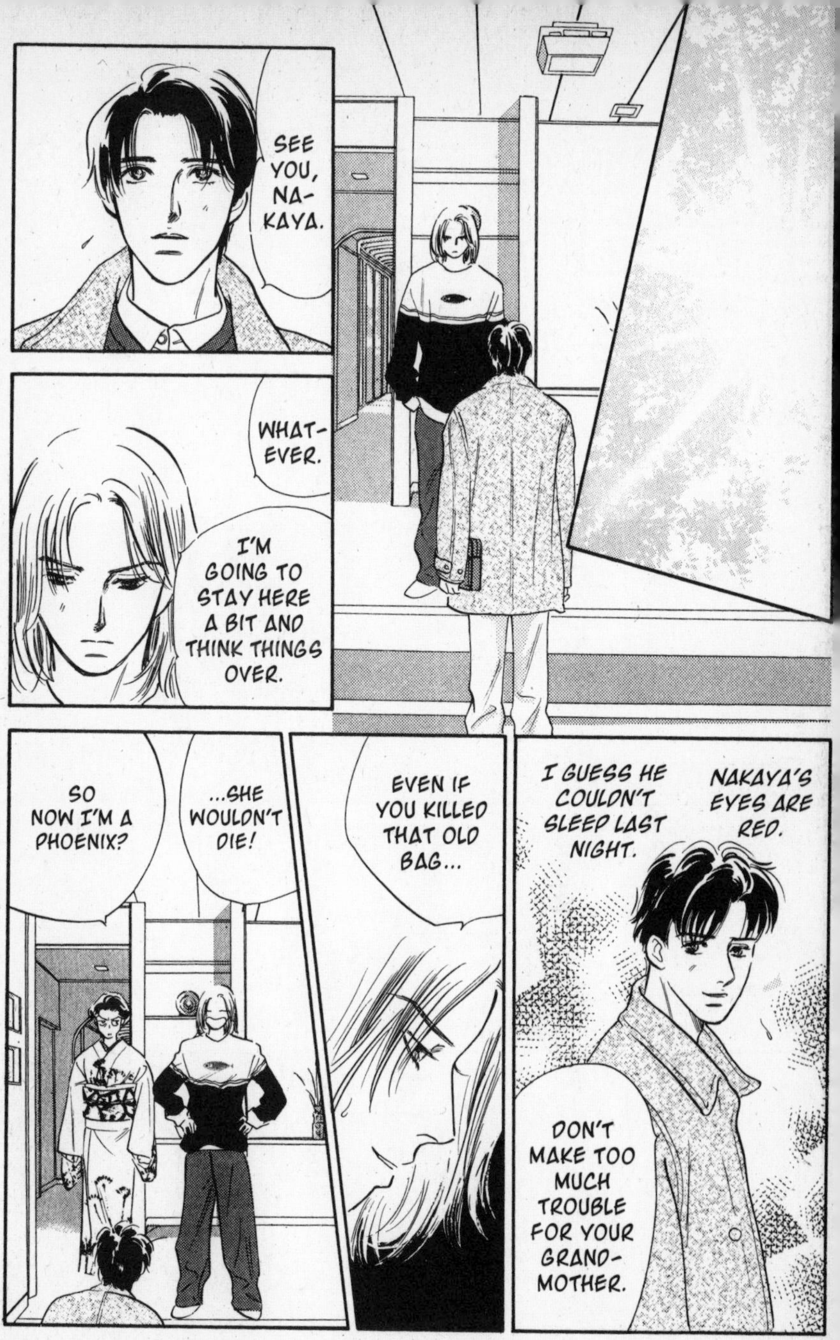
SEE YOU, NAKAYA.
WHATEVER.
I'M GOING TO STAY HERE A BIT AND THINK THINGS OVER.
NAKAYA'S EYES ARE RED.
I GUESS HE COULDN'T SLEEP LAST NIGHT.
DON'T MAKE TOO MUCH TROUBLE FOR YOUR GRANDMOTHER.
EVEN IF YOU KILLED THAT OLD BAG...
...SHE WOULDN'T DIE!
SO NOW I'M A PHOENIX?

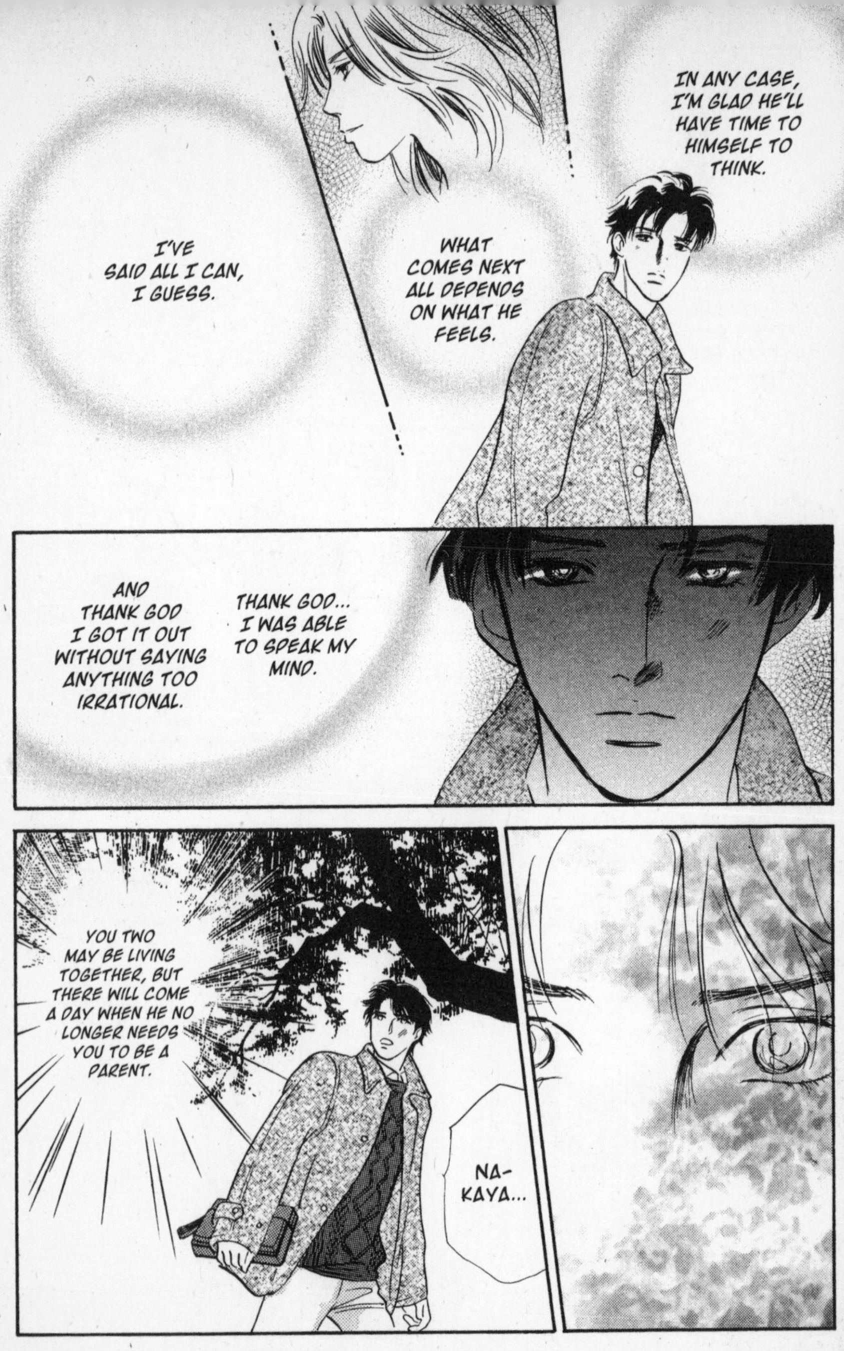
IN ANY CASE, I'M GLAD HE'LL HAVE TIME TO HIMSELF TO THINK.
WHAT COMES NEXT ALL DEPENDS ON WHAT HE FEELS.
I'VE SAID ALL I CAN, I GUESS.
THANK GOD... I WAS ABLE TO SPEAK MY MIND.
AND THANK GOD I GOT IT OUT WITHOUT SAYING ANYTHING TOO IRRATIONAL.
NA-KAYA...
YOU TWO MAY BE LIVING TOGETHER, BUT THERE WILL COME A DAY WHEN HE NO LONGER NEEDS YOU TO BE A PARENT.

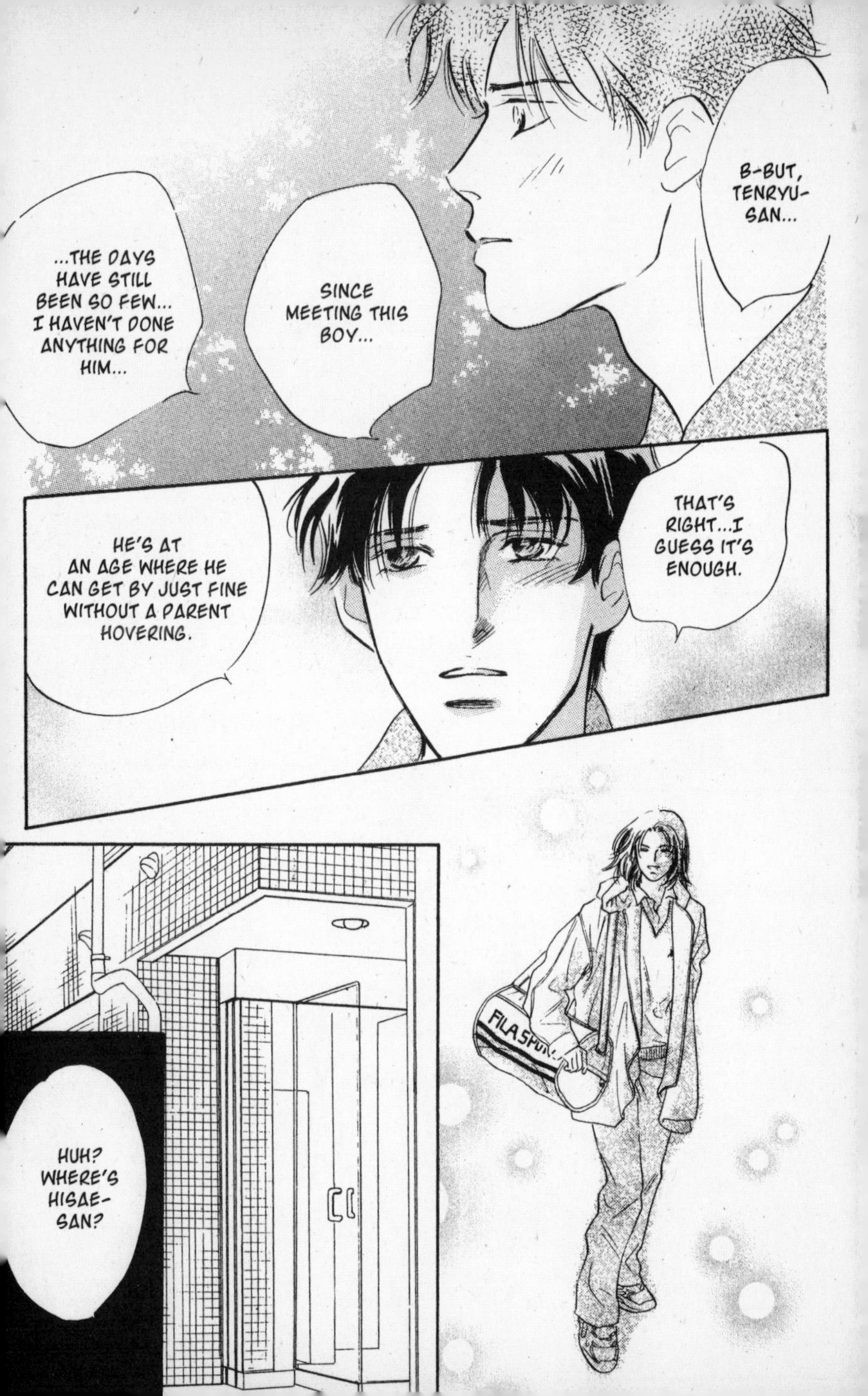
B-BUT, TENRYU-SAN...
SINCE MEETING THIS BOY...
...THE DAYS HAVE STILL BEEN SO FEW... I HAVEN'T DONE ANYTHING FOR HIM...
THAT'S RIGHT...I GUESS IT'S ENOUGH.
HE'S AT AN AGE WHERE HE CAN GET BY JUST FINE WITHOUT A PARENT HOVERING.
HUH? WHERE'S HISAE-SAN?
FILA SPOR

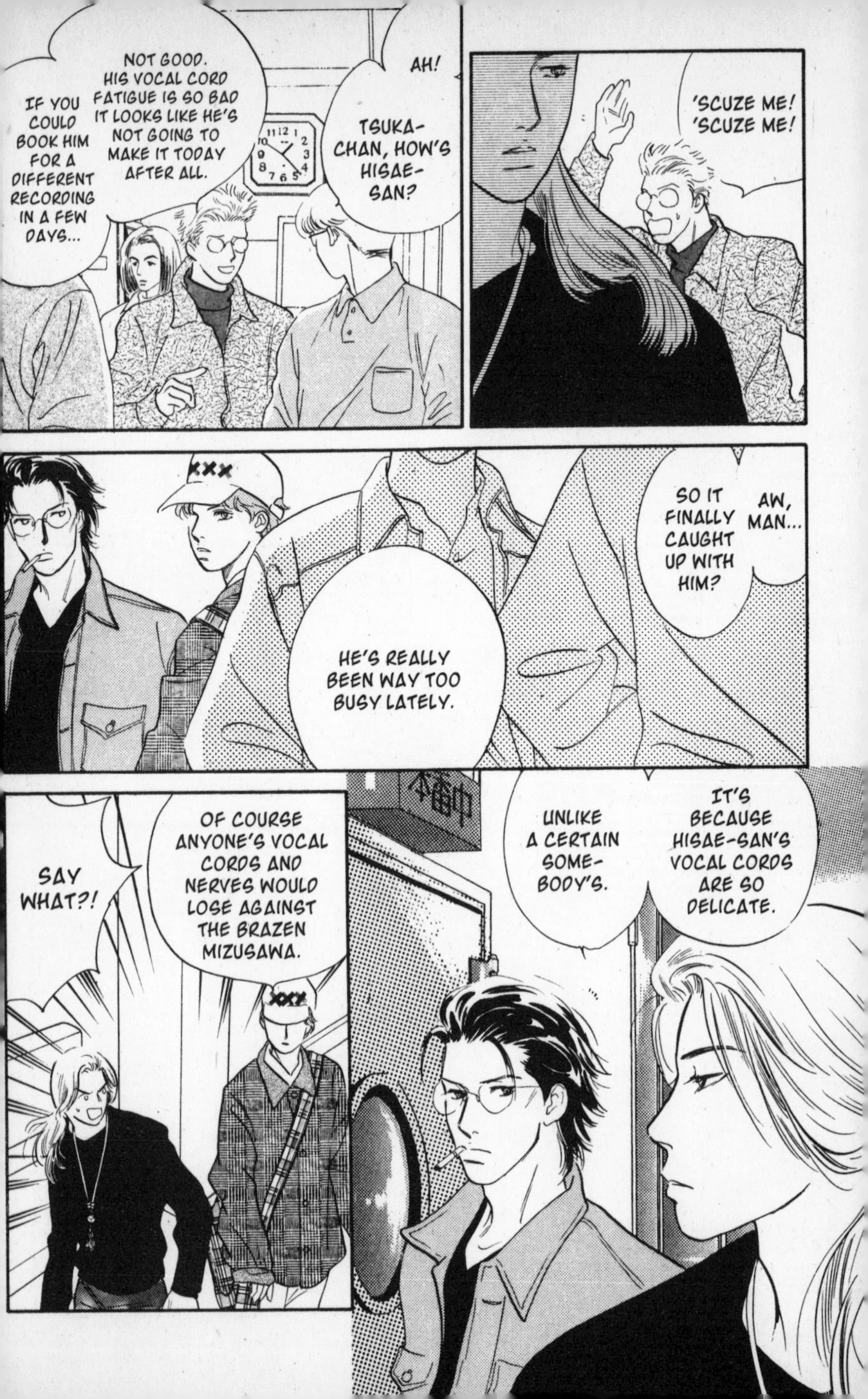
'SCUZE ME! 'SCUZE ME!
AH!
TSUKA-CHAN, HOW'S HISAE-SAN?
NOT GOOD. HIS VOCAL CORD FATIGUE IS SO BAD IT LOOKS LIKE HE'S NOT GOING TO MAKE IT TODAY AFTER ALL.
IF YOU COULD BOOK HIM FOR A DIFFERENT RECORDING IN A FEW DAYS...
AW, MAN...
SO IT FINALLY CAUGHT UP WITH HIM?
HE'S REALLY BEEN WAY TOO BUSY LATELY.
IT'S BECAUSE HISAE-SAN'S VOCAL CORDS ARE SO DELICATE.
UNLIKE A CERTAIN SOMEBODY'S.
OF COURSE ANYONE'S VOCAL CORDS AND NERVES WOULD LOSE AGAINST THE BRAZEN MIZUSAWA.
SAY WHAT?!

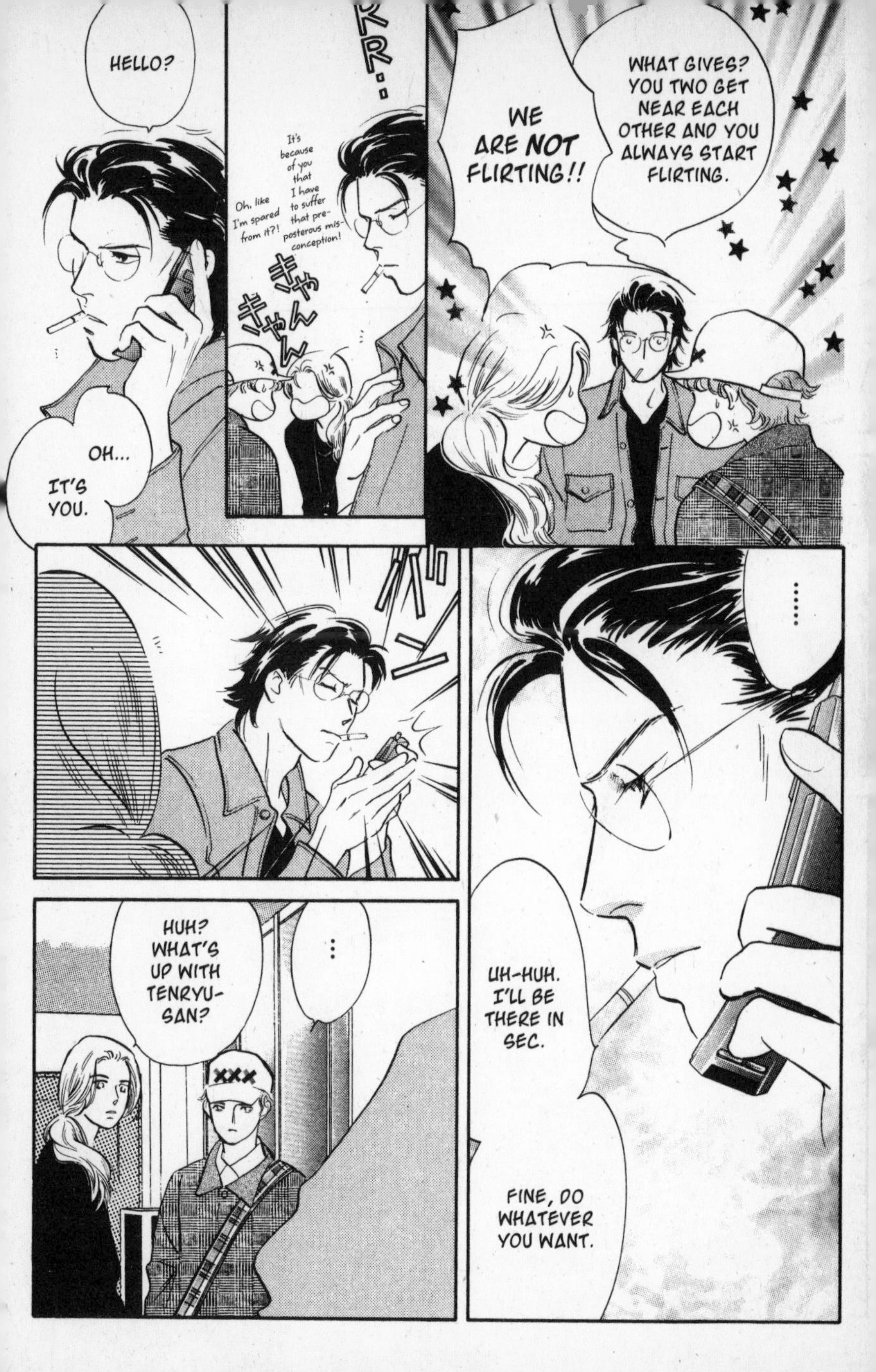
WHAT GIVES? YOU TWO GET NEAR EACH OTHER AND YOU ALWAYS START FLIRTING.
WE ARE **NOT** FLIRTING!!
RR..
It's because of you that I have to suffer that preposterous misconception!
Oh, like I'm spared from it?!
きゃんきゃん
HELLO?
OH... IT'S YOU.
......
UH-HUH. I'LL BE THERE IN SEC.
FINE, DO WHATEVER YOU WANT.
HUH? WHAT'S UP WITH TENRYU-SAN?
...

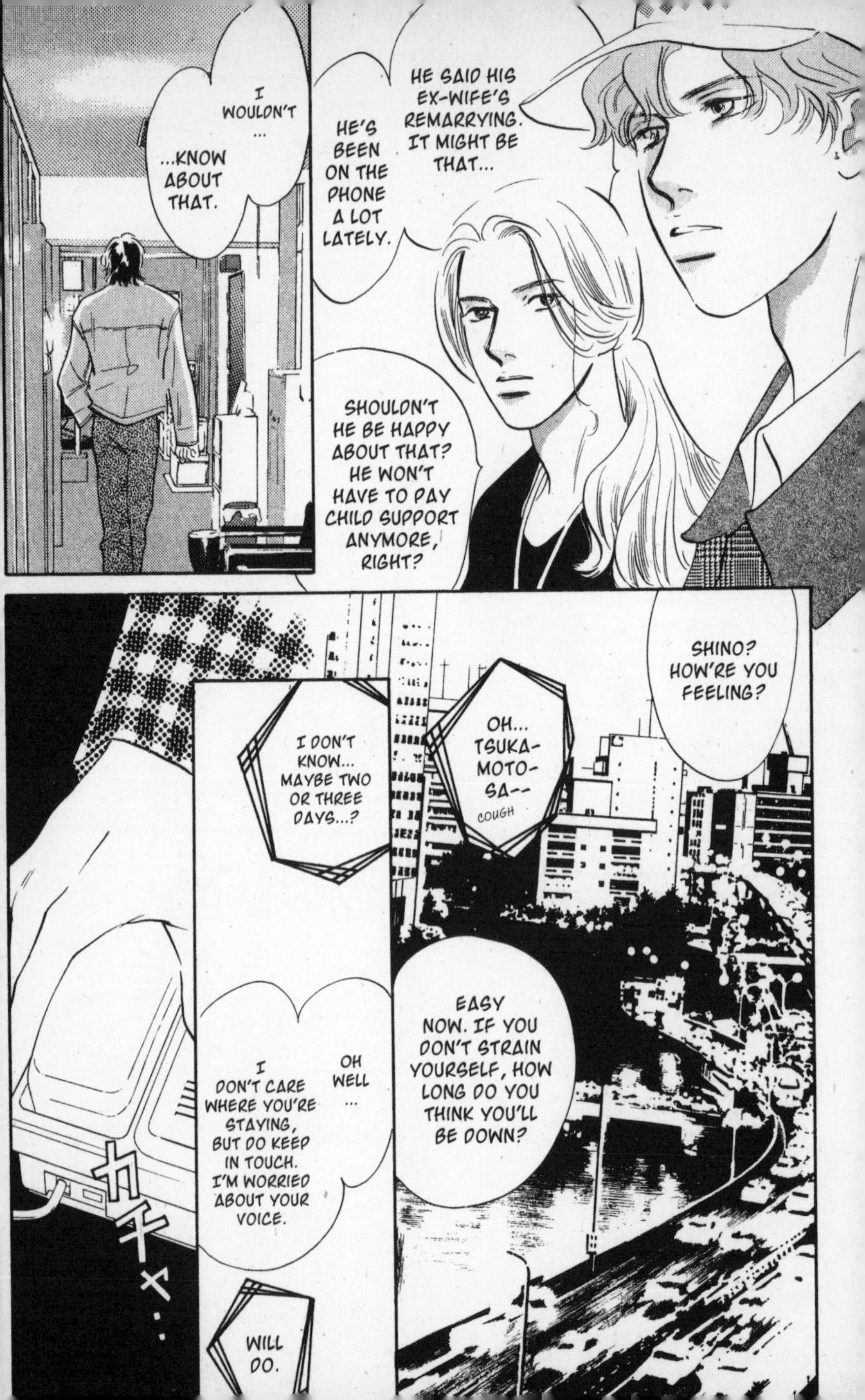
HE SAID HIS EX-WIFE'S REMARRYING. IT MIGHT BE THAT...
HE'S BEEN ON THE PHONE A LOT LATELY.
SHOULDN'T HE BE HAPPY ABOUT THAT? HE WON'T HAVE TO PAY CHILD SUPPORT ANYMORE, RIGHT?
I WOULDN'T ...
...KNOW ABOUT THAT.
SHINO? HOW'RE YOU FEELING?
OH... TSUKA-MOTO-SA-- COUGH
EASY NOW. IF YOU DON'T STRAIN YOURSELF, HOW LONG DO YOU THINK YOU'LL BE DOWN?
I DON'T KNOW... MAYBE TWO OR THREE DAYS...?
OH WELL ...
I DON'T CARE WHERE YOU'RE STAYING, BUT DO KEEP IN TOUCH. I'M WORRIED ABOUT YOUR VOICE.
WILL DO.
カチャ‥

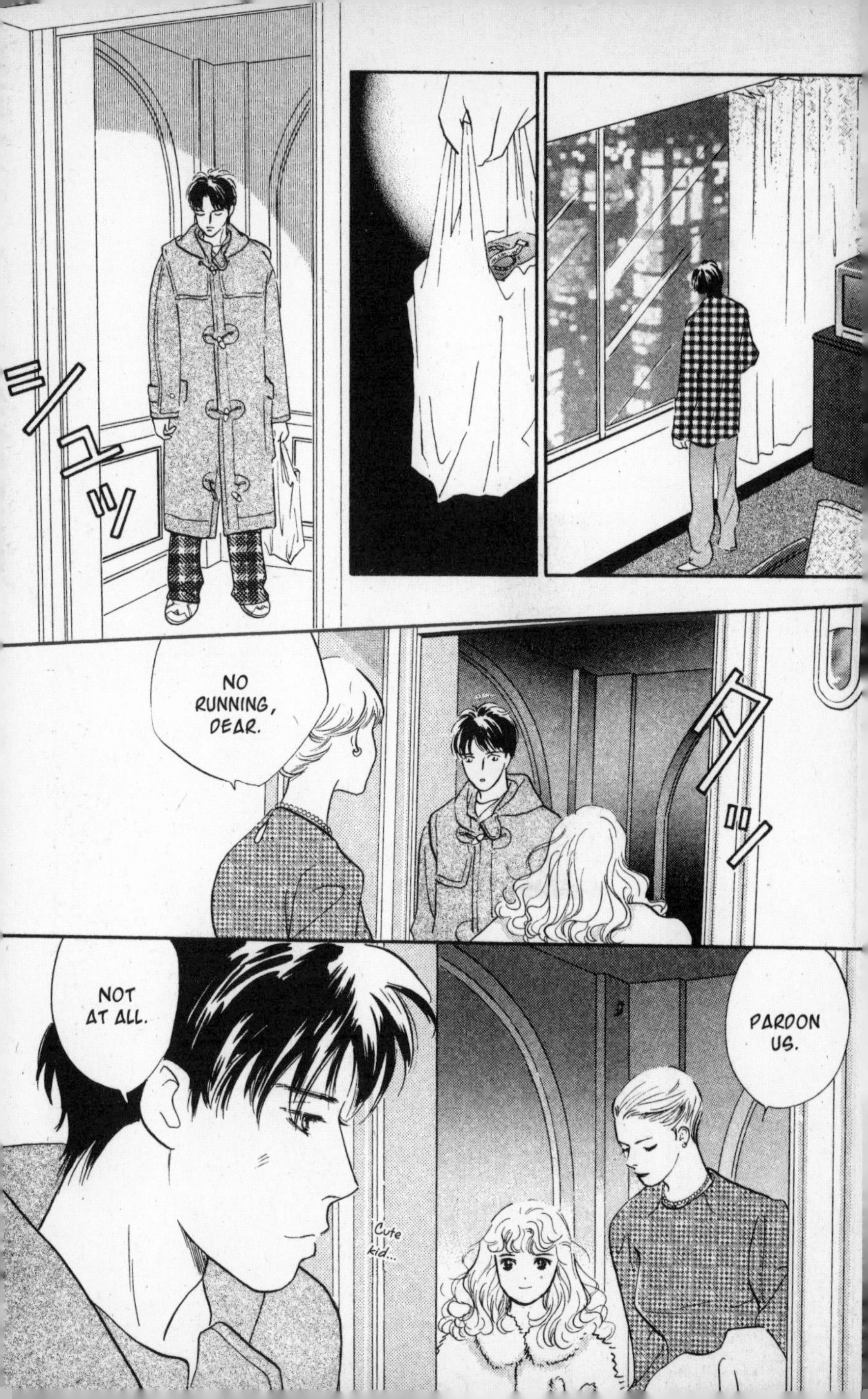
NO RUNNING, DEAR.
PARDON US.
Cute kid...
NOT AT ALL.

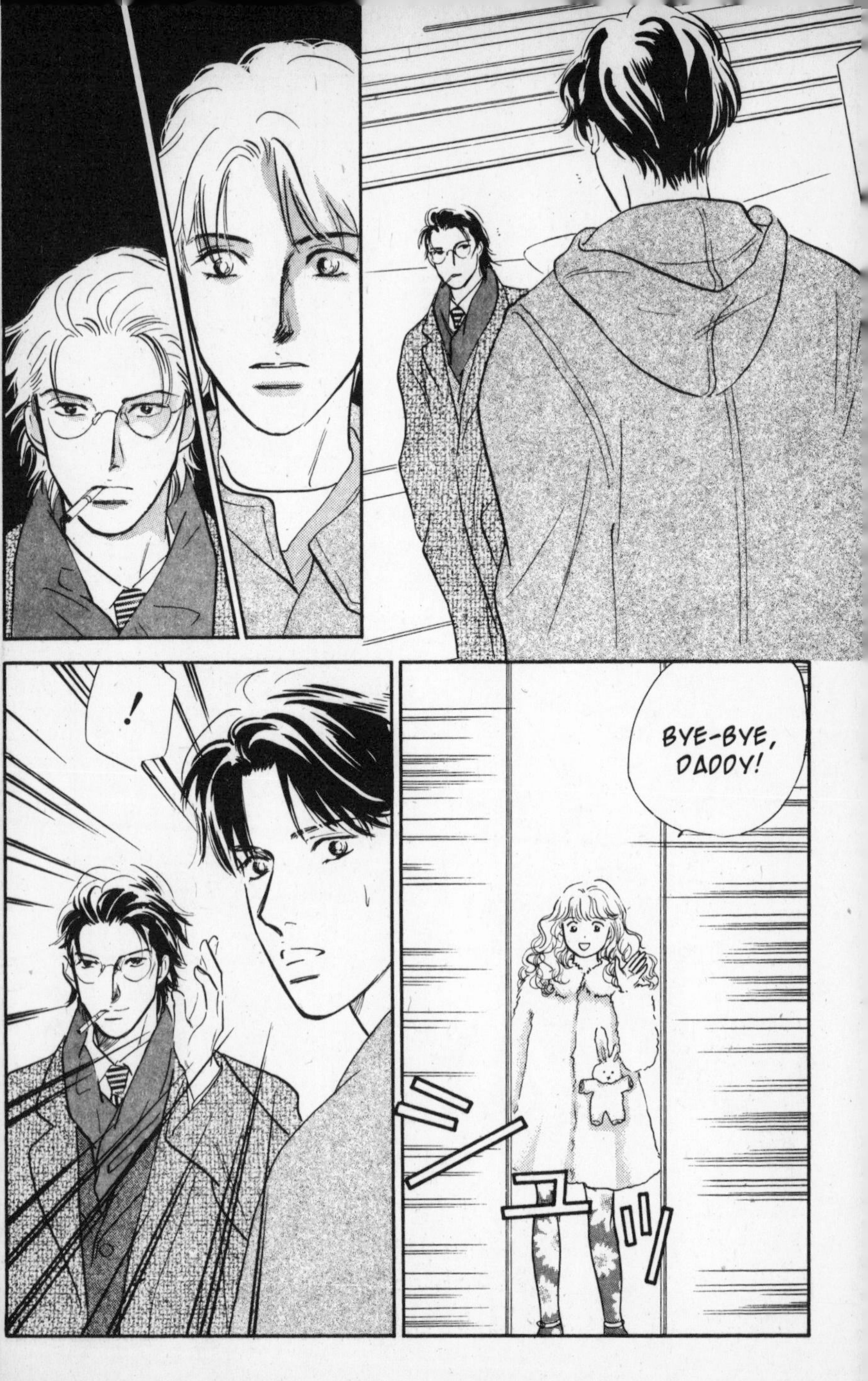
!
BYE-BYE, DADDY!

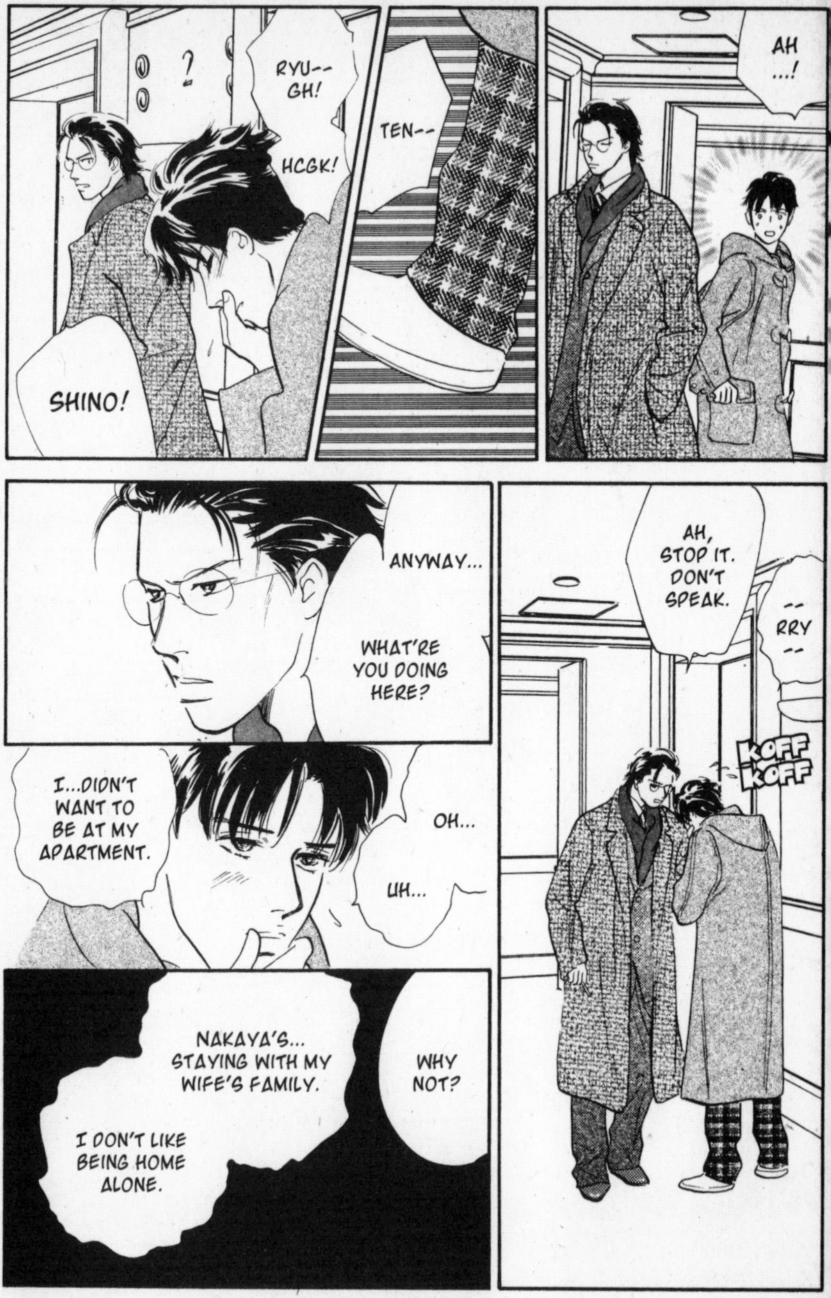
AH ...!
TEN--
RYU--GH!
HCGK!
?
SHINO!
--RRY--
AH, STOP IT. DON'T SPEAK.
KOFF KOFF
ANYWAY...
WHAT'RE YOU DOING HERE?
OH...
UH...
I...DIDN'T WANT TO BE AT MY APARTMENT.
WHY NOT?
NAKAYA'S... STAYING WITH MY WIFE'S FAMILY.
I DON'T LIKE BEING HOME ALONE.

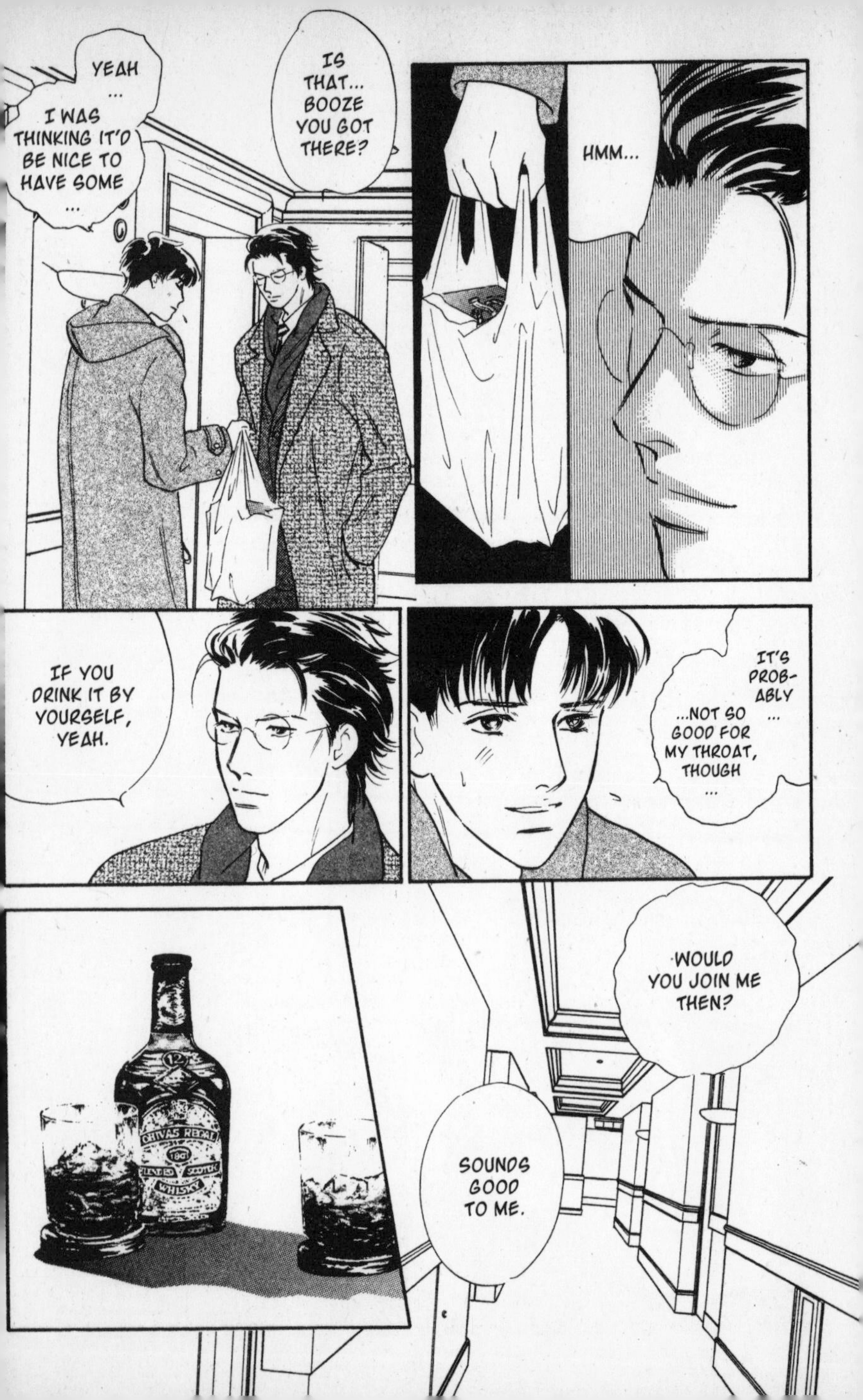
HMM...
IS THAT... BOOZE YOU GOT THERE?
YEAH ... I WAS THINKING IT'D BE NICE TO HAVE SOME ...
IT'S PROBABLY ... ...NOT SO GOOD FOR MY THROAT, THOUGH ...
IF YOU DRINK IT BY YOURSELF, YEAH.
WOULD YOU JOIN ME THEN?
SOUNDS GOOD TO ME.
CHIVAS REGAL
BLENDED SCOTCH WHISKY

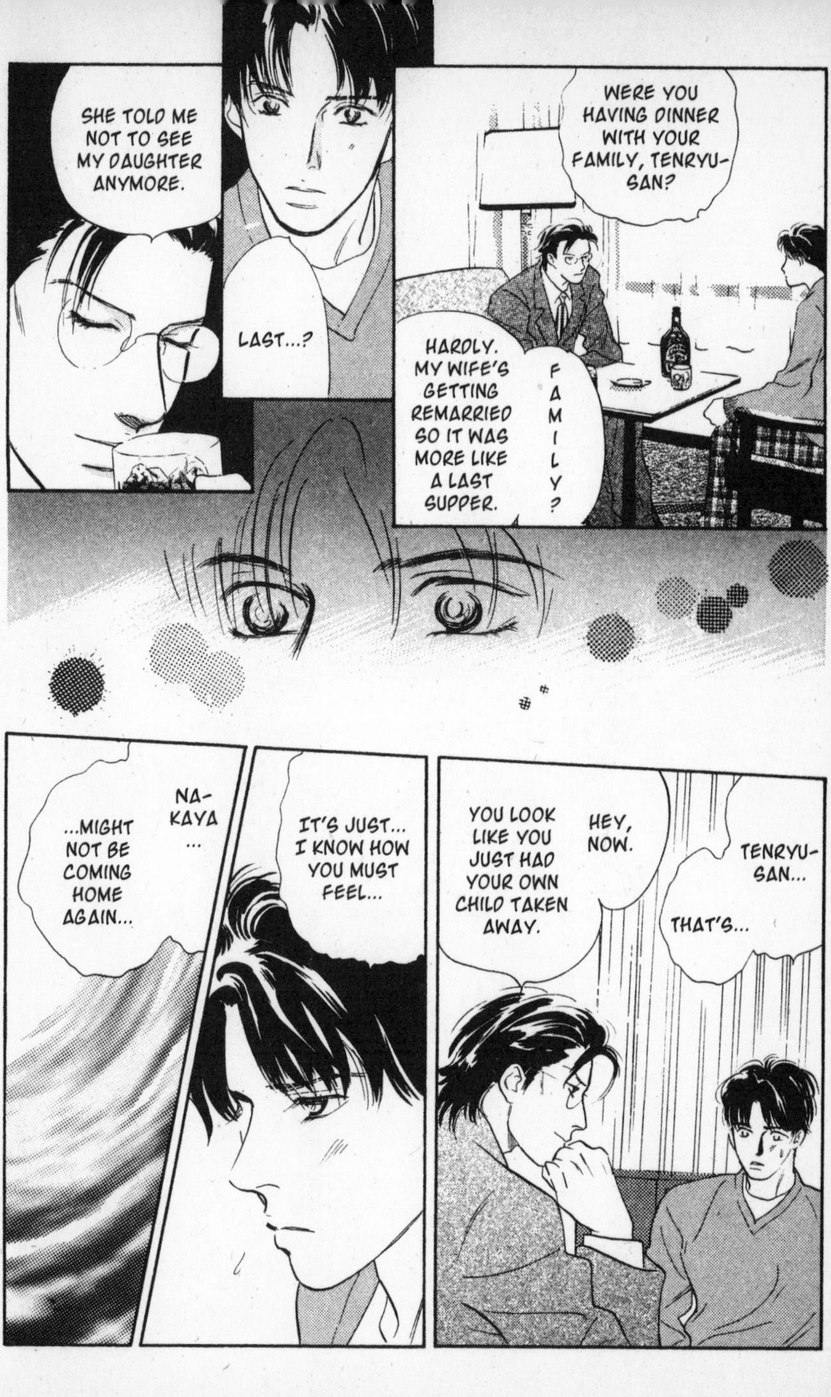
WERE YOU HAVING DINNER WITH YOUR FAMILY, TENRYU-SAN?
HARDLY. MY WIFE'S GETTING REMARRIED SO IT WAS MORE LIKE A LAST SUPPER.
FAMILY?
LAST...?
SHE TOLD ME NOT TO SEE MY DAUGHTER ANYMORE.
TENRYU-SAN...
THAT'S...
HEY, NOW.
YOU LOOK LIKE YOU JUST HAD YOUR OWN CHILD TAKEN AWAY.
IT'S JUST... I KNOW HOW YOU MUST FEEL...
NA-KAYA...
...MIGHT NOT BE COMING HOME AGAIN...

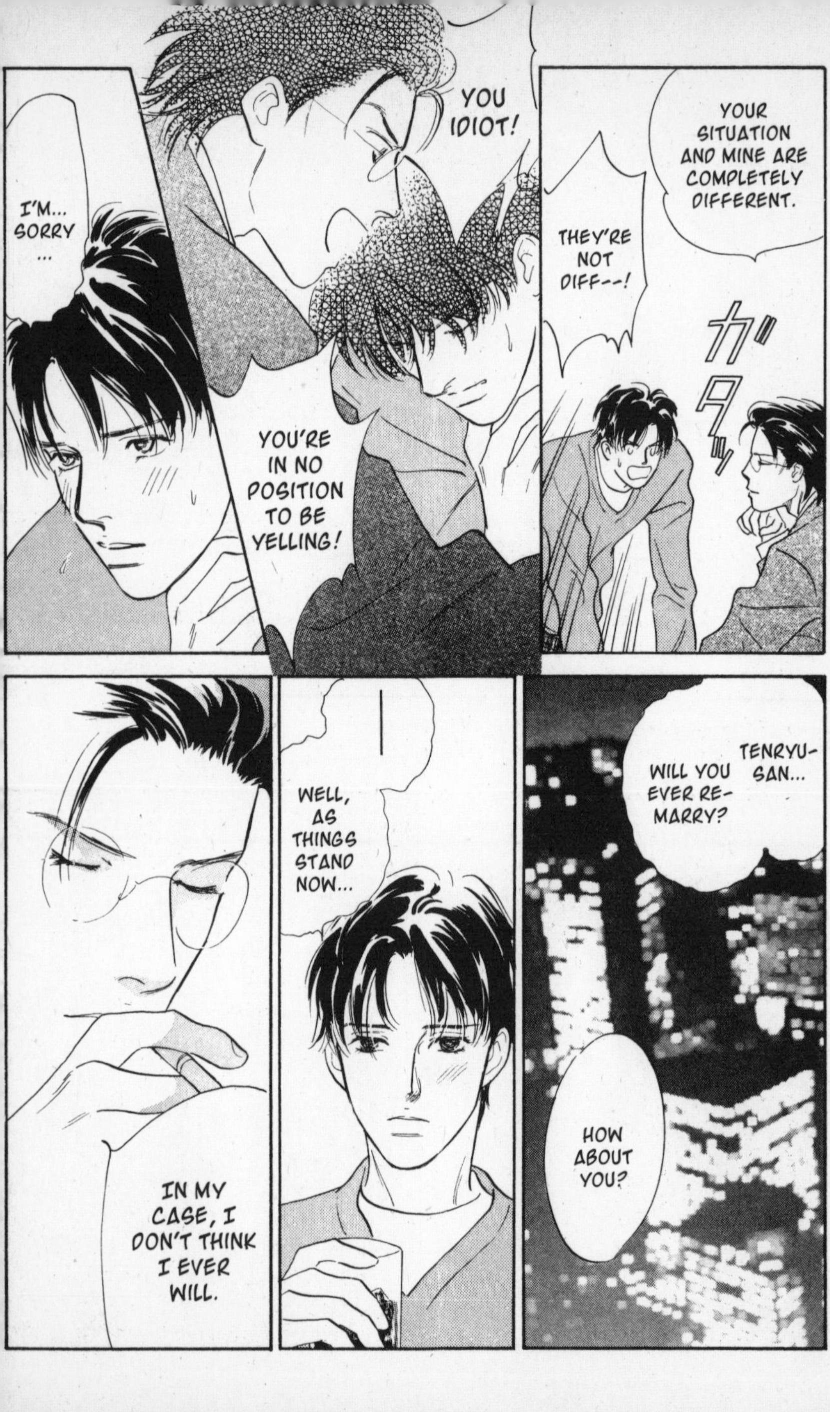
YOUR SITUATION AND MINE ARE COMPLETELY DIFFERENT.
THEY'RE NOT DIFF--!
ガタッ
YOU IDIOT!
YOU'RE IN NO POSITION TO BE YELLING!
I'M... SORRY ...
TENRYU-SAN...
WILL YOU EVER RE-MARRY?
HOW ABOUT YOU?
WELL, AS THINGS STAND NOW...
IN MY CASE, I DON'T THINK I EVER WILL.

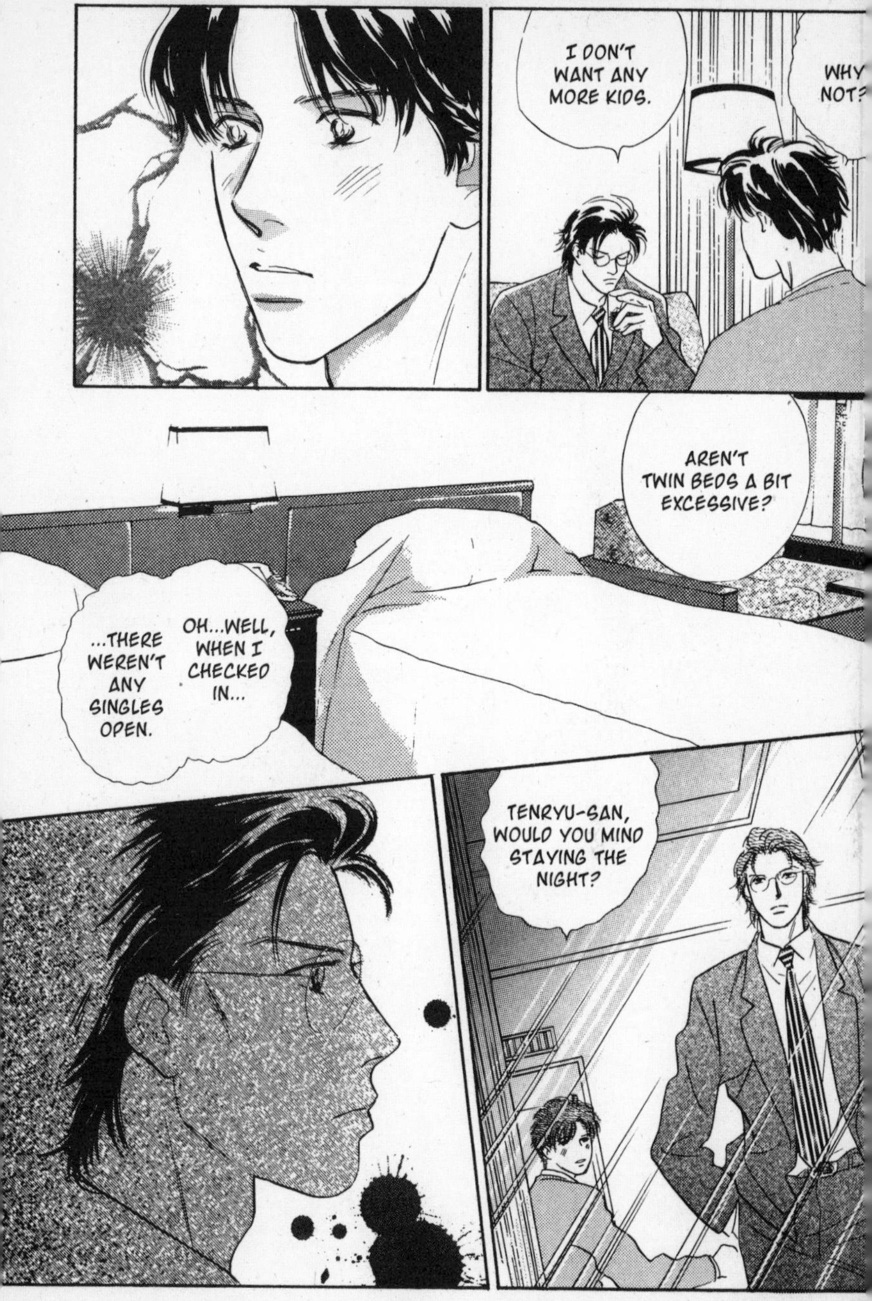
WHY NOT?
I DON'T WANT ANY MORE KIDS.
AREN'T TWIN BEDS A BIT EXCESSIVE?
OH...WELL, WHEN I CHECKED IN...
...THERE WEREN'T ANY SINGLES OPEN.
TENRYU-SAN, WOULD YOU MIND STAYING THE NIGHT?

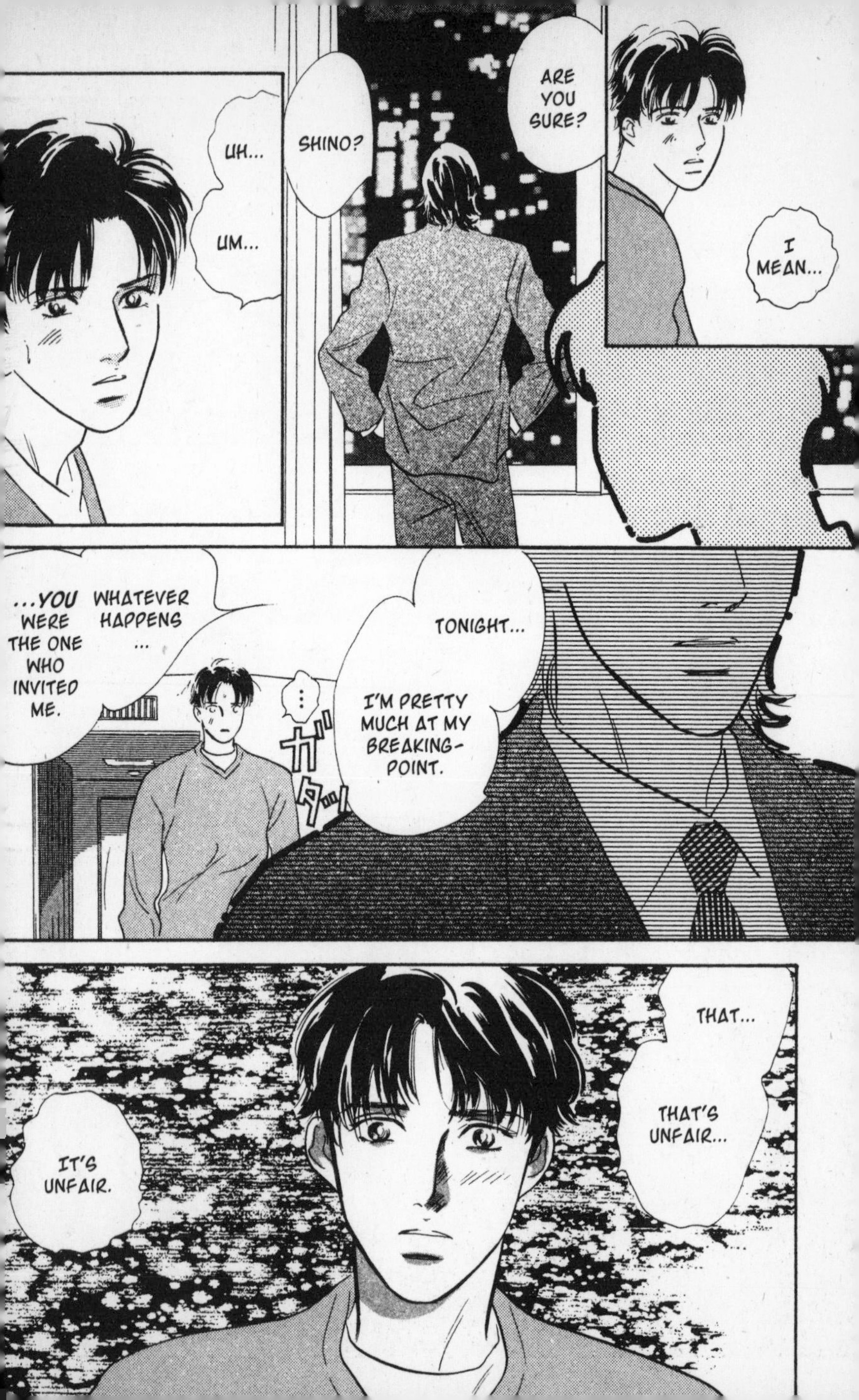
ARE YOU SURE?
I MEAN...
SHINO?
UH...
UM...
TONIGHT...
I'M PRETTY MUCH AT MY BREAKING-POINT.
...
ガタッ
WHATEVER HAPPENS ...
...YOU WERE THE ONE WHO INVITED ME.
THAT...
THAT'S UNFAIR...
IT'S UNFAIR.

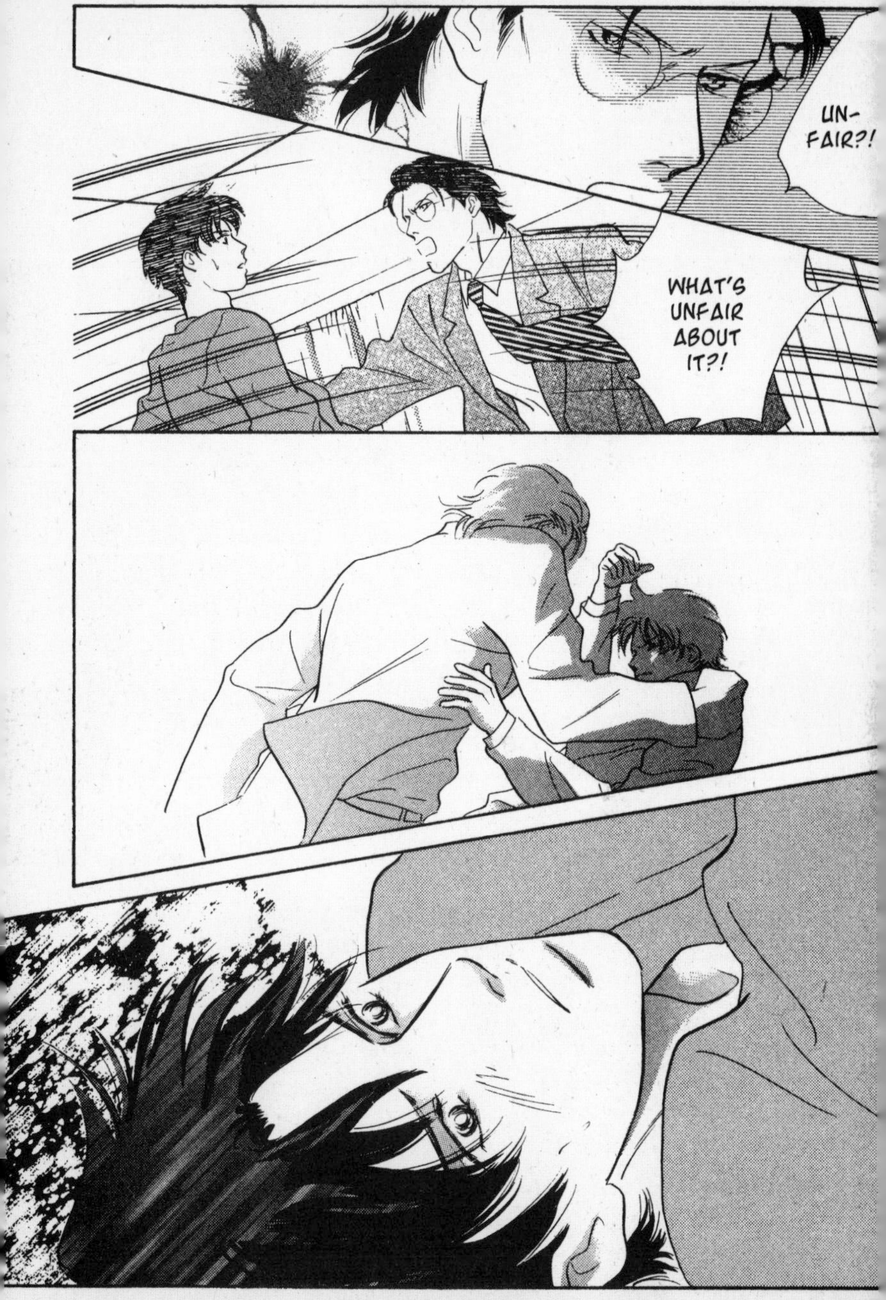
UN-
FAIR?!
WHAT'S UNFAIR ABOUT IT?!

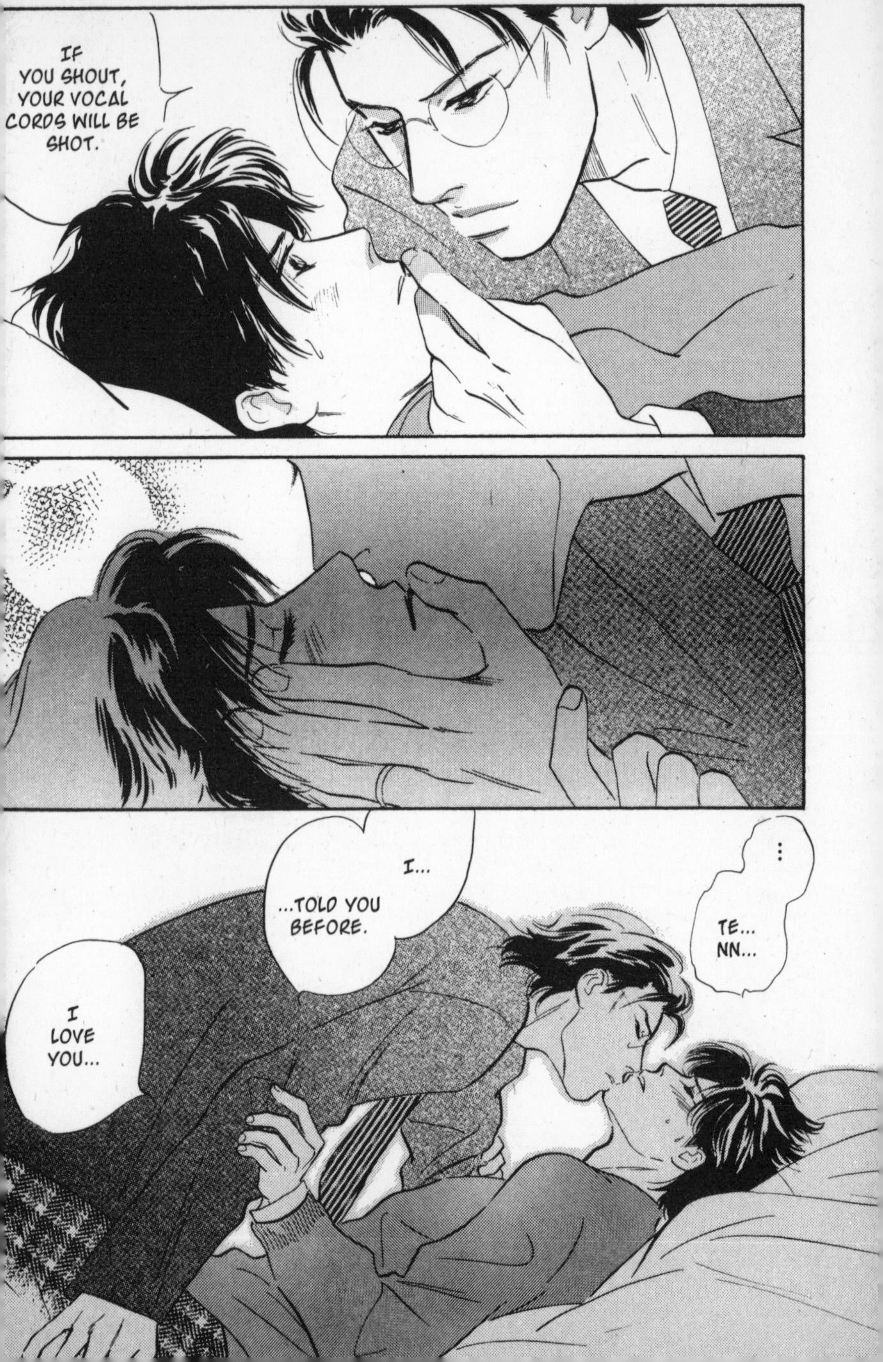
IF YOU SHOUT, YOUR VOCAL CORDS WILL BE SHOT.
...
TE... NN...
I...
...TOLD YOU BEFORE.
I LOVE YOU...

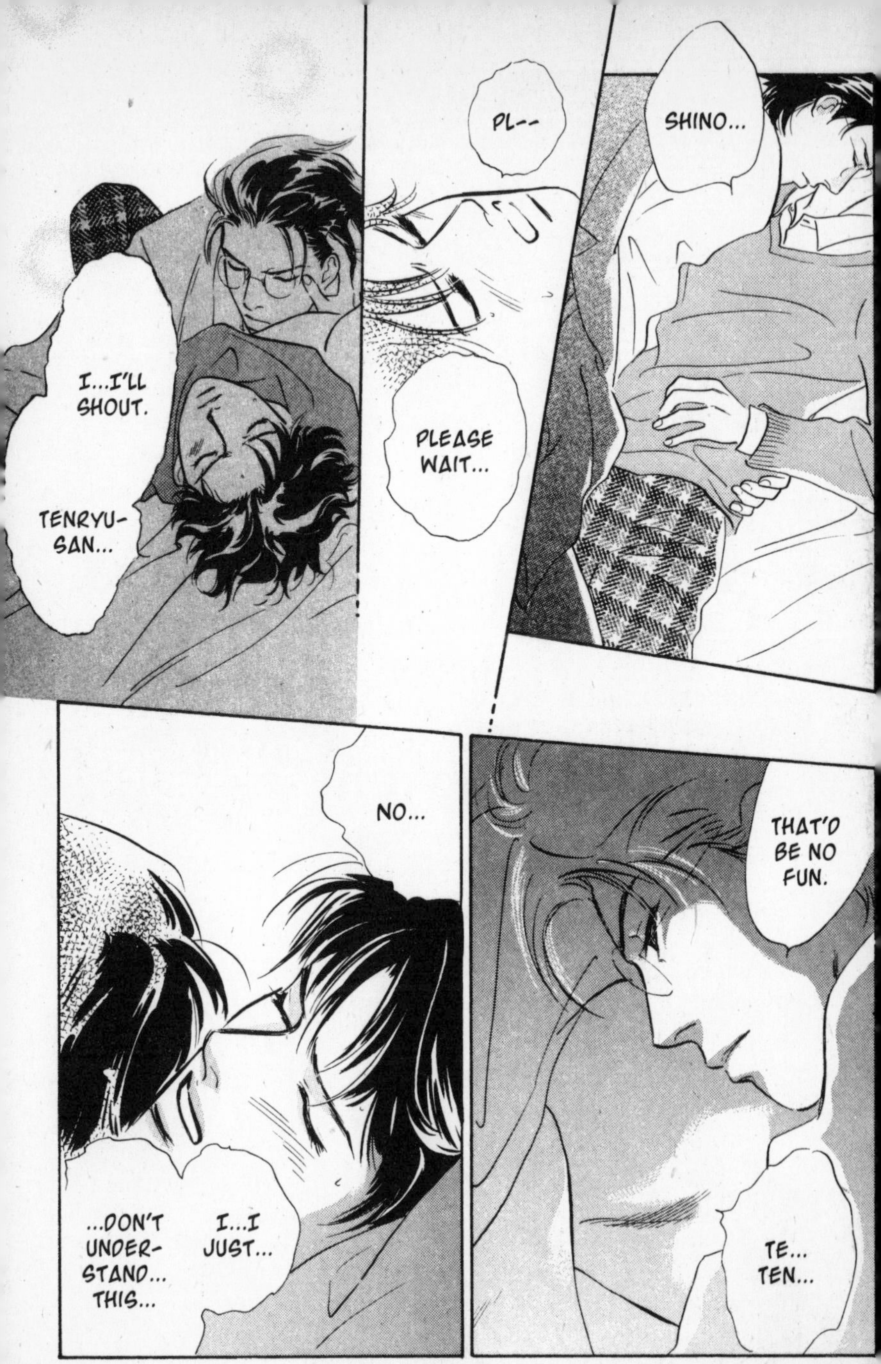
SHINO...
PL--
PLEASE WAIT...
I...I'LL SHOUT.
TENRYU-SAN...
THAT'D BE NO FUN.
TE... TEN...
NO...
I...I JUST...
...DON'T UNDER-STAND... THIS...

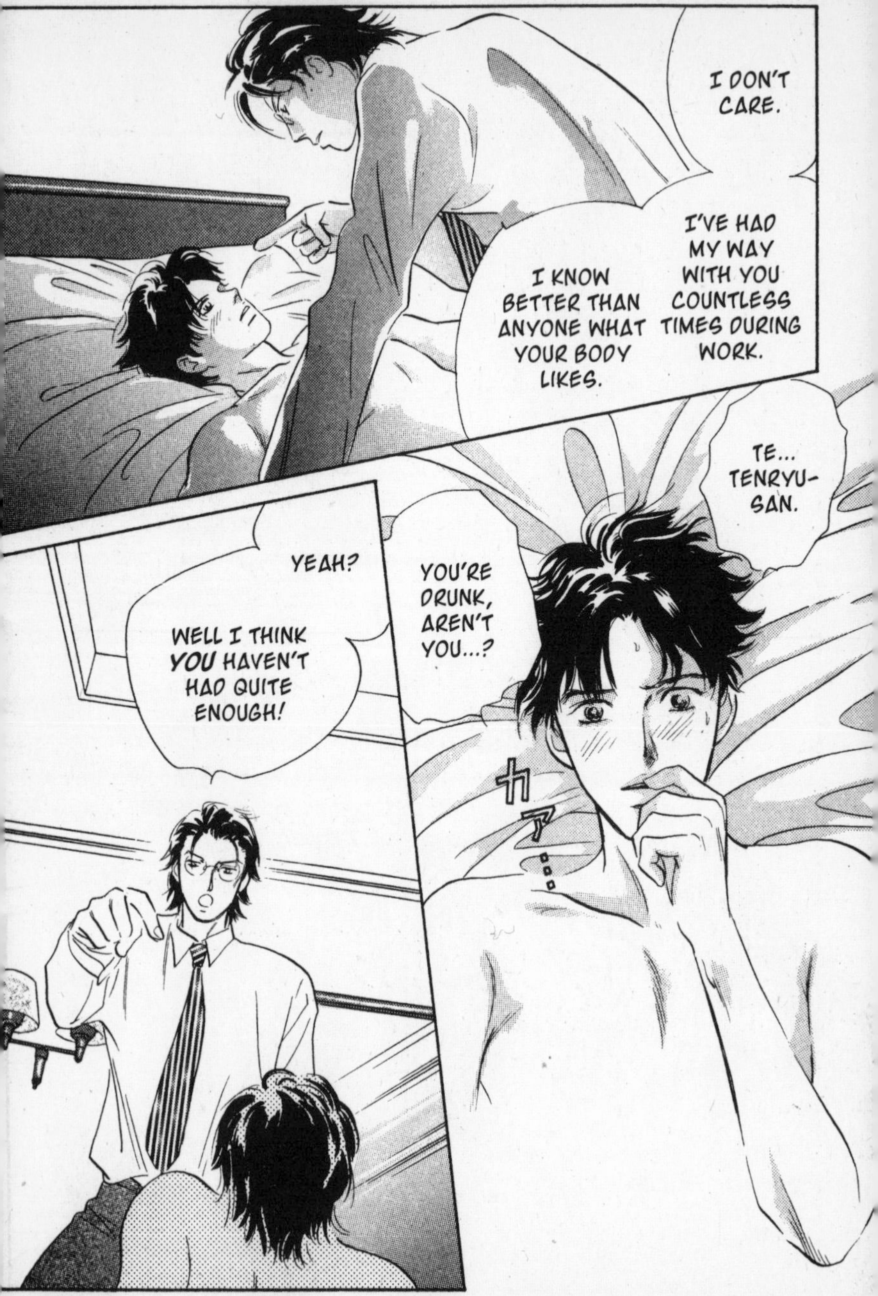

I DON'T CARE.
I'VE HAD MY WAY WITH YOU COUNTLESS TIMES DURING WORK.
I KNOW BETTER THAN ANYONE WHAT YOUR BODY LIKES.
TE... TENRYU-SAN.
YOU'RE DRUNK, AREN'T YOU...?
カァ...
YEAH?
WELL I THINK *YOU* HAVEN'T HAD QUITE ENOUGH!

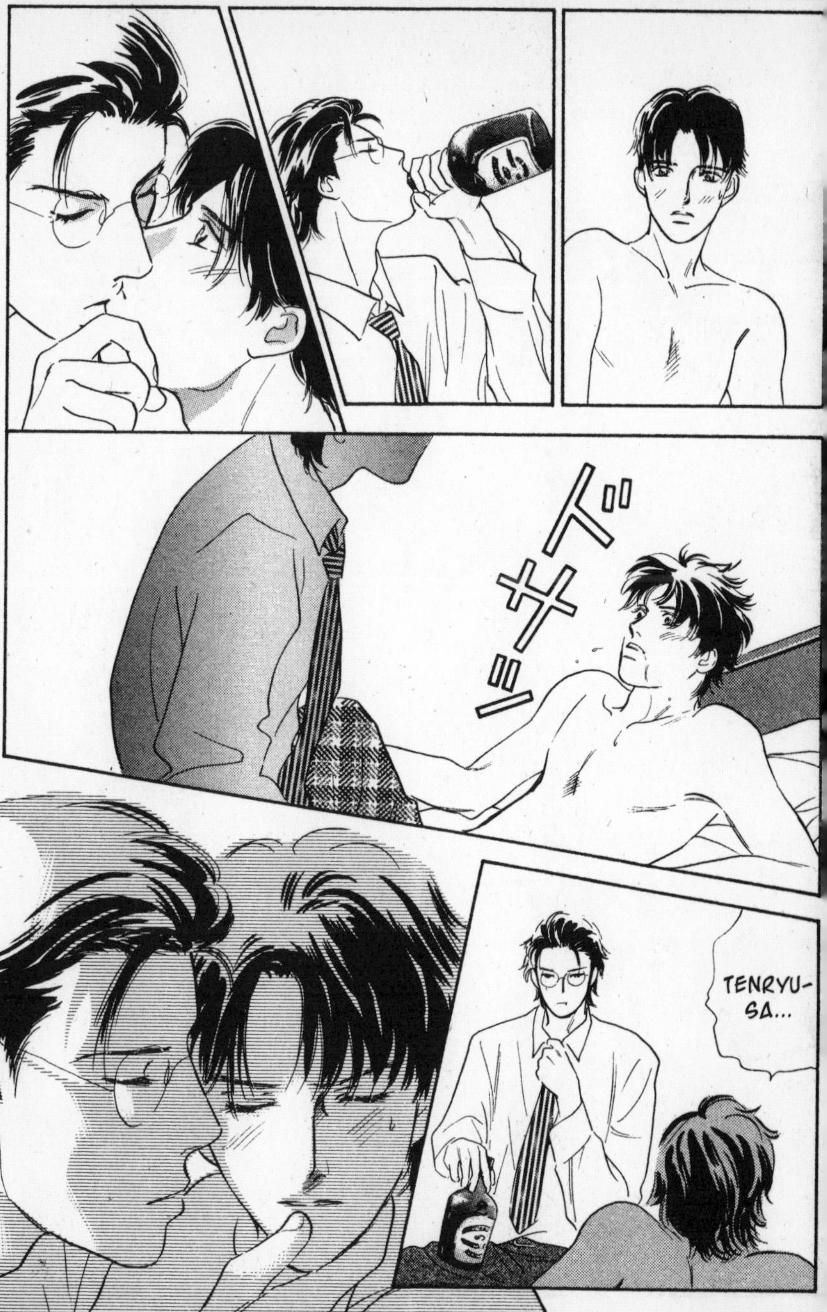
ズサッ
TENRYU-SA...

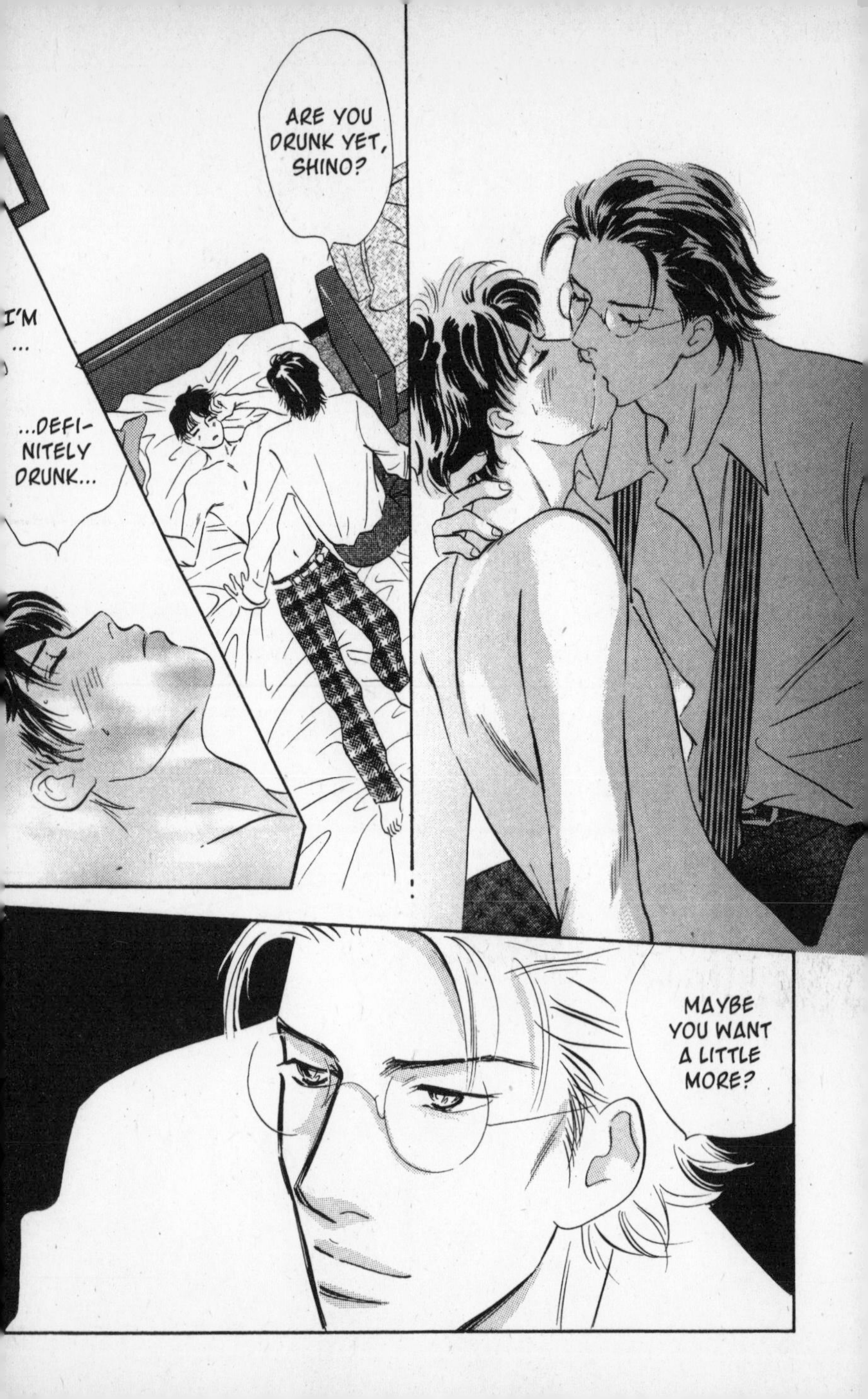
ARE YOU DRUNK YET, SHINO?
I'M ...
...DEFINITELY DRUNK...
MAYBE YOU WANT A LITTLE MORE?

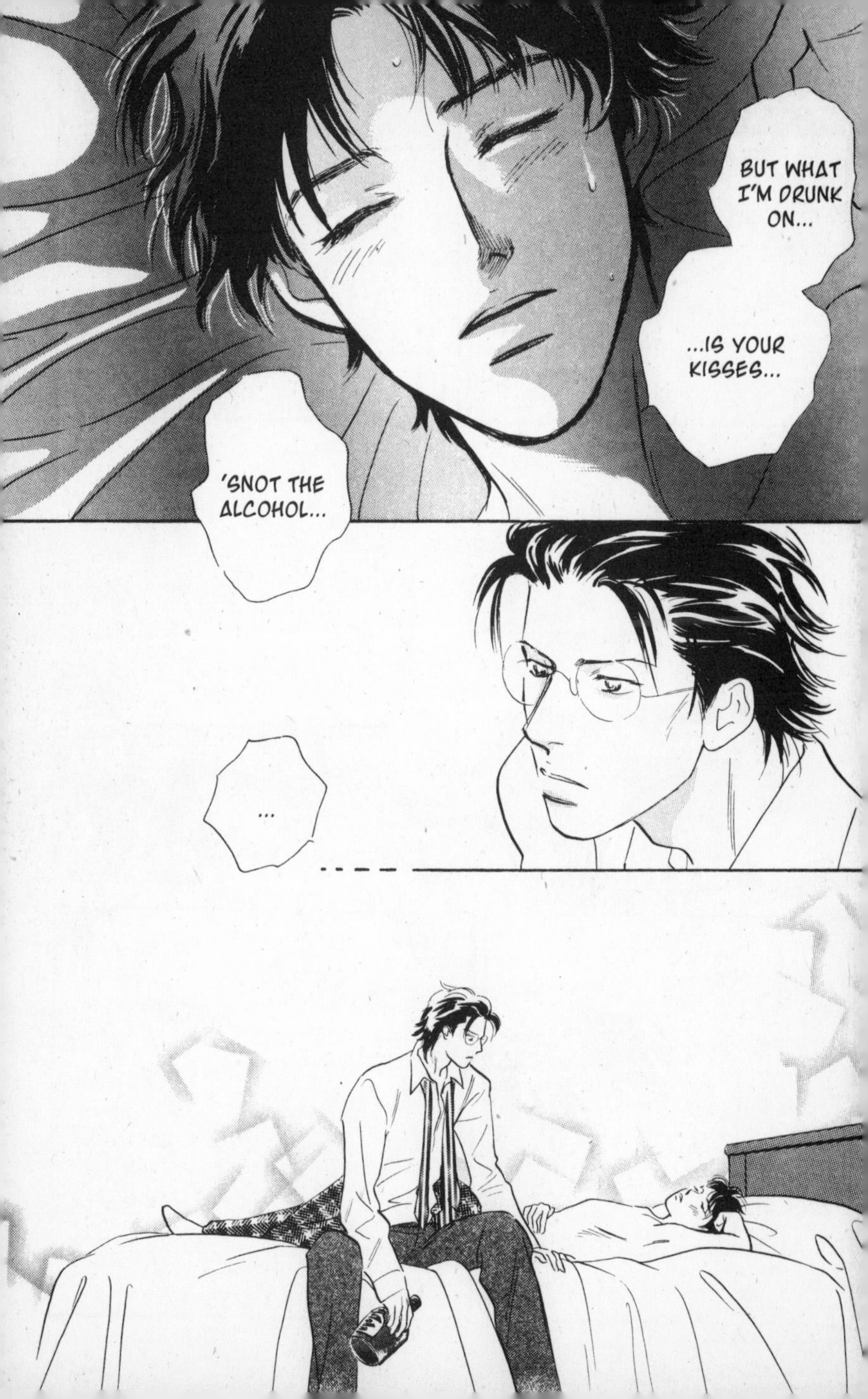
BUT WHAT I'M DRUNK ON...
...IS YOUR KISSES...
'SNOT THE ALCOHOL...
...

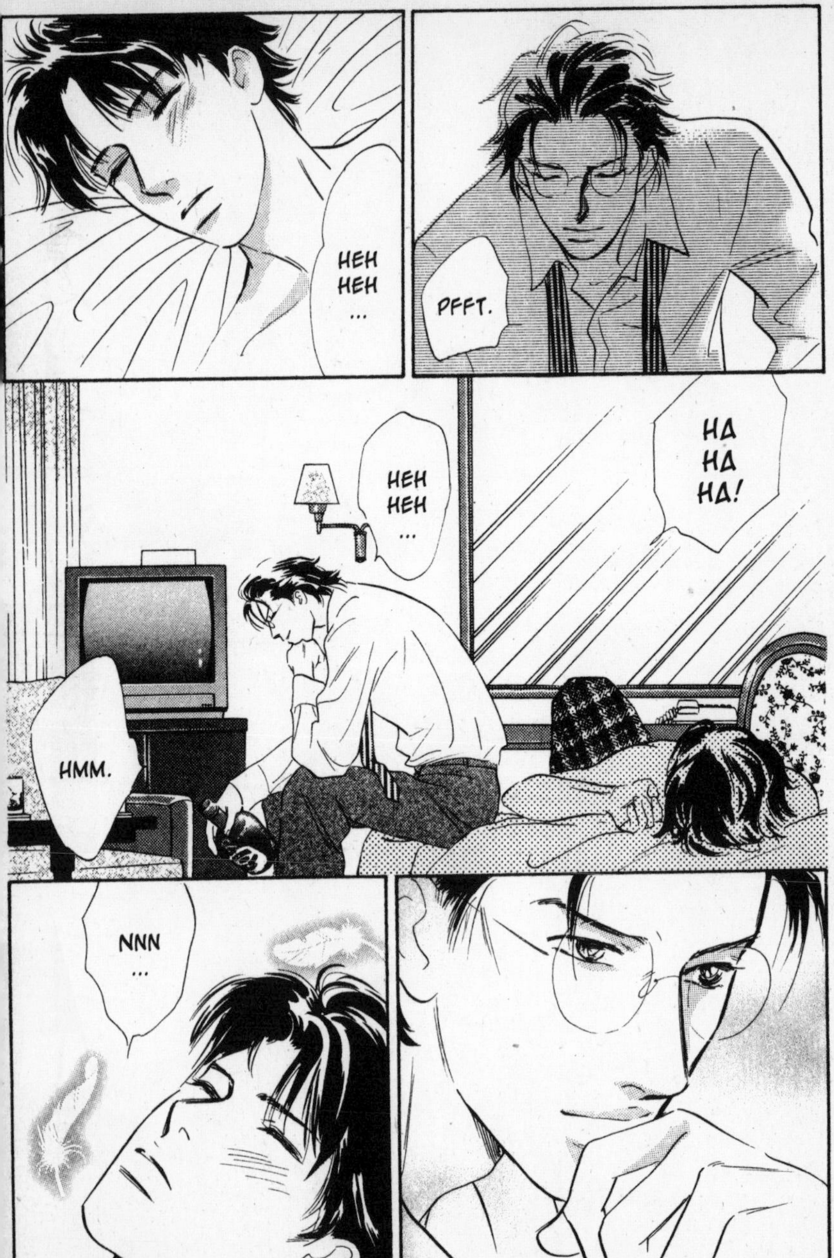
PFFT.
HEH HEH ...
HA HA HA!
HEH HEH ...
HMM.
NNN ...

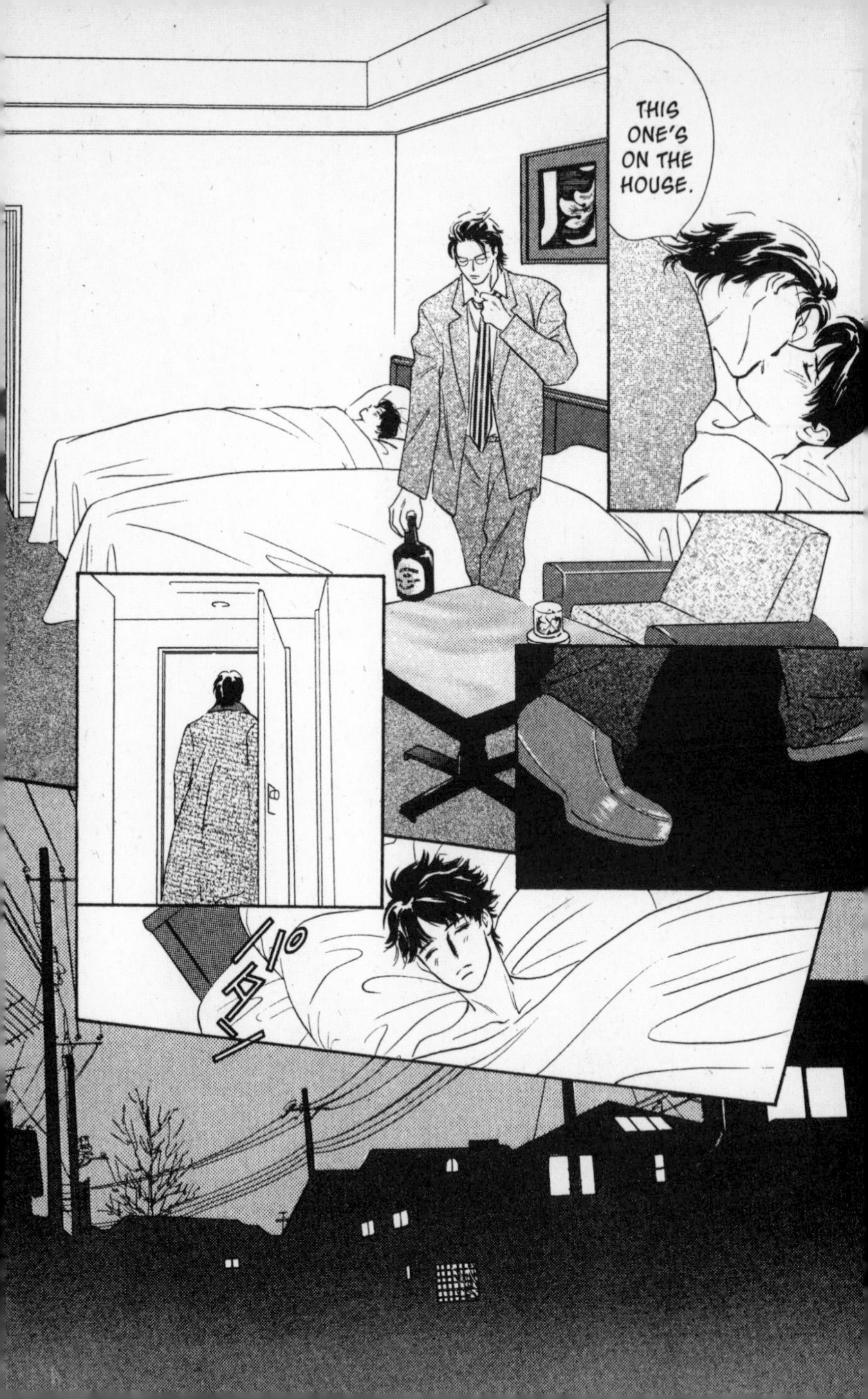
THIS ONE'S ON THE HOUSE.
パタン

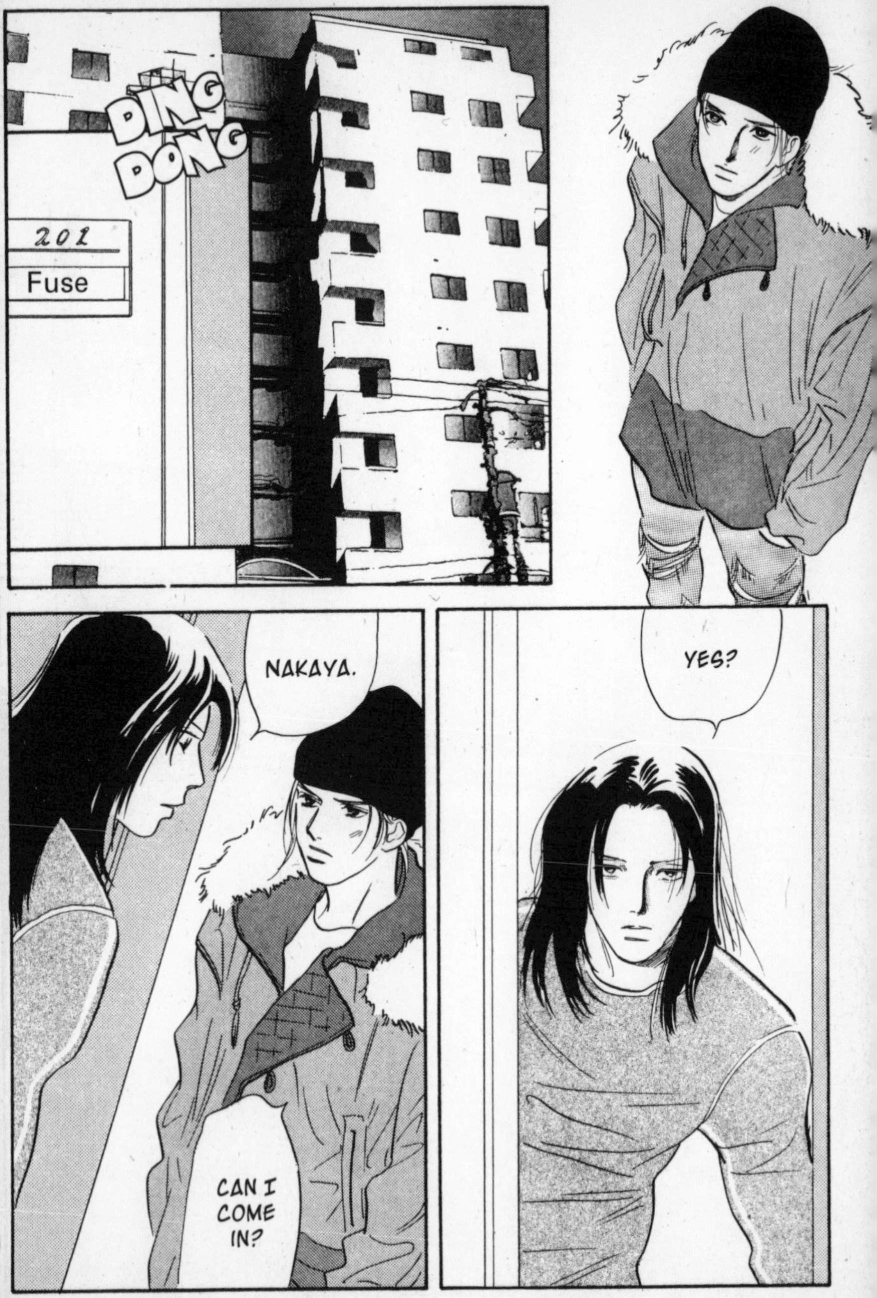
DING DONG
201
Fuse
YES?
NAKAYA.
CAN I COME IN?

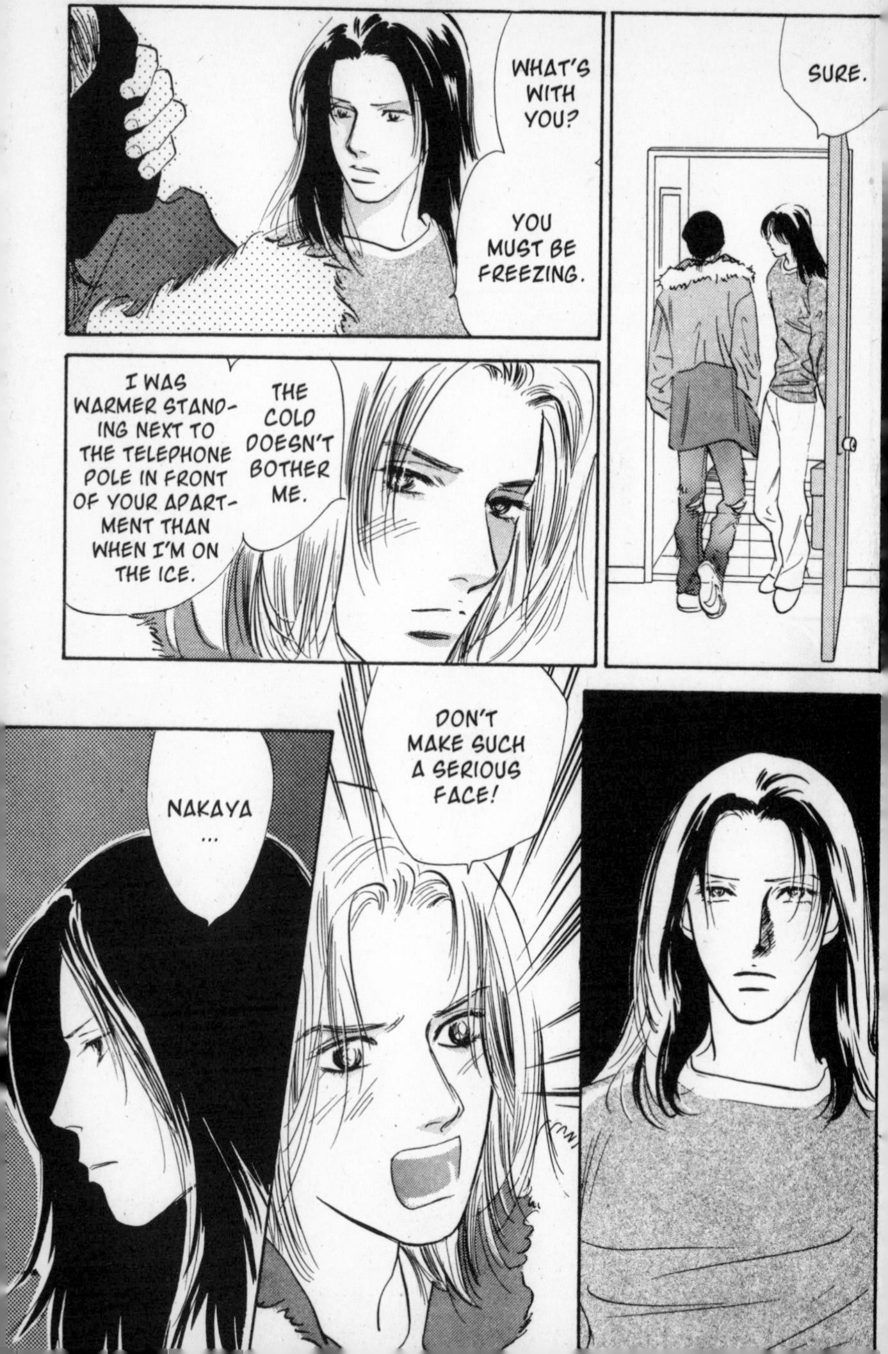
SURE.
WHAT'S WITH YOU?
YOU MUST BE FREEZING.
THE COLD DOESN'T BOTHER ME.
I WAS WARMER STANDING NEXT TO THE TELEPHONE POLE IN FRONT OF YOUR APARTMENT THAN WHEN I'M ON THE ICE.
DON'T MAKE SUCH A SERIOUS FACE!
NAKAYA ...

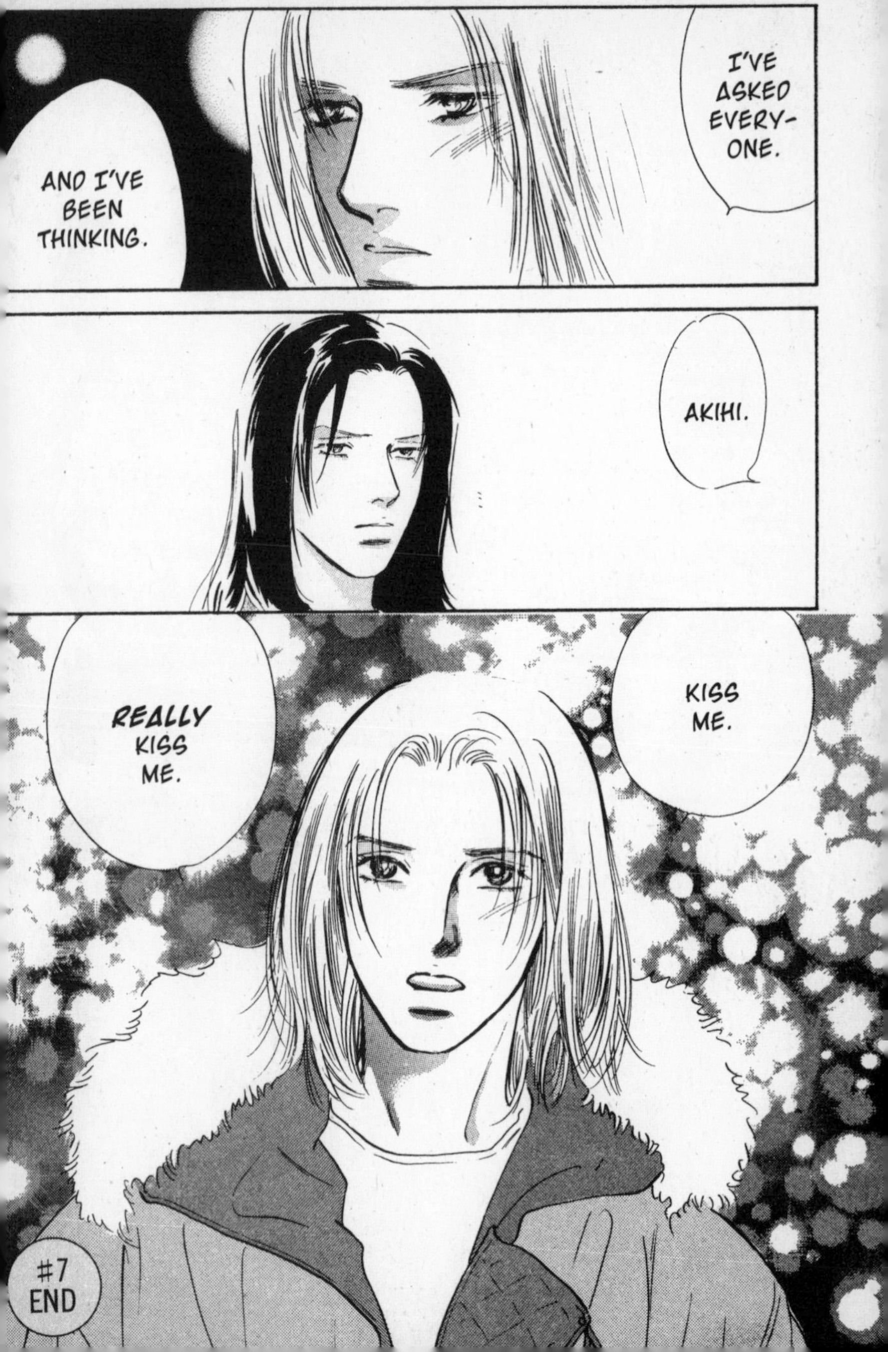
I'VE ASKED EVERY-ONE.
AND I'VE BEEN THINKING.
AKIHI.
KISS ME.
REALLY KISS ME.
#7 END

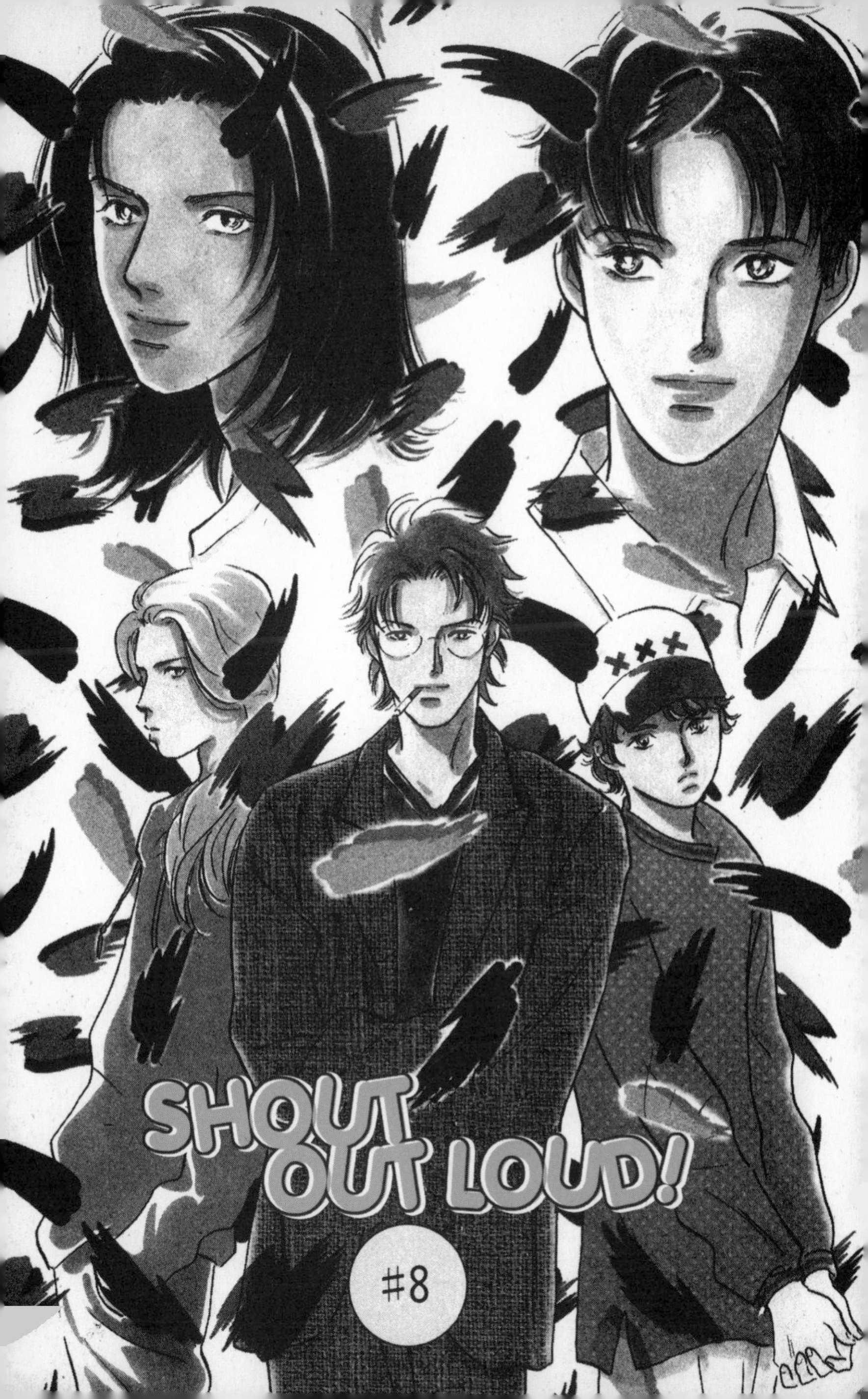
SHOUT OUT LOUD!
#8

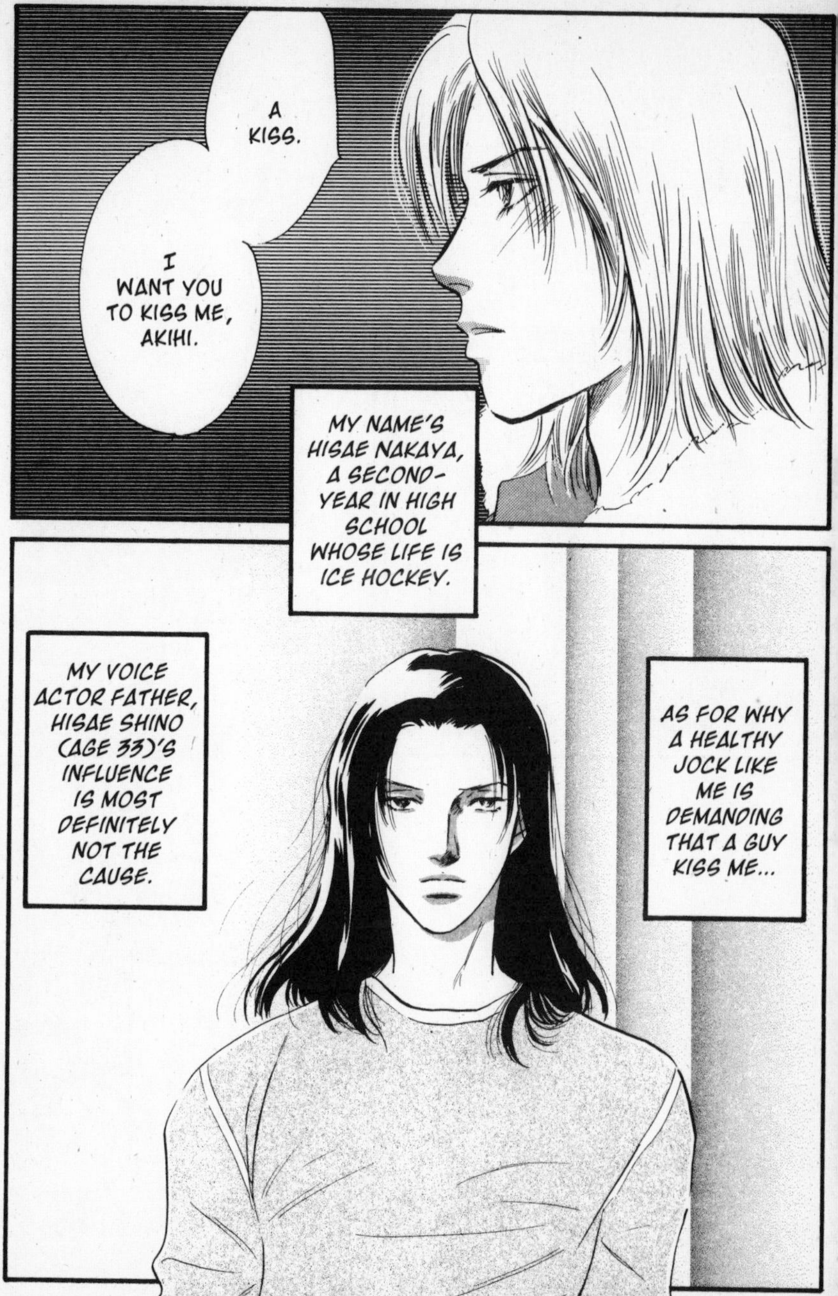
A KISS.
I WANT YOU TO KISS ME, AKIHI.
MY NAME'S HISAE NAKAYA, A SECOND-YEAR IN HIGH SCHOOL WHOSE LIFE IS ICE HOCKEY.
AS FOR WHY A HEALTHY JOCK LIKE ME IS DEMANDING THAT A GUY KISS ME...
MY VOICE ACTOR FATHER, HISAE SHINO (AGE 33)'S INFLUENCE IS MOST DEFINITELY NOT THE CAUSE.

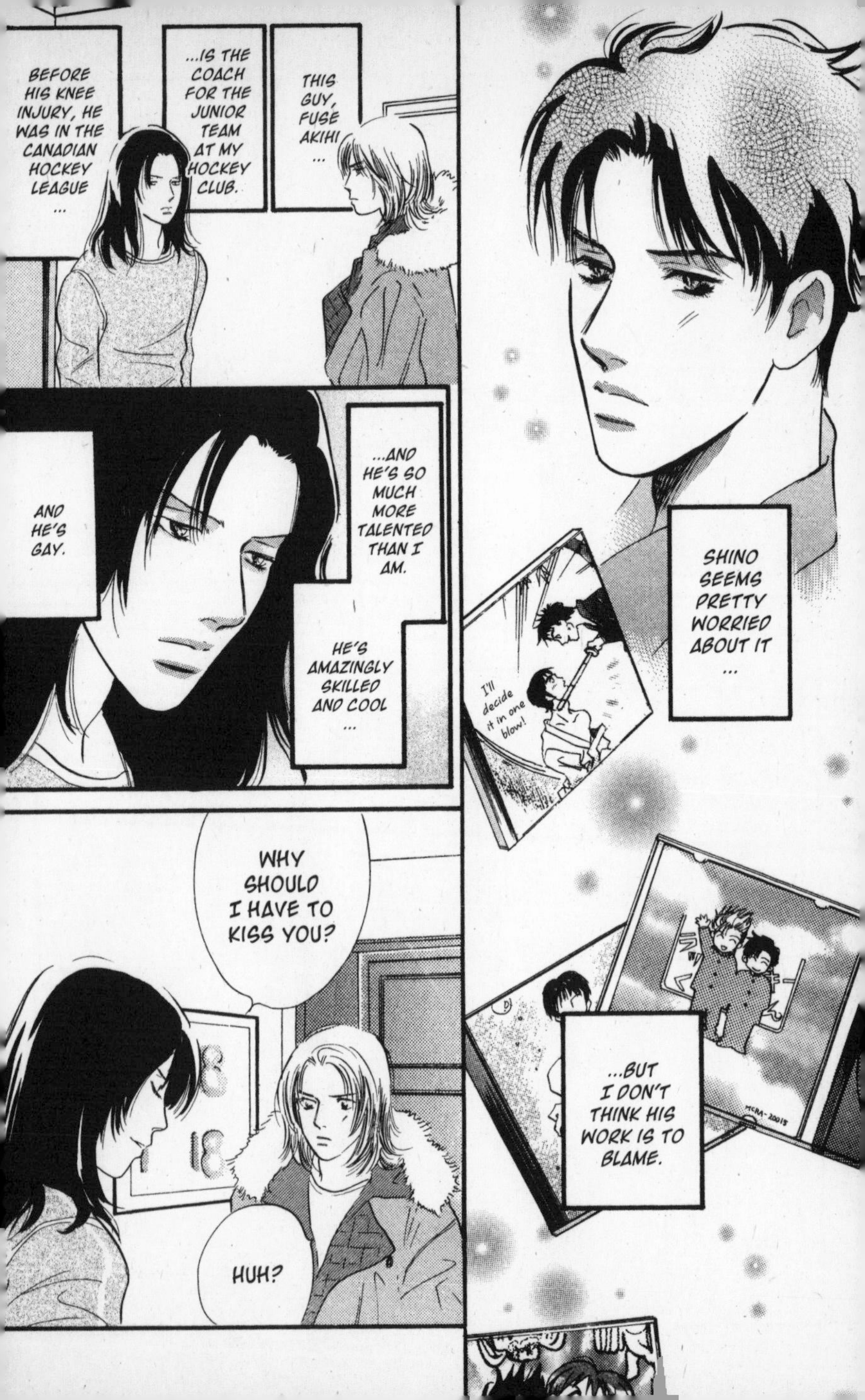
SHINO SEEMS PRETTY WORRIED ABOUT IT ...
I'll decide it in one blow!
...BUT I DON'T THINK HIS WORK IS TO BLAME.
THIS GUY, FUSE AKIHI ...
...IS THE COACH FOR THE JUNIOR TEAM AT MY HOCKEY CLUB.
BEFORE HIS KNEE INJURY, HE WAS IN THE CANADIAN HOCKEY LEAGUE ...
...AND HE'S SO MUCH MORE TALENTED THAN I AM.
HE'S AMAZINGLY SKILLED AND COOL ...
AND HE'S GAY.
WHY SHOULD I HAVE TO KISS YOU?
HUH?

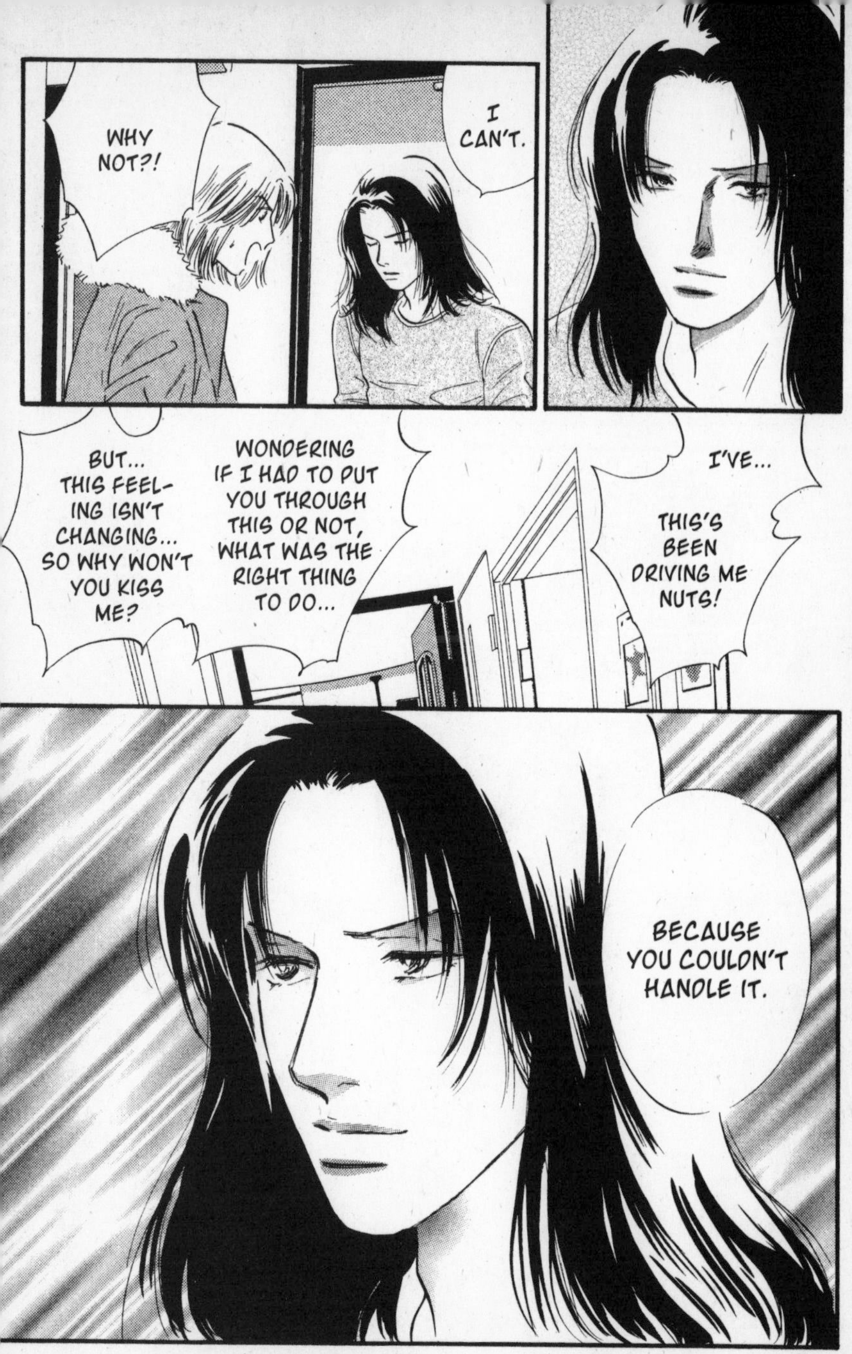
I CAN'T.
WHY NOT?!
I'VE...
THIS'S BEEN DRIVING ME NUTS!
WONDERING IF I HAD TO PUT YOU THROUGH THIS OR NOT, WHAT WAS THE RIGHT THING TO DO...
BUT... THIS FEEL-ING ISN'T CHANGING... SO WHY WON'T YOU KISS ME?
BECAUSE YOU COULDN'T HANDLE IT.

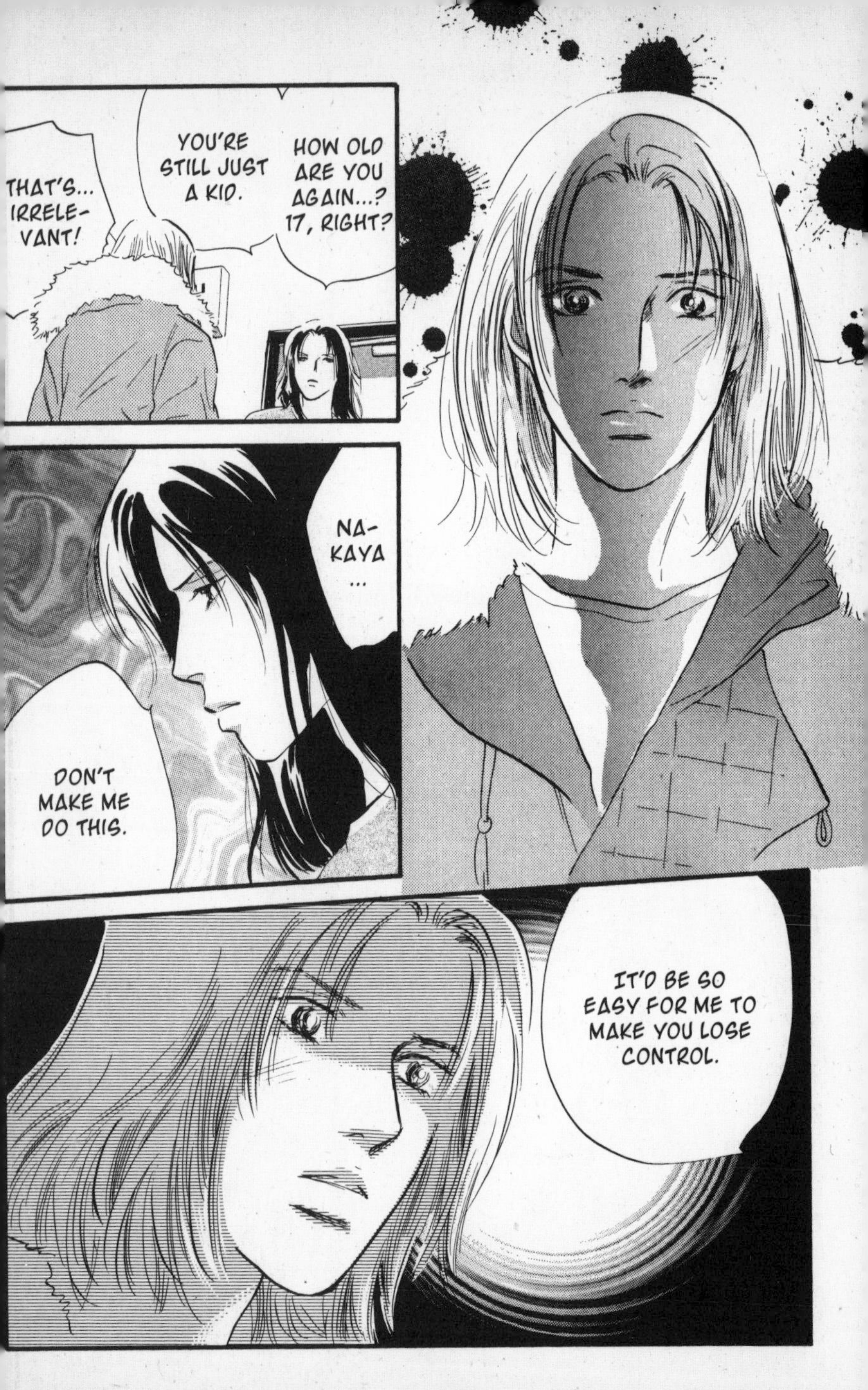
HOW OLD ARE YOU AGAIN...? 17, RIGHT?
YOU'RE STILL JUST A KID.
THAT'S... IRRELEVANT!
NAKAYA...
DON'T MAKE ME DO THIS.
IT'D BE SO EASY FOR ME TO MAKE YOU LOSE CONTROL.

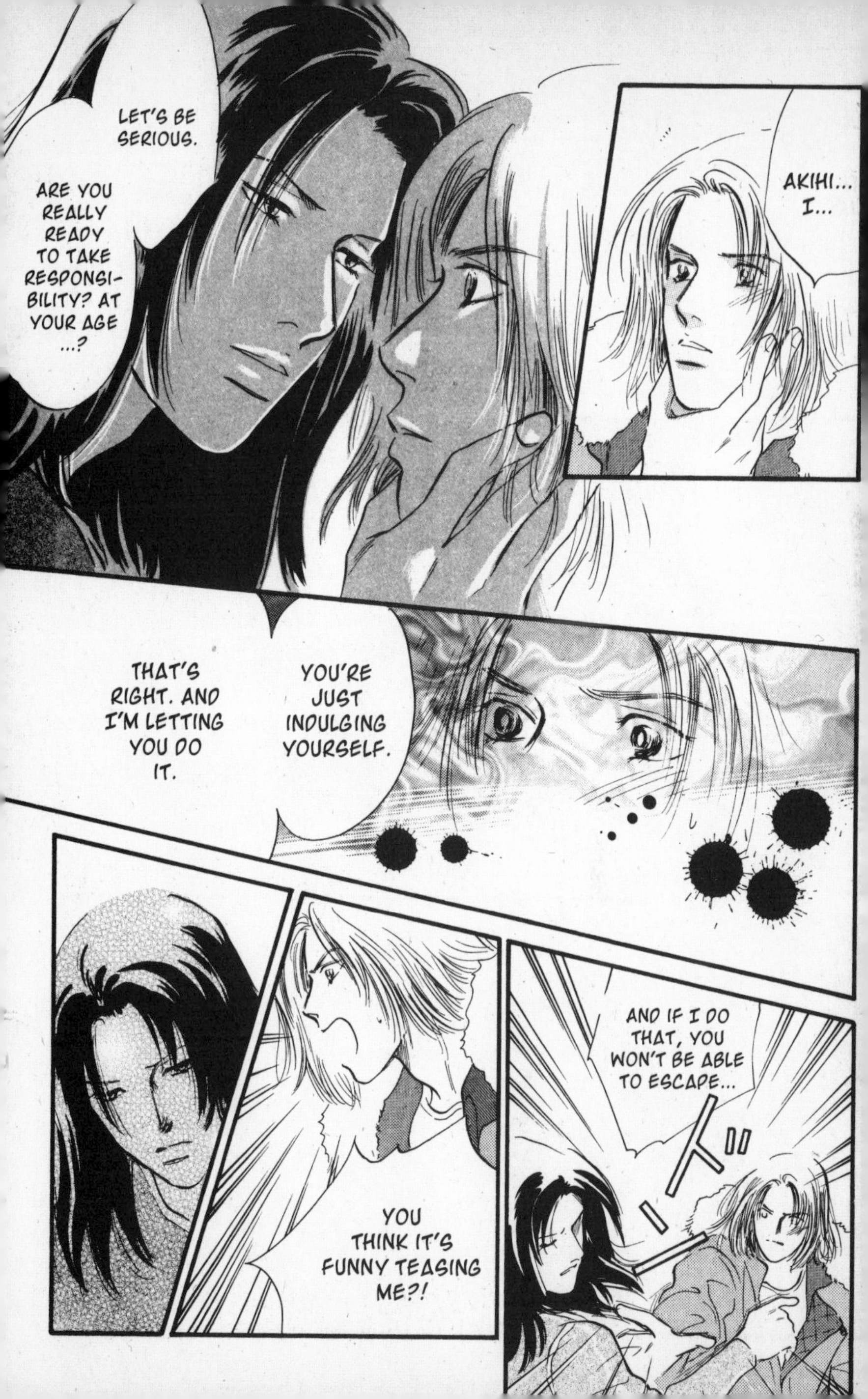
AKIHI... I...
LET'S BE SERIOUS.
ARE YOU REALLY READY TO TAKE RESPONSIBILITY? AT YOUR AGE ...?
YOU'RE JUST INDULGING YOURSELF.
THAT'S RIGHT. AND I'M LETTING YOU DO IT.
AND IF I DO THAT, YOU WON'T BE ABLE TO ESCAPE...
YOU THINK IT'S FUNNY TEASING ME?!

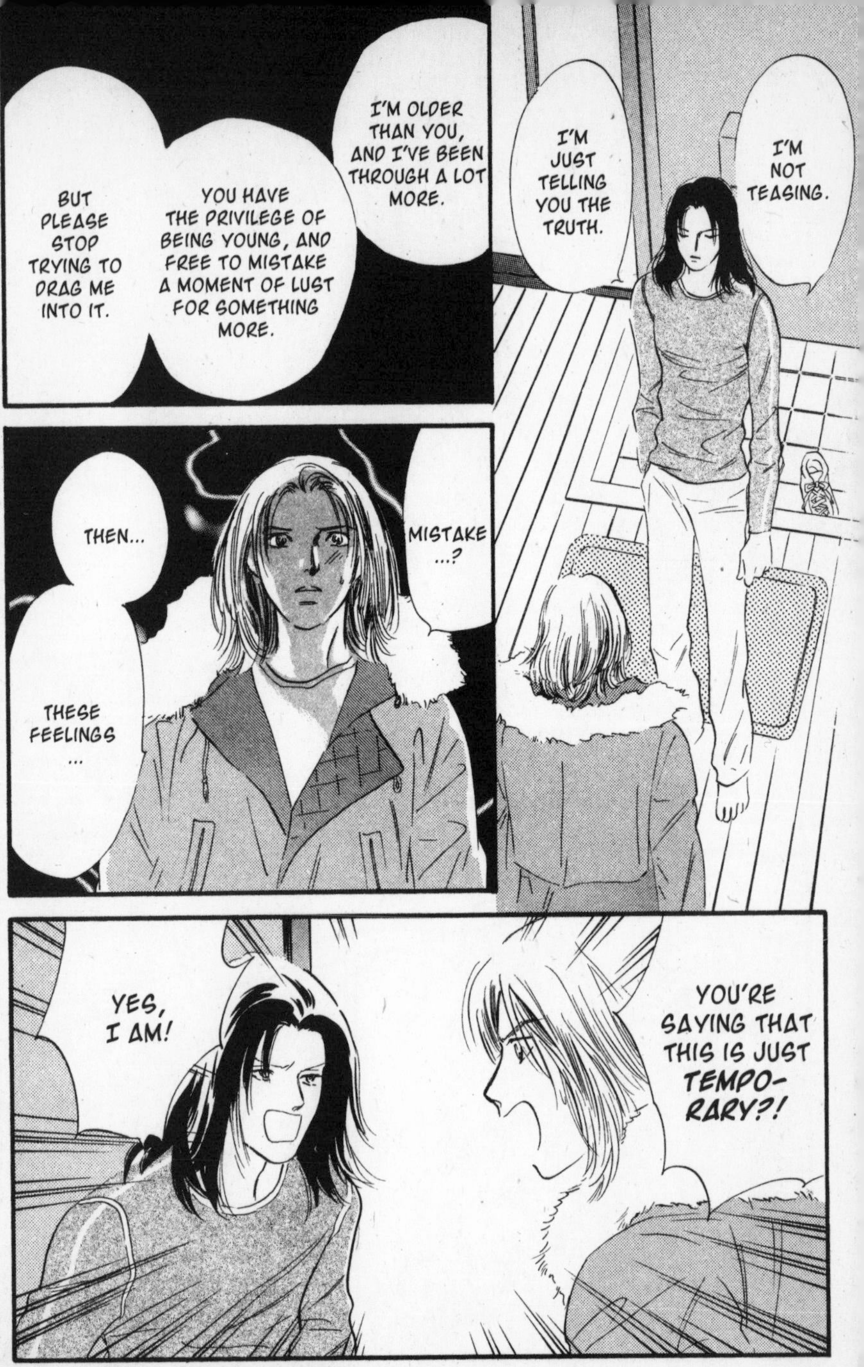
I'M NOT TEASING.
I'M JUST TELLING YOU THE TRUTH.
I'M OLDER THAN YOU, AND I'VE BEEN THROUGH A LOT MORE.
YOU HAVE THE PRIVILEGE OF BEING YOUNG, AND FREE TO MISTAKE A MOMENT OF LUST FOR SOMETHING MORE.
BUT PLEASE STOP TRYING TO DRAG ME INTO IT.
MISTAKE ...?
THEN...
THESE FEELINGS ...
YOU'RE SAYING THAT THIS IS JUST *TEMPORARY?!*
YES, I AM!

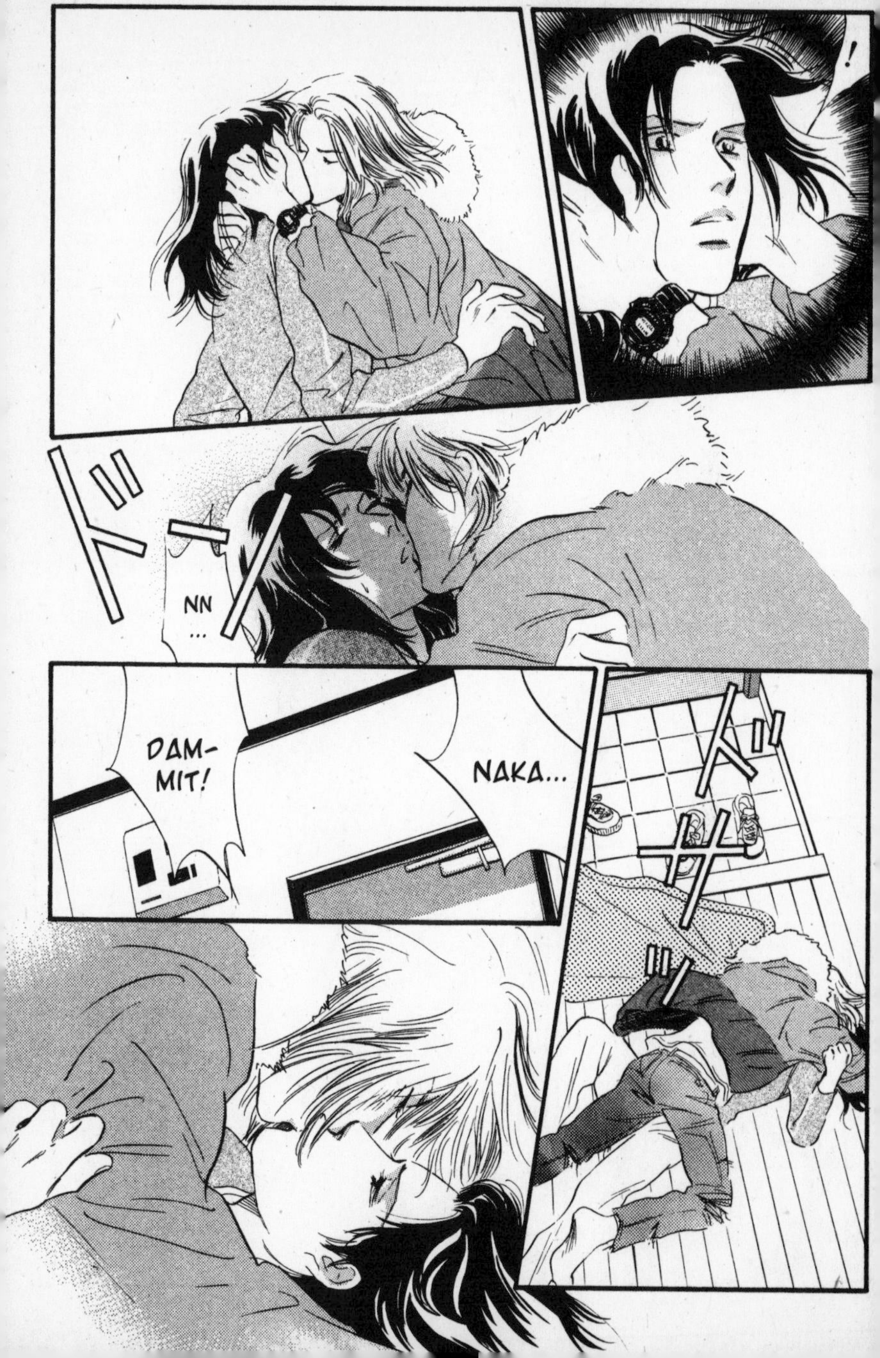
!
NN ...
NAKA...
DAM-
MIT!

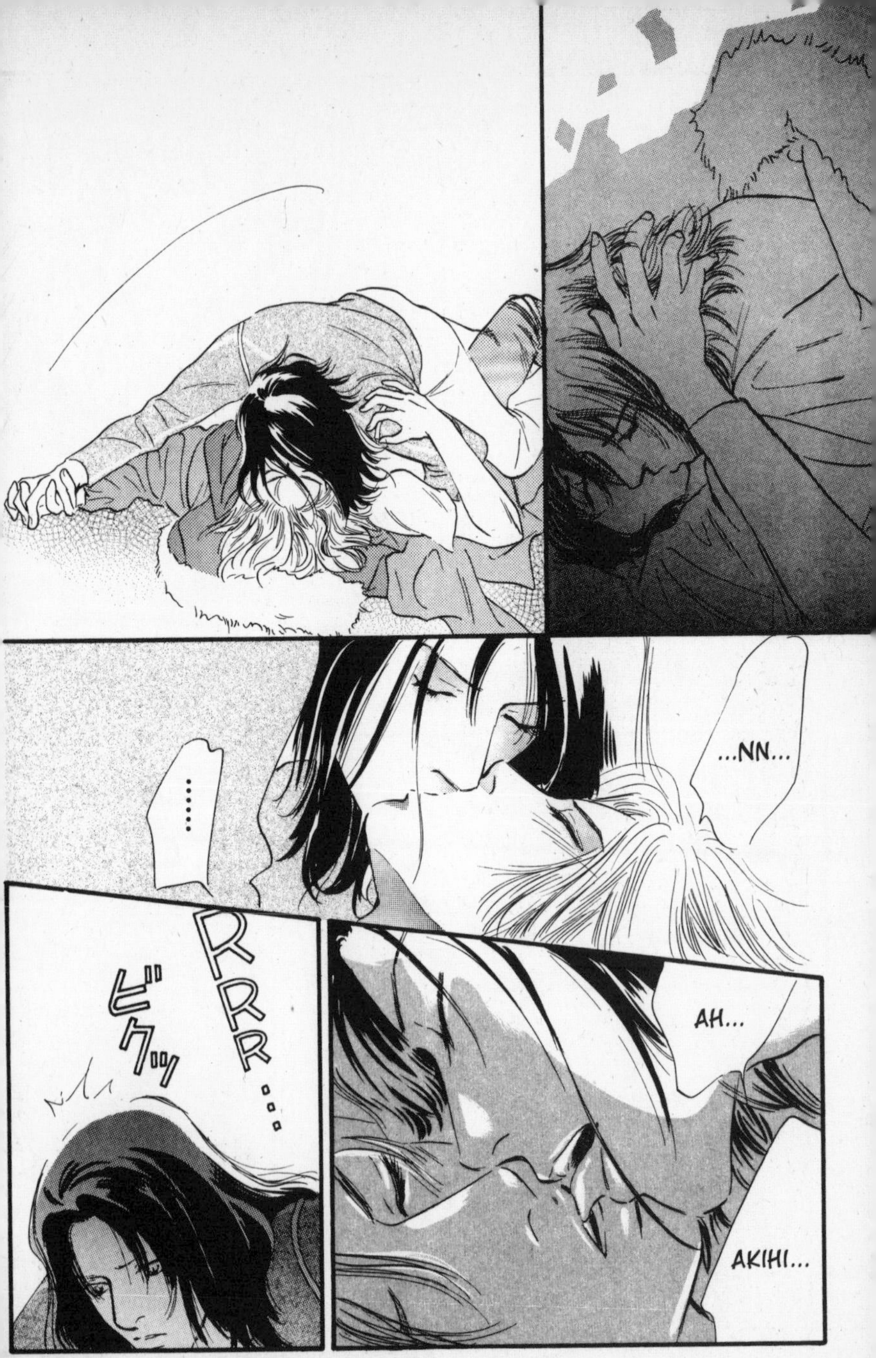

...NN...
......
AH...
AKIHI...
RRR...
ビクッ

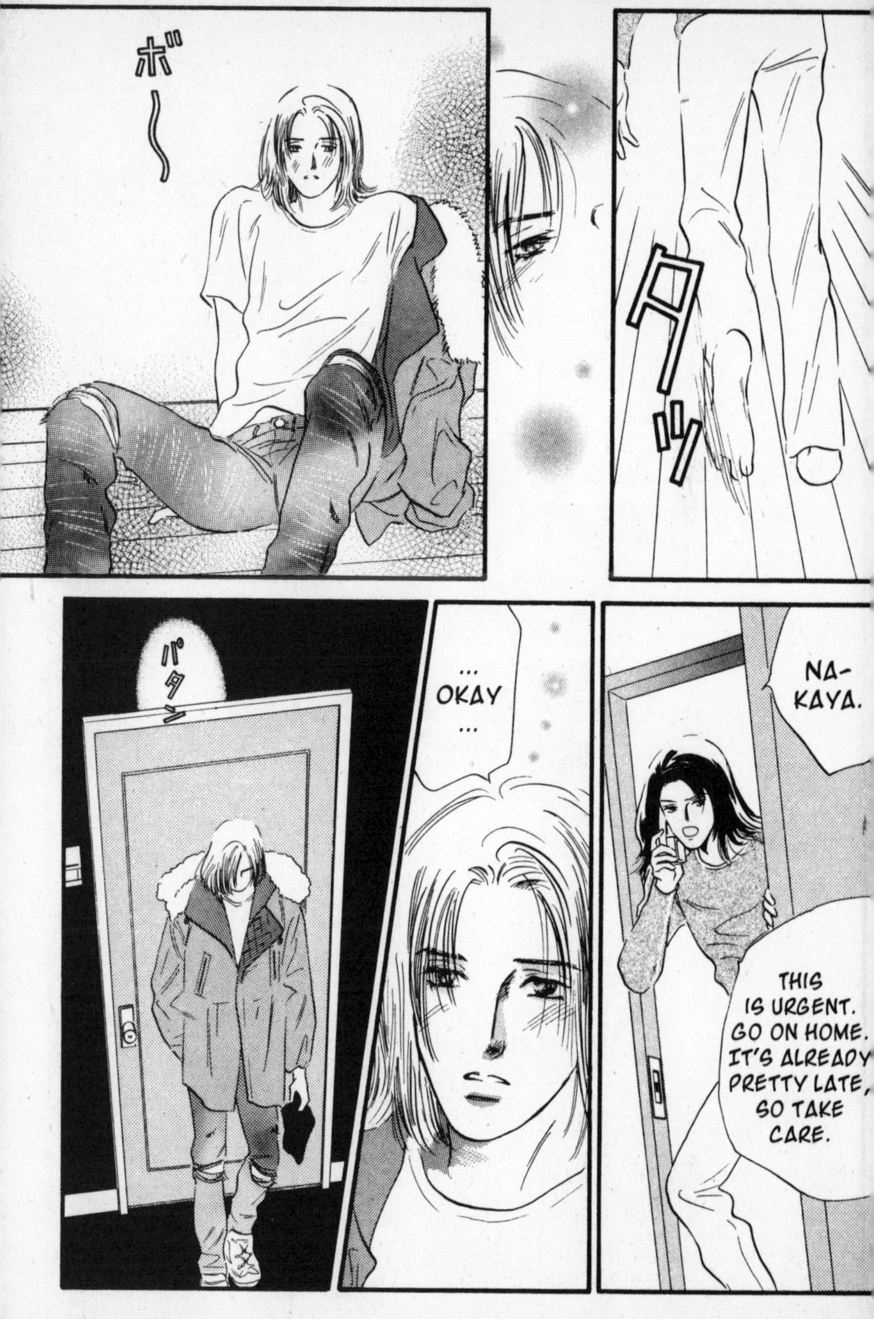
タッ
ボ〜〜
NA-KAYA.
THIS IS URGENT. GO ON HOME. IT'S ALREADY PRETTY LATE, SO TAKE CARE.
...OKAY...
パタン

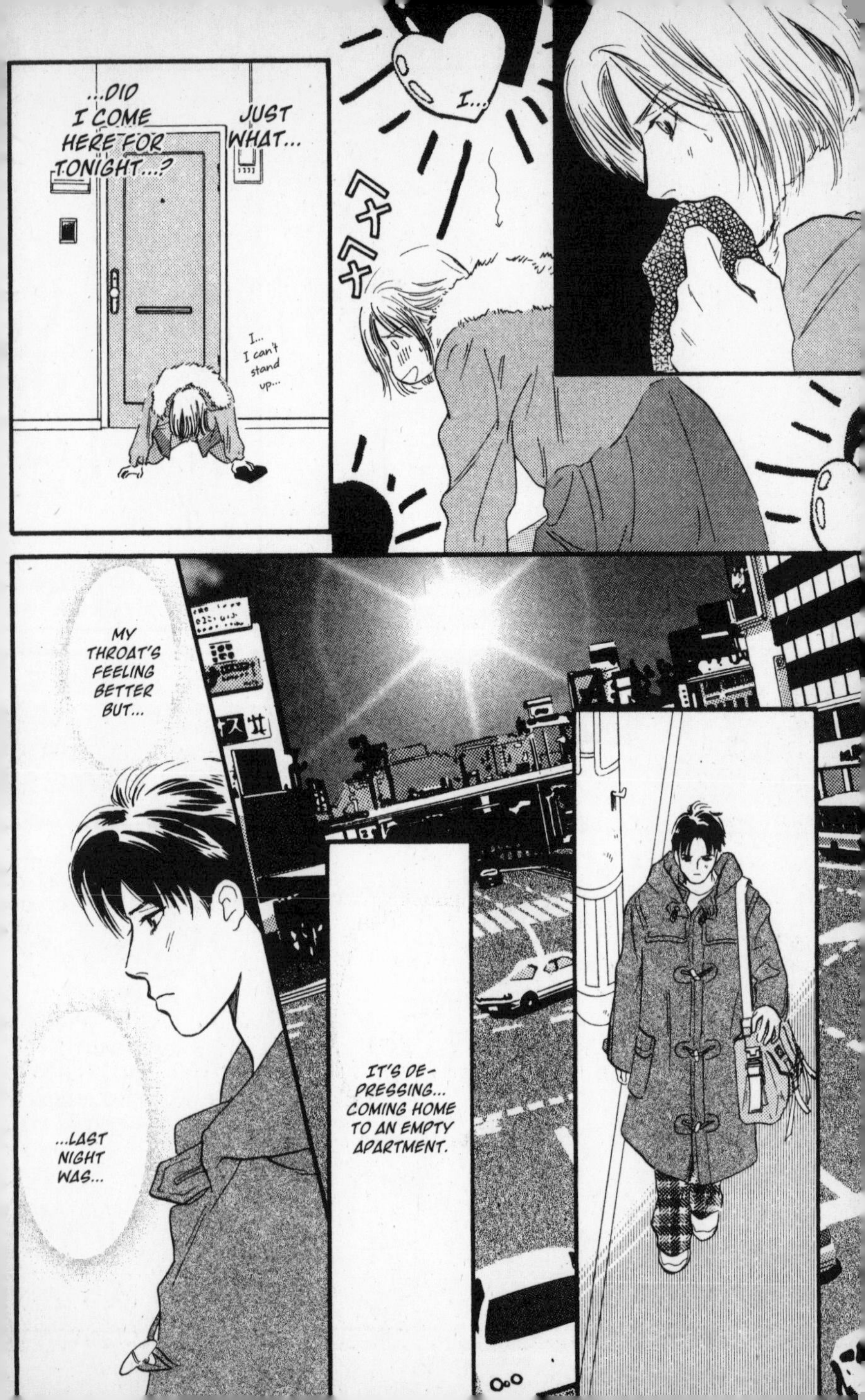
I...
JUST WHAT...
...DID I COME HERE FOR TONIGHT...?
I... I can't stand up...
IT'S DE-PRESSING... COMING HOME TO AN EMPTY APARTMENT.
MY THROAT'S FEELING BETTER BUT...
...LAST NIGHT WAS...

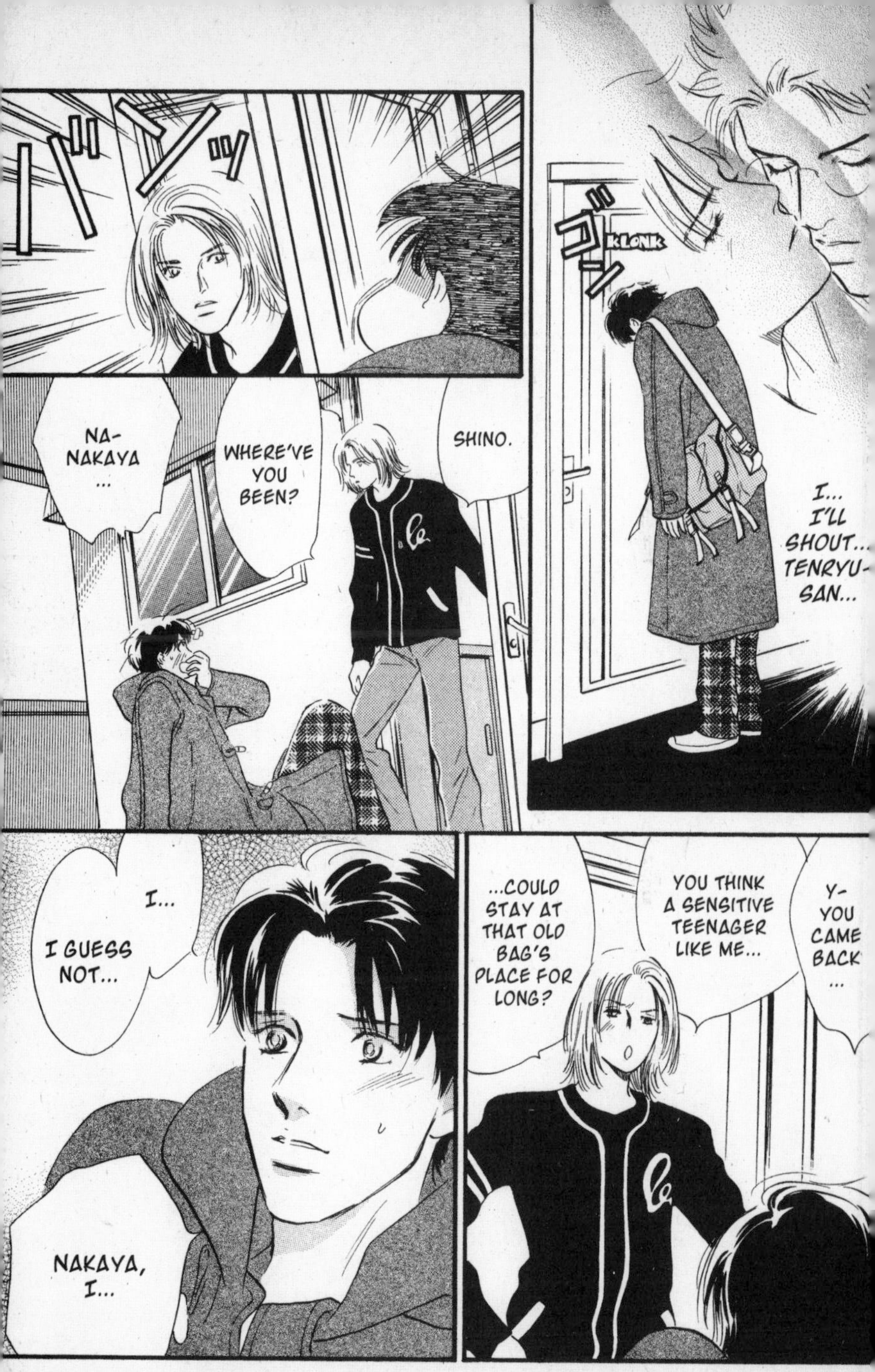
KLONK
I... I'LL SHOUT... TENRYU-SAN...
SHINO.
WHERE'VE YOU BEEN?
NA-NAKAYA...
Y-YOU CAME BACK...
YOU THINK A SENSITIVE TEENAGER LIKE ME...
...COULD STAY AT THAT OLD BAG'S PLACE FOR LONG?
I...
I GUESS NOT...
NAKAYA, I...

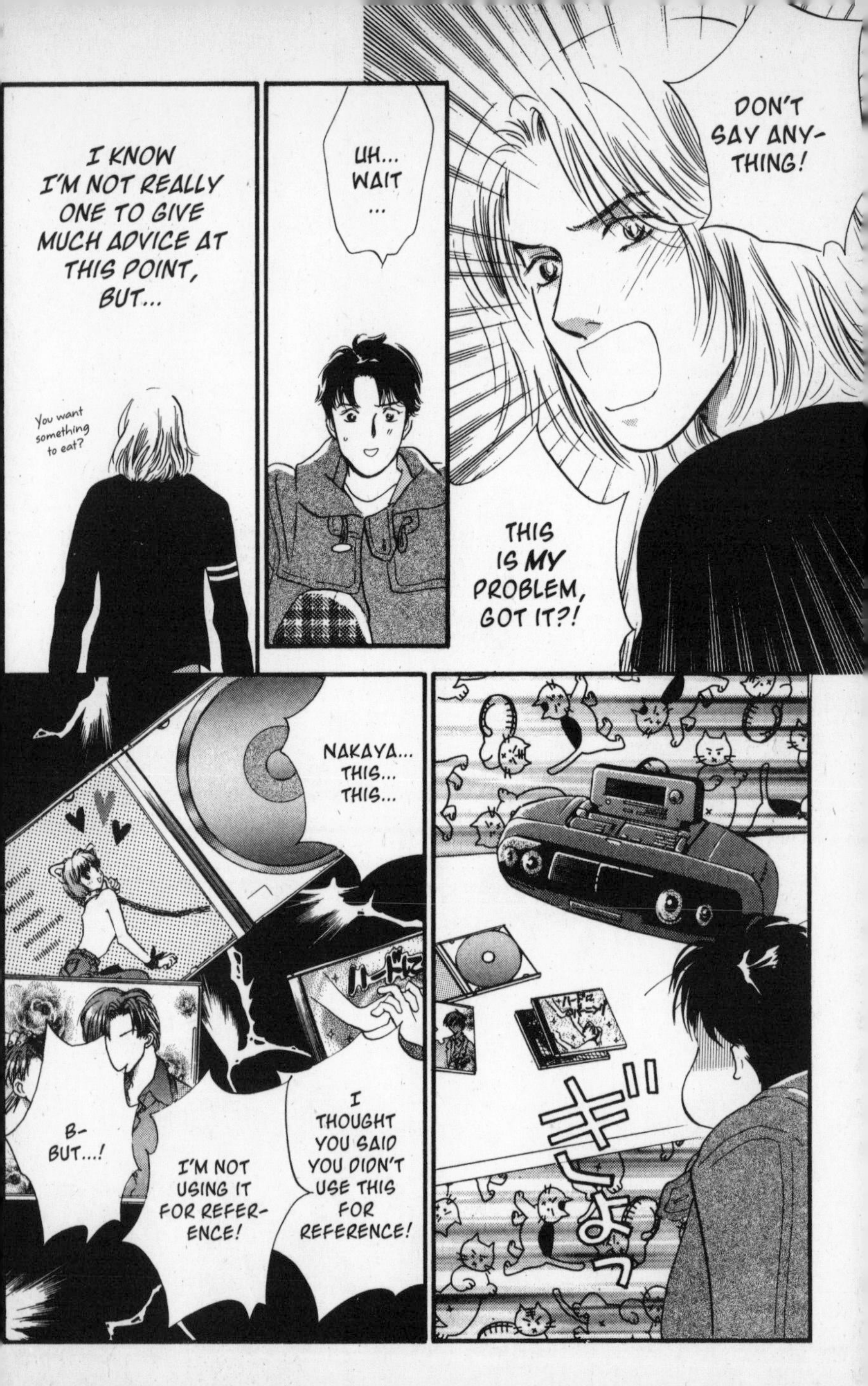
DON'T SAY ANY-THING!
THIS IS MY PROBLEM, GOT IT?!
UH... WAIT ...
I KNOW I'M NOT REALLY ONE TO GIVE MUCH ADVICE AT THIS POINT, BUT...
You want something to eat?
ギょっ
NAKAYA... THIS... THIS...
I THOUGHT YOU SAID YOU DIDN'T USE THIS FOR REFERENCE!
I'M NOT USING IT FOR REFERENCE!
B- BUT...!

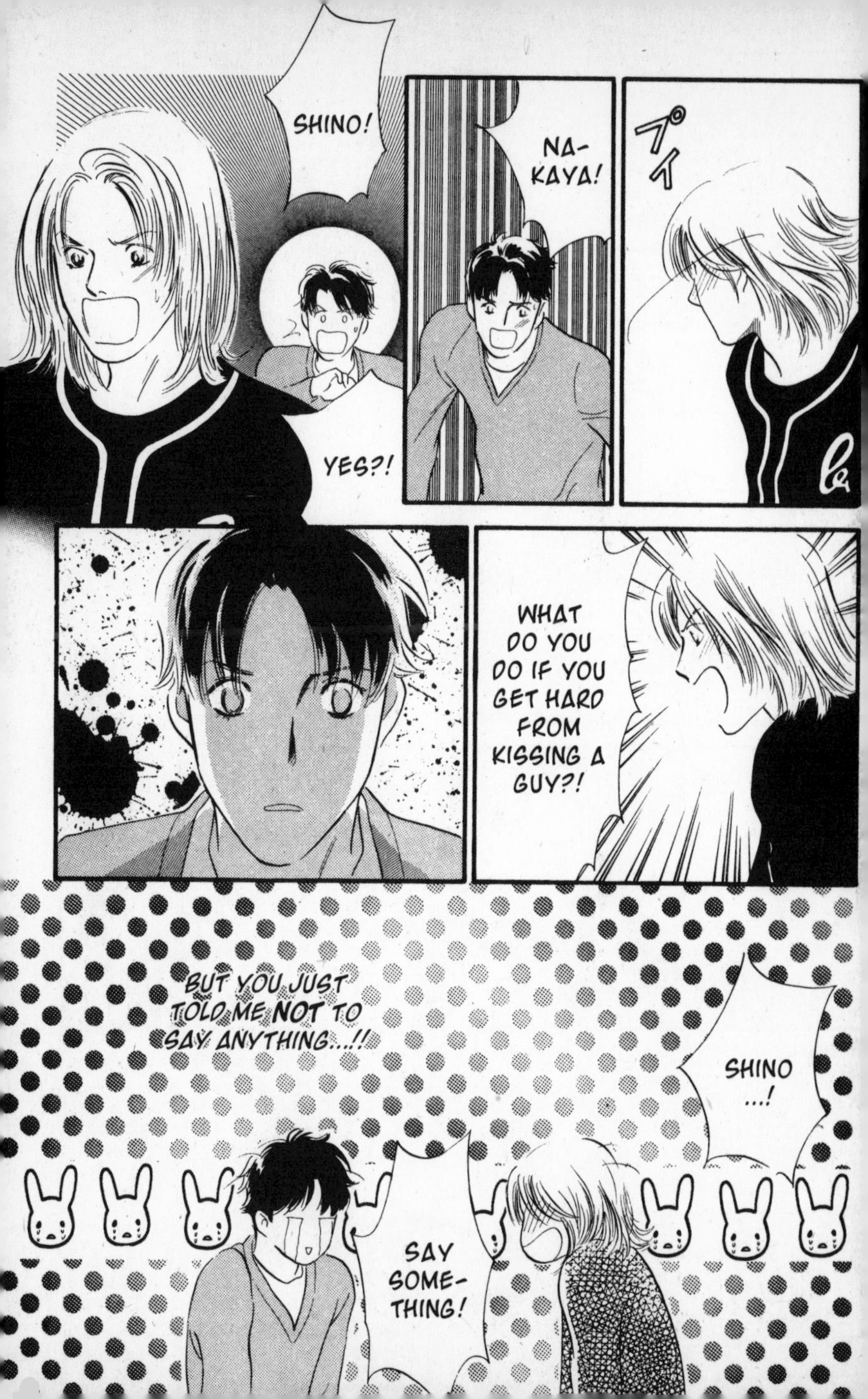
ペイ
NA-KAYA!
SHINO!
YES?!
WHAT DO YOU DO IF YOU GET HARD FROM KISSING A GUY?!
SHINO ...!
SAY SOME-THING!
BUT YOU JUST TOLD ME **NOT** TO SAY ANYTHING...!!

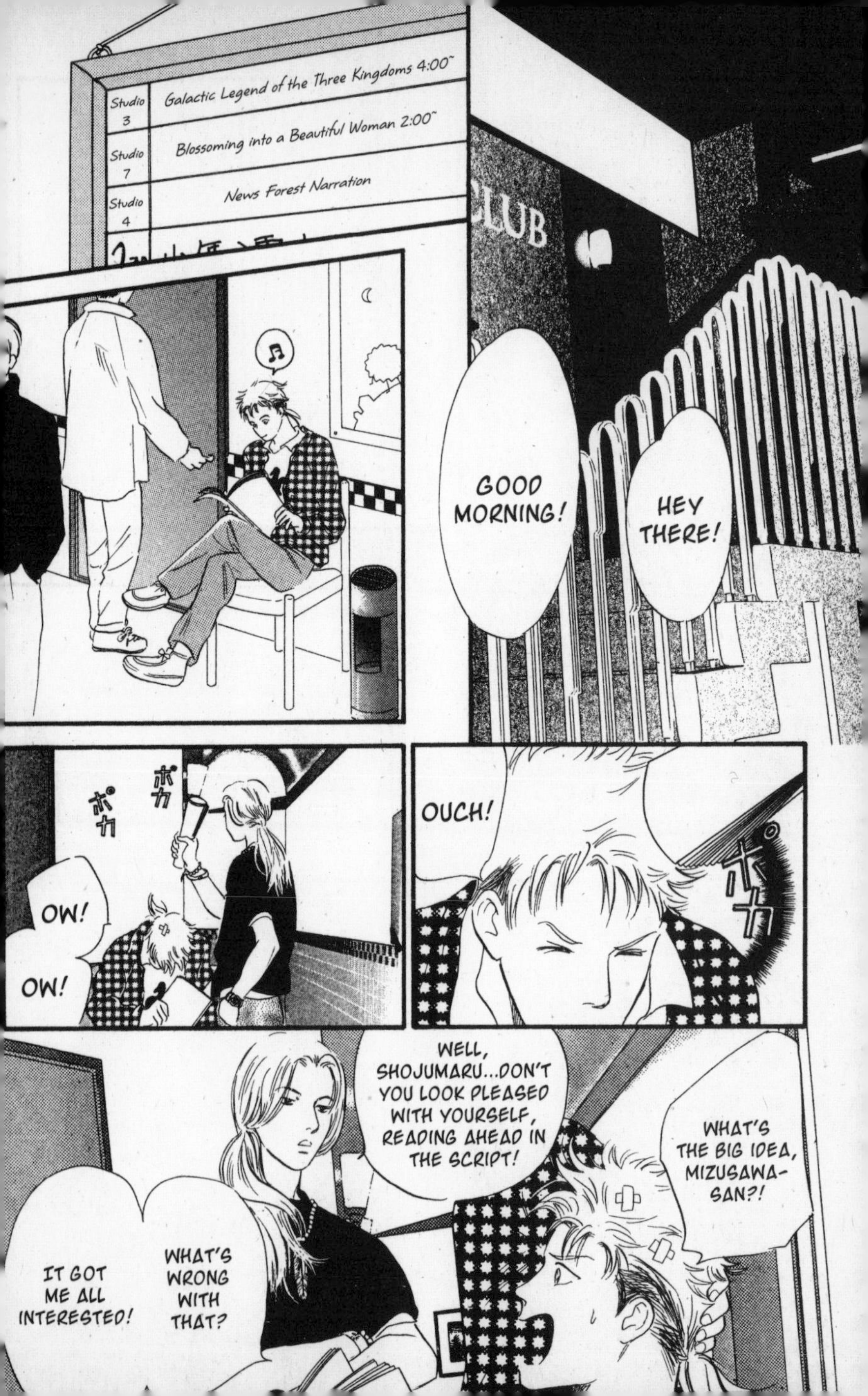
HEY THERE!
GOOD MORNING!
Studio 3 Galactic Legend of the Three Kingdoms 4:00~
Studio 7 Blossoming into a Beautiful Woman 2:00~
Studio 4 News Forest Narration
♪
OUCH!
ポカ
ポカ
ポカ
OW!
OW!
WHAT'S THE BIG IDEA, MIZUSAWA-SAN?!
WELL, SHOJUMARU...DON'T YOU LOOK PLEASED WITH YOURSELF, READING AHEAD IN THE SCRIPT!
WHAT'S WRONG WITH THAT?
IT GOT ME ALL INTERESTED!

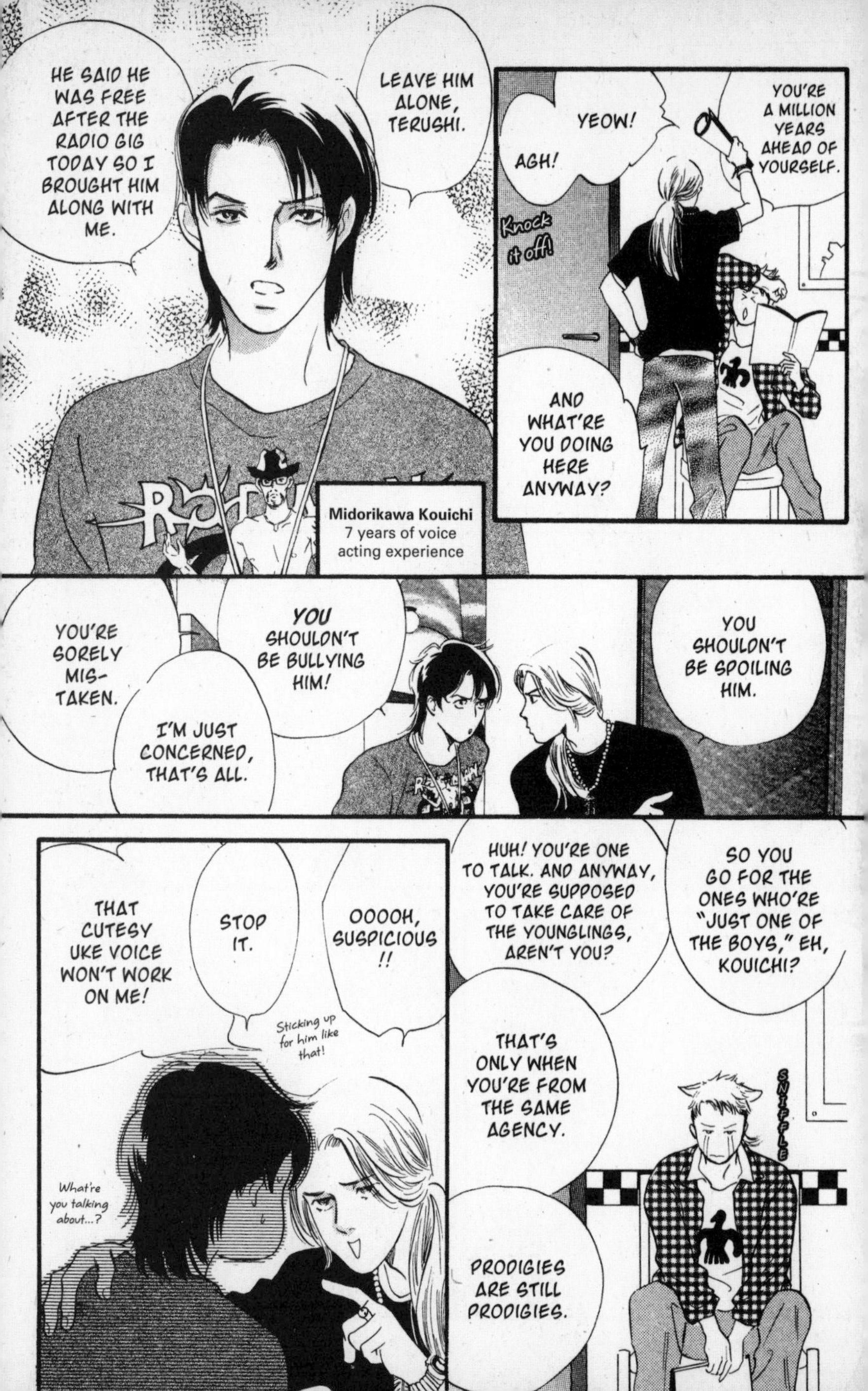
YOU'RE A MILLION YEARS AHEAD OF YOURSELF.
YEOW!
AGH!
Knock it off!
AND WHAT'RE YOU DOING HERE ANYWAY?
LEAVE HIM ALONE, TERUSHI.
HE SAID HE WAS FREE AFTER THE RADIO GIG TODAY SO I BROUGHT HIM ALONG WITH ME.
Midorikawa Kouichi 7 years of voice acting experience
YOU SHOULDN'T BE SPOILING HIM.
YOU SHOULDN'T BE BULLYING HIM!
YOU'RE SORELY MIS-TAKEN.
I'M JUST CONCERNED, THAT'S ALL.
SO YOU GO FOR THE ONES WHO'RE "JUST ONE OF THE BOYS," EH, KOUICHI?
HUH! YOU'RE ONE TO TALK. AND ANYWAY, YOU'RE SUPPOSED TO TAKE CARE OF THE YOUNGLINGS, AREN'T YOU?
SNIFFLE
THAT'S ONLY WHEN YOU'RE FROM THE SAME AGENCY.
PRODIGIES ARE STILL PRODIGIES.
OOOOH, SUSPICIOUS!!
Sticking up for him like that!
STOP IT.
THAT CUTESY UKE VOICE WON'T WORK ON ME!
What're you talking about...?

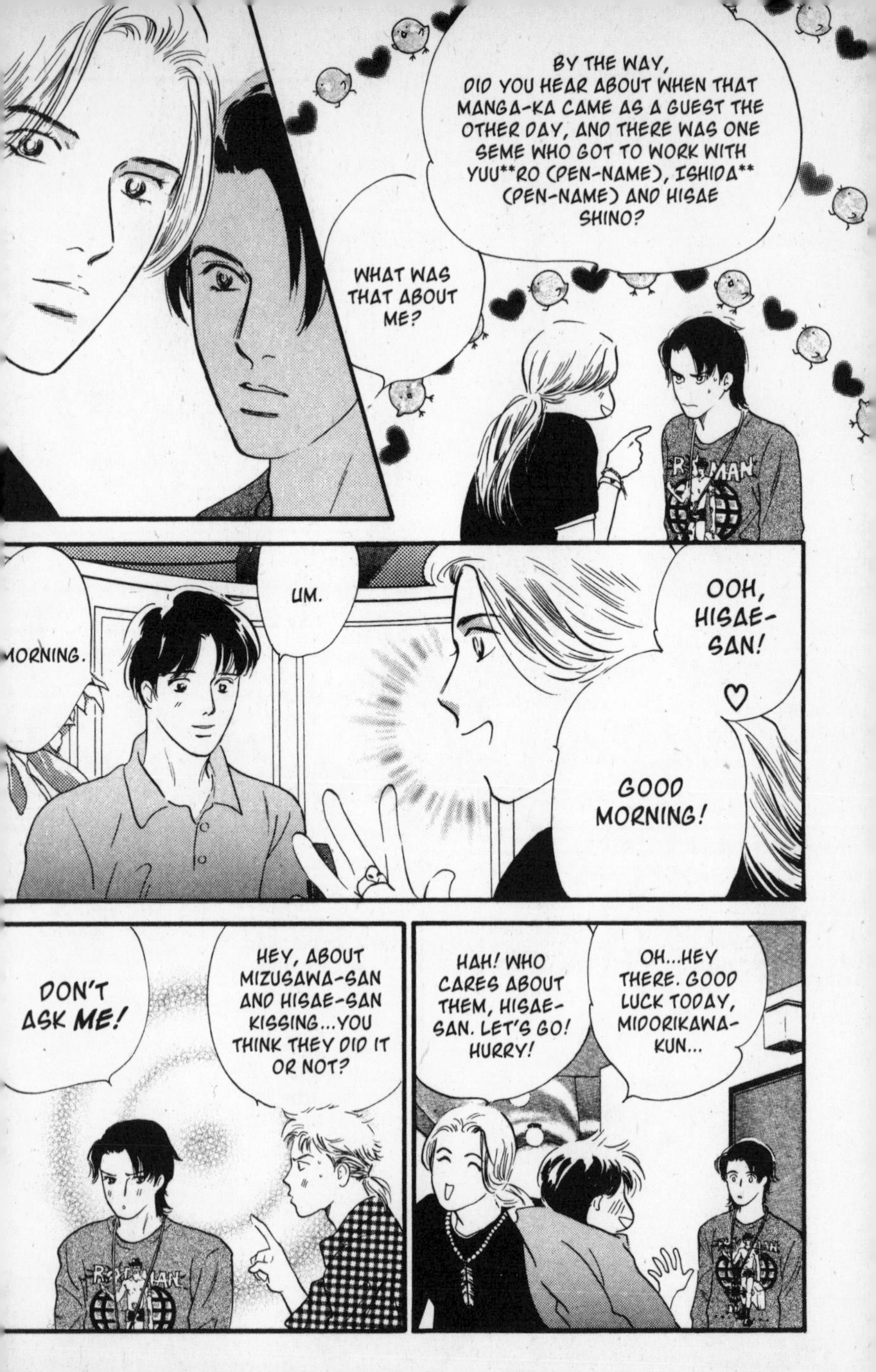
BY THE WAY, DID YOU HEAR ABOUT WHEN THAT MANGA-KA CAME AS A GUEST THE OTHER DAY, AND THERE WAS ONE SEME WHO GOT TO WORK WITH YUU**RO (PEN-NAME), ISHIDA** (PEN-NAME) AND HISAE SHINO?
WHAT WAS THAT ABOUT ME?
OOH, HISAE-SAN! ♡
GOOD MORNING!
UM.
MORNING.
OH...HEY THERE. GOOD LUCK TODAY, MIDORIKAWA-KUN...
HAH! WHO CARES ABOUT THEM, HISAE-SAN. LET'S GO! HURRY!
HEY, ABOUT MIZUSAWA-SAN AND HISAE-SAN KISSING...YOU THINK THEY DID IT OR NOT?
DON'T ASK *ME*!

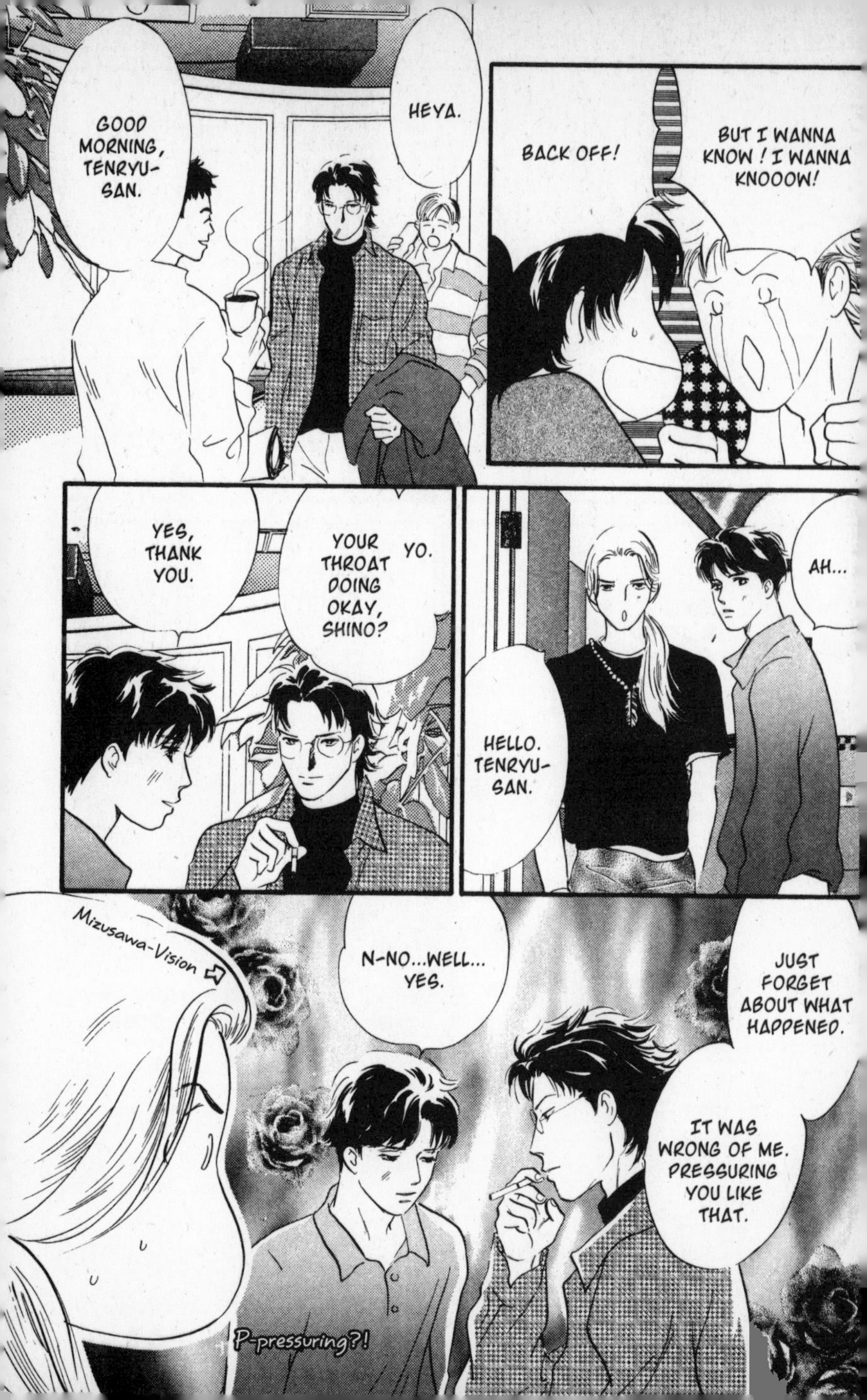
BUT I WANNA KNOW ! I WANNA KNOOOW!
BACK OFF!
HEYA.
GOOD MORNING, TENRYU-SAN.
AH...
HELLO. TENRYU-SAN.
YO.
YOUR THROAT DOING OKAY, SHINO?
YES, THANK YOU.
JUST FORGET ABOUT WHAT HAPPENED.
IT WAS WRONG OF ME. PRESSURING YOU LIKE THAT.
N-NO...WELL... YES.
Mizusawa-Vision
P-pressuring?!

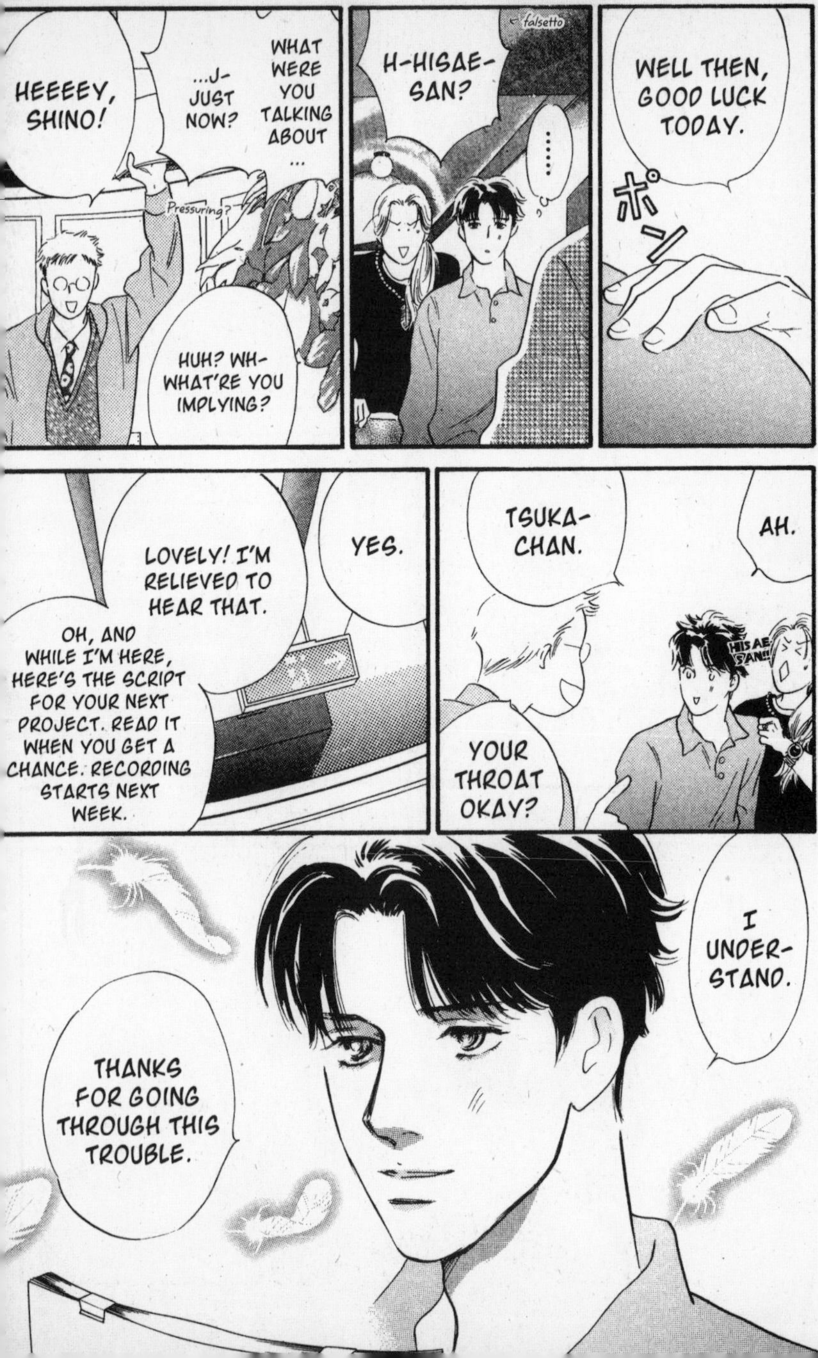
WELL THEN, GOOD LUCK TODAY.
ポン
falsetto
H-HISAE-SAN?
......
WHAT WERE YOU TALKING ABOUT ...
...J- JUST NOW?
HEEEEY, SHINO!
Pressuring?
HUH? WH-WHAT'RE YOU IMPLYING?
AH.
TSUKA-CHAN.
HISAE-SAN!!
YOUR THROAT OKAY?
YES.
LOVELY! I'M RELIEVED TO HEAR THAT.
OH, AND WHILE I'M HERE, HERE'S THE SCRIPT FOR YOUR NEXT PROJECT. READ IT WHEN YOU GET A CHANCE. RECORDING STARTS NEXT WEEK.
I UNDER-STAND.
THANKS FOR GOING THROUGH THIS TROUBLE.

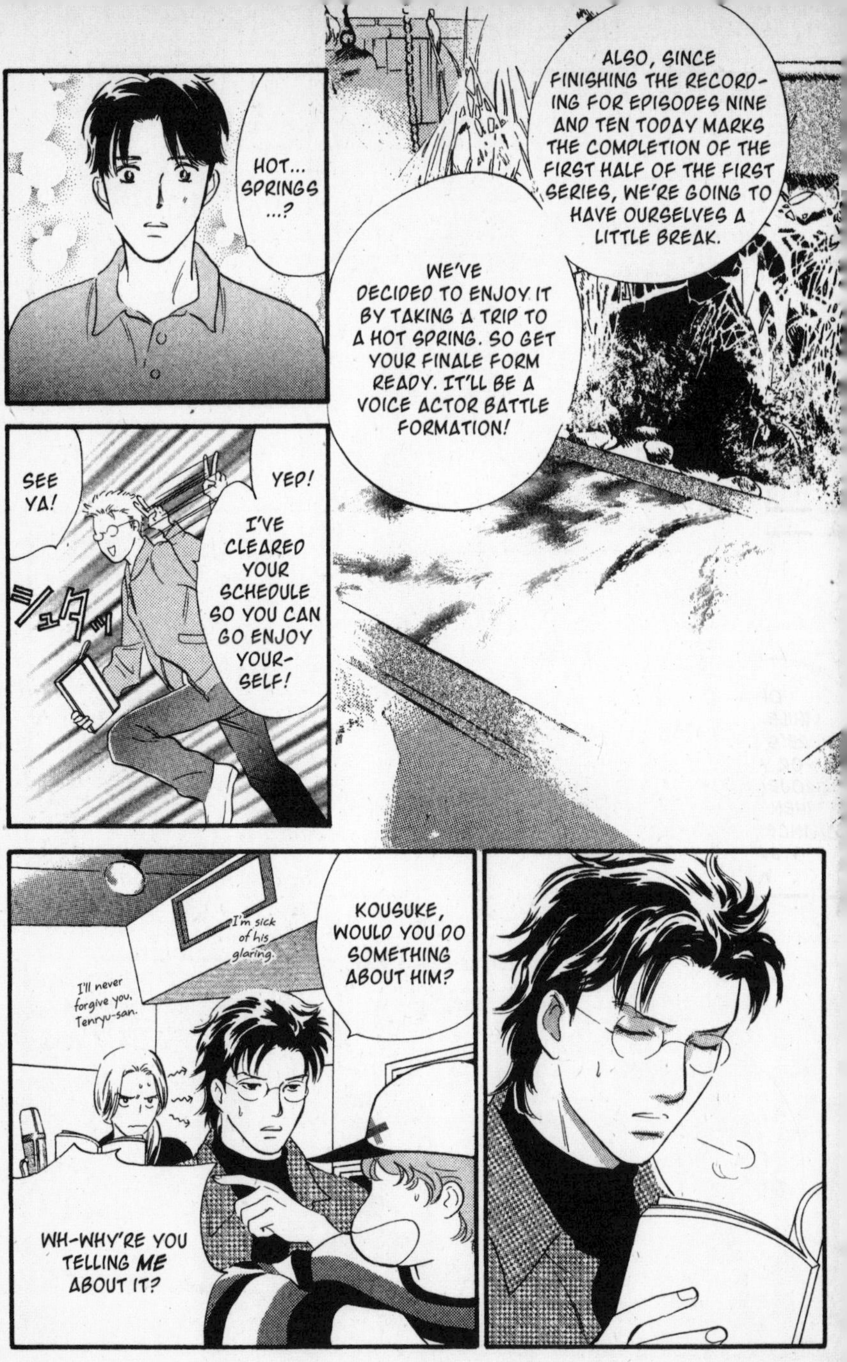
ALSO, SINCE FINISHING THE RECORDING FOR EPISODES NINE AND TEN TODAY MARKS THE COMPLETION OF THE FIRST HALF OF THE FIRST SERIES, WE'RE GOING TO HAVE OURSELVES A LITTLE BREAK.
WE'VE DECIDED TO ENJOY IT BY TAKING A TRIP TO A HOT SPRING. SO GET YOUR FINALE FORM READY. IT'LL BE A VOICE ACTOR BATTLE FORMATION!
HOT... SPRINGS ...?
YEP!
I'VE CLEARED YOUR SCHEDULE SO YOU CAN GO ENJOY YOURSELF!
SEE YA!
シュタッ
KOUSUKE, WOULD YOU DO SOMETHING ABOUT HIM?
I'm sick of his glaring.
I'll never forgive you, Tenryu-san.
WH-WHY'RE YOU TELLING *ME* ABOUT IT?

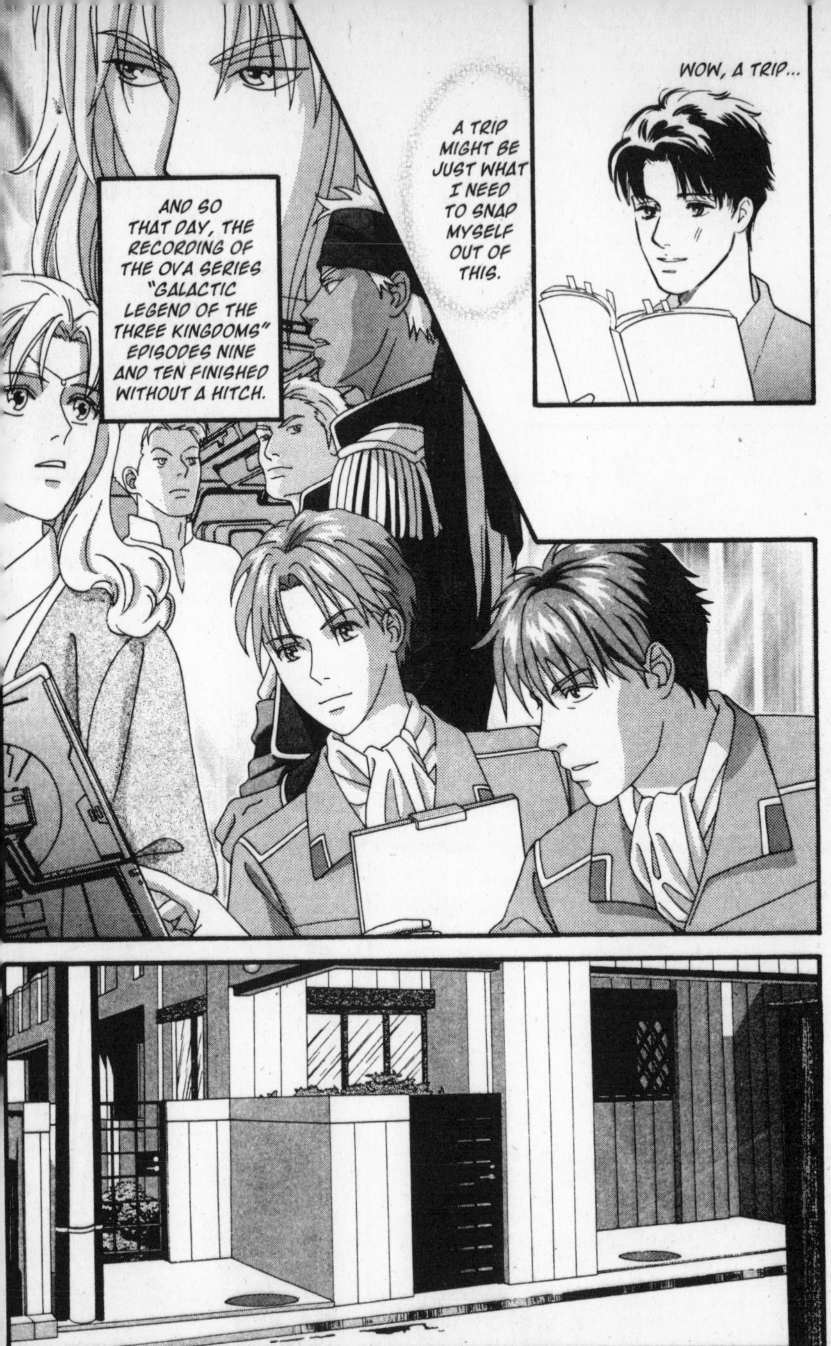
WOW, A TRIP...
A TRIP MIGHT BE JUST WHAT I NEED TO SNAP MYSELF OUT OF THIS.
AND SO THAT DAY, THE RECORDING OF THE OVA SERIES "GALACTIC LEGEND OF THE THREE KINGDOMS" EPISODES NINE AND TEN FINISHED WITHOUT A HITCH.

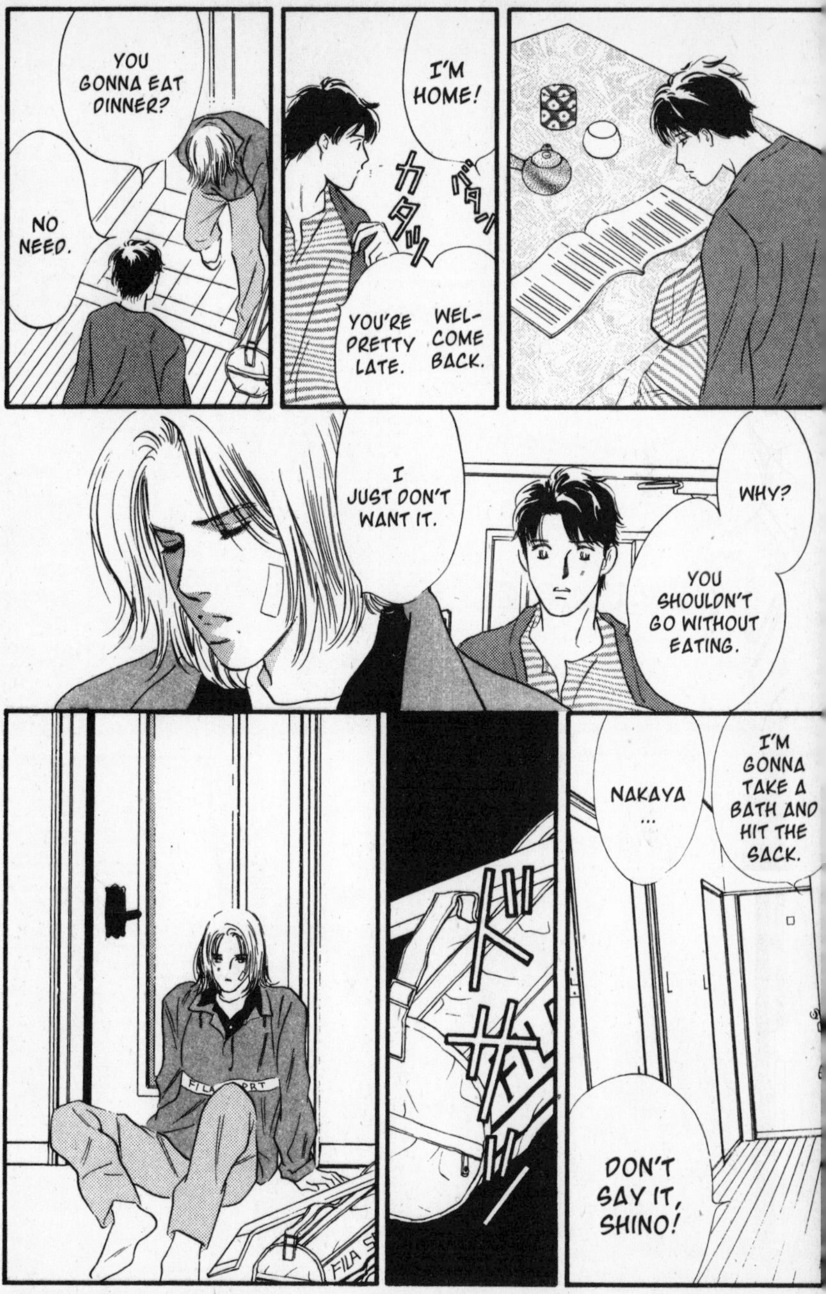
I'M HOME!
バタッ
カタッ
WEL-COME BACK.
YOU'RE PRETTY LATE.
YOU GONNA EAT DINNER?
NO NEED.
WHY?
YOU SHOULDN'T GO WITHOUT EATING.
I JUST DON'T WANT IT.
I'M GONNA TAKE A BATH AND HIT THE SACK.
NAKAYA ...
DON'T SAY IT, SHINO!

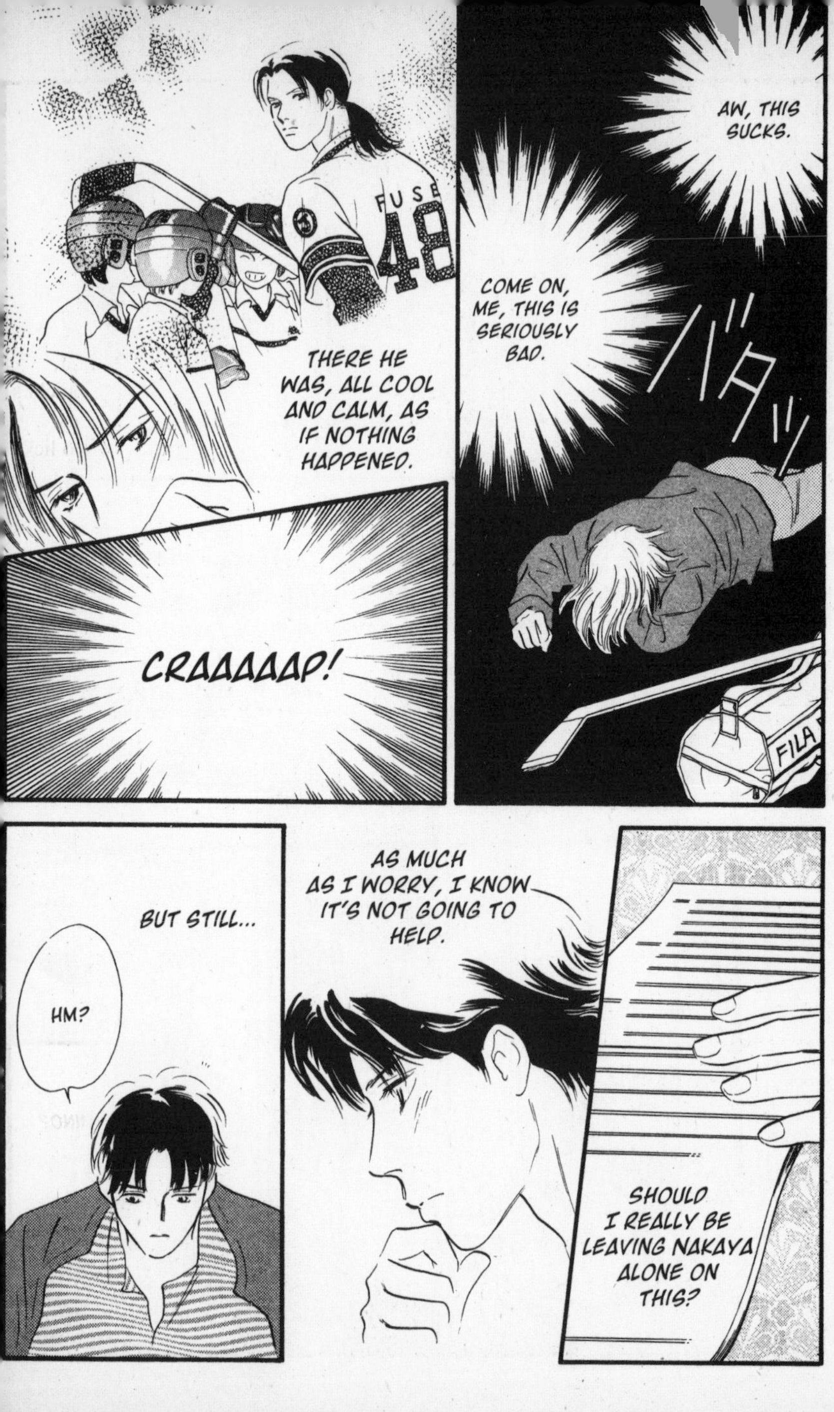
AW, THIS SUCKS.
COME ON, ME, THIS IS SERIOUSLY BAD.
バタッ
FILA
FUSE 48
THERE HE WAS, ALL COOL AND CALM, AS IF NOTHING HAPPENED.
CRAAAAAAP!
AS MUCH AS I WORRY, I KNOW IT'S NOT GOING TO HELP.
SHOULD I REALLY BE LEAVING NAKAYA ALONE ON THIS?
BUT STILL...
HM?

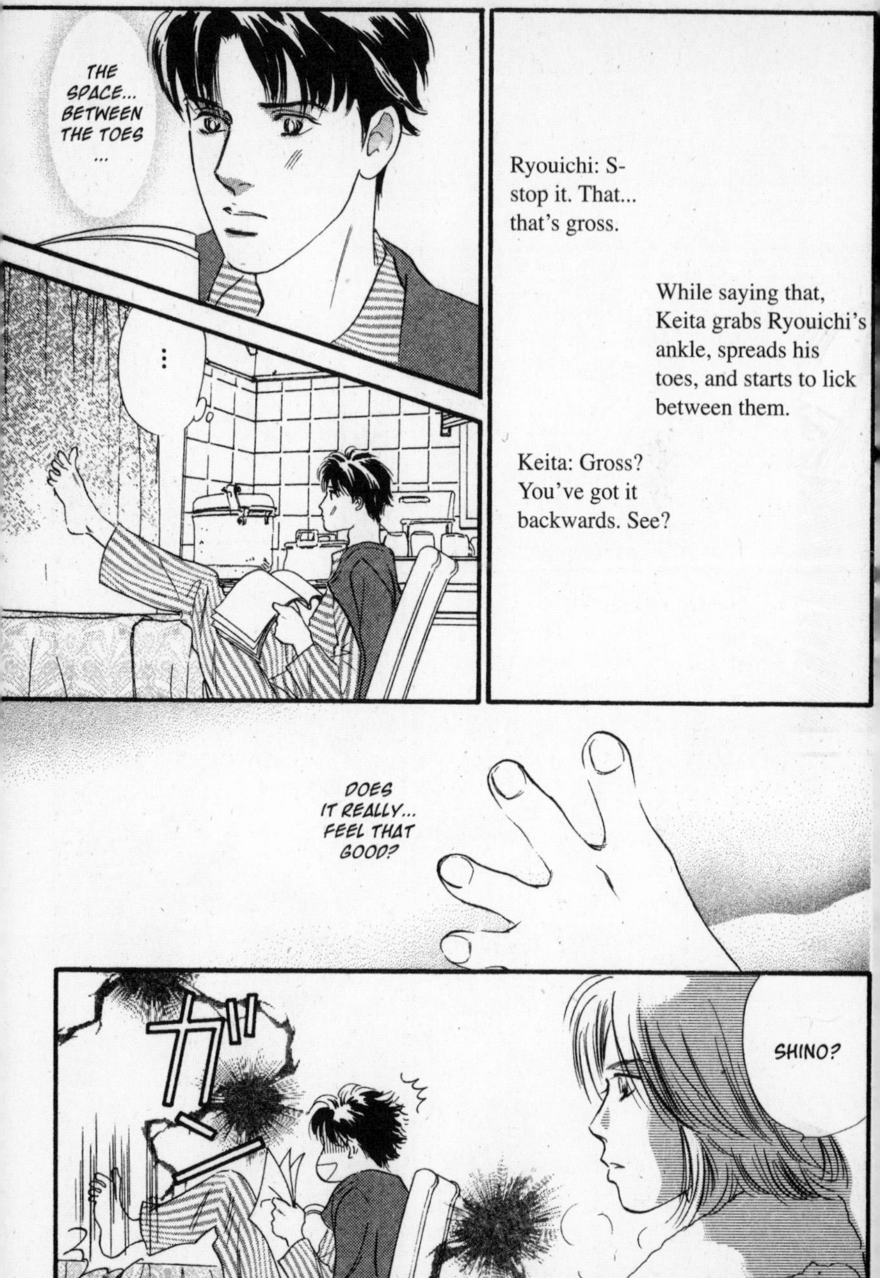
Ryouichi: S-stop it. That... that's gross.
While saying that, Keita grabs Ryouichi's ankle, spreads his toes, and starts to lick between them.
Keita: Gross? You've got it backwards. See?
THE SPACE... BETWEEN THE TOES ...
...
DOES IT REALLY... FEEL THAT GOOD?
SHINO?

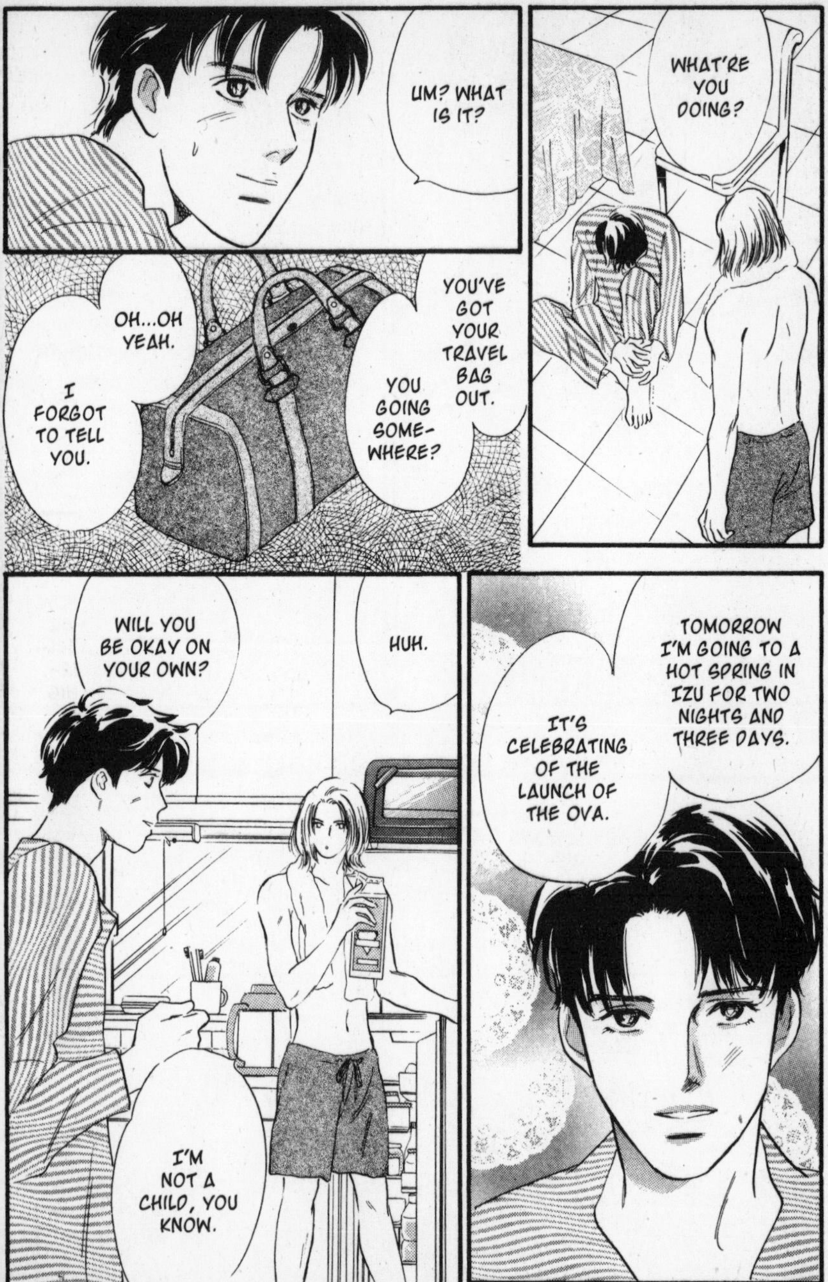
WHAT'RE YOU DOING?
UM? WHAT IS IT?
YOU'VE GOT YOUR TRAVEL BAG OUT.
YOU GOING SOME-WHERE?
OH...OH YEAH.
I FORGOT TO TELL YOU.
TOMORROW I'M GOING TO A HOT SPRING IN IZU FOR TWO NIGHTS AND THREE DAYS.
IT'S CELEBRATING OF THE LAUNCH OF THE OVA.
HUH.
WILL YOU BE OKAY ON YOUR OWN?
I'M NOT A CHILD, YOU KNOW.

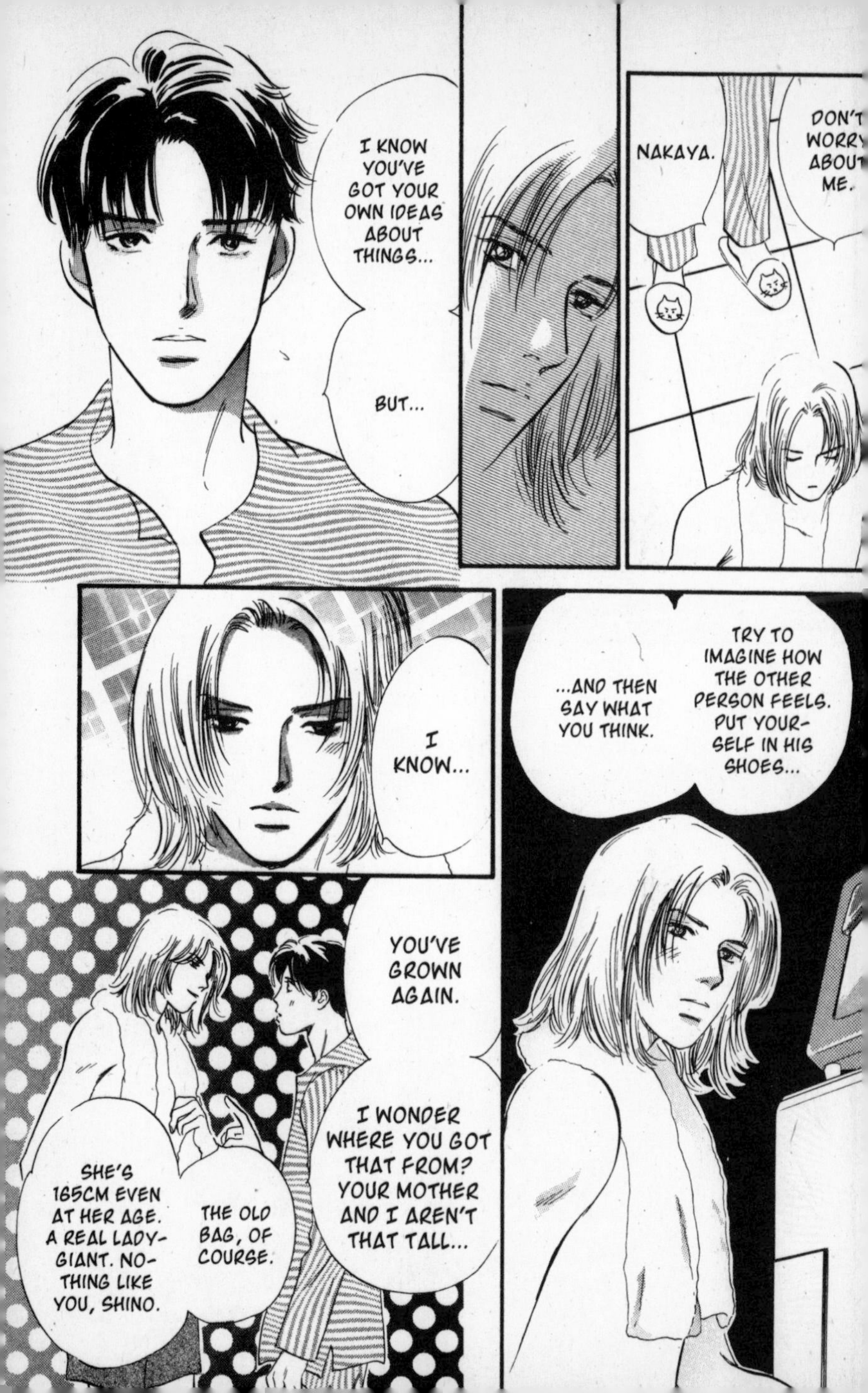
DON'T WORRY ABOUT ME.
NAKAYA.
I KNOW YOU'VE GOT YOUR OWN IDEAS ABOUT THINGS...
BUT...
TRY TO IMAGINE HOW THE OTHER PERSON FEELS. PUT YOUR-SELF IN HIS SHOES...
...AND THEN SAY WHAT YOU THINK.
I KNOW...
YOU'VE GROWN AGAIN.
I WONDER WHERE YOU GOT THAT FROM? YOUR MOTHER AND I AREN'T THAT TALL...
THE OLD BAG, OF COURSE.
SHE'S 165CM EVEN AT HER AGE. A REAL LADY-GIANT. NO-THING LIKE YOU, SHINO.

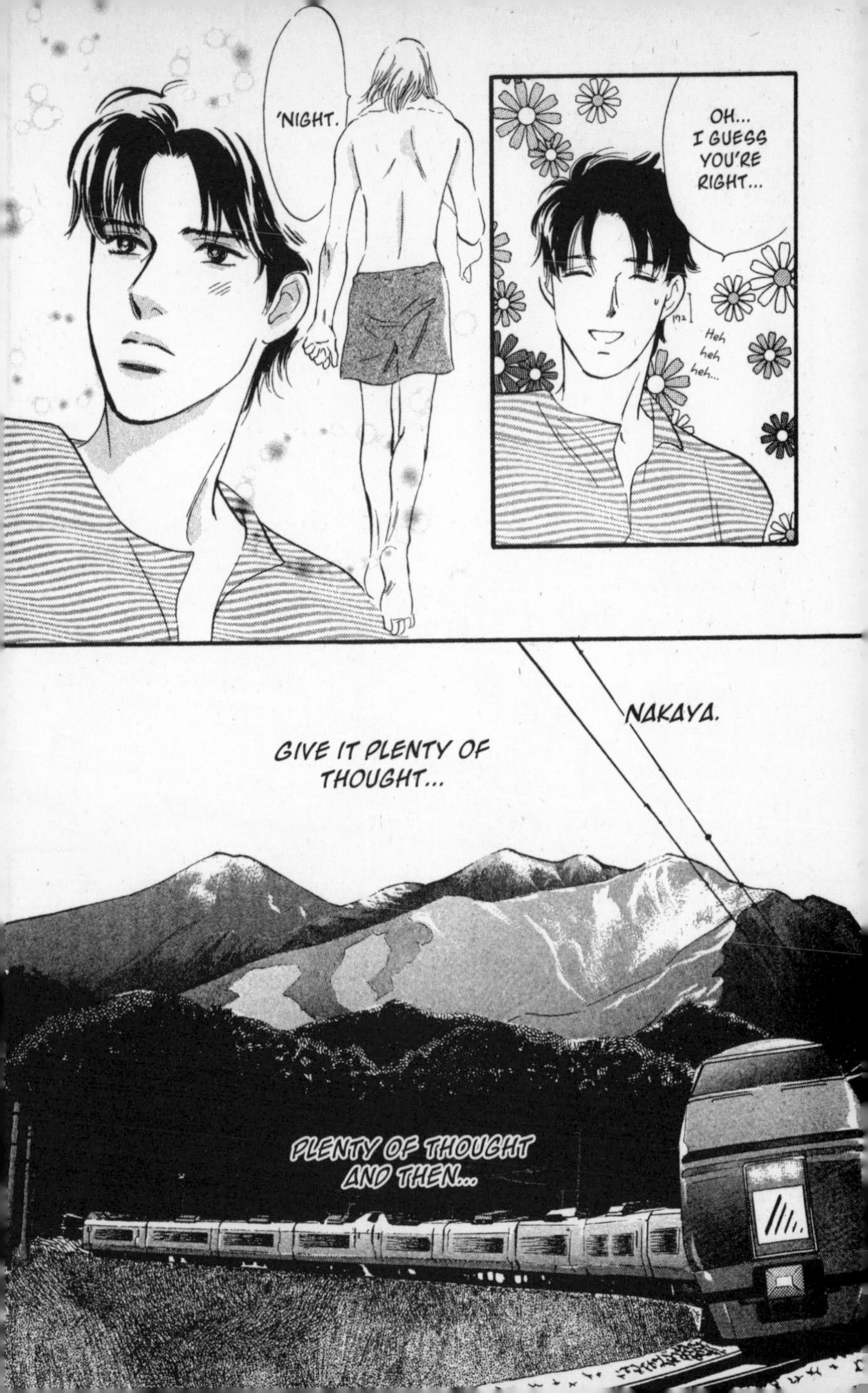
OH... I GUESS YOU'RE RIGHT...
Heh heh heh...
'NIGHT.
NAKAYA.
GIVE IT PLENTY OF THOUGHT...
PLENTY OF THOUGHT AND THEN...

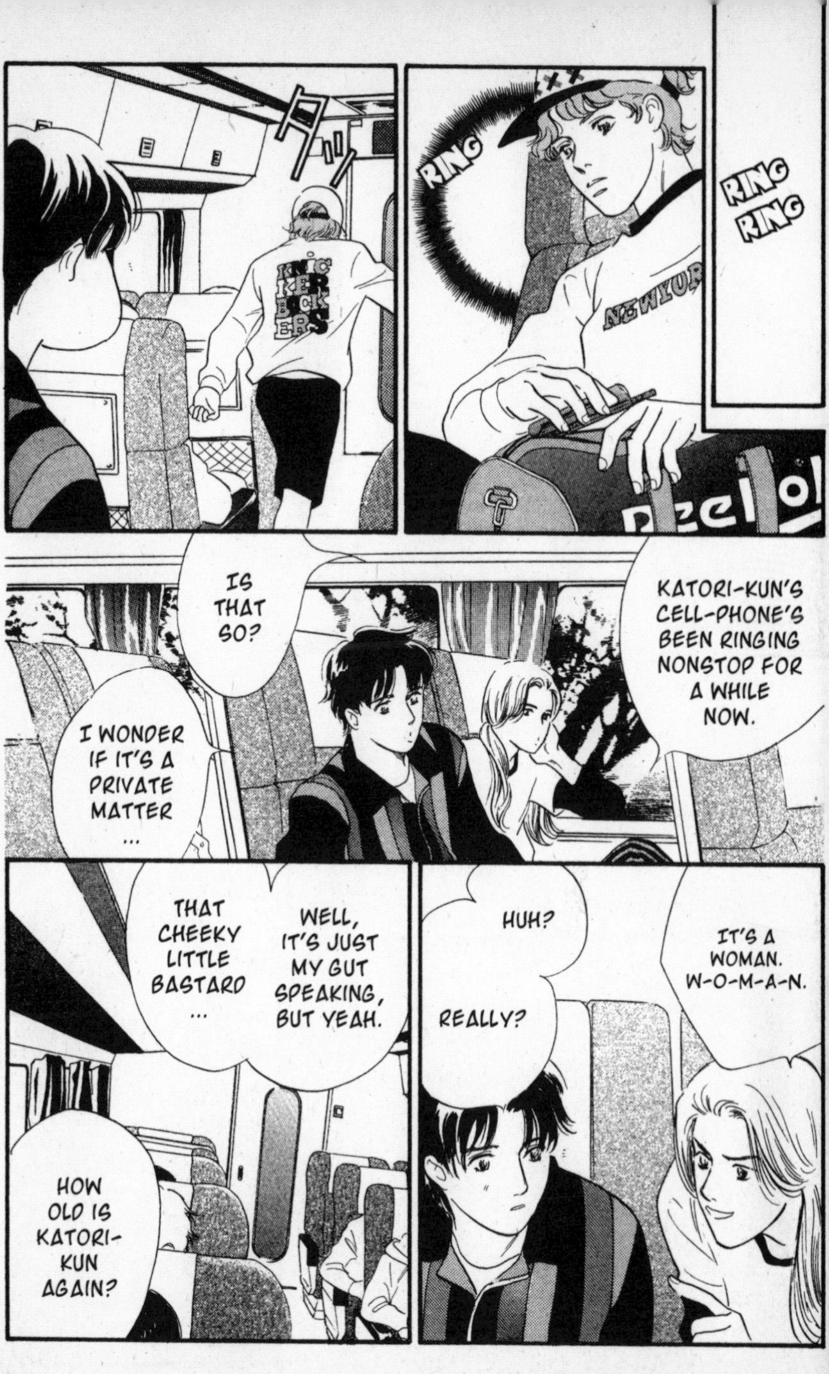
RING RING
RING
KATORI-KUN'S CELL-PHONE'S BEEN RINGING NONSTOP FOR A WHILE NOW.
IS THAT SO?
I WONDER IF IT'S A PRIVATE MATTER ...
IT'S A WOMAN. W-O-M-A-N.
HUH?
REALLY?
WELL, IT'S JUST MY GUT SPEAKING, BUT YEAH.
THAT CHEEKY LITTLE BASTARD ...
HOW OLD IS KATORI-KUN AGAIN?

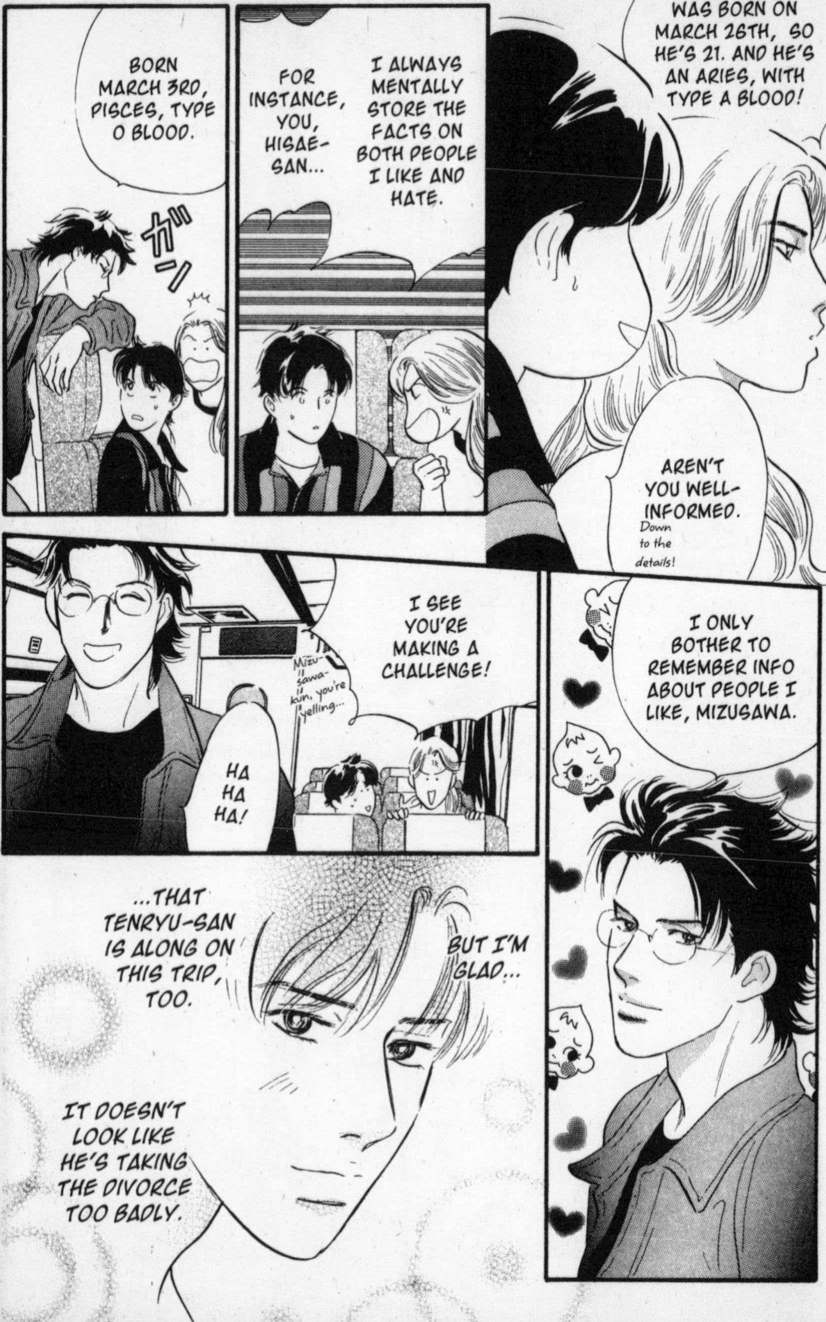
WELL, HE WAS BORN ON MARCH 26TH, SO HE'S 21. AND HE'S AN ARIES, WITH TYPE A BLOOD!
AREN'T YOU WELL-INFORMED.
Down to the details!
I ALWAYS MENTALLY STORE THE FACTS ON BOTH PEOPLE I LIKE AND HATE.
FOR INSTANCE, YOU, HISAE-SAN...
BORN MARCH 3RD, PISCES, TYPE O BLOOD.
ガーン
I ONLY BOTHER TO REMEMBER INFO ABOUT PEOPLE I LIKE, MIZUSAWA.
I SEE YOU'RE MAKING A CHALLENGE!
Mizu-sawa-kun, you're yelling...
HA HA HA HA!
BUT I'M GLAD...
...THAT TENRYU-SAN IS ALONG ON THIS TRIP, TOO.
IT DOESN'T LOOK LIKE HE'S TAKING THE DIVORCE TOO BADLY.

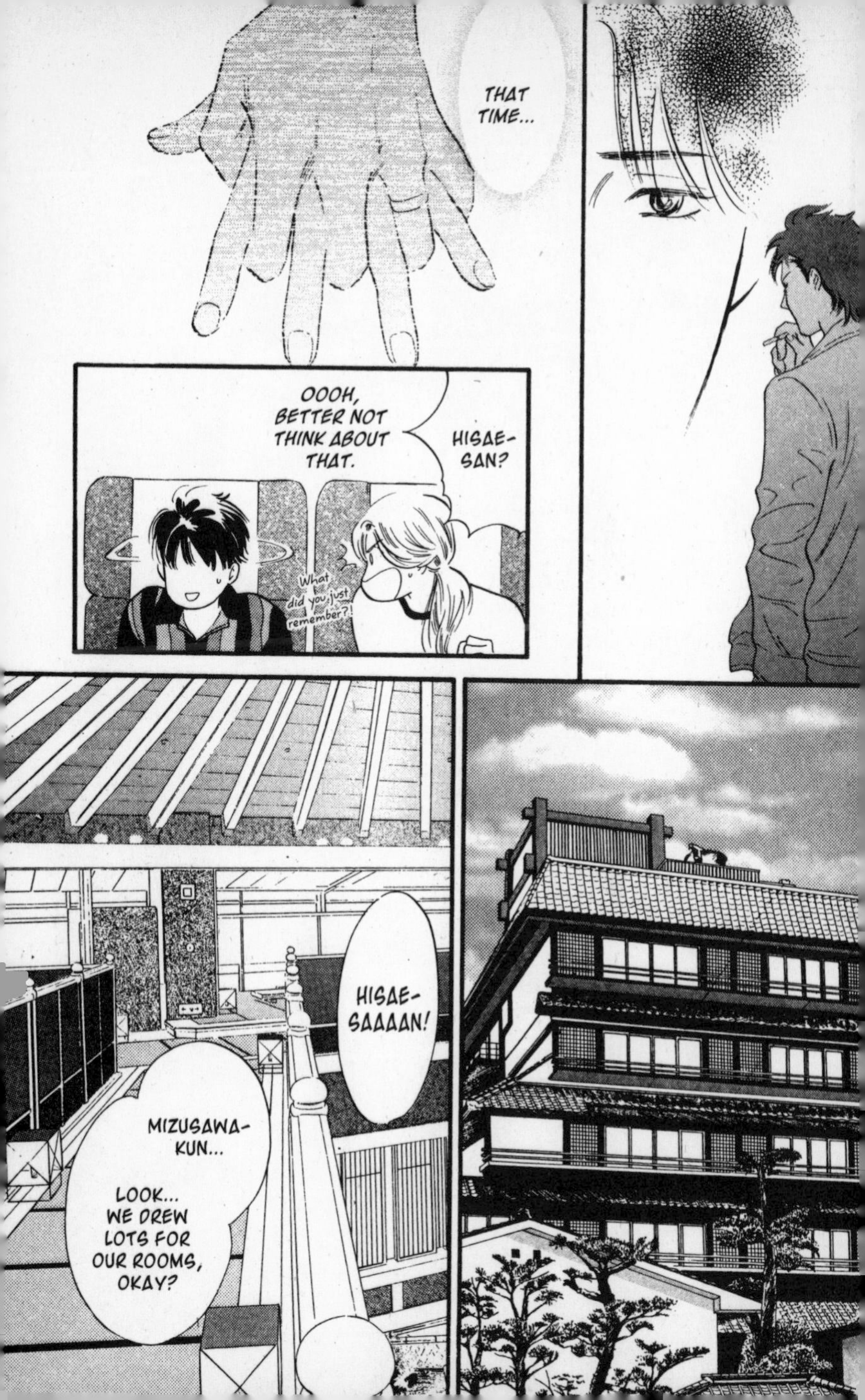
THAT TIME...
HISAE-SAN?
OOOH, BETTER NOT THINK ABOUT THAT.
What did you just remember?!
HISAE-SAAAAN!
MIZUSAWA-KUN...
LOOK... WE DREW LOTS FOR OUR ROOMS, OKAY?

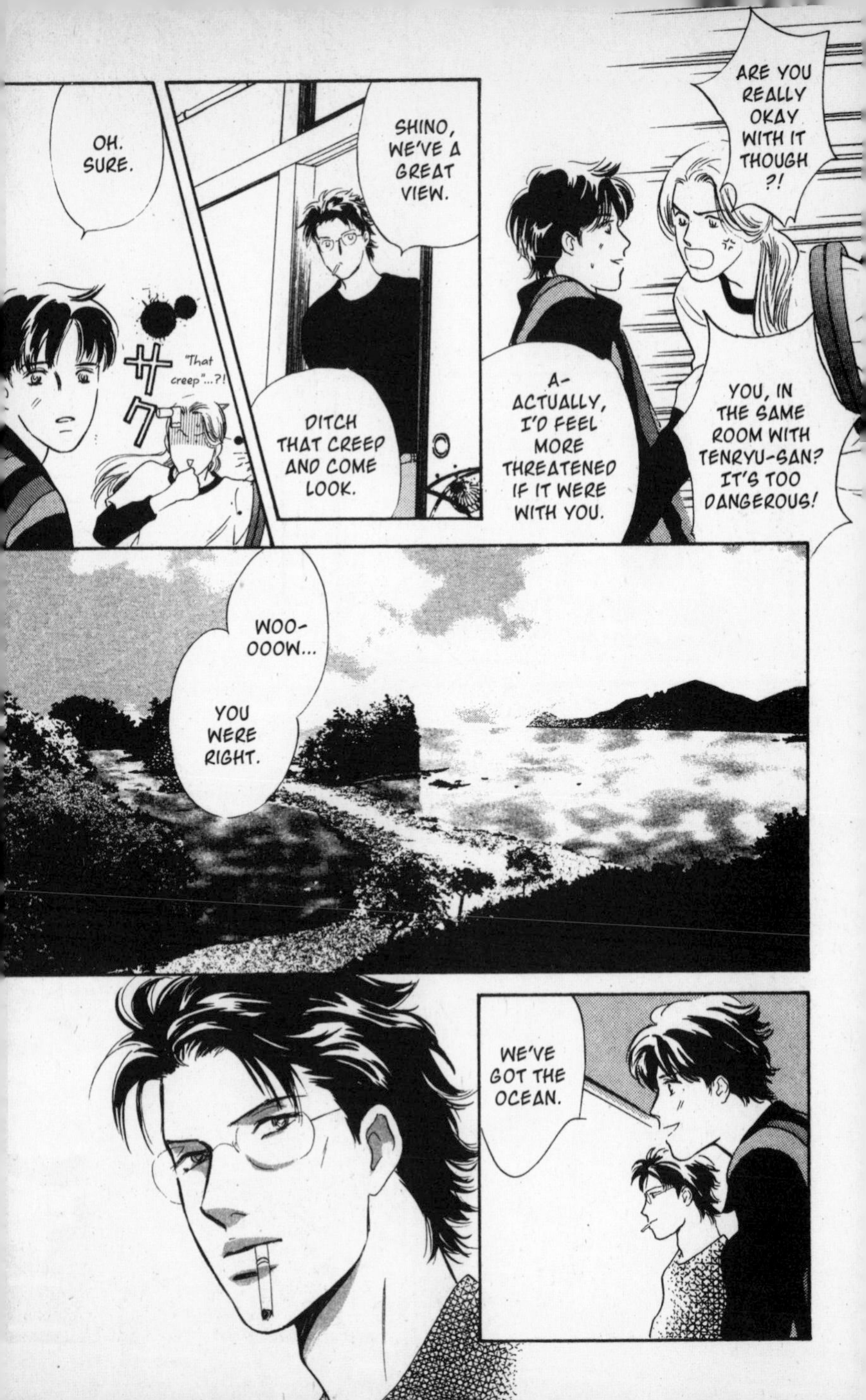
ARE YOU REALLY OKAY WITH IT THOUGH?!
YOU, IN THE SAME ROOM WITH TENRYU-SAN? IT'S TOO DANGEROUS!
A- ACTUALLY, I'D FEEL MORE THREATENED IF IT WERE WITH YOU.
SHINO, WE'VE A GREAT VIEW.
DITCH THAT CREEP AND COME LOOK.
OH. SURE.
サク
"That creep"...?!
WOO- OOOW...
YOU WERE RIGHT.
WE'VE GOT THE OCEAN.

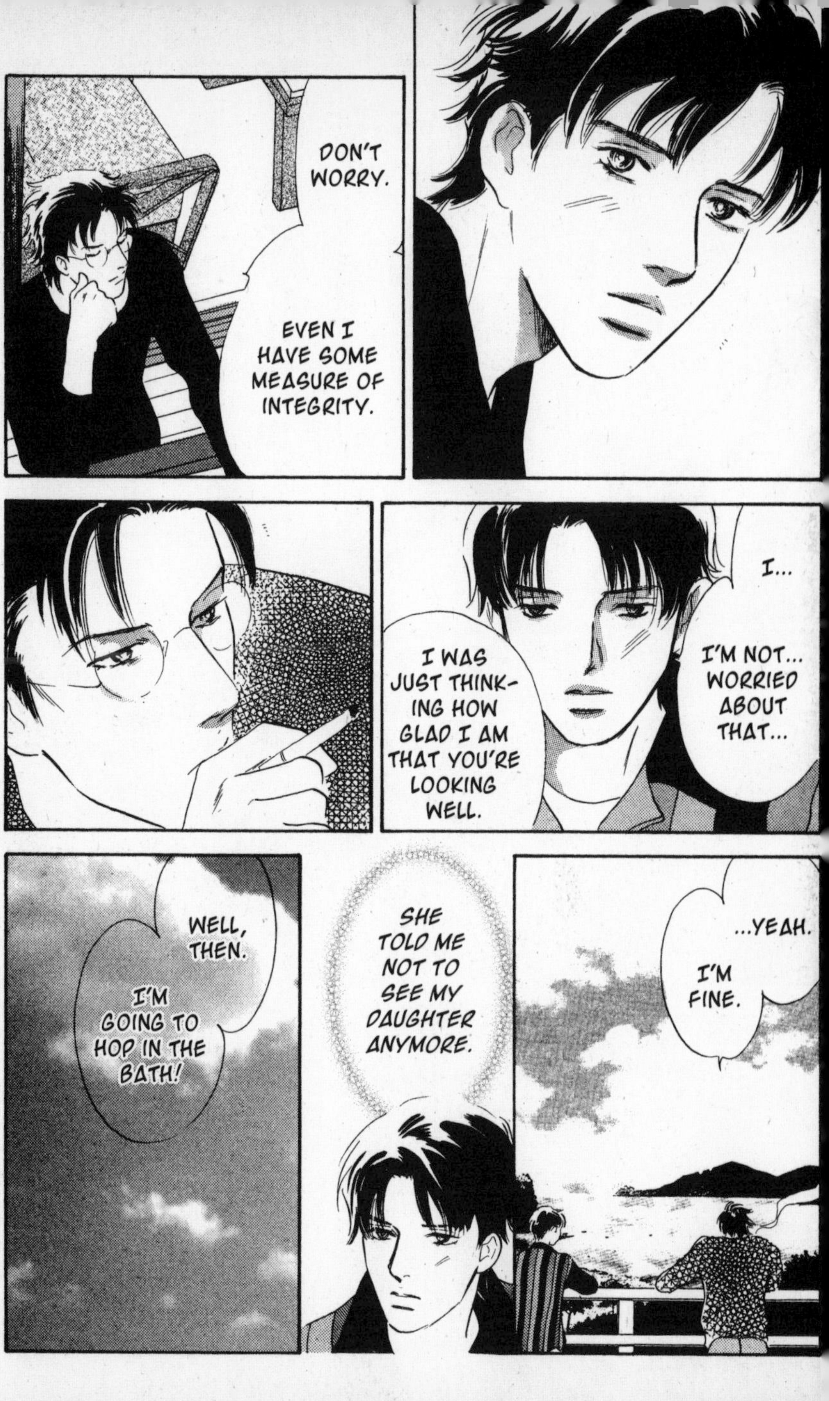
DON'T WORRY.
EVEN I HAVE SOME MEASURE OF INTEGRITY.
I...
I'M NOT... WORRIED ABOUT THAT...
I WAS JUST THINKING HOW GLAD I AM THAT YOU'RE LOOKING WELL.
...YEAH.
I'M FINE.
SHE TOLD ME NOT TO SEE MY DAUGHTER ANYMORE.
WELL, THEN.
I'M GOING TO HOP IN THE BATH!

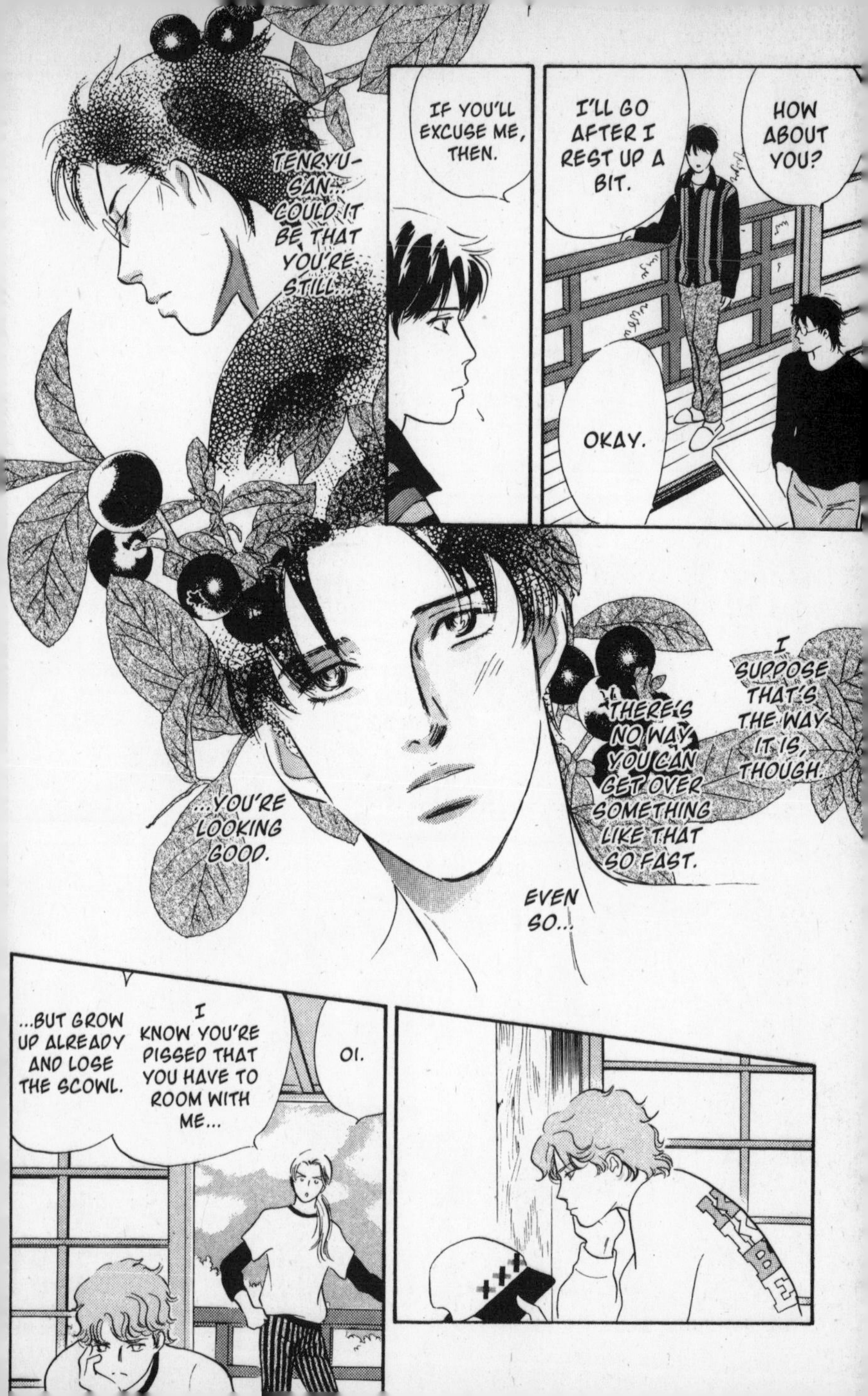
HOW ABOUT YOU?
I'LL GO AFTER I REST UP A BIT.
OKAY.
IF YOU'LL EXCUSE ME, THEN.
TENRYU-SAN... COULD IT BE THAT YOU'RE STILL...
I SUPPOSE THAT'S THE WAY IT IS, THOUGH.
THERE'S NO WAY YOU CAN GET OVER SOMETHING LIKE THAT SO FAST.
EVEN SO...
...YOU'RE LOOKING GOOD.
OI.
I KNOW YOU'RE PISSED THAT YOU HAVE TO ROOM WITH ME...
...BUT GROW UP ALREADY AND LOSE THE SCOWL.

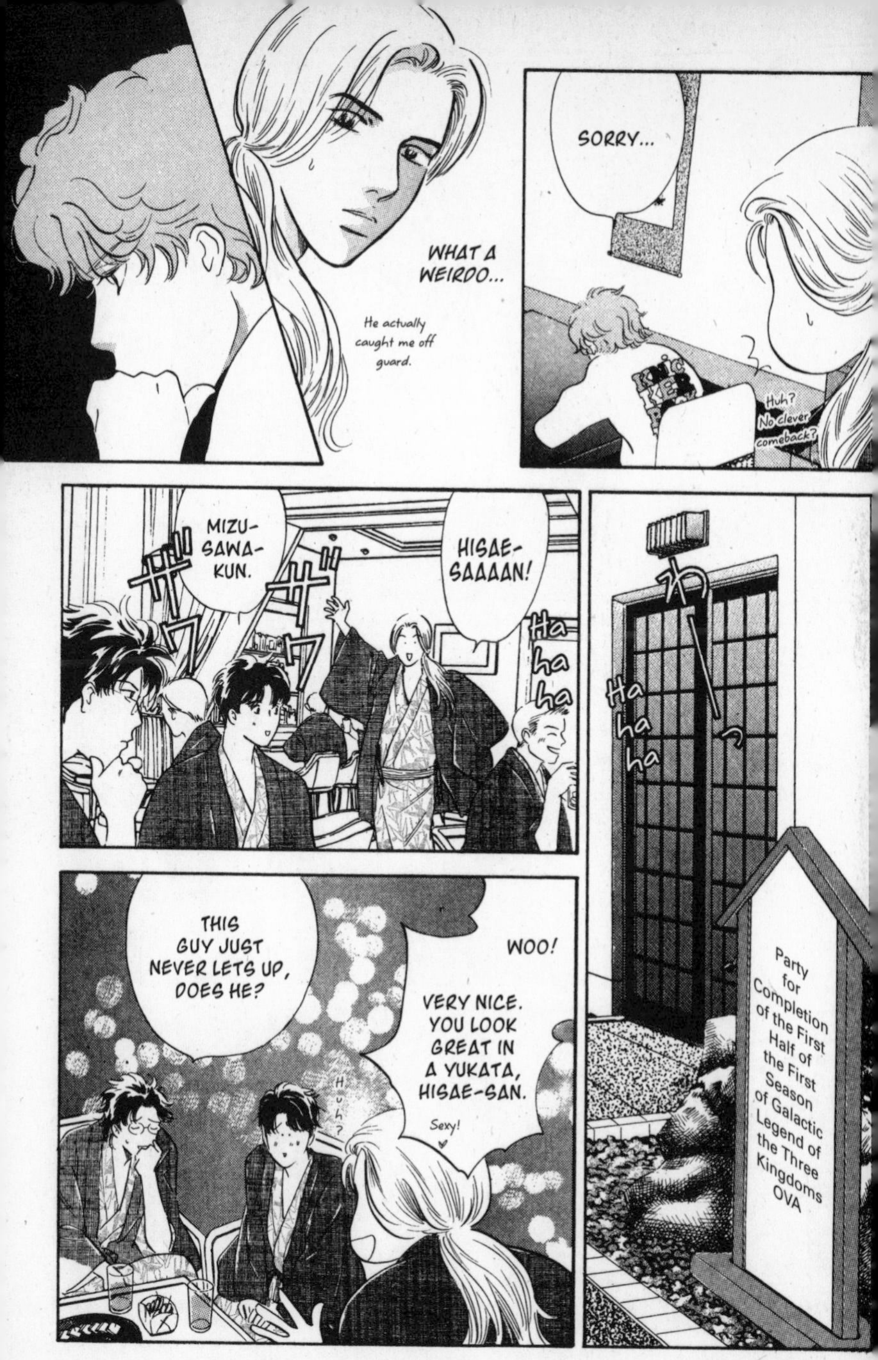
SORRY...
Huh? No clever comeback?
WHAT A WEIRDO...
He actually caught me off guard.
Ha ha ha
Party for Completion of the First Half of the First Season of Galactic Legend of the Three Kingdoms OVA
HISAE-SAAAAN!
Ha ha ha
MIZU-SAWA-KUN.
WOO!
VERY NICE. YOU LOOK GREAT IN A YUKATA, HISAE-SAN.
Sexy!
Huh?
THIS GUY JUST NEVER LETS UP, DOES HE?

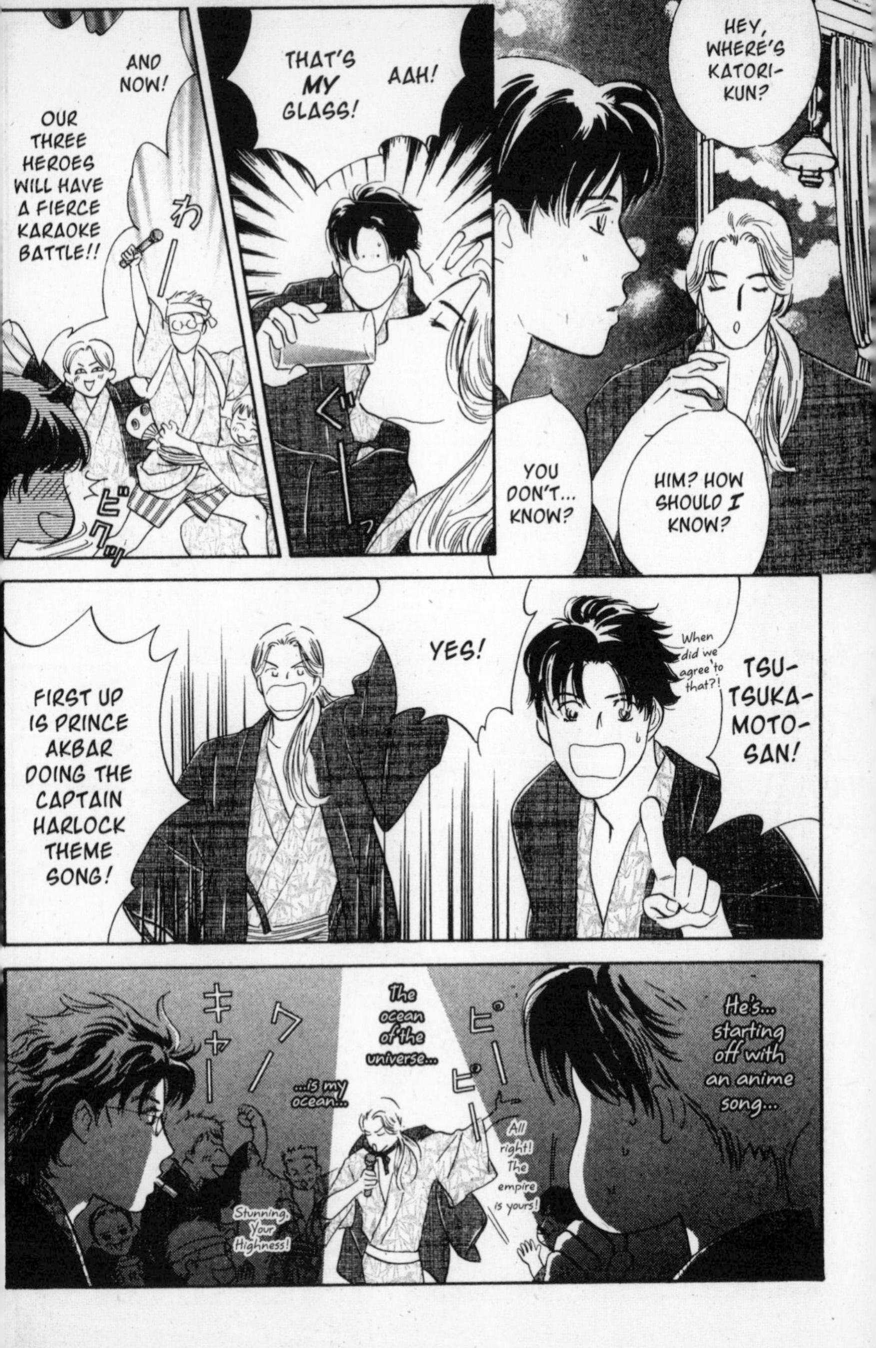
HEY, WHERE'S KATORI-KUN?
HIM? HOW SHOULD I KNOW?
YOU DON'T... KNOW?
AAH!
THAT'S MY GLASS!
AND NOW!
OUR THREE HEROES WILL HAVE A FIERCE KARAOKE BATTLE!!
わー
ビクッ
TSU-TSUKA-MOTO-SAN!
When did we agree to that?!
YES!
FIRST UP IS PRINCE AKBAR DOING THE CAPTAIN HARLOCK THEME SONG!
He's... starting off with an anime song...
All right! The empire is yours!
ピーピー
The ocean of the universe...
...is my ocean...
キャー
Stunning, Your Highness!

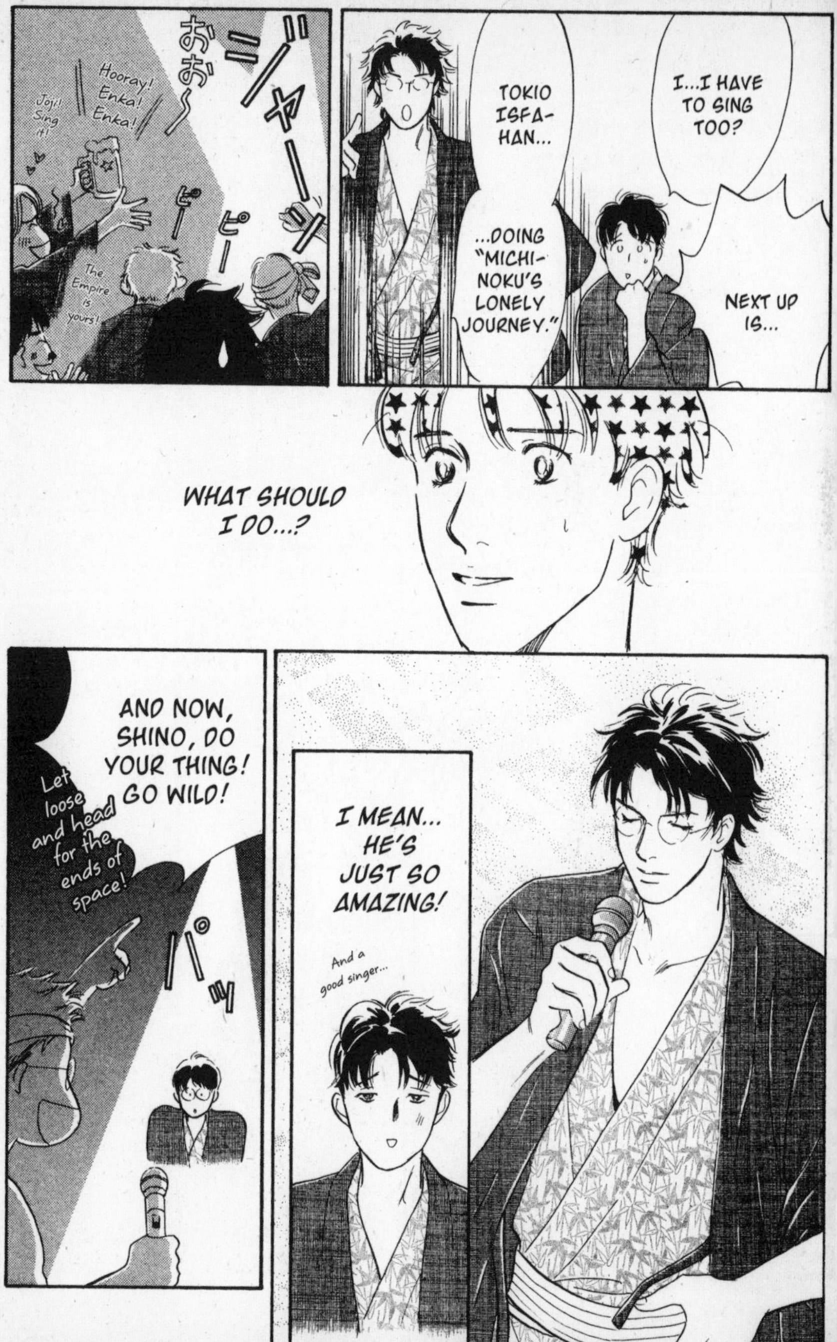

I...I HAVE TO SING TOO?
NEXT UP IS...
TOKIO ISFA-HAN...
...DOING "MICHI-NOKU'S LONELY JOURNEY."
ジャーンッ
おお~
ピーピー
Hooray! Enka! Enka!
Joji! Sing it!
The Empire is yours!
WHAT SHOULD I DO...?
I MEAN... HE'S JUST SO AMAZING!
And a good singer...
AND NOW, SHINO, DO YOUR THING! GO WILD!
Let loose and head for the ends of space!
パッ

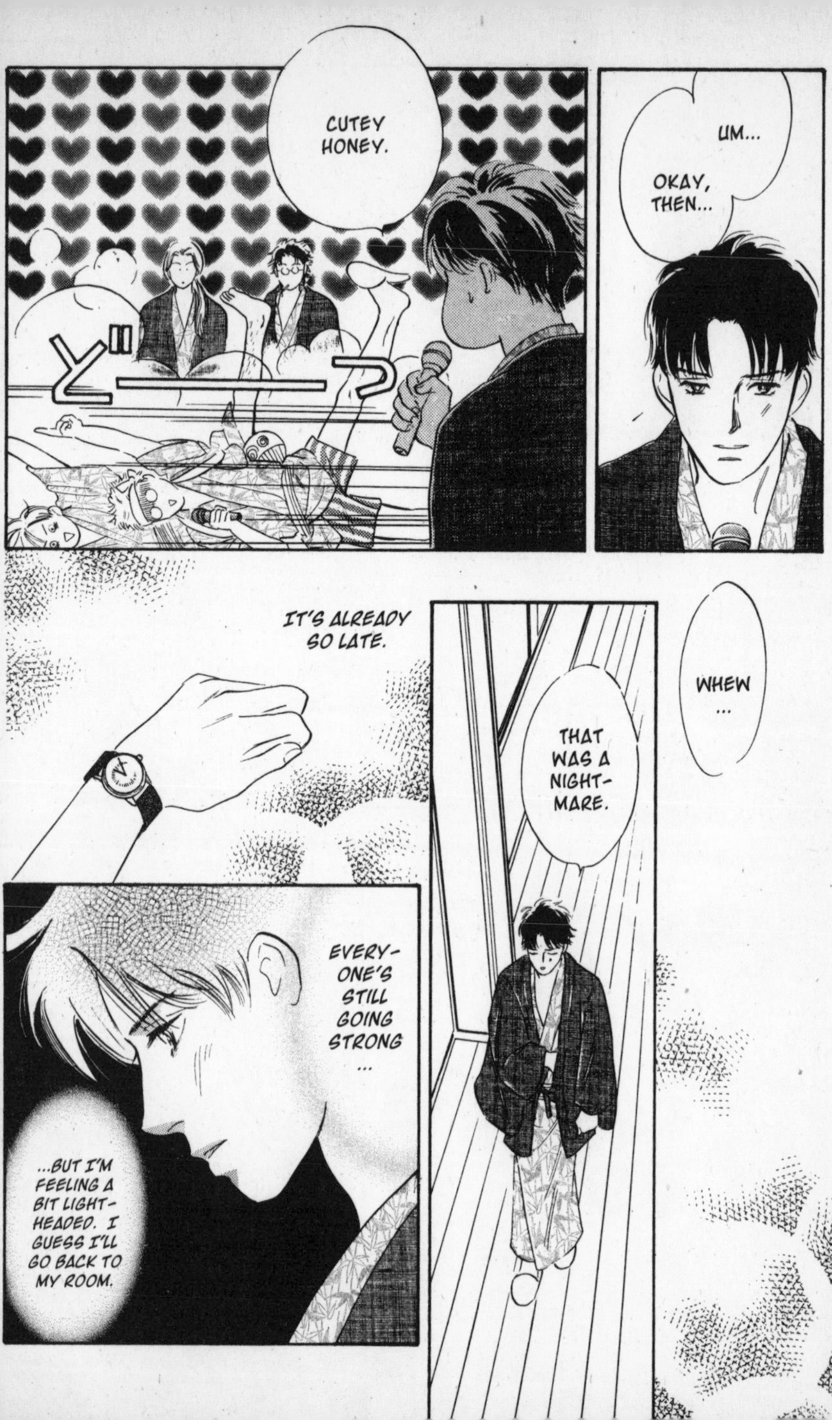
UM...
OKAY, THEN...
CUTEY HONEY.
ドーン
WHEW ...
THAT WAS A NIGHT-MARE.
IT'S ALREADY SO LATE.
EVERY-ONE'S STILL GOING STRONG ...
...BUT I'M FEELING A BIT LIGHT-HEADED. I GUESS I'LL GO BACK TO MY ROOM.

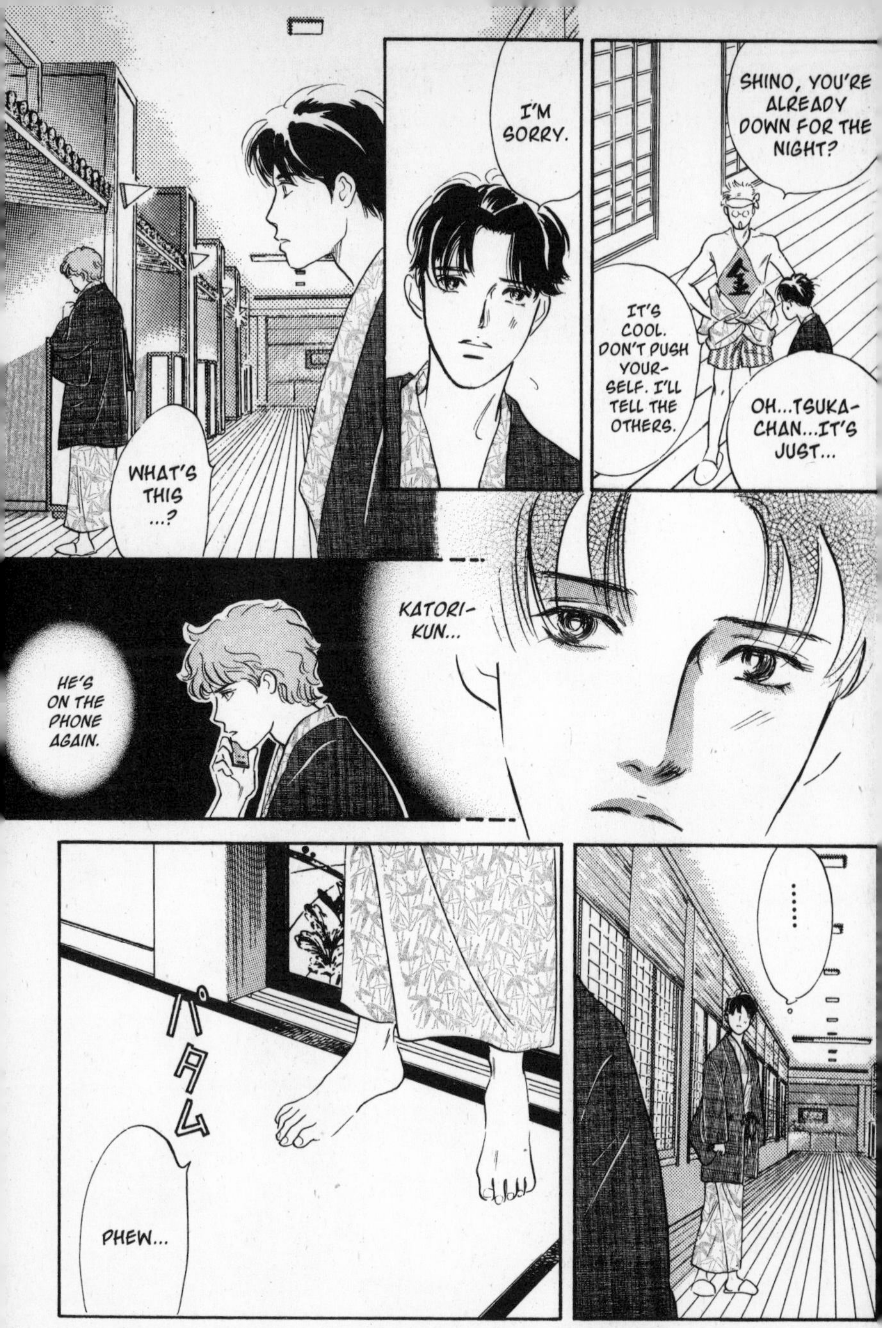
SHINO, YOU'RE ALREADY DOWN FOR THE NIGHT?
OH...TSUKA-CHAN...IT'S JUST...
IT'S COOL. DON'T PUSH YOUR-SELF. I'LL TELL THE OTHERS.
I'M SORRY.
WHAT'S THIS ...?
KATORI-KUN...
HE'S ON THE PHONE AGAIN.
......
パタム
PHEW...

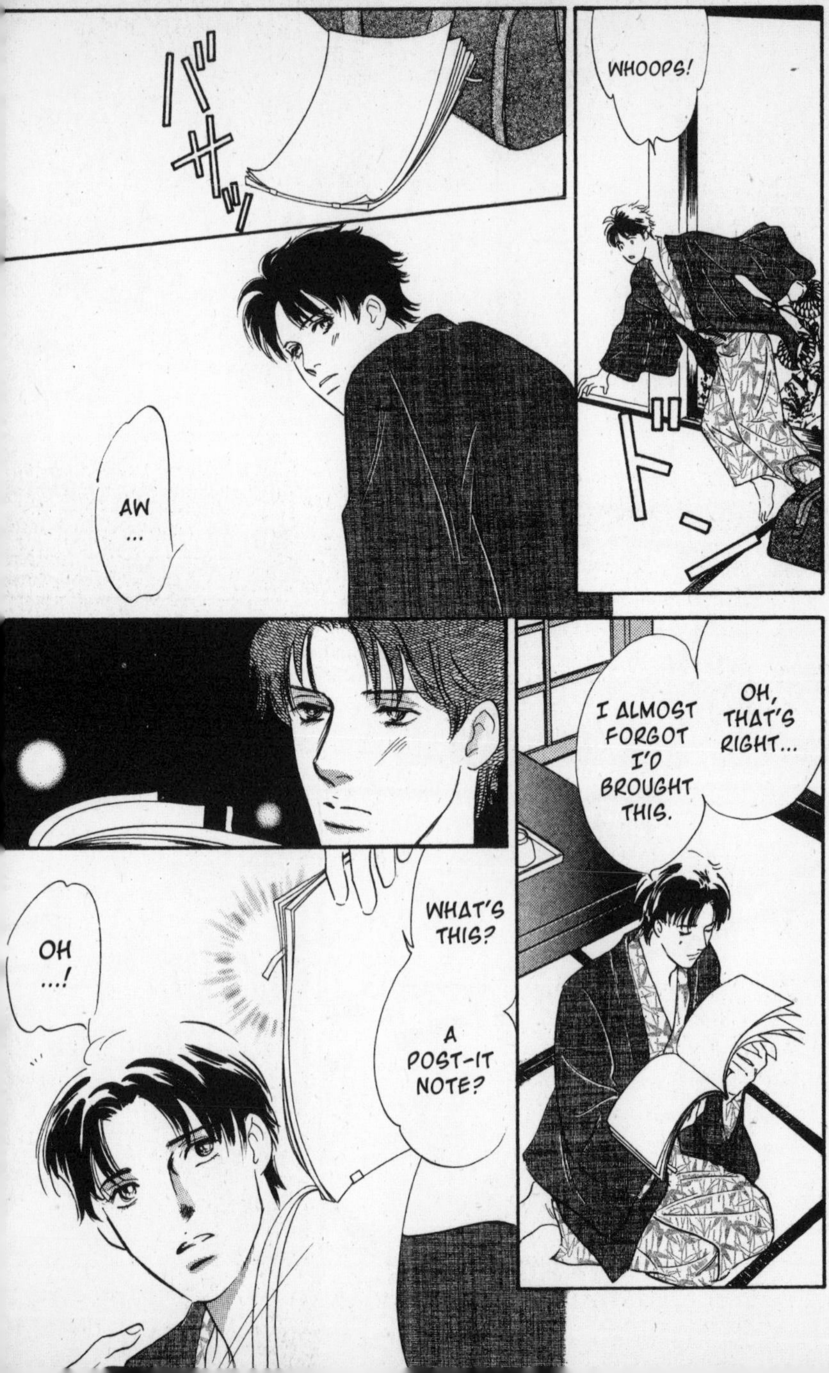
WHOOPS!
バサッ
AW ...
OH, THAT'S RIGHT...
I ALMOST FORGOT I'D BROUGHT THIS.
WHAT'S THIS?
A POST-IT NOTE?
OH ...!

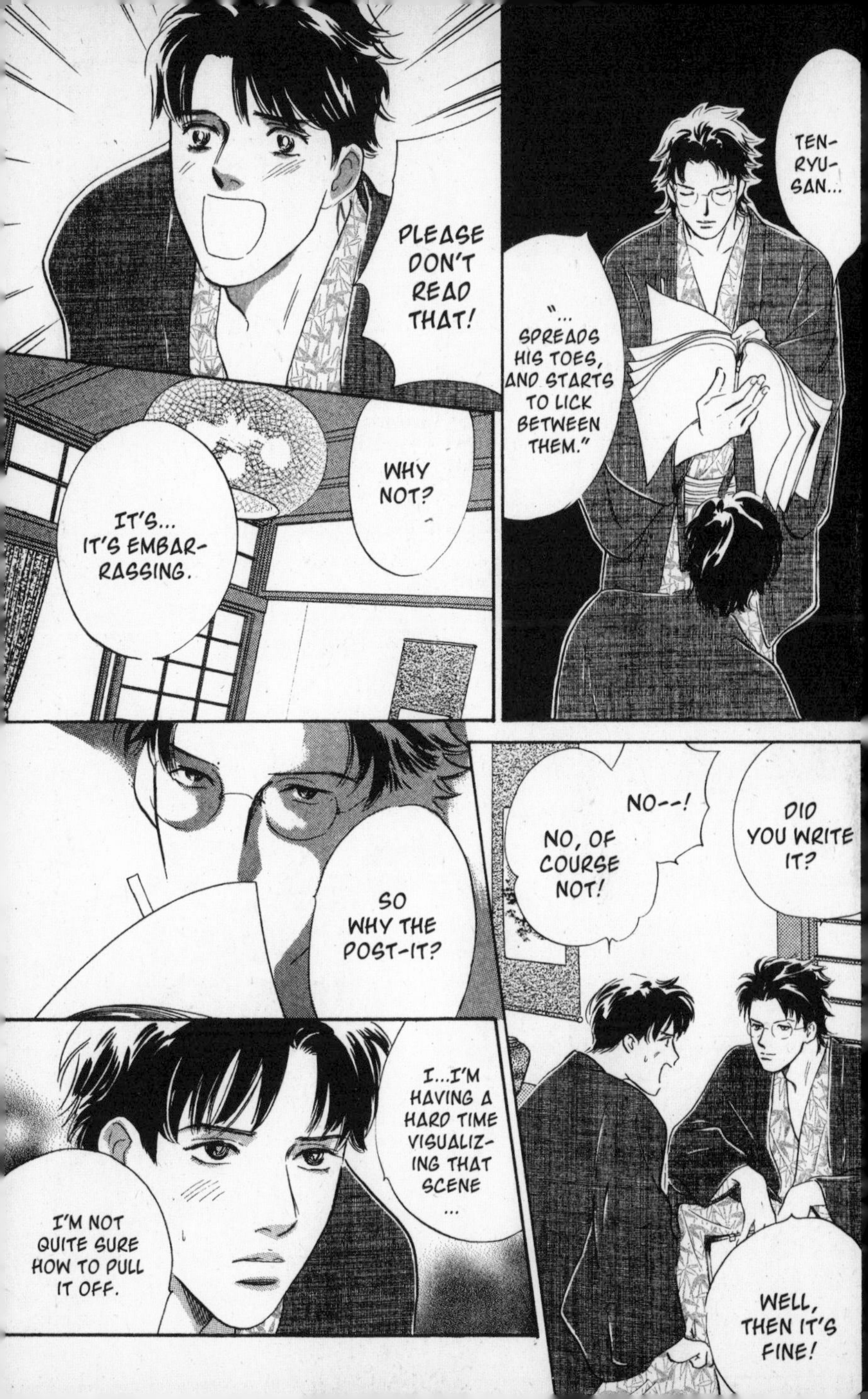
TEN-RYU-SAN...
"... SPREADS HIS TOES, AND STARTS TO LICK BETWEEN THEM."
PLEASE DON'T READ THAT!
WHY NOT?
IT'S... IT'S EMBARRASSING.
DID YOU WRITE IT?
NO--!
NO, OF COURSE NOT!
WELL, THEN IT'S FINE!
SO WHY THE POST-IT?
I...I'M HAVING A HARD TIME VISUALIZING THAT SCENE ...
I'M NOT QUITE SURE HOW TO PULL IT OFF.

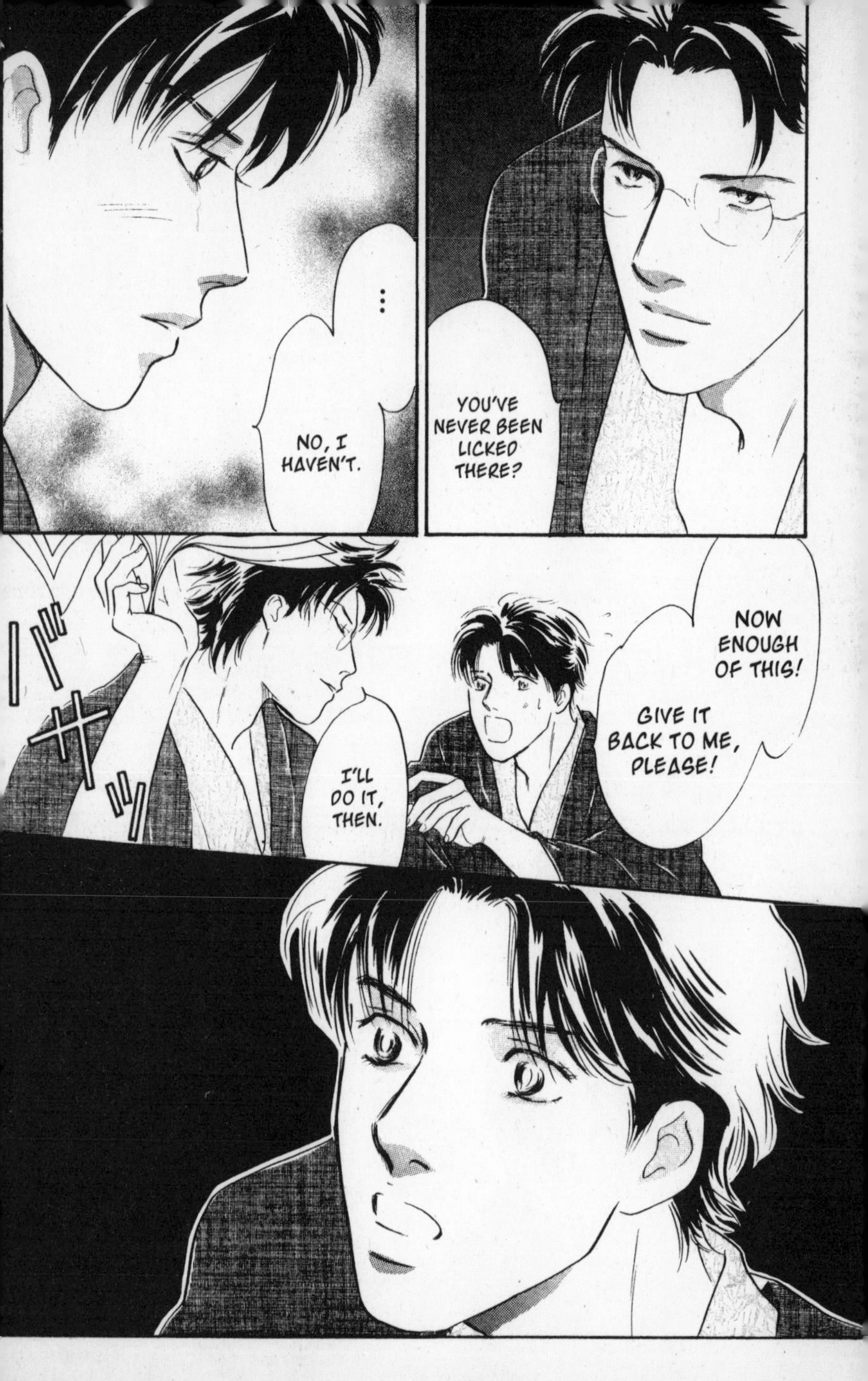
YOU'VE NEVER BEEN LICKED THERE?
...
NO, I HAVEN'T.
NOW ENOUGH OF THIS!
GIVE IT BACK TO ME, PLEASE!
I'LL DO IT, THEN.

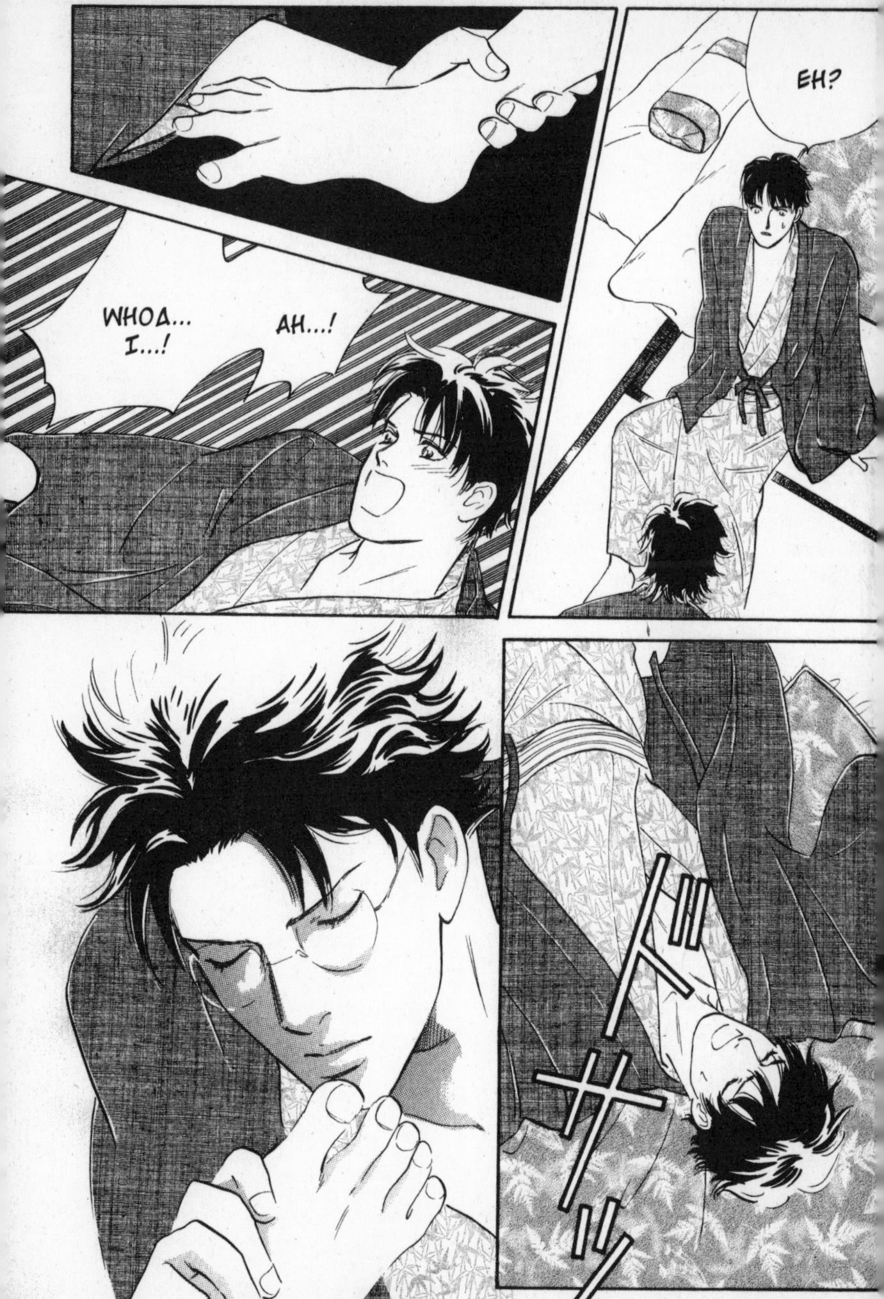
EH?
AH...!
WHOA...
I...!

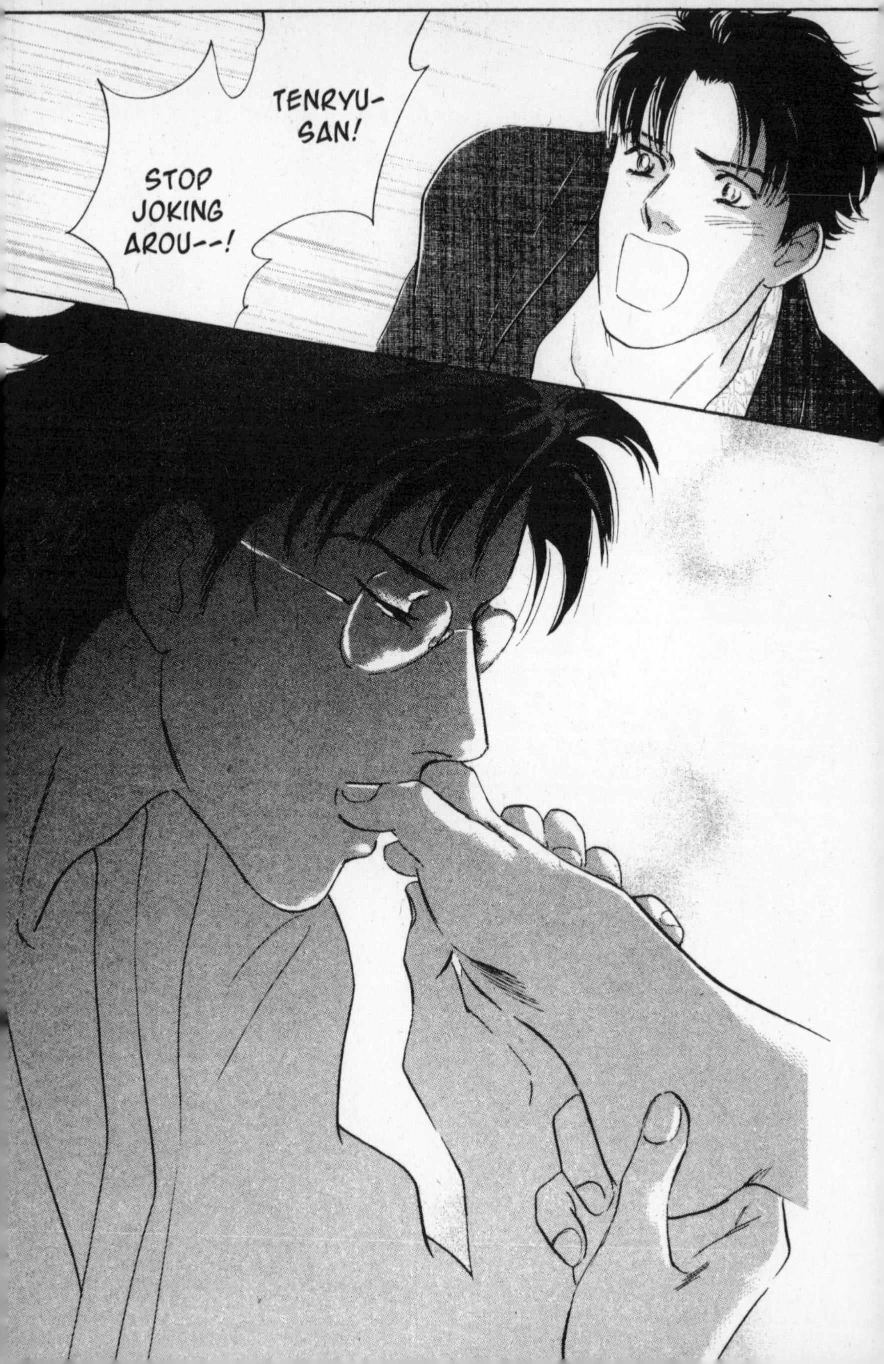
TENRYU-SAN!
STOP JOKING AROU--!

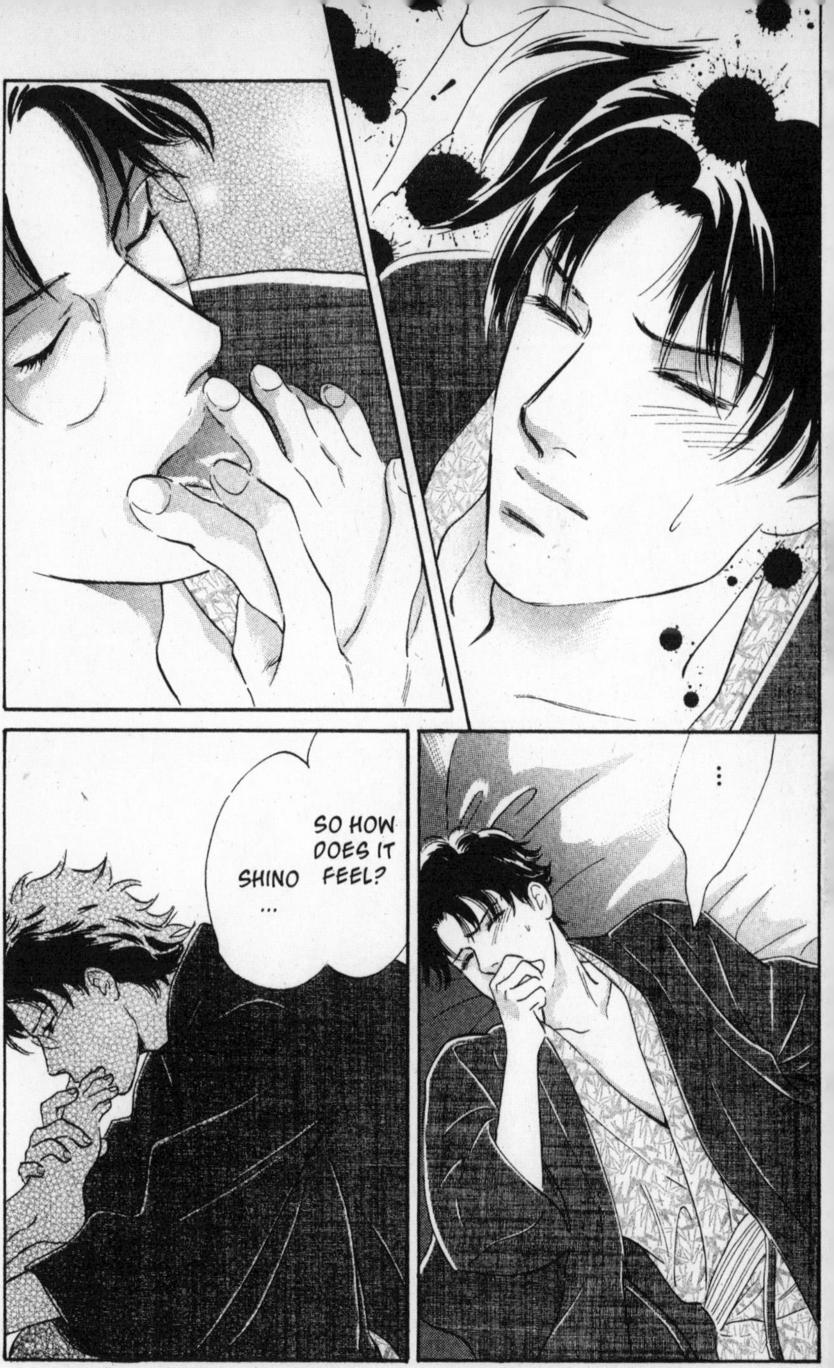
!
...
SO HOW DOES IT FEEL?
SHINO ...

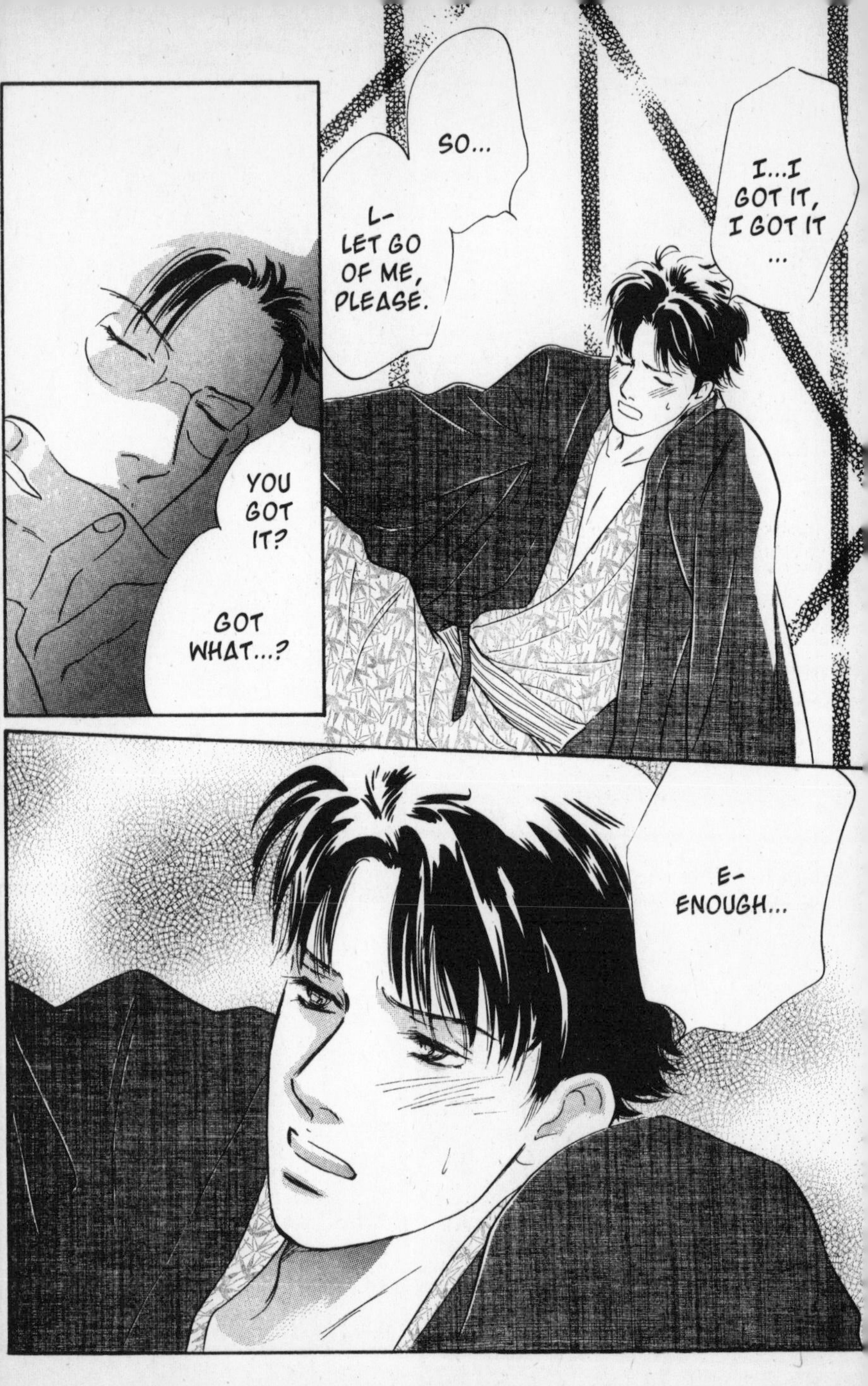
I...I GOT IT, I GOT IT ...
SO... L- LET GO OF ME, PLEASE.
YOU GOT IT? GOT WHAT...?
E- ENOUGH...

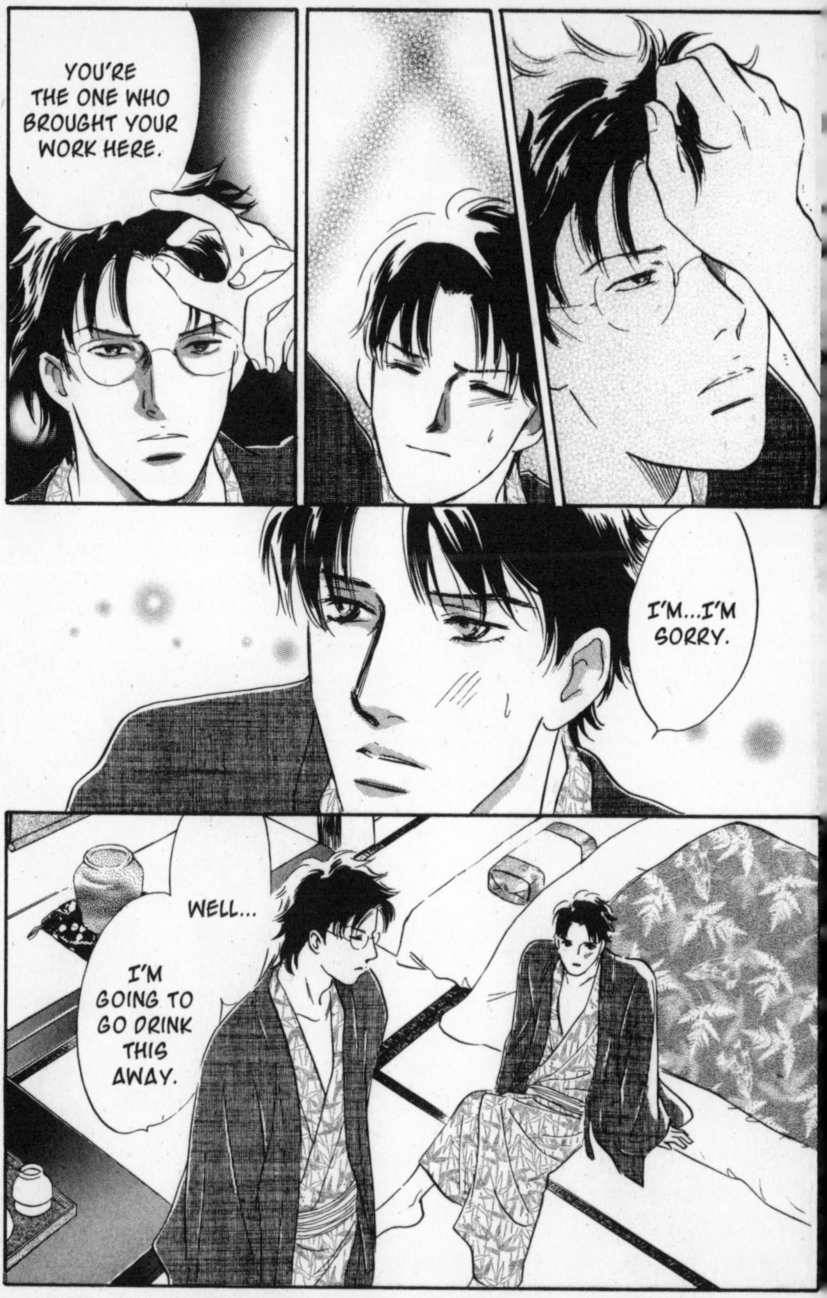
YOU'RE THE ONE WHO BROUGHT YOUR WORK HERE.
I'M...I'M SORRY.
WELL...
I'M GOING TO GO DRINK THIS AWAY.

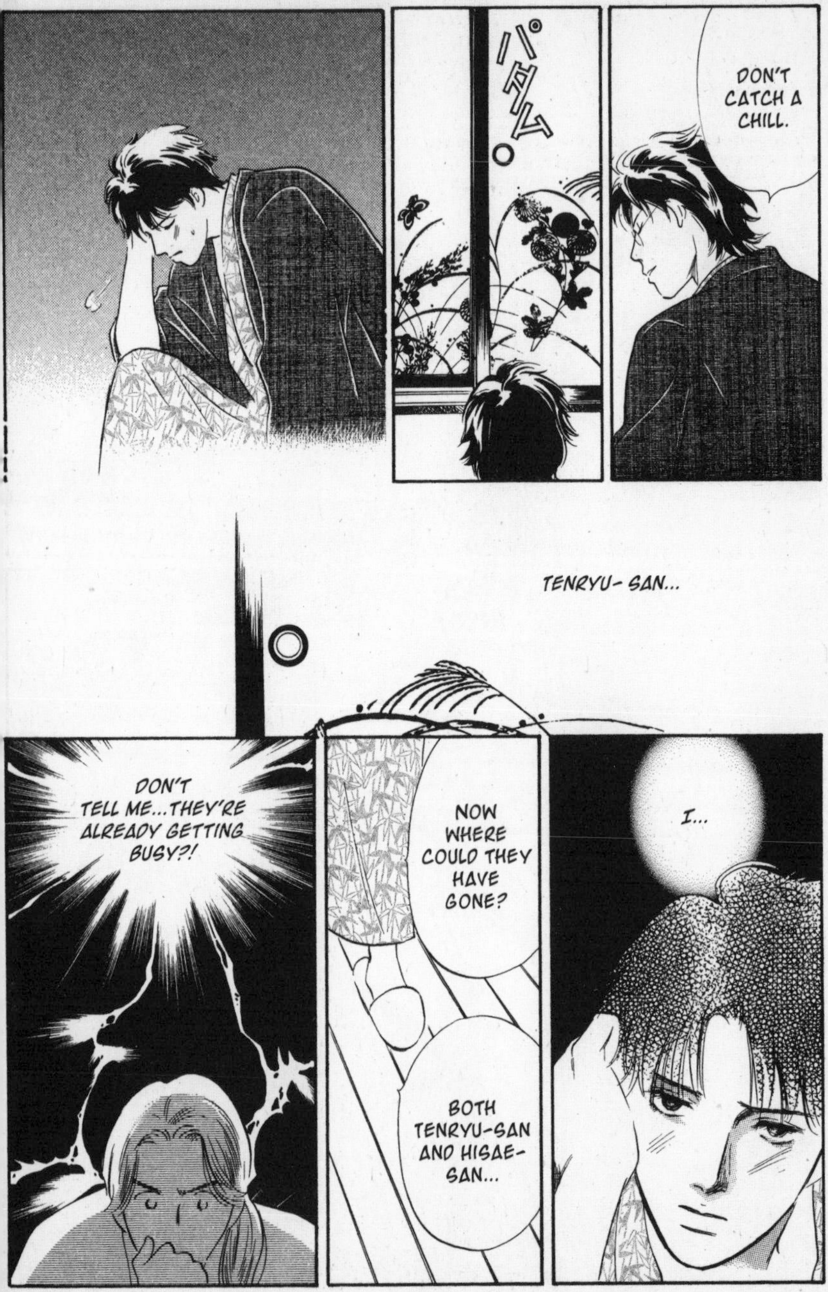
DON'T CATCH A CHILL.
パタン。
TENRYU- SAN...
I...
NOW WHERE COULD THEY HAVE GONE?
BOTH TENRYU-SAN AND HISAE-SAN...
DON'T TELL ME...THEY'RE ALREADY GETTING BUSY?!

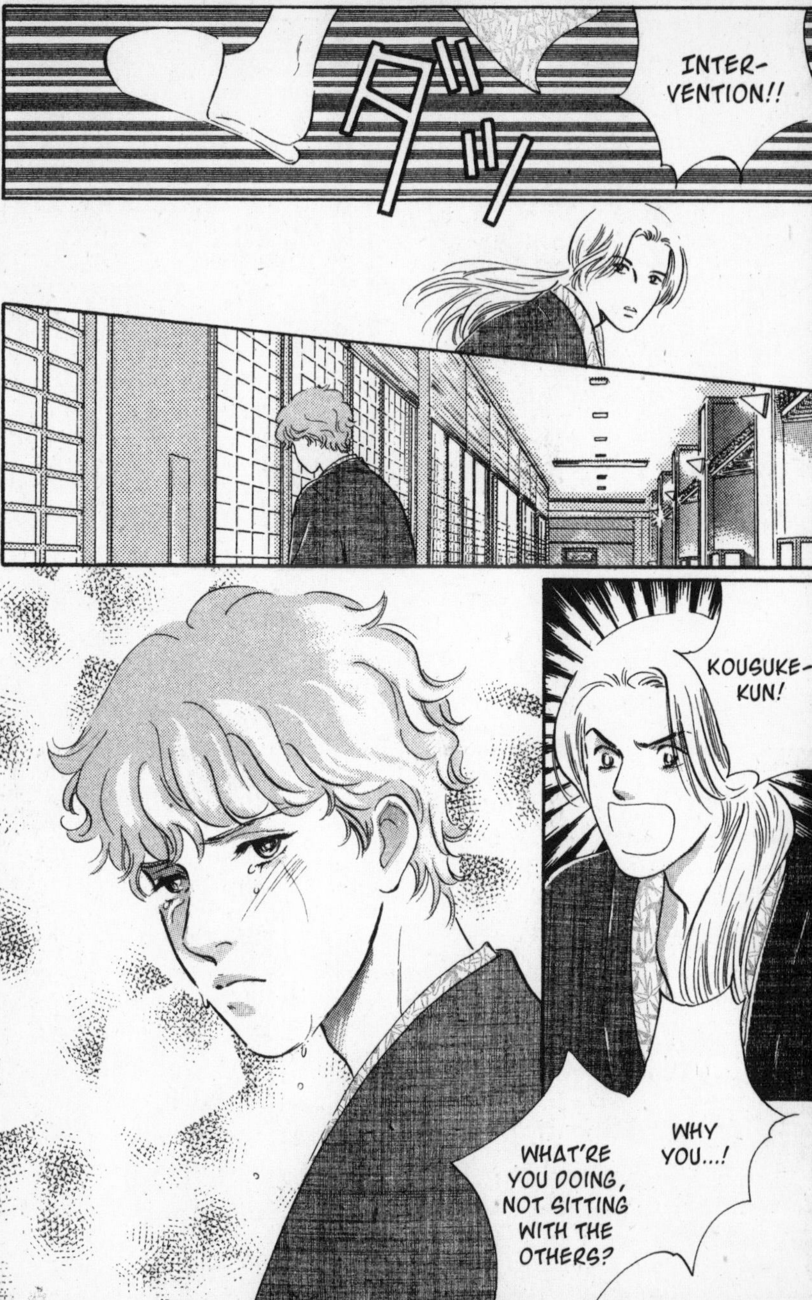
INTER-VENTION!!
ダッ
KOUSUKE-KUN!
WHY YOU...!
WHAT'RE YOU DOING, NOT SITTING WITH THE OTHERS?

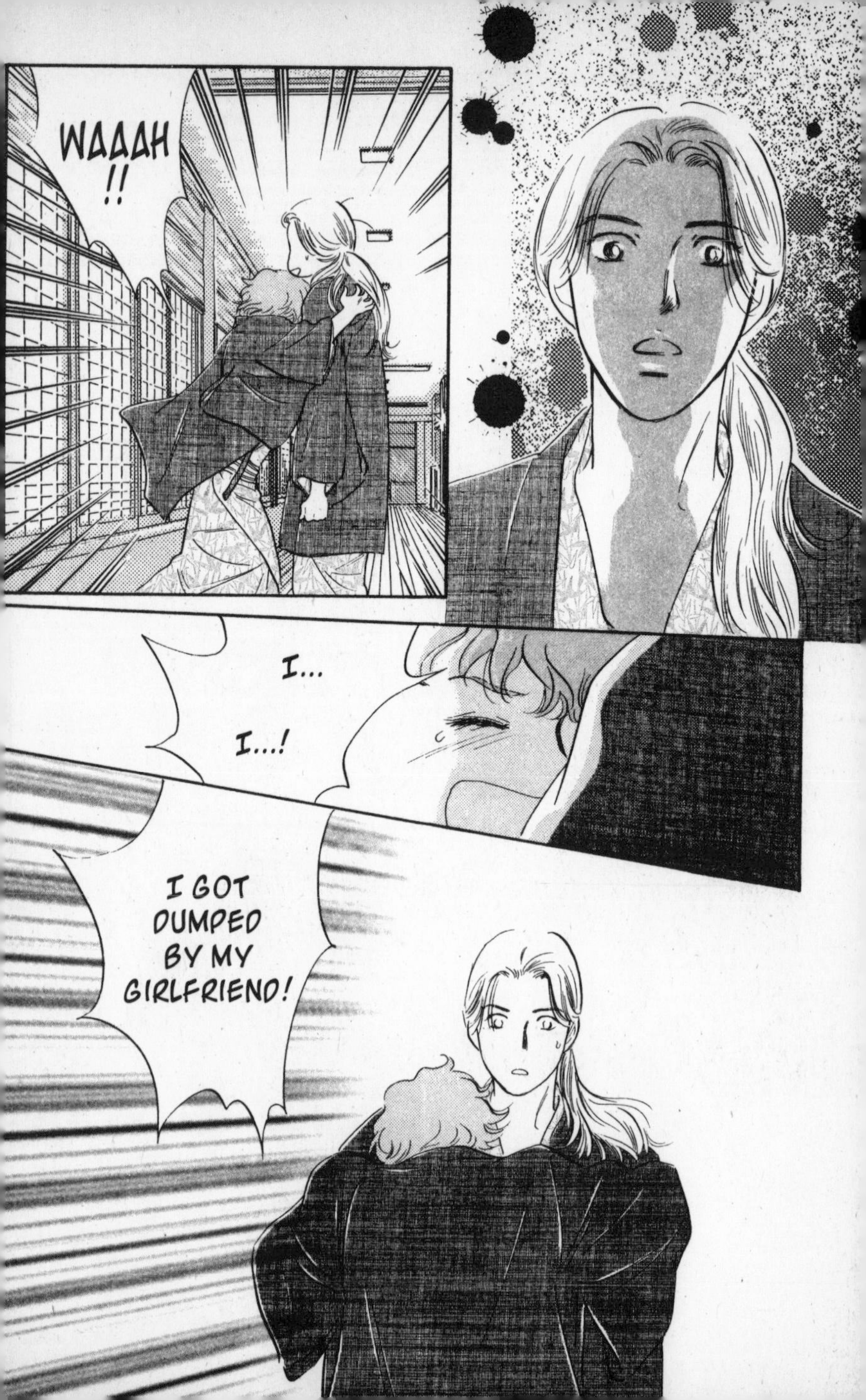
WAAAH !!
I...
I...!
I GOT DUMPED BY MY GIRLFRIEND!

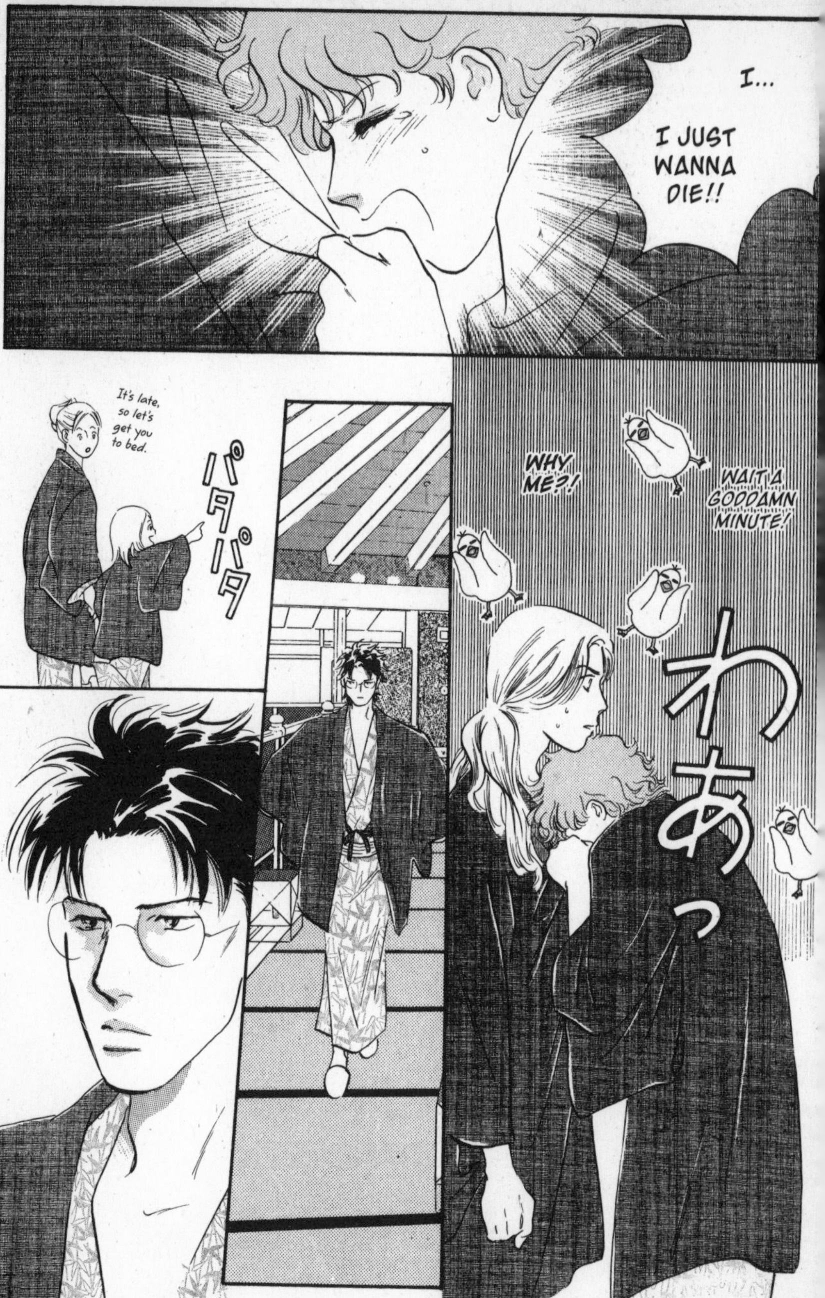
I...
I JUST WANNA DIE!!
WAIT A GODDAMN MINUTE!
WHY ME?!
わあっ
It's late, so let's get you to bed.
パタパタ

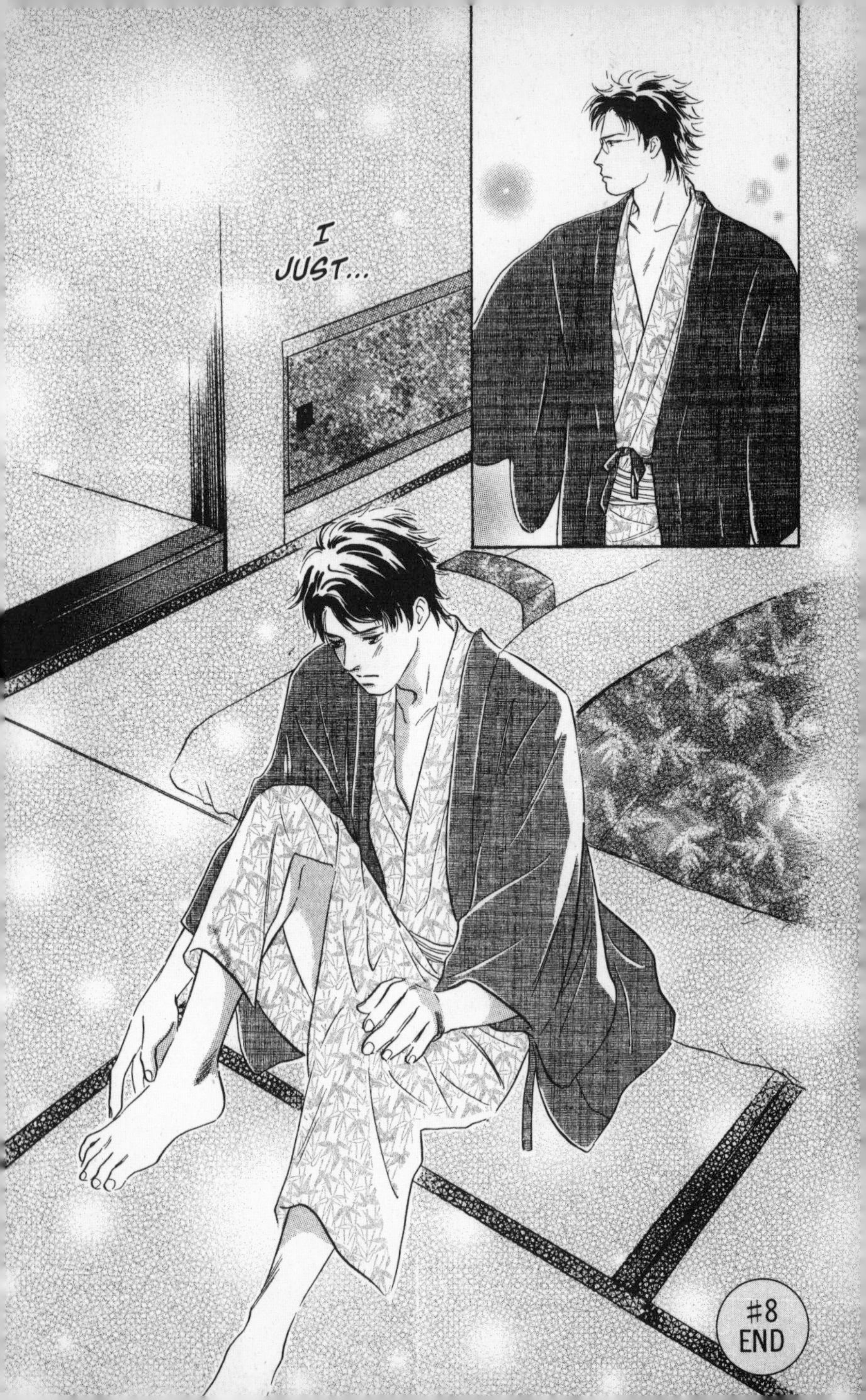
I JUST...
#8 END

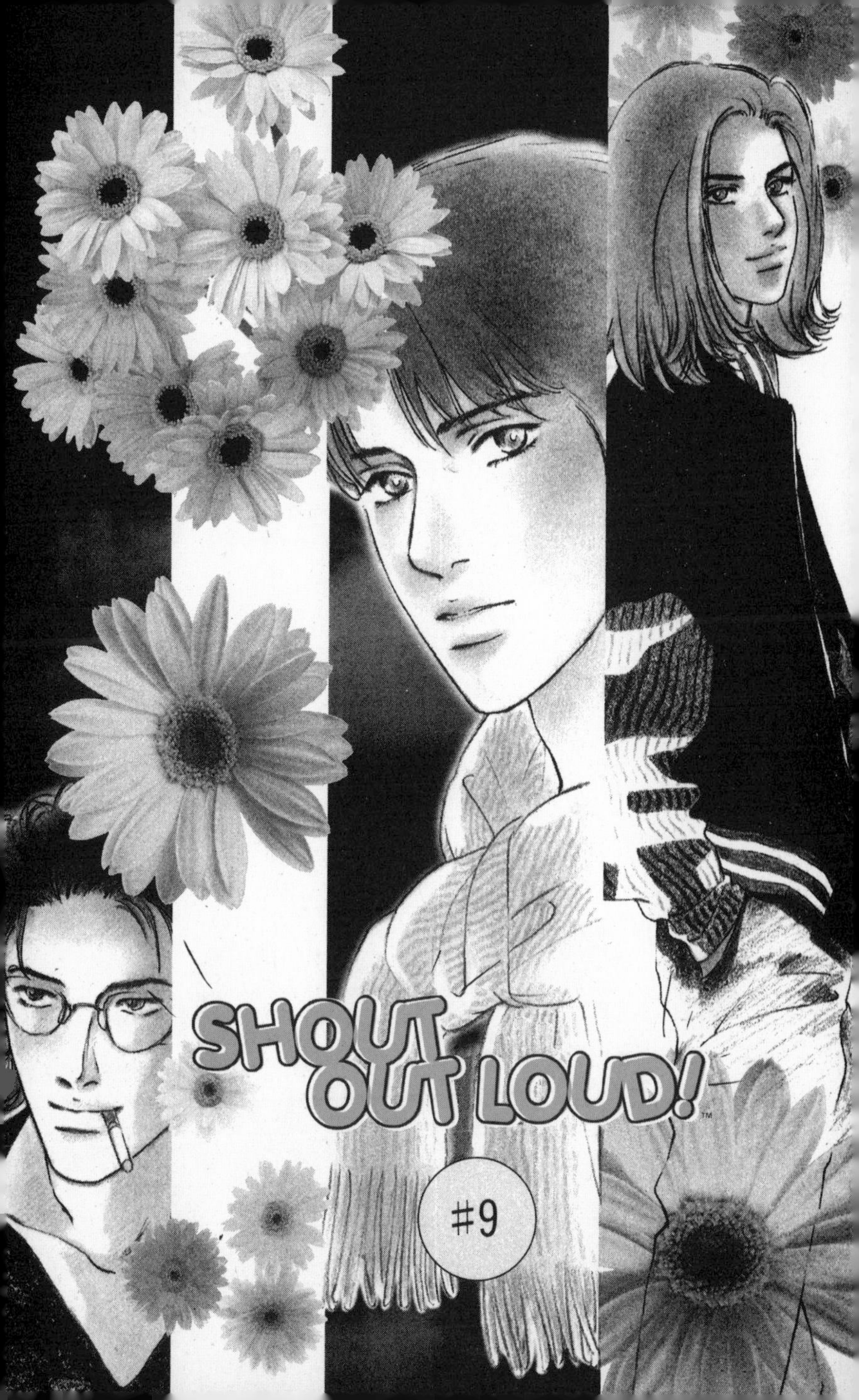
SHOUT OUT LOUD!™
#9

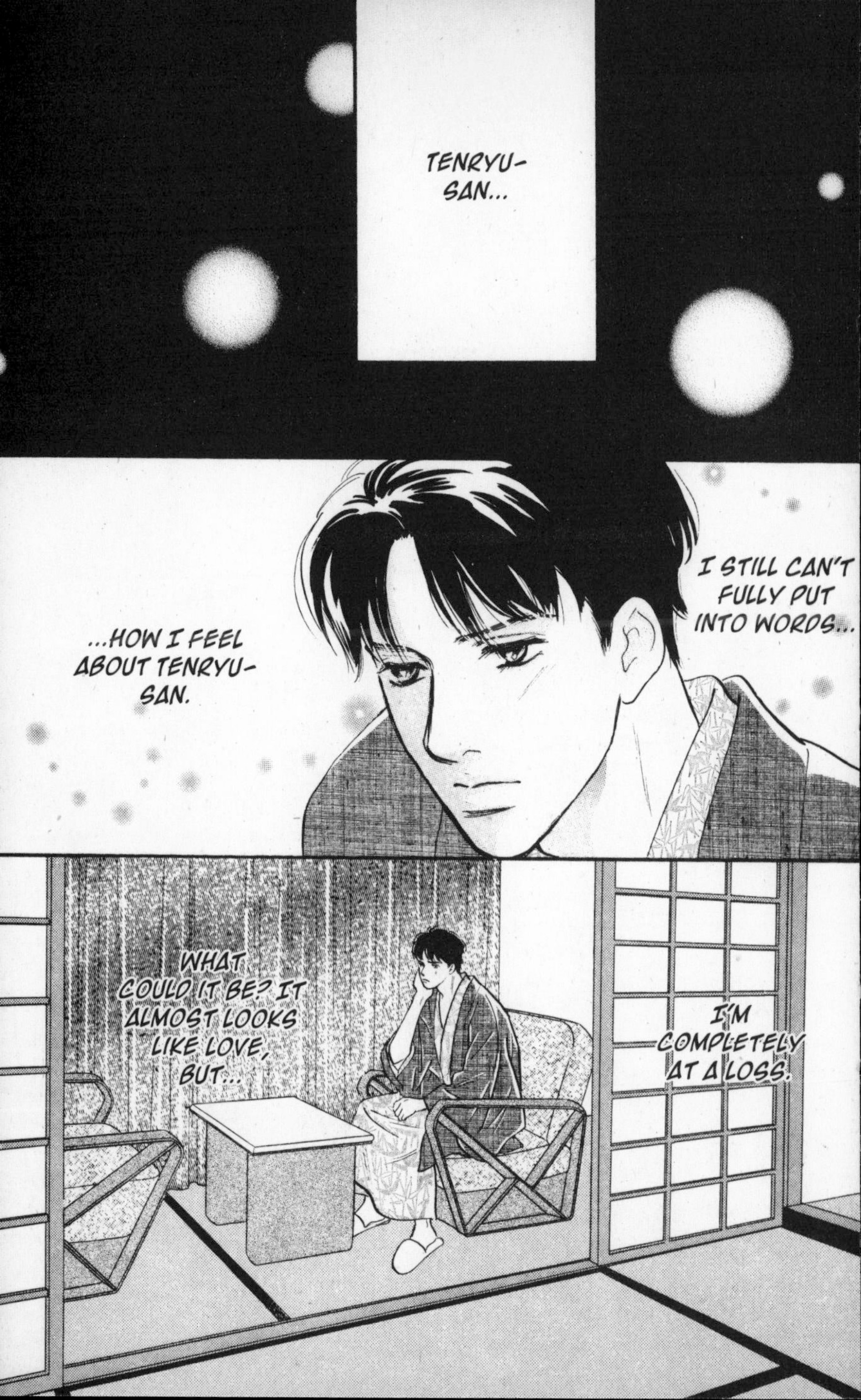
TENRYU-SAN...
I STILL CAN'T FULLY PUT INTO WORDS...
...HOW I FEEL ABOUT TENRYU-SAN.
I'M COMPLETELY AT A LOSS.
WHAT COULD IT BE? IT ALMOST LOOKS LIKE LOVE, BUT...

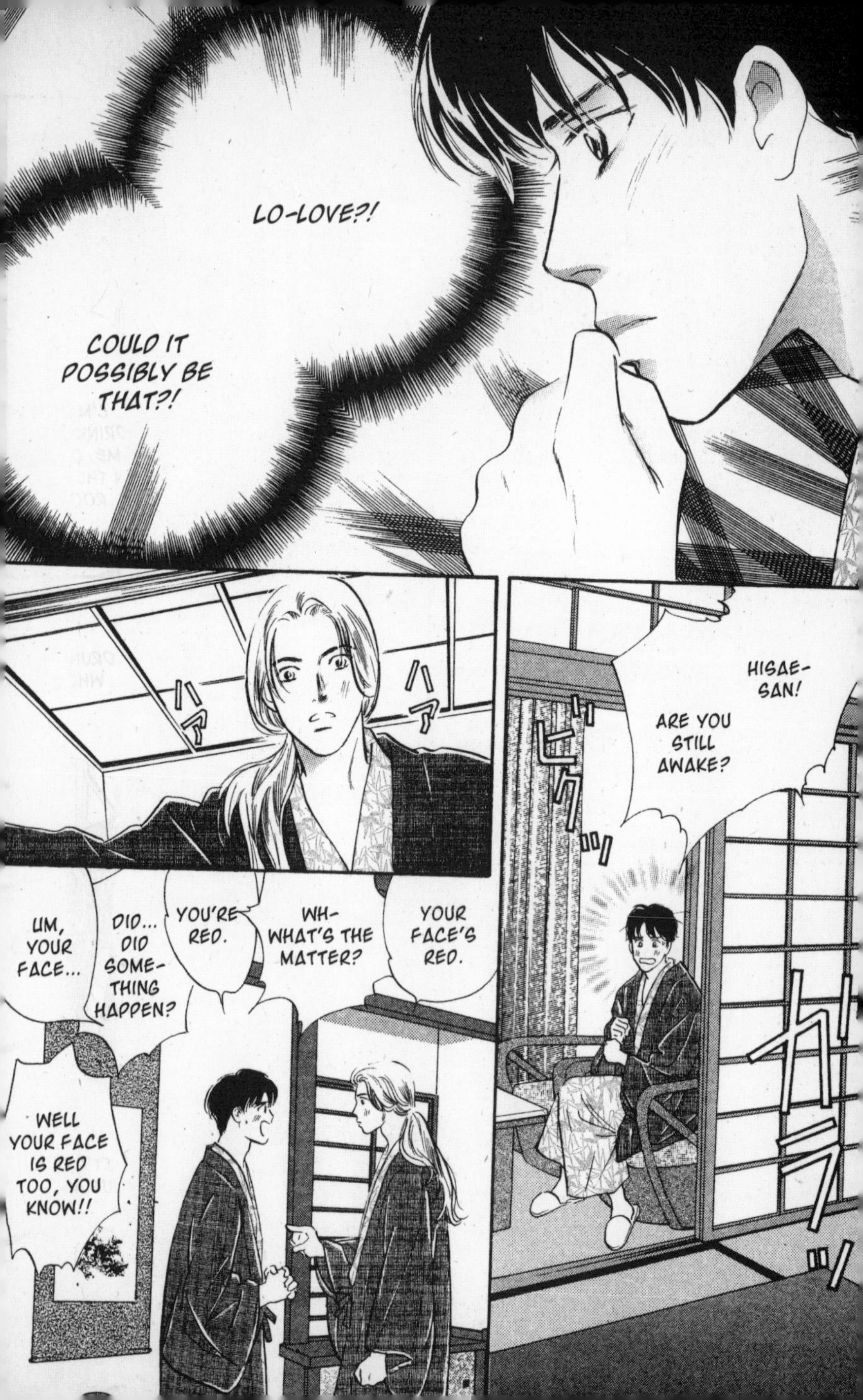
LO-LOVE?!
COULD IT POSSIBLY BE THAT?!
HISAE-SAN!
ARE YOU STILL AWAKE?
ビクッ
ガラッ
ハア
ハア
YOUR FACE'S RED.
WH-WHAT'S THE MATTER?
YOU'RE RED.
DID... DID SOME-THING HAPPEN?
UM, YOUR FACE...
WELL YOUR FACE IS RED TOO, YOU KNOW!!

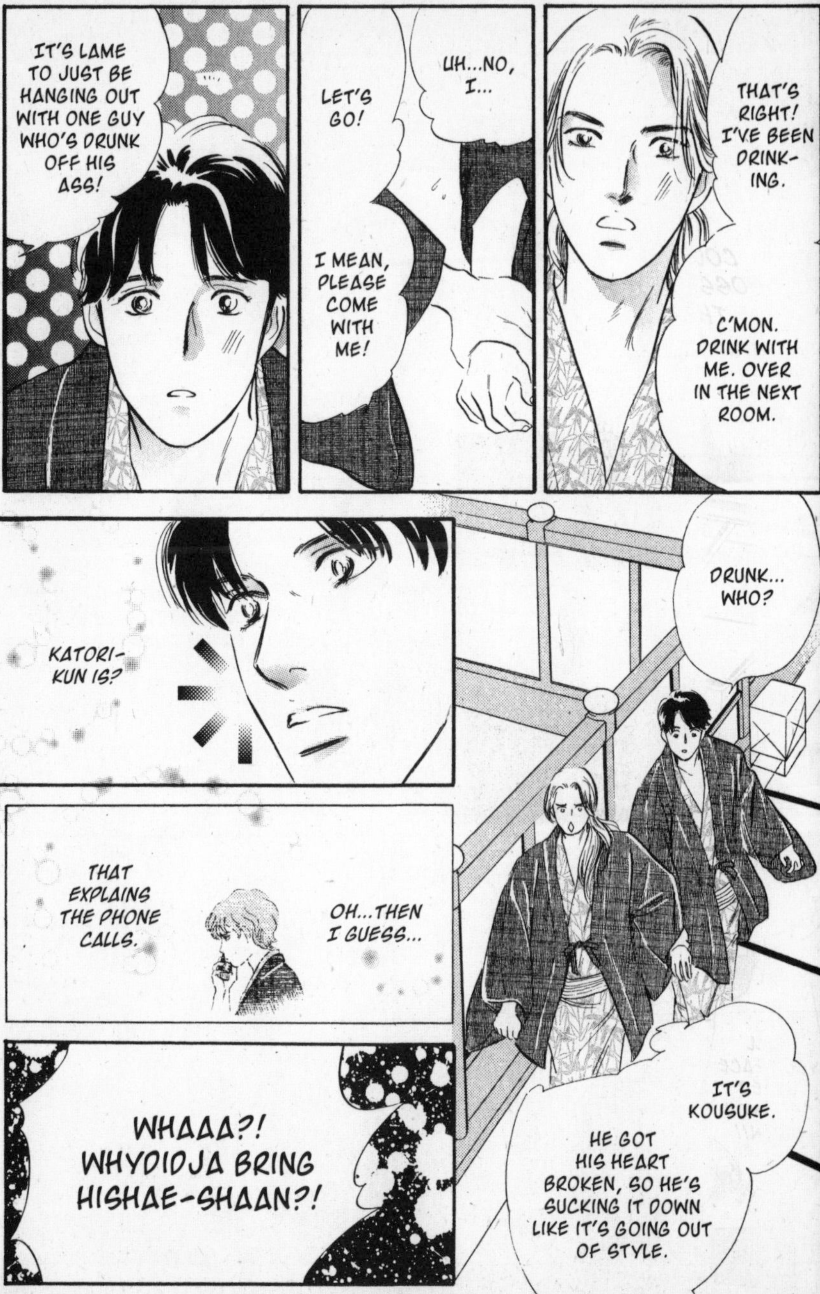
THAT'S RIGHT! I'VE BEEN DRINK-ING.
C'MON. DRINK WITH ME. OVER IN THE NEXT ROOM.
UH...NO, I...
LET'S GO!
I MEAN, PLEASE COME WITH ME!
IT'S LAME TO JUST BE HANGING OUT WITH ONE GUY WHO'S DRUNK OFF HIS ASS!
DRUNK... WHO?
IT'S KOUSUKE.
HE GOT HIS HEART BROKEN, SO HE'S SUCKING IT DOWN LIKE IT'S GOING OUT OF STYLE.
KATORI-KUN IS?
OH...THEN I GUESS...
THAT EXPLAINS THE PHONE CALLS.
WHAAA?! WHYDIDJA BRING HISHAE-SHAAN?!

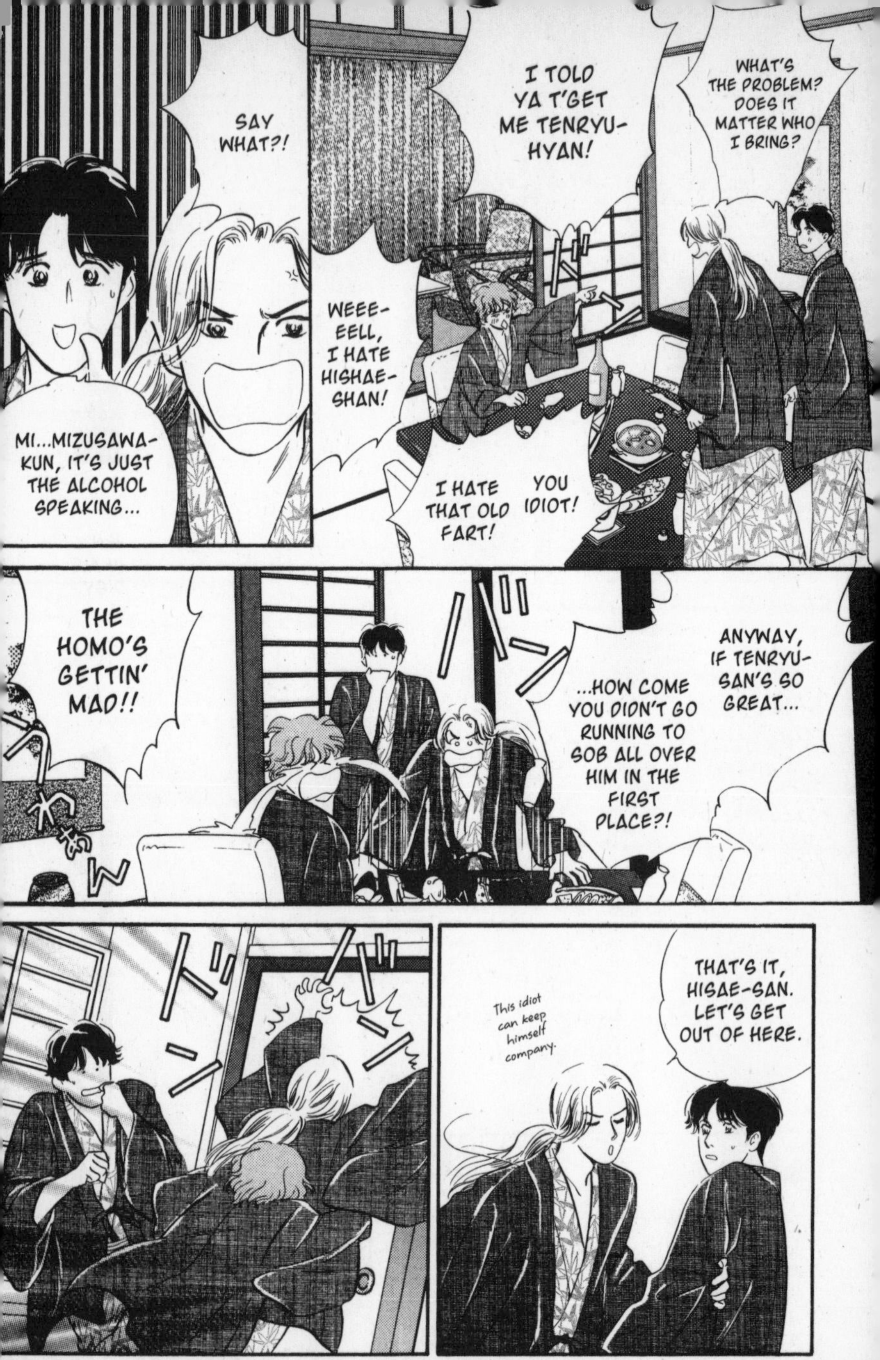
WHAT'S THE PROBLEM? DOES IT MATTER WHO I BRING?
I TOLD YA T'GET ME TENRYU-HYAN!
WEEE-EELL, I HATE HISHAE-SHAN!
YOU IDIOT!
I HATE THAT OLD FART!
SAY WHAT?!
MI...MIZUSAWA-KUN, IT'S JUST THE ALCOHOL SPEAKING...
ANYWAY, IF TENRYU-SAN'S SO GREAT...
...HOW COME YOU DIDN'T GO RUNNING TO SOB ALL OVER HIM IN THE FIRST PLACE?!
THE HOMO'S GETTIN' MAD!!
THAT'S IT, HISAE-SAN. LET'S GET OUT OF HERE.
This idiot can keep himself company.

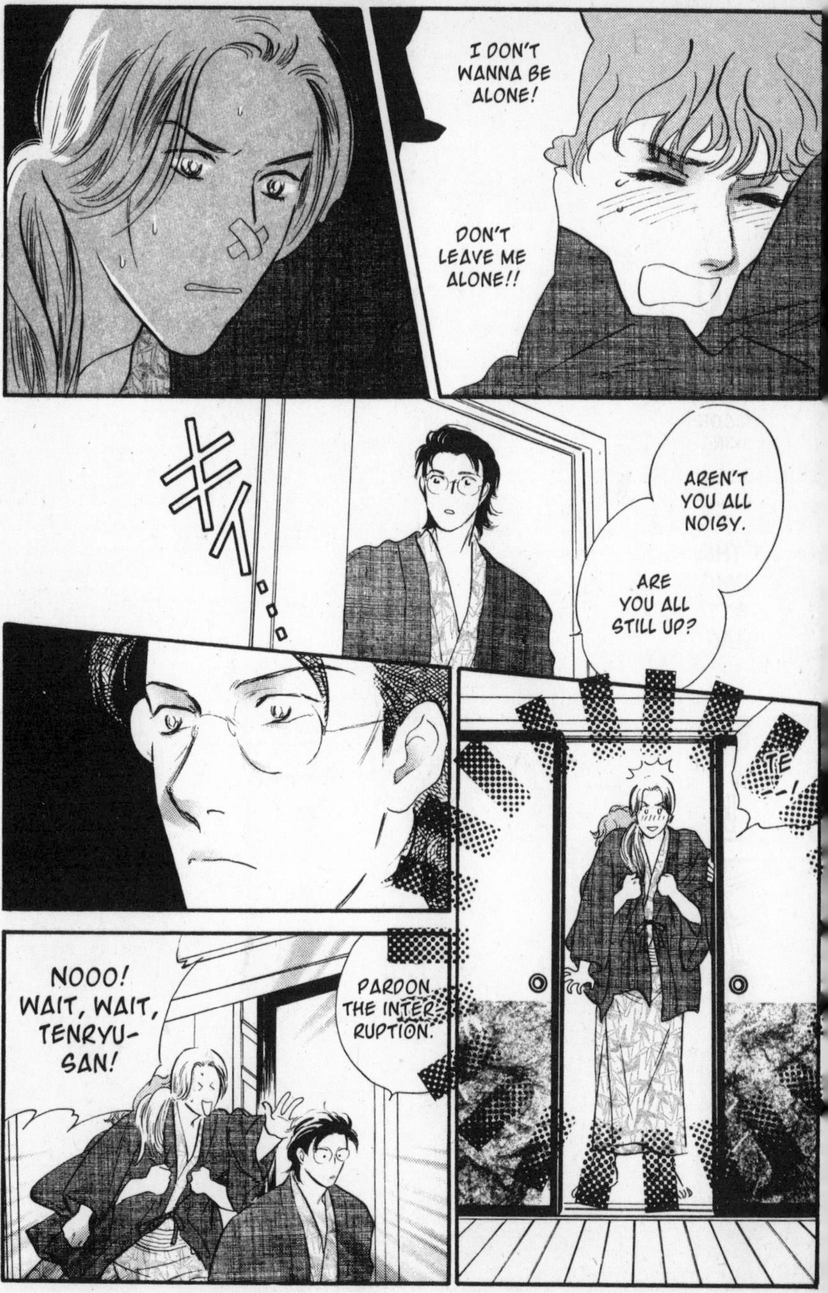
I DON'T WANNA BE ALONE!
DON'T LEAVE ME ALONE!!
キイ...
AREN'T YOU ALL NOISY.
ARE YOU ALL STILL UP?
TE--!
PARDON THE INTER-RUPTION.
NOOO! WAIT, WAIT, TENRYU-SAN!

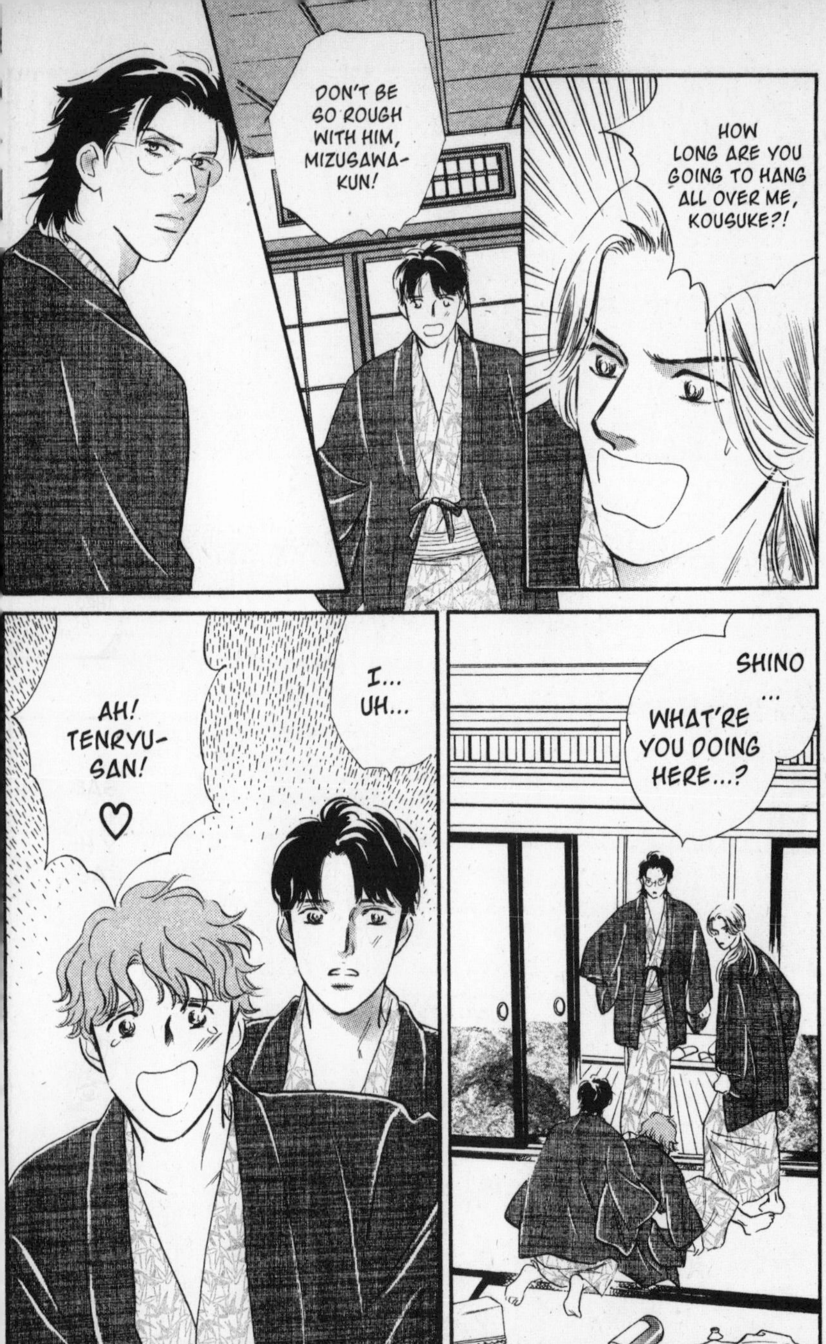
HOW LONG ARE YOU GOING TO HANG ALL OVER ME, KOUSUKE?!
DON'T BE SO ROUGH WITH HIM, MIZUSAWA-KUN!
SHINO ... WHAT'RE YOU DOING HERE...?
I... UH...
AH! TENRYU-SAN! ♡

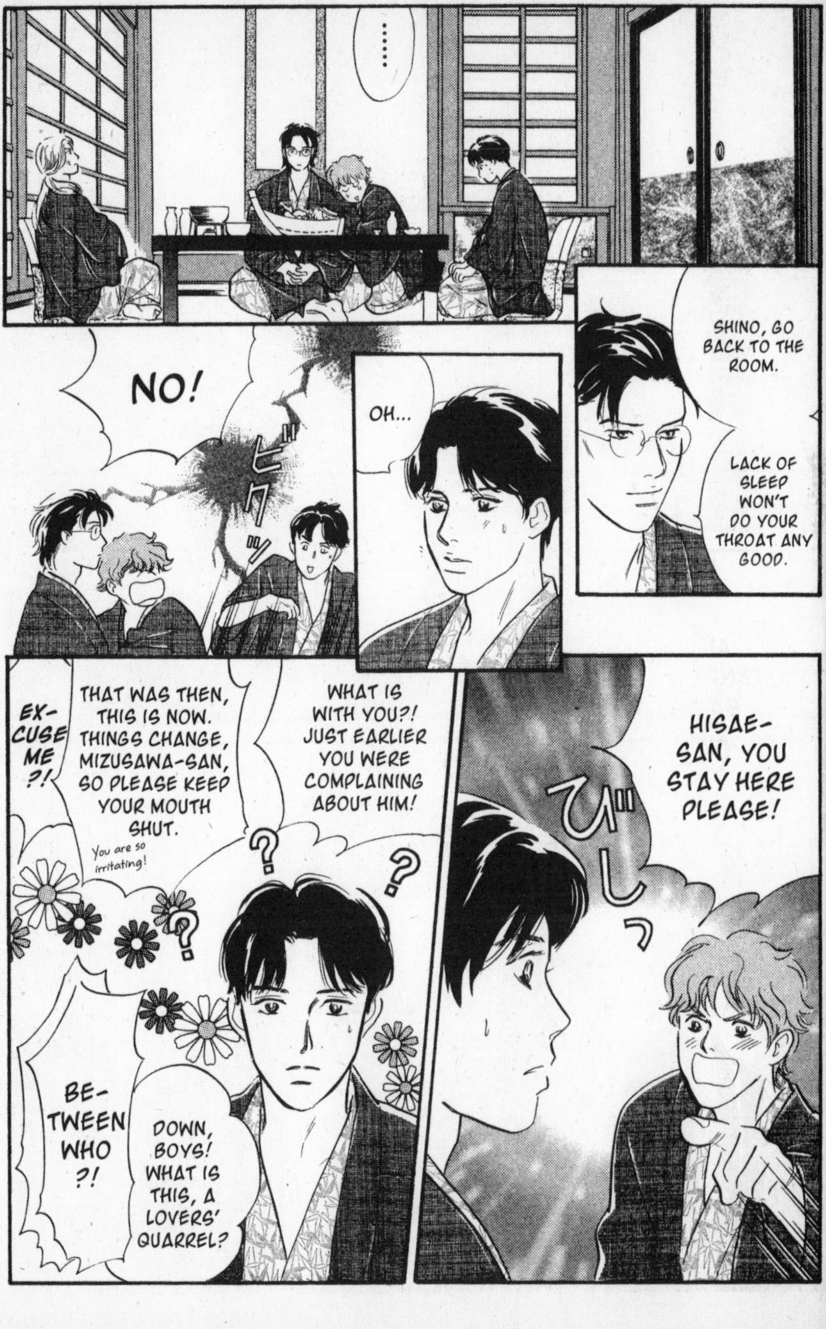
......
SHINO, GO BACK TO THE ROOM.
LACK OF SLEEP WON'T DO YOUR THROAT ANY GOOD.
OH...
ビクッ
NO!
HISAE-SAN, YOU STAY HERE PLEASE!
びしっ
WHAT IS WITH YOU?! JUST EARLIER YOU WERE COMPLAINING ABOUT HIM!
THAT WAS THEN, THIS IS NOW. THINGS CHANGE, MIZUSAWA-SAN, SO PLEASE KEEP YOUR MOUTH SHUT.
You are so irritating!
EX-CUSE ME?!
DOWN, BOYS! WHAT IS THIS, A LOVERS' QUARREL?
BE-TWEEN WHO?!

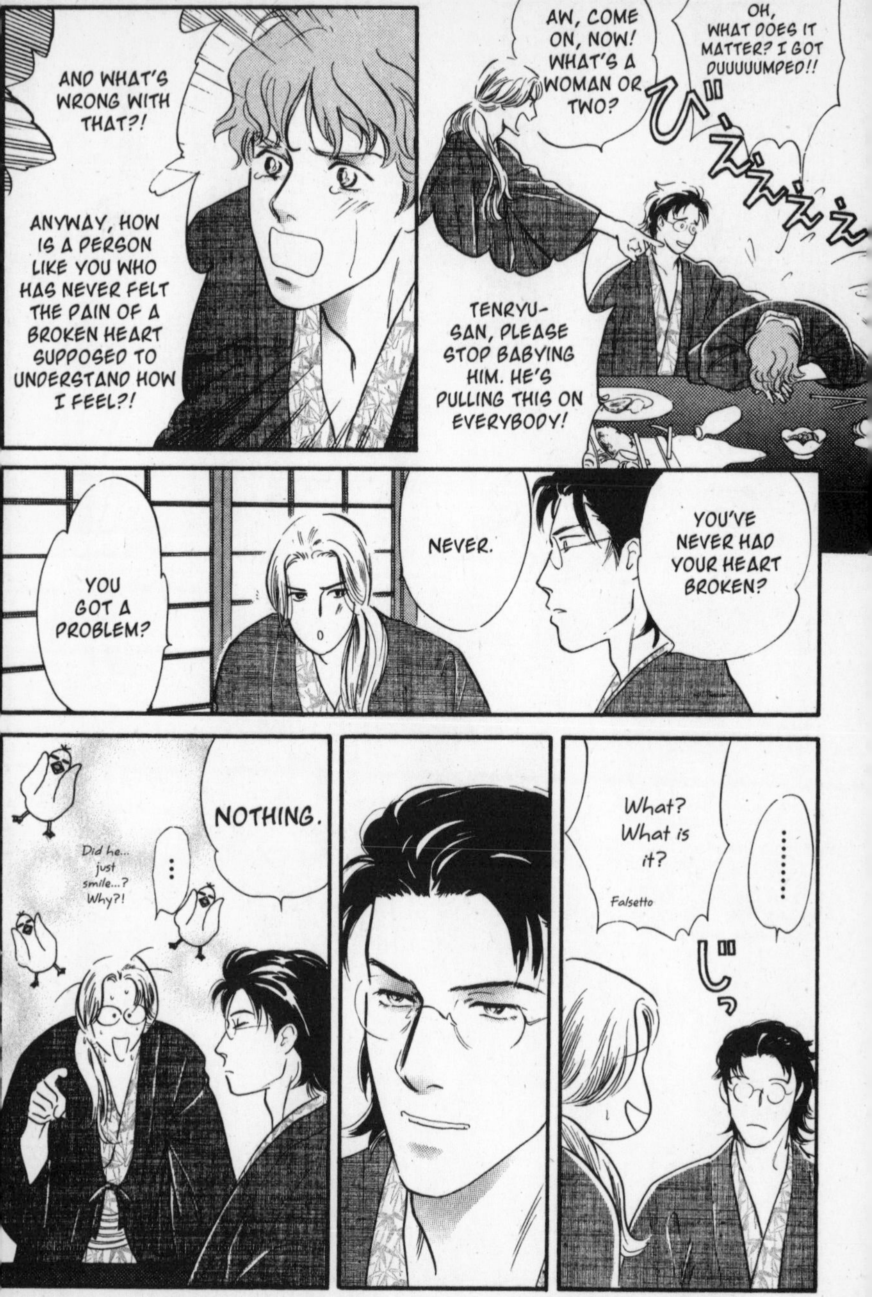
OH, WHAT DOES IT MATTER? I GOT DUUUUUMPED!!
AW, COME ON, NOW! WHAT'S A WOMAN OR TWO?
TENRYU-SAN, PLEASE STOP BABYING HIM. HE'S PULLING THIS ON EVERYBODY!
AND WHAT'S WRONG WITH THAT?!
ANYWAY, HOW IS A PERSON LIKE YOU WHO HAS NEVER FELT THE PAIN OF A BROKEN HEART SUPPOSED TO UNDERSTAND HOW I FEEL?!
YOU'VE NEVER HAD YOUR HEART BROKEN?
NEVER.
YOU GOT A PROBLEM?
What? What is it?
Falsetto
....
NOTHING.
...
Did he... just smile...? Why?!

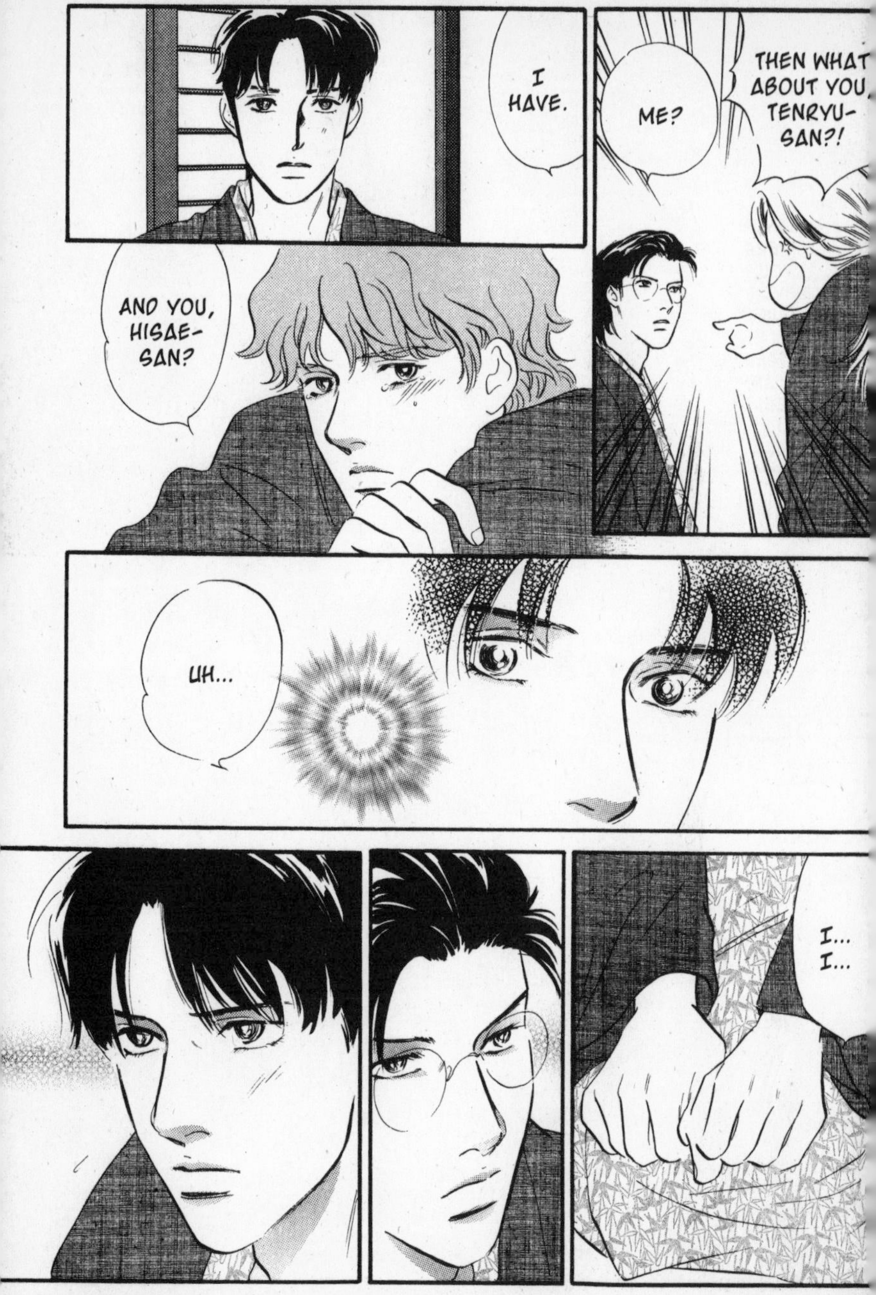
THEN WHAT ABOUT YOU, TENRYU-SAN?!
ME?
I HAVE.
AND YOU, HISAE-SAN?
UH...
I... I...

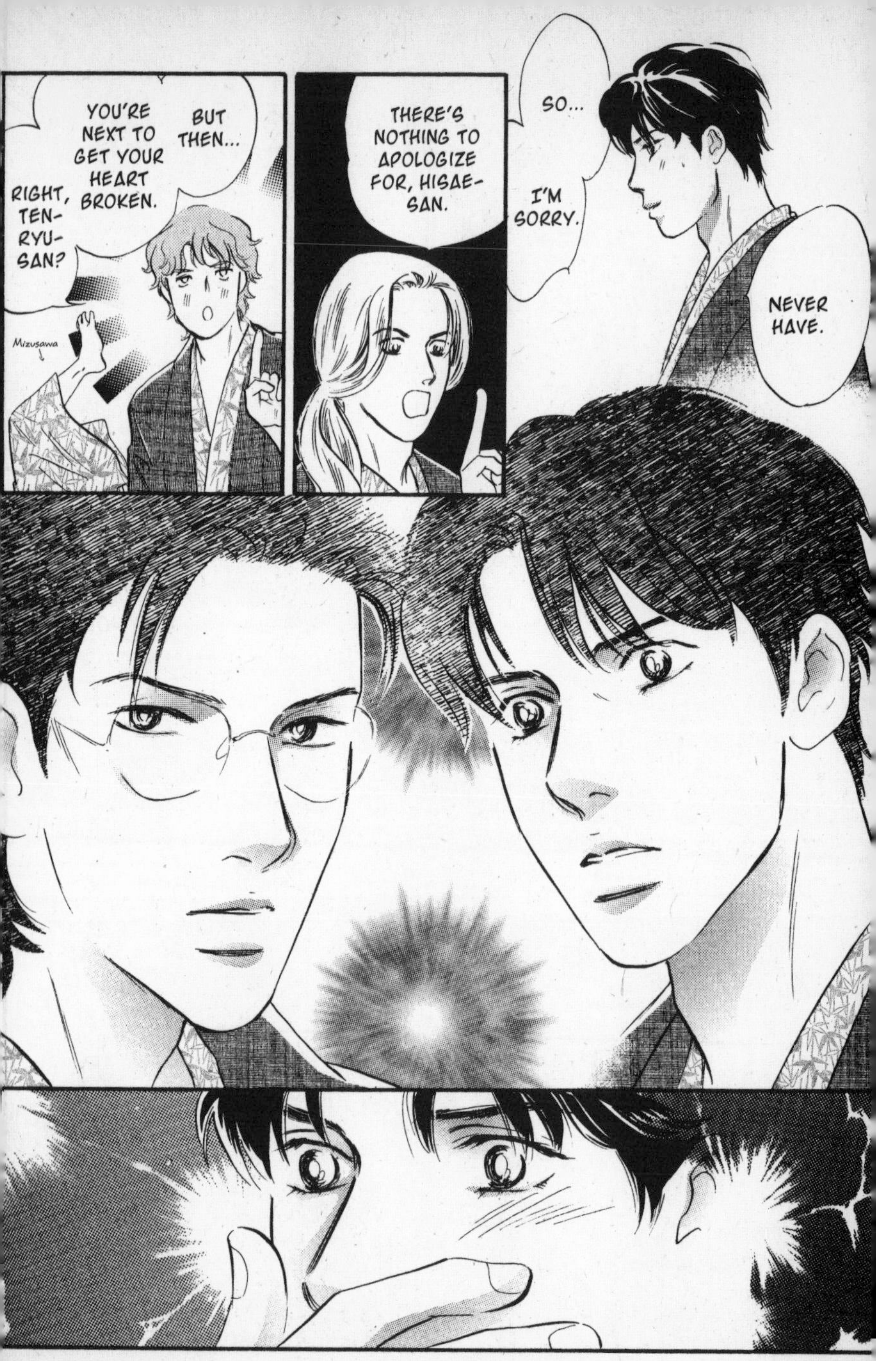
SO... I'M SORRY.
THERE'S NOTHING TO APOLOGIZE FOR, HISAE-SAN.
BUT THEN... YOU'RE NEXT TO GET YOUR HEART BROKEN. RIGHT, TEN-RYU-SAN?
Mizusawa
NEVER HAVE.

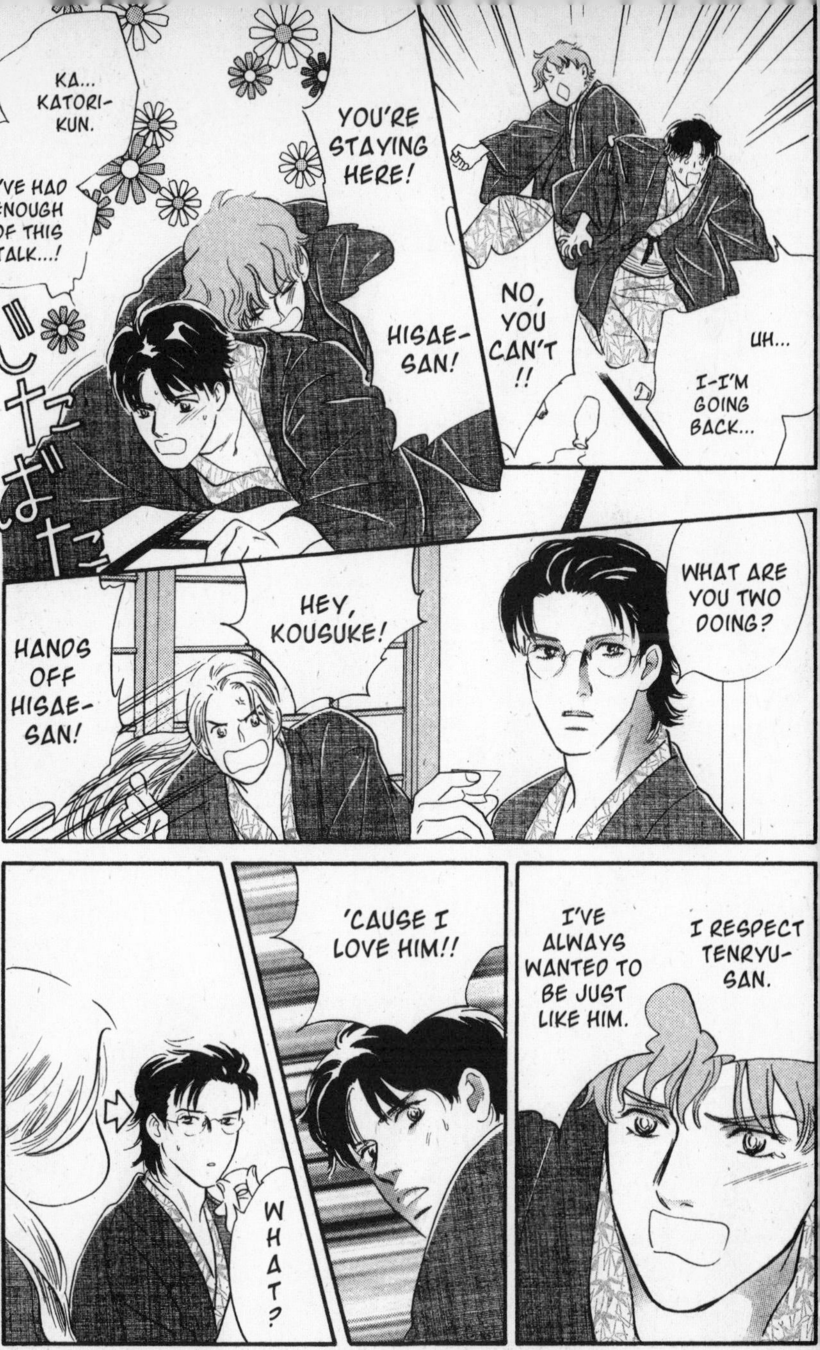
UH...
I-I'M GOING BACK...
NO, YOU CAN'T!!
HISAE-SAN!
YOU'RE STAYING HERE!
KA... KATORI-KUN.
I'VE HAD ENOUGH OF THIS TALK...!
じたばた
WHAT ARE YOU TWO DOING?
HEY, KOUSUKE!
HANDS OFF HISAE-SAN!
I RESPECT TENRYU-SAN.
I'VE ALWAYS WANTED TO BE JUST LIKE HIM.
'CAUSE I LOVE HIM!!
WHAT?

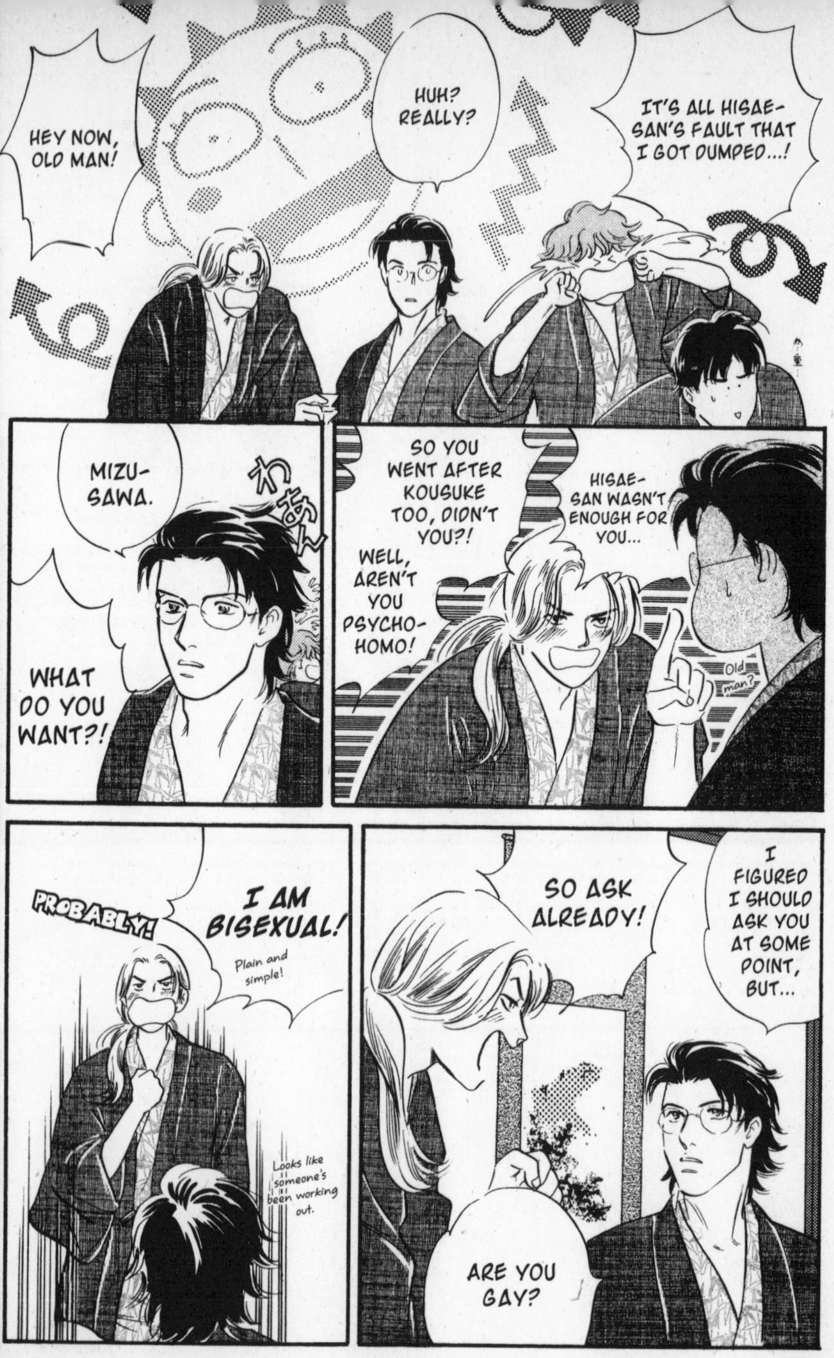
IT'S ALL HISAE-SAN'S FAULT THAT I GOT DUMPED...!
HUH? REALLY?
HEY NOW, OLD MAN!
HISAE-SAN WASN'T ENOUGH FOR YOU...
SO YOU WENT AFTER KOUSUKE TOO, DIDN'T YOU?!
WELL, AREN'T YOU PSYCHO-HOMO!
Old man?
MIZU-SAWA.
わあん
WHAT DO YOU WANT?!
I FIGURED I SHOULD ASK YOU AT SOME POINT, BUT...
SO ASK ALREADY!
ARE YOU GAY?
I AM BISEXUAL!
PROBABLY!
Plain and simple!
Looks like someone's been working out.

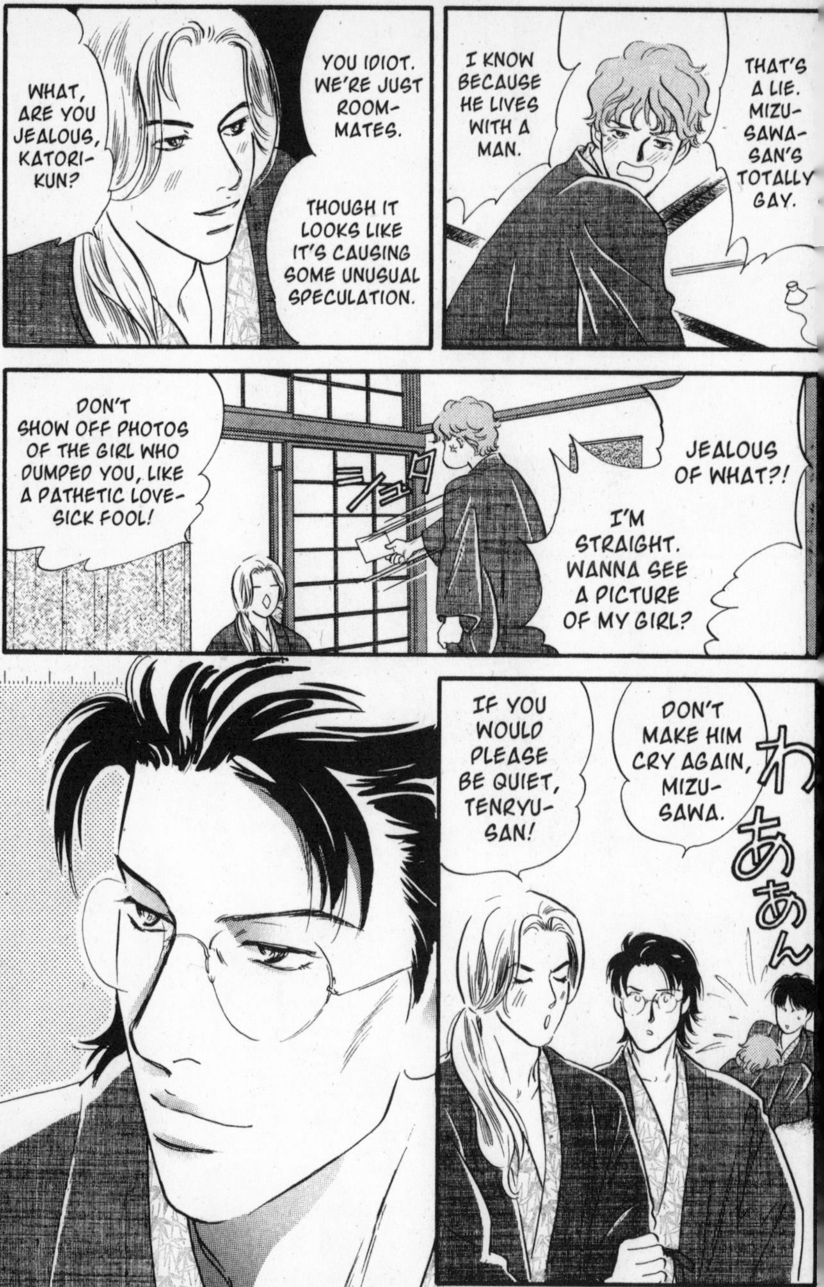
THAT'S A LIE. MIZUSAWA-SAN'S TOTALLY GAY.
I KNOW BECAUSE HE LIVES WITH A MAN.
YOU IDIOT. WE'RE JUST ROOMMATES.
THOUGH IT LOOKS LIKE IT'S CAUSING SOME UNUSUAL SPECULATION.
WHAT, ARE YOU JEALOUS, KATORI-KUN?
JEALOUS OF WHAT?!
I'M STRAIGHT. WANNA SEE A PICTURE OF MY GIRL?
DON'T SHOW OFF PHOTOS OF THE GIRL WHO DUMPED YOU, LIKE A PATHETIC LOVE-SICK FOOL!
わああん
DON'T MAKE HIM CRY AGAIN, MIZUSAWA.
IF YOU WOULD PLEASE BE QUIET, TENRYU-SAN!

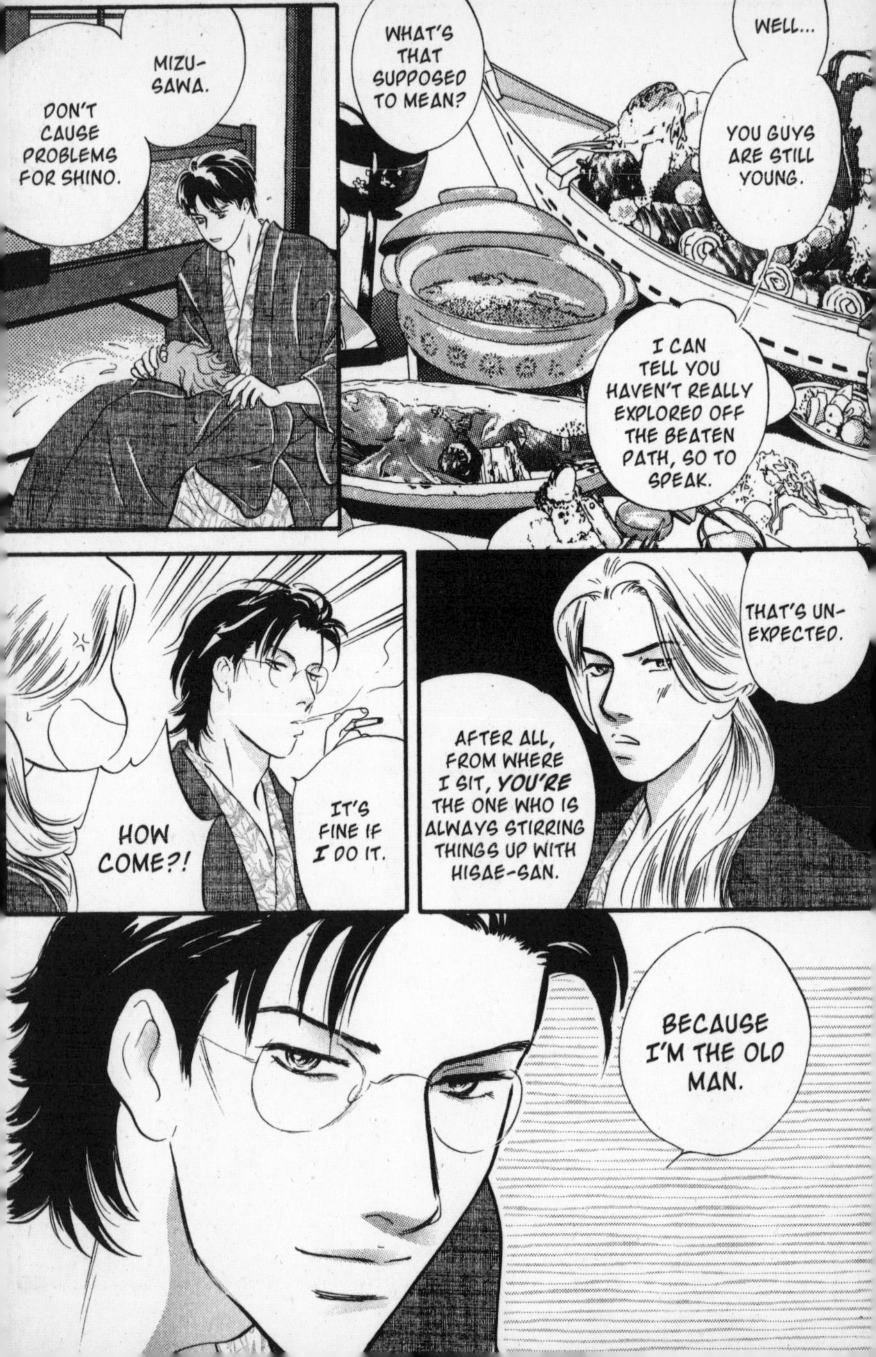
WELL...
WHAT'S THAT SUPPOSED TO MEAN?
YOU GUYS ARE STILL YOUNG.
I CAN TELL YOU HAVEN'T REALLY EXPLORED OFF THE BEATEN PATH, SO TO SPEAK.
MIZU-SAWA.
DON'T CAUSE PROBLEMS FOR SHINO.
THAT'S UN-EXPECTED.
AFTER ALL, FROM WHERE I SIT, *YOU'RE* THE ONE WHO IS ALWAYS STIRRING THINGS UP WITH HISAE-SAN.
IT'S FINE IF *I* DO IT.
HOW COME?!
BECAUSE I'M THE OLD MAN.

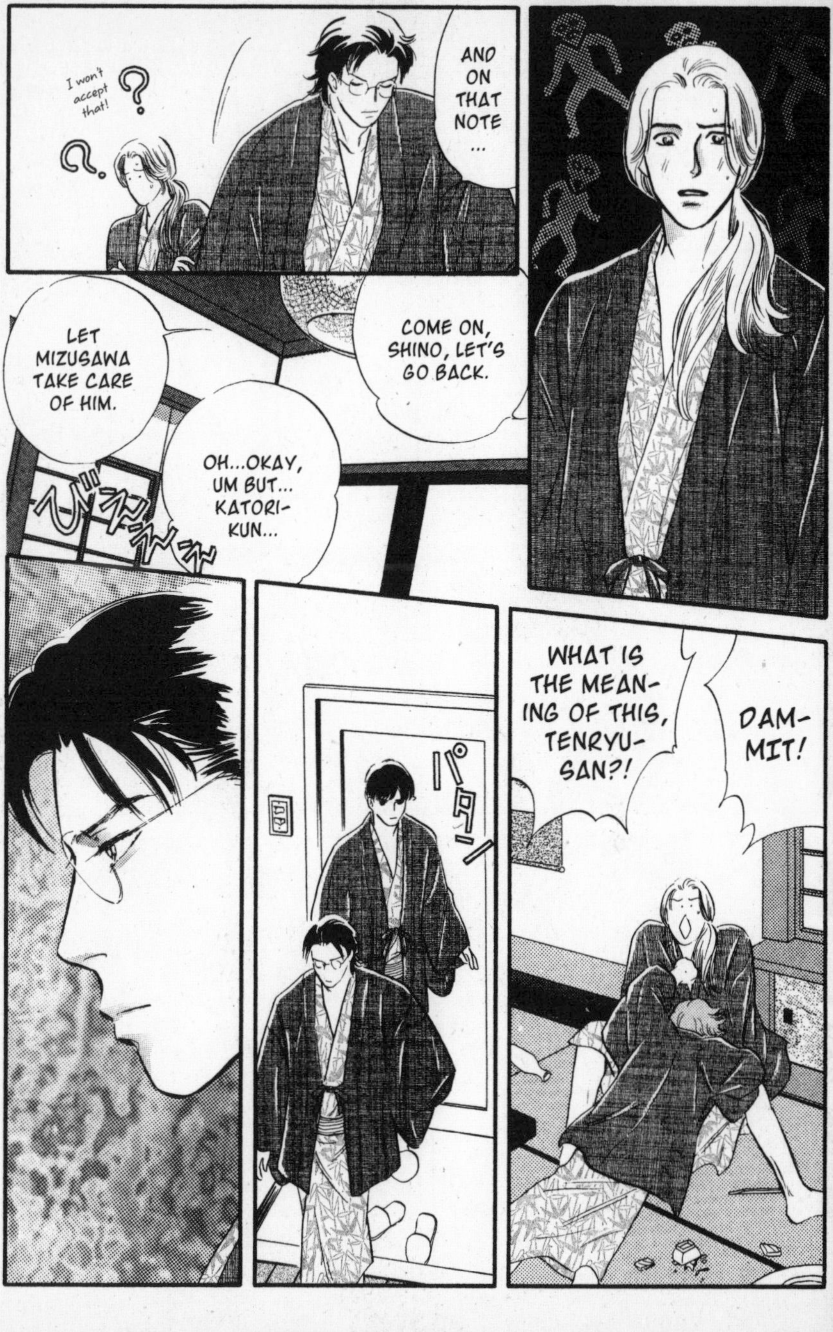
AND ON THAT NOTE ...
I won't accept that!
COME ON, SHINO, LET'S GO BACK.
LET MIZUSAWA TAKE CARE OF HIM.
OH...OKAY, UM BUT... KATORI-KUN...
DAM-MIT!
WHAT IS THE MEAN-ING OF THIS, TENRYU-SAN?!
パタ―

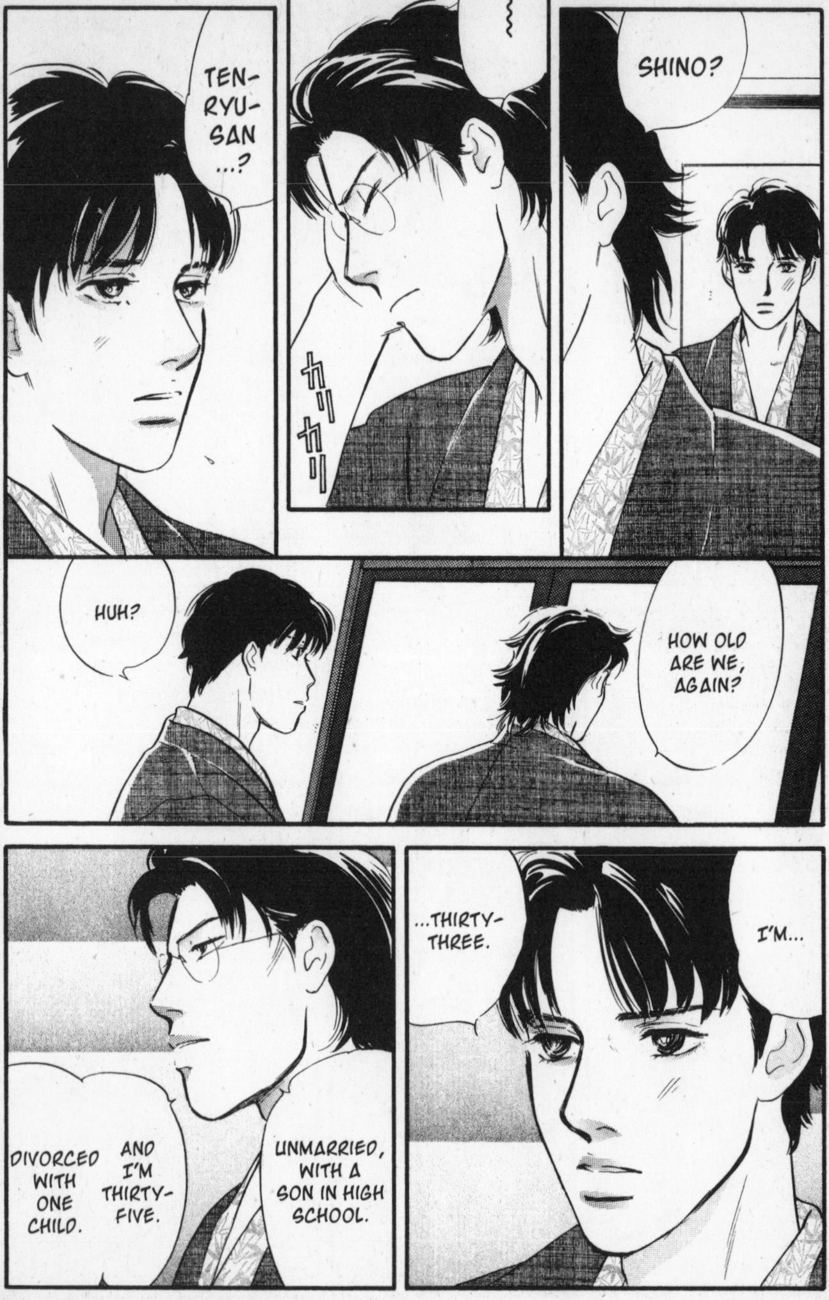
SHINO?
カリカリ
TEN-RYU-SAN ...?
HOW OLD ARE WE, AGAIN?
HUH?
I'M...
...THIRTY-THREE.
UNMARRIED, WITH A SON IN HIGH SCHOOL.
AND I'M THIRTY-FIVE.
DIVORCED WITH ONE CHILD.

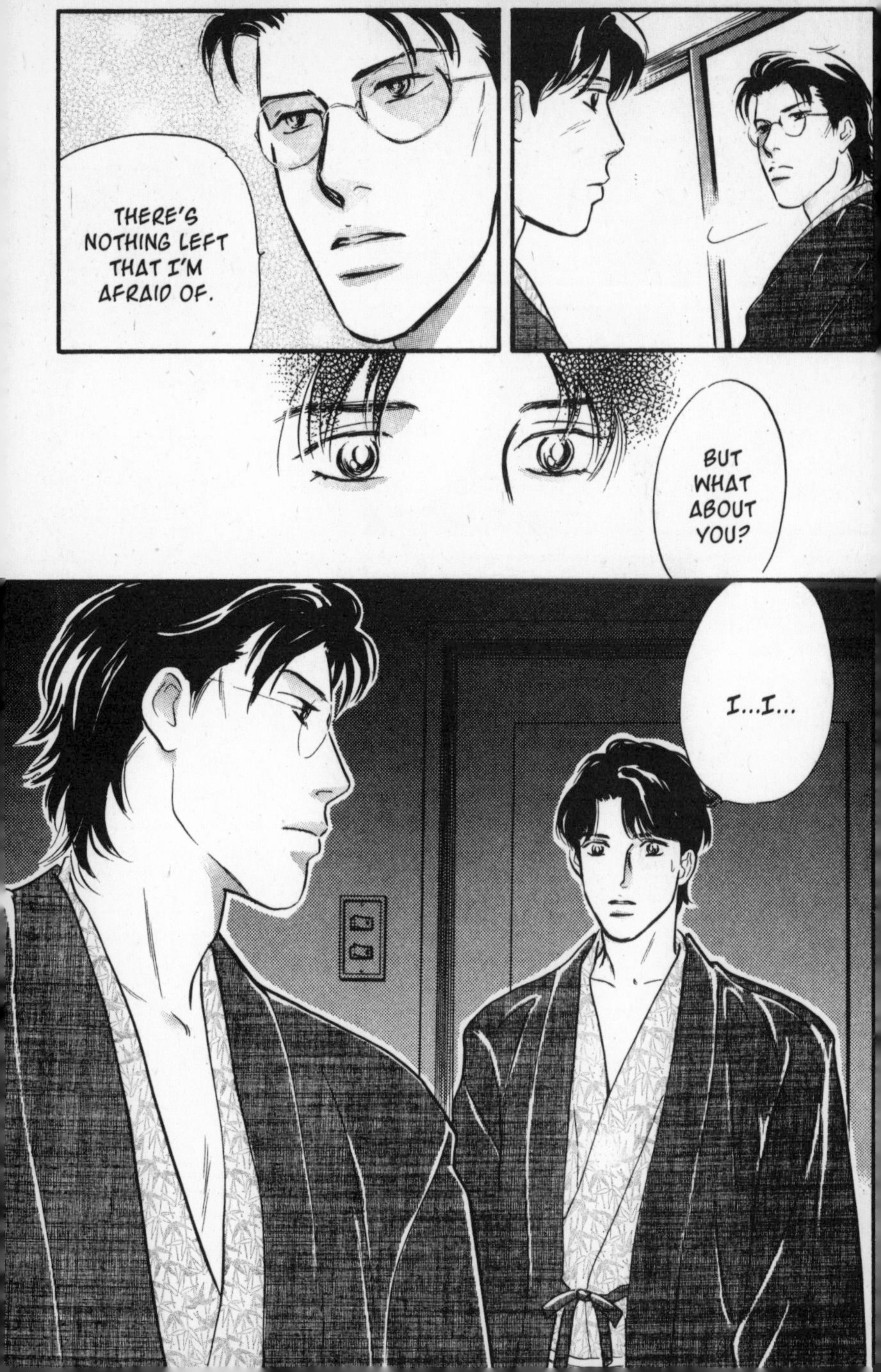
THERE'S NOTHING LEFT THAT I'M AFRAID OF.
BUT WHAT ABOUT YOU?
I...I...

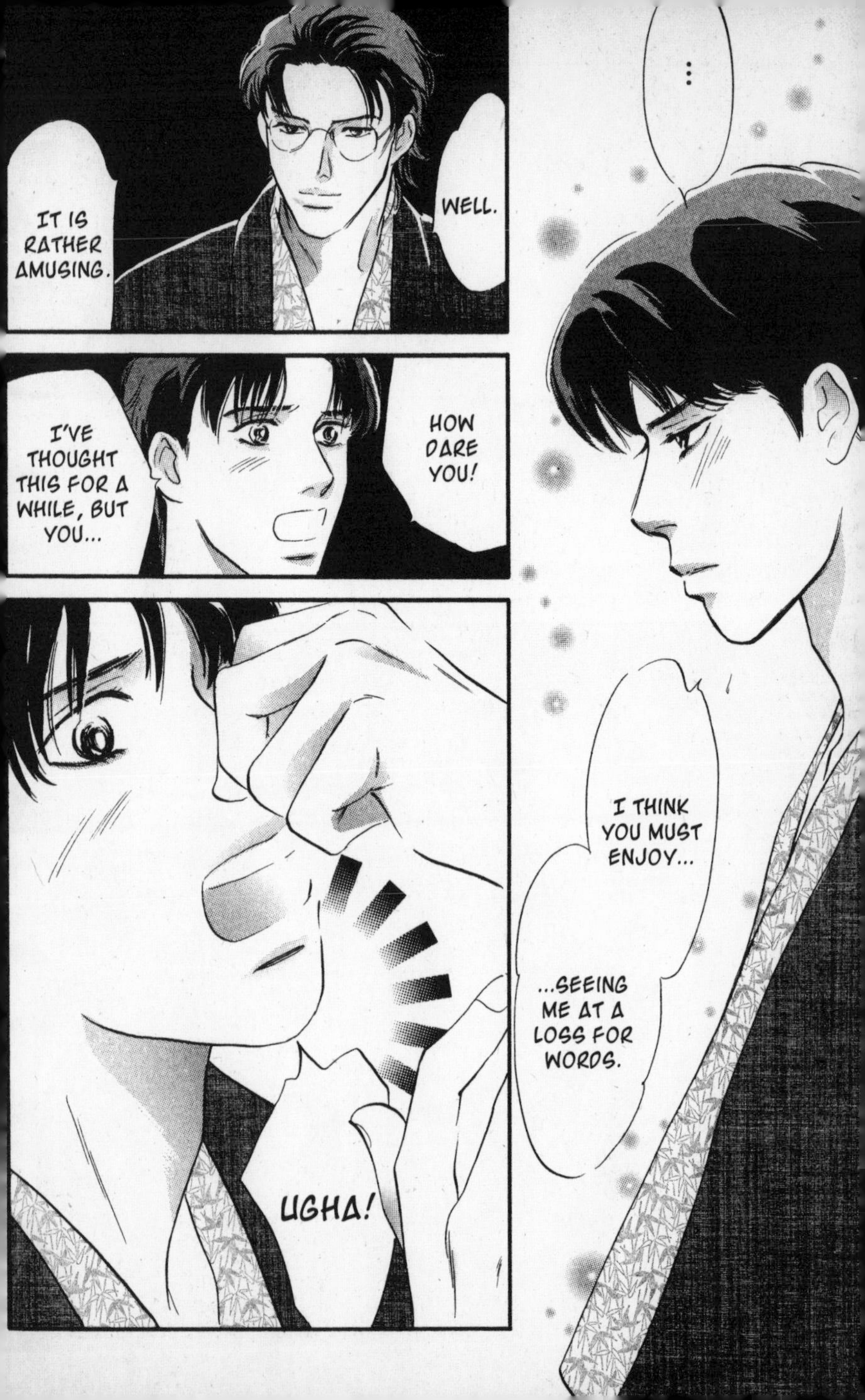
...
I THINK YOU MUST ENJOY...
...SEEING ME AT A LOSS FOR WORDS.
WELL.
IT IS RATHER AMUSING.
HOW DARE YOU!
I'VE THOUGHT THIS FOR A WHILE, BUT YOU...
UGHA!

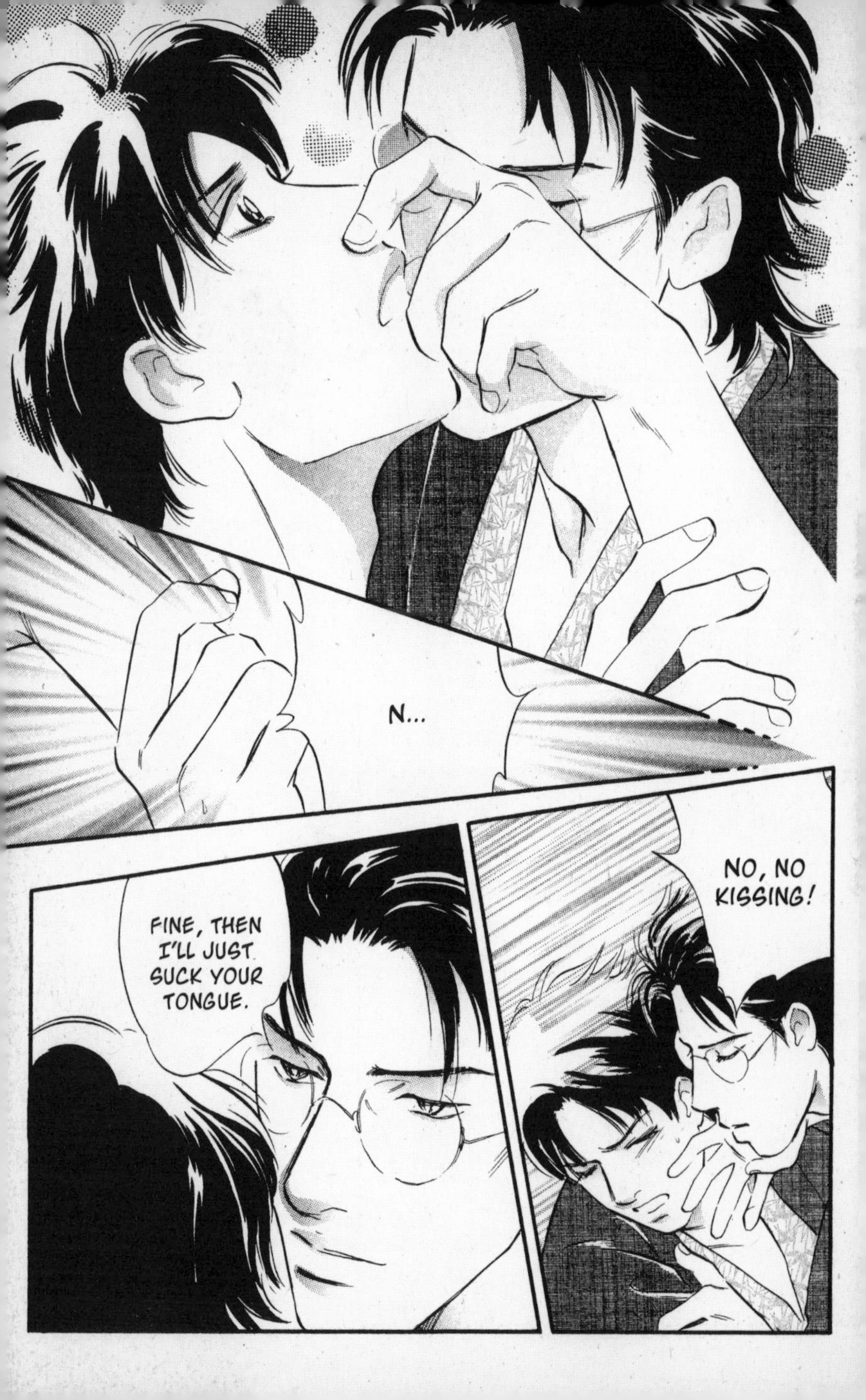
N...
NO, NO KISSING!
FINE, THEN I'LL JUST SUCK YOUR TONGUE.

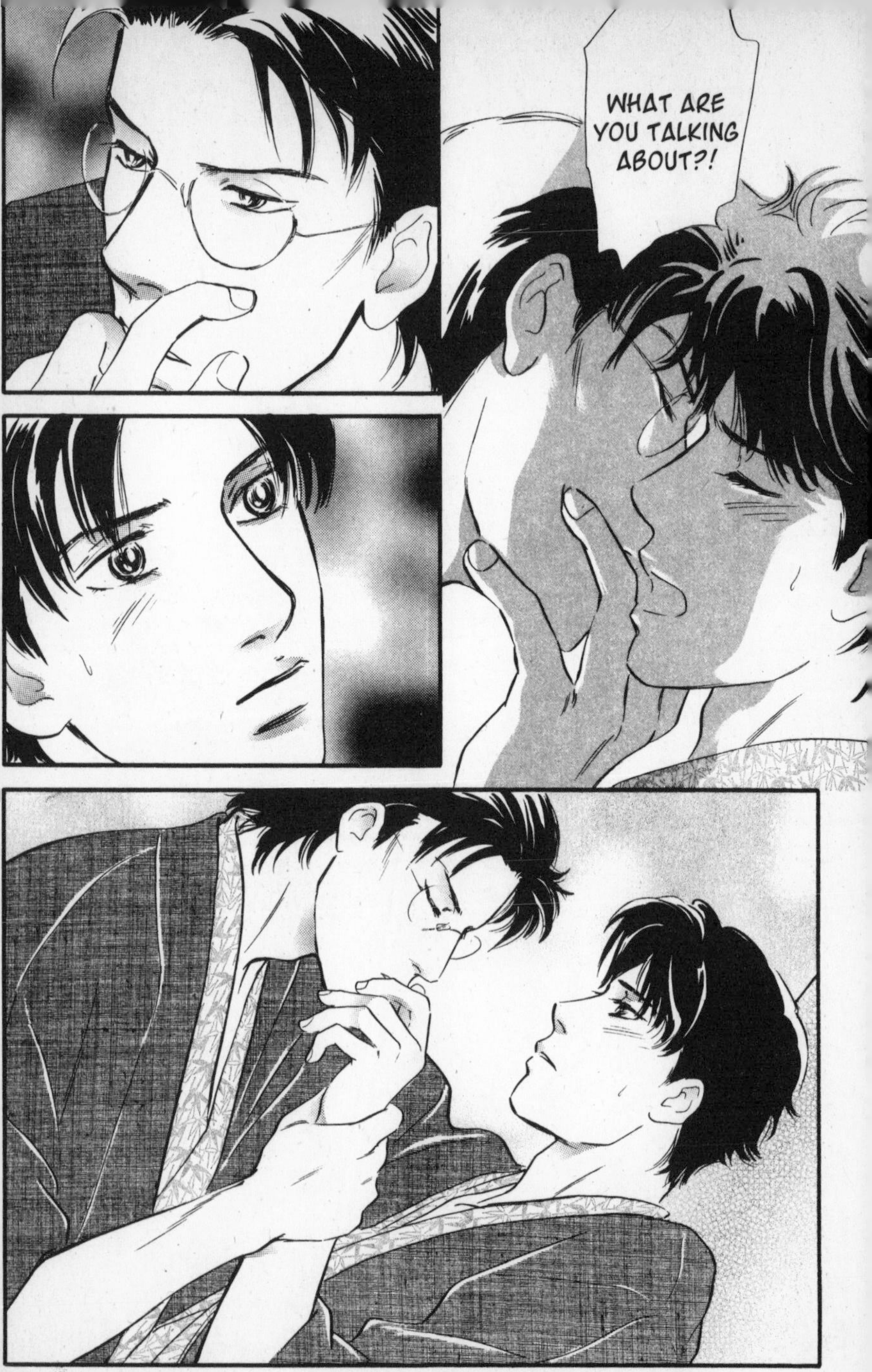
WHAT ARE YOU TALKING ABOUT?!

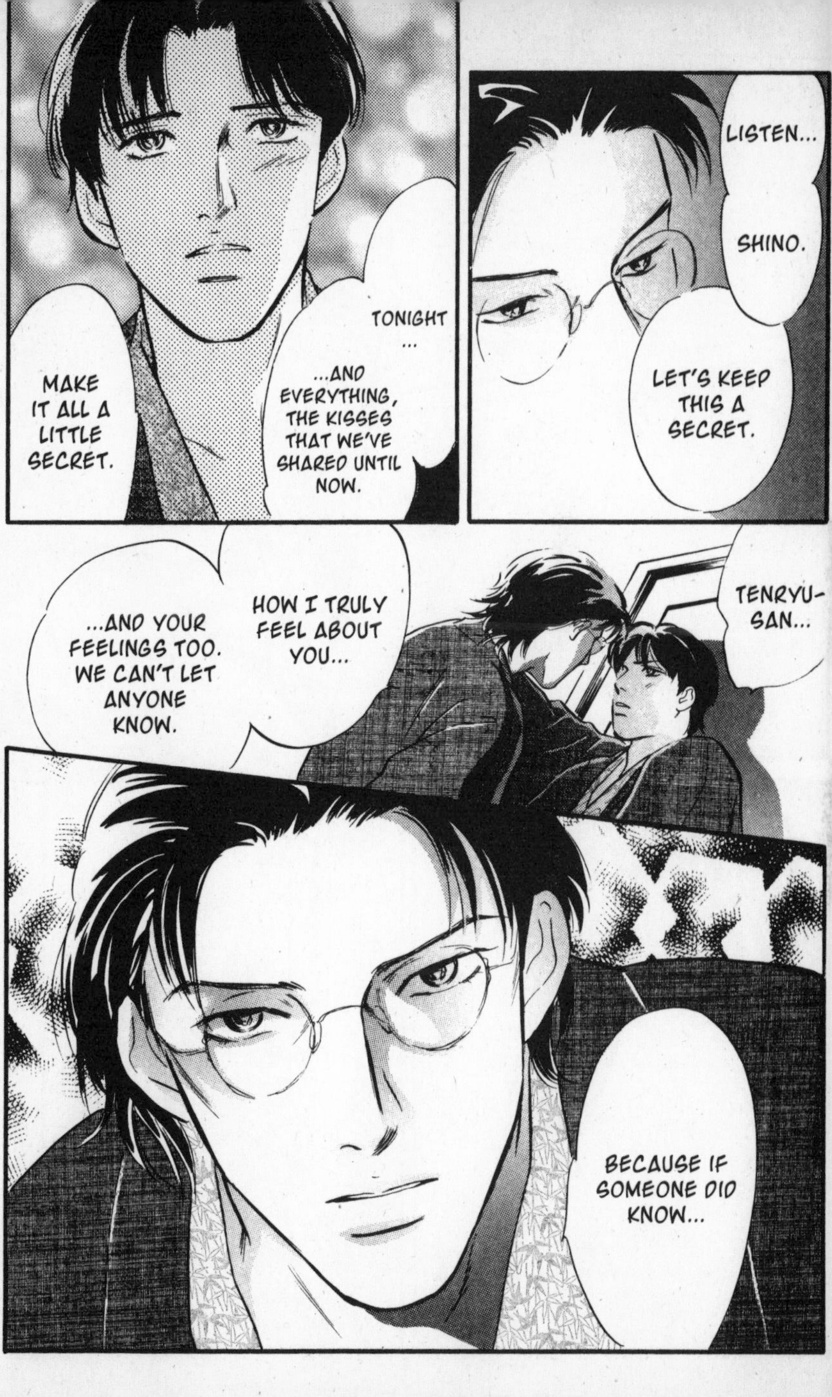
LISTEN...
SHINO.
LET'S KEEP THIS A SECRET.
TONIGHT ...
...AND EVERYTHING, THE KISSES THAT WE'VE SHARED UNTIL NOW.
MAKE IT ALL A LITTLE SECRET.
TENRYU-SAN...
HOW I TRULY FEEL ABOUT YOU...
...AND YOUR FEELINGS TOO. WE CAN'T LET ANYONE KNOW.
BECAUSE IF SOMEONE DID KNOW...

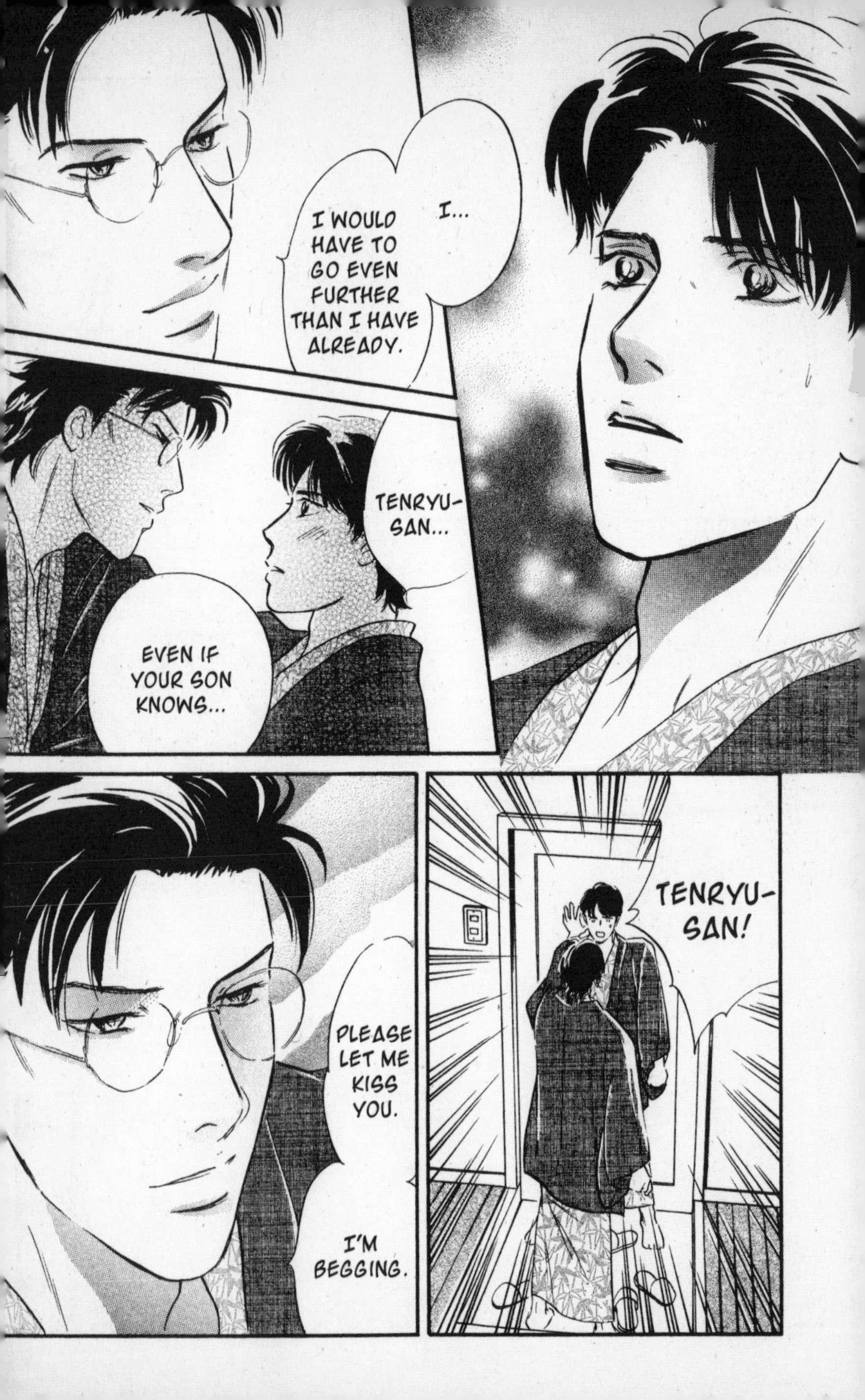
I...
I WOULD HAVE TO GO EVEN FURTHER THAN I HAVE ALREADY.
TENRYU-SAN...
EVEN IF YOUR SON KNOWS...
TENRYU-SAN!
PLEASE LET ME KISS YOU.
I'M BEGGING.

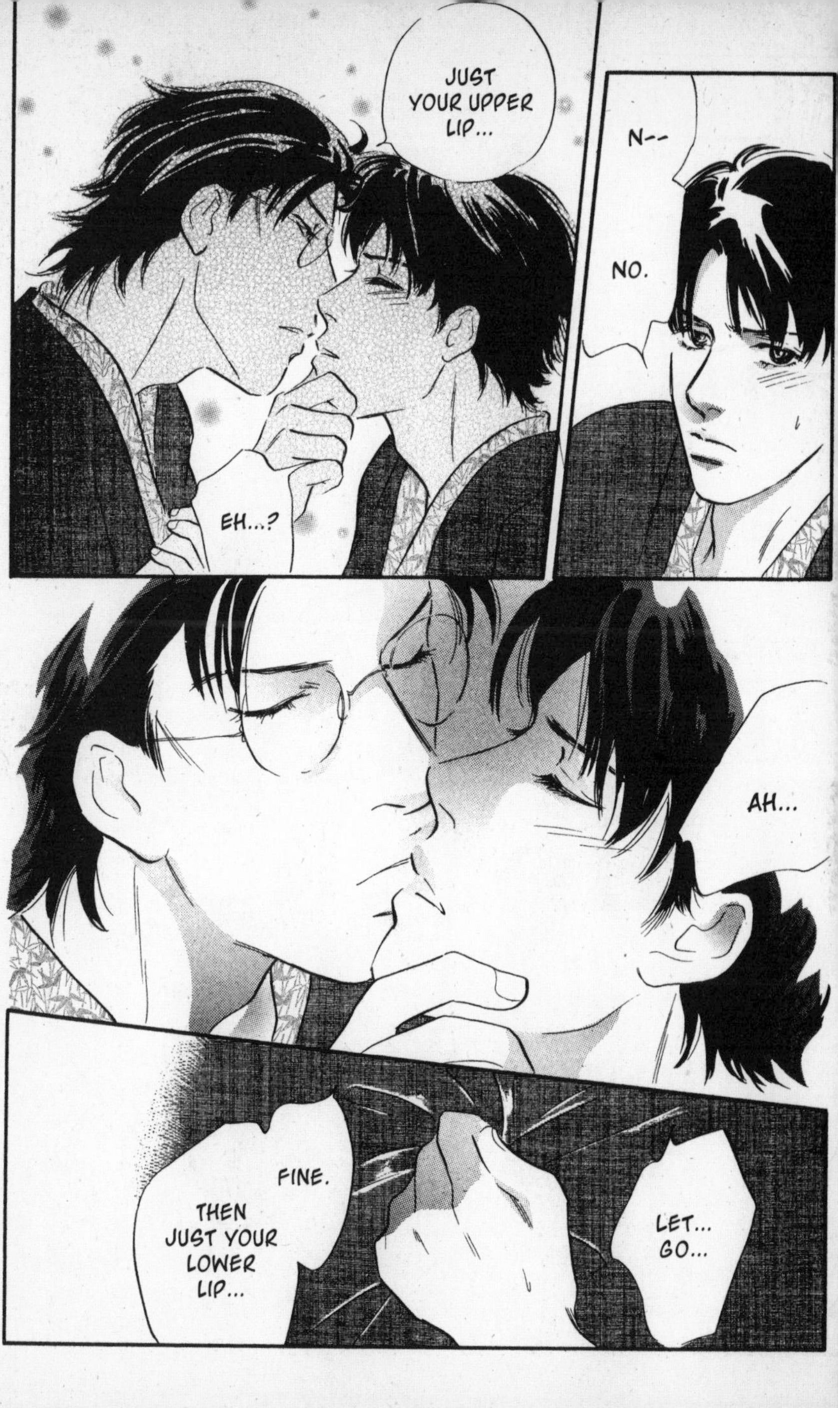
N--
NO.
JUST YOUR UPPER LIP...
EH...?
AH...
LET... GO...
FINE.
THEN JUST YOUR LOWER LIP...

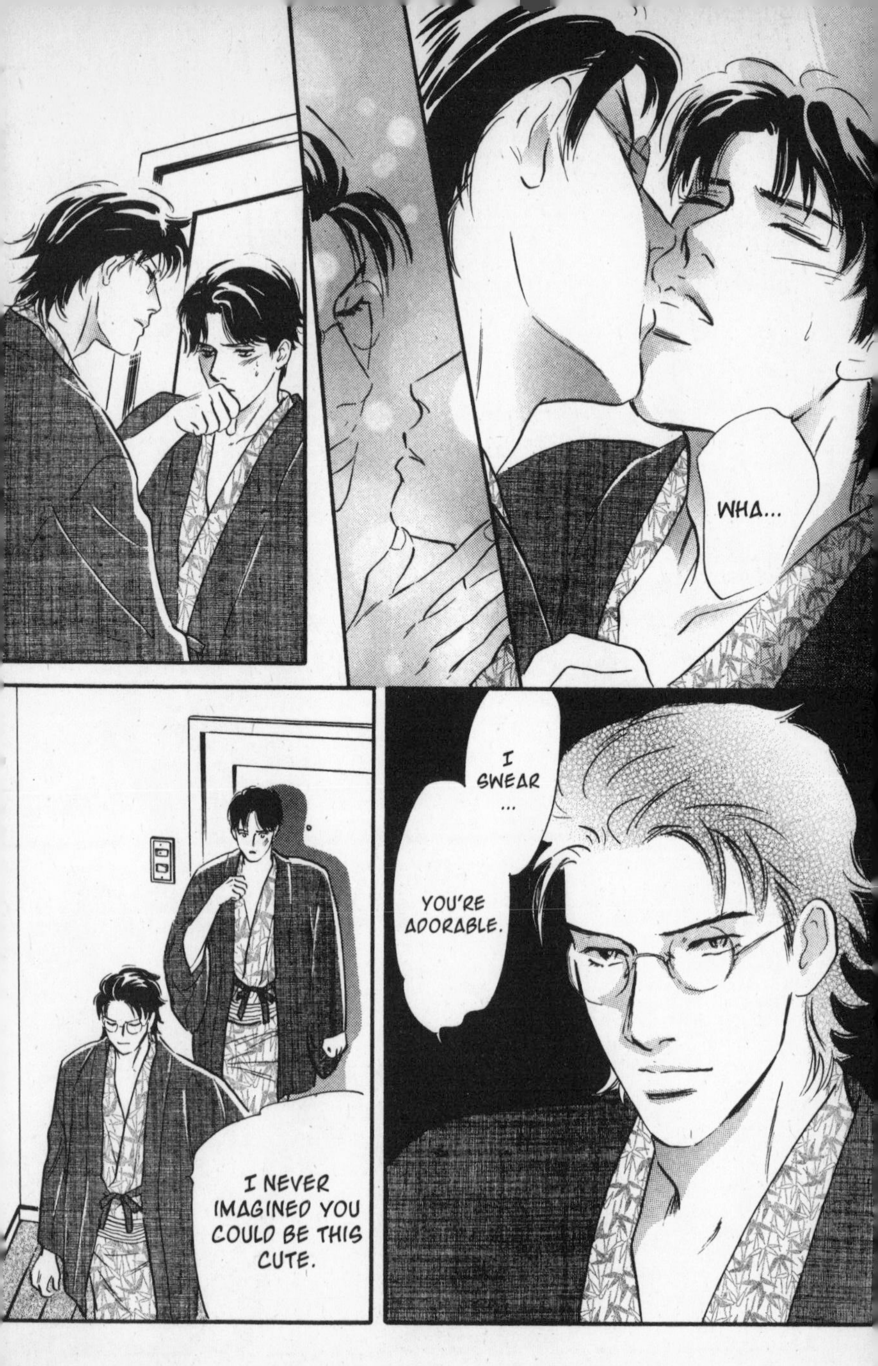
WHA...
I SWEAR ...
YOU'RE ADORABLE.
I NEVER IMAGINED YOU COULD BE THIS CUTE.

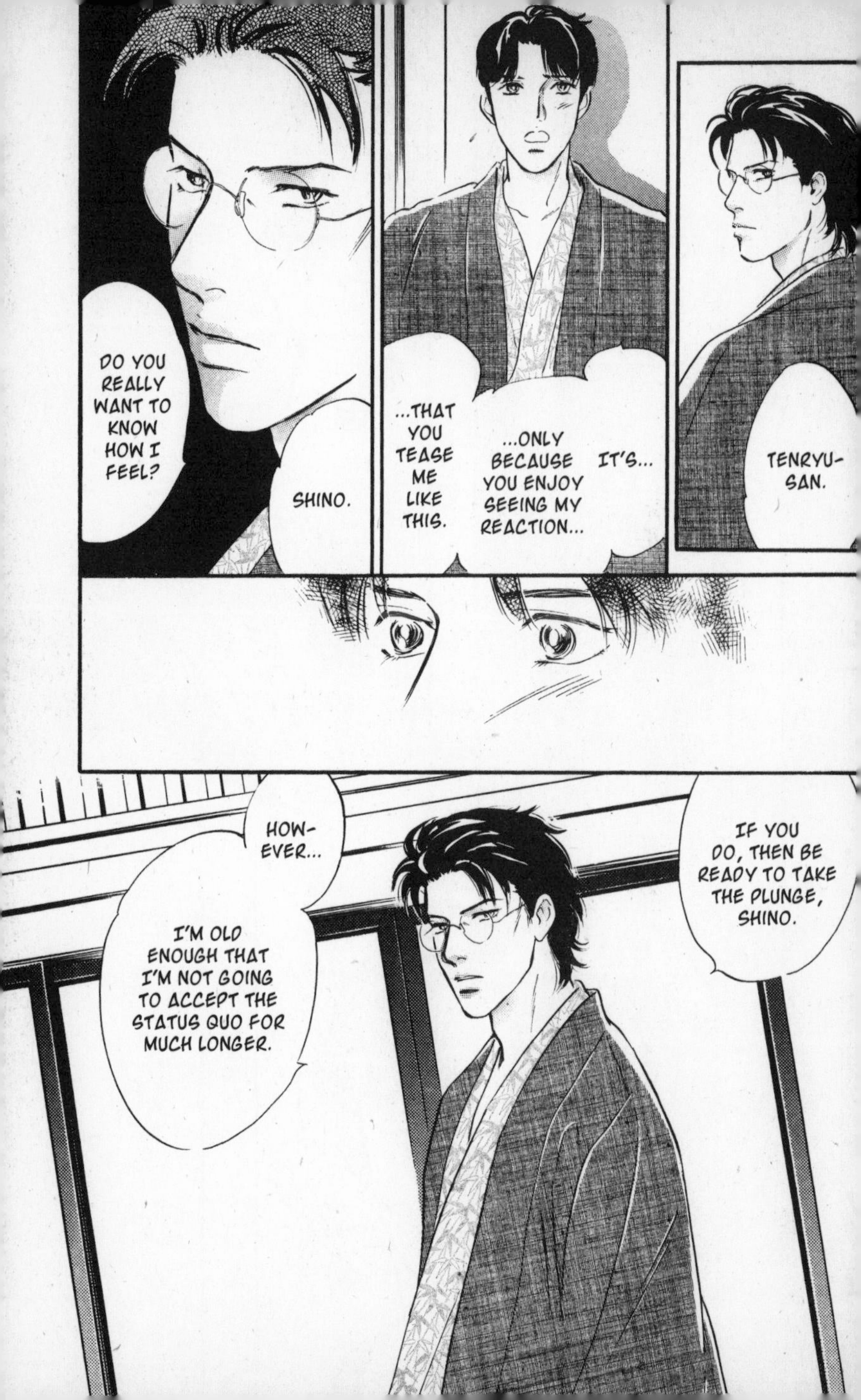
TENRYU-SAN.
IT'S...
...ONLY BECAUSE YOU ENJOY SEEING MY REACTION...
...THAT YOU TEASE ME LIKE THIS.
SHINO.
DO YOU REALLY WANT TO KNOW HOW I FEEL?
IF YOU DO, THEN BE READY TO TAKE THE PLUNGE, SHINO.
HOW-EVER...
I'M OLD ENOUGH THAT I'M NOT GOING TO ACCEPT THE STATUS QUO FOR MUCH LONGER.

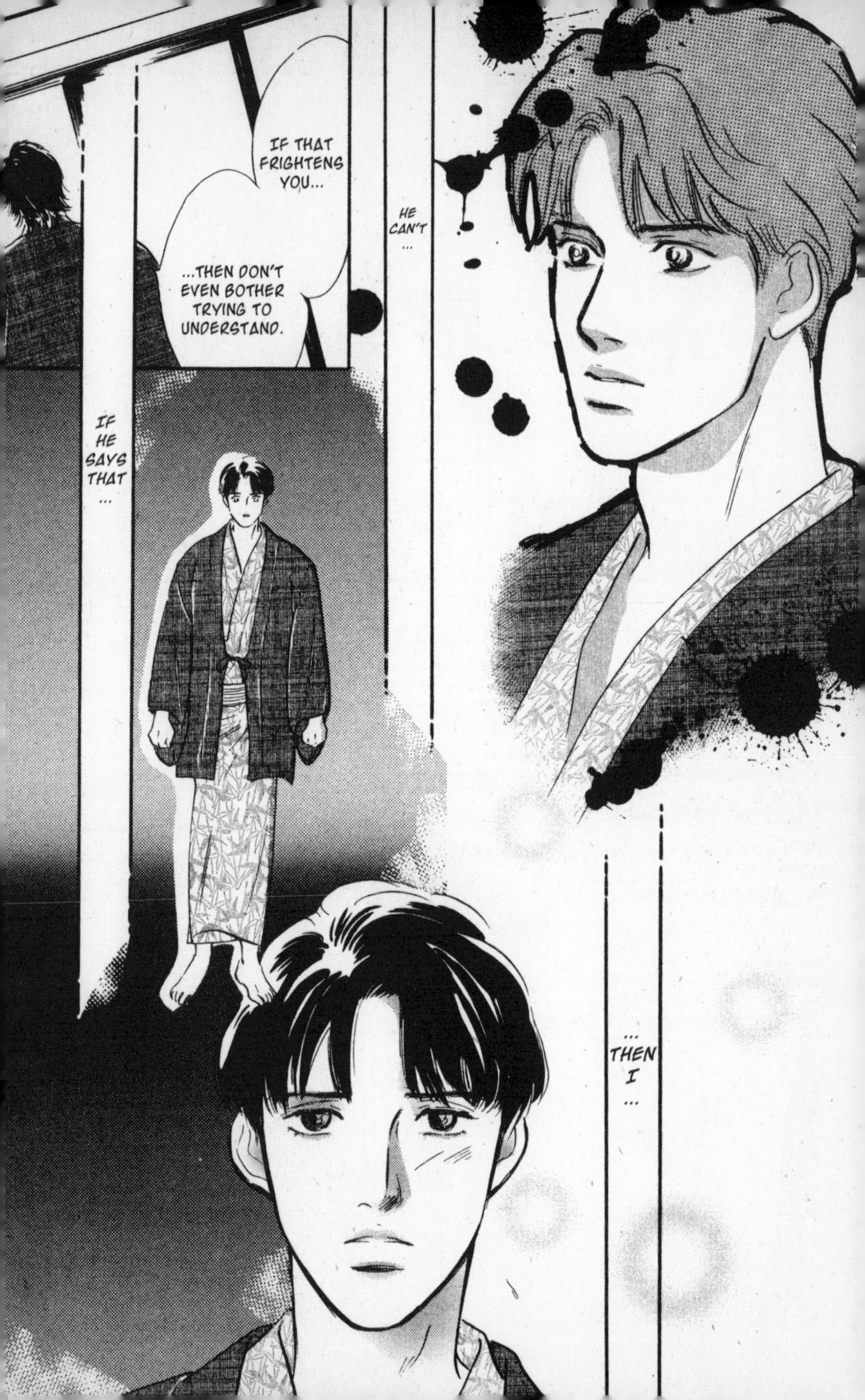
HE CAN'T ...
IF THAT FRIGHTENS YOU...
...THEN DON'T EVEN BOTHER TRYING TO UNDERSTAND.
IF HE SAYS THAT ...
... THEN I ...

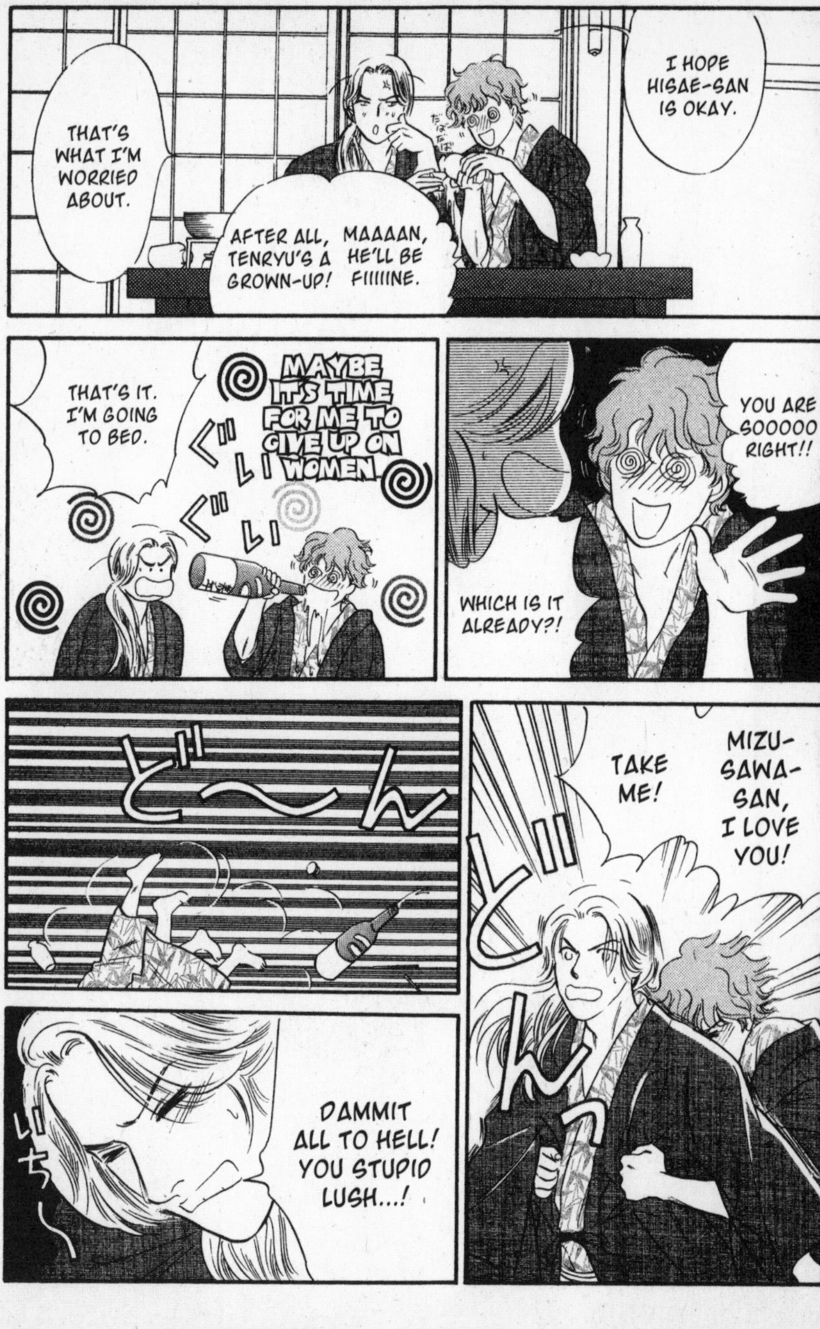
I HOPE HISAE-SAN IS OKAY.
MAAAAN, HE'LL BE FIIIIINE.
AFTER ALL, TENRYU'S A GROWN-UP!
THAT'S WHAT I'M WORRIED ABOUT.
YOU ARE SOOOOO RIGHT!!
WHICH IS IT ALREADY?!
MAYBE IT'S TIME FOR ME TO GIVE UP ON WOMEN.
THAT'S IT. I'M GOING TO BED.
MIZU-SAWA-SAN, I LOVE YOU!
TAKE ME!
DAMMIT ALL TO HELL! YOU STUPID LUSH...!

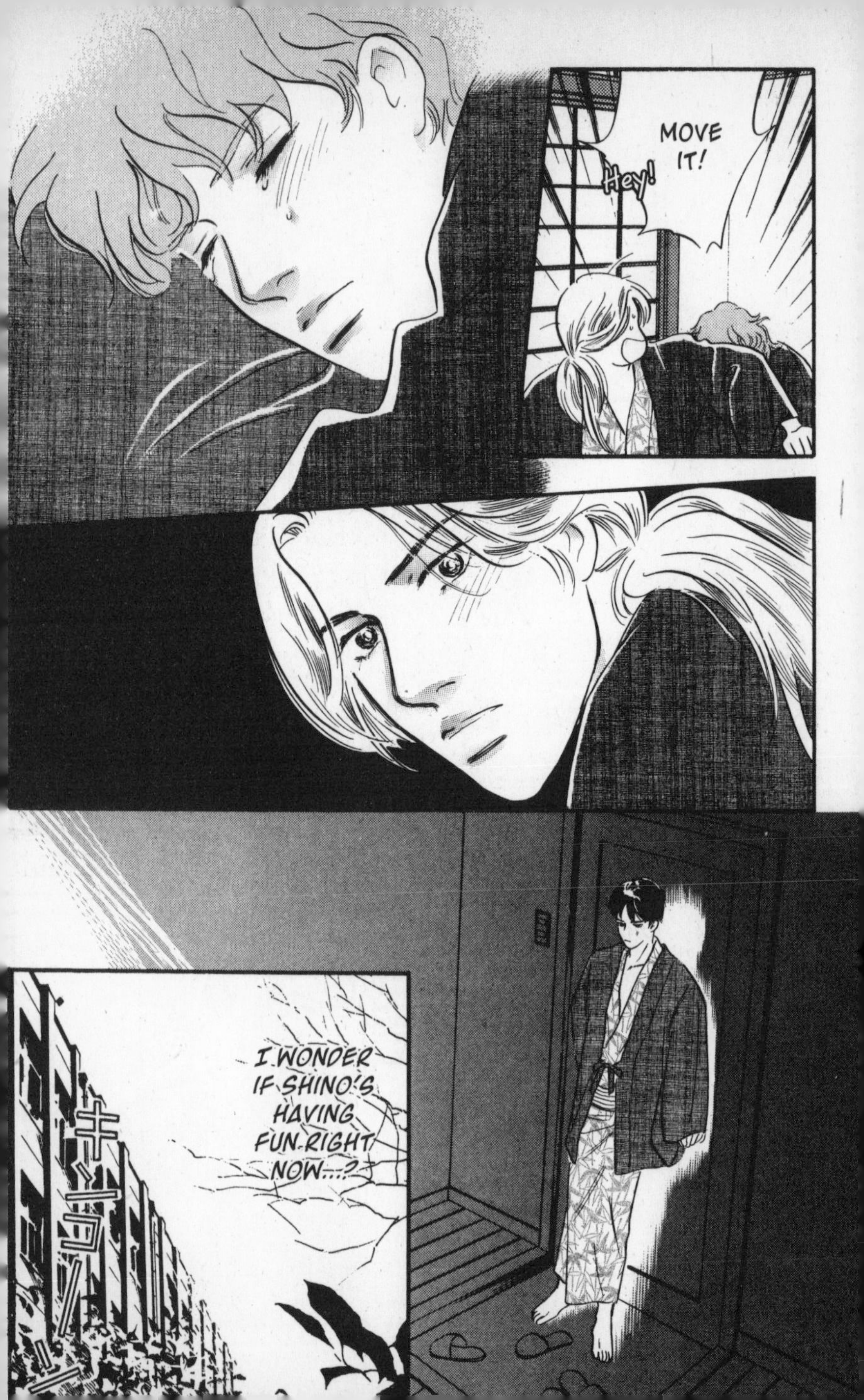
MOVE IT!
Hey!
I WONDER IF SHINO'S HAVING FUN RIGHT NOW...?

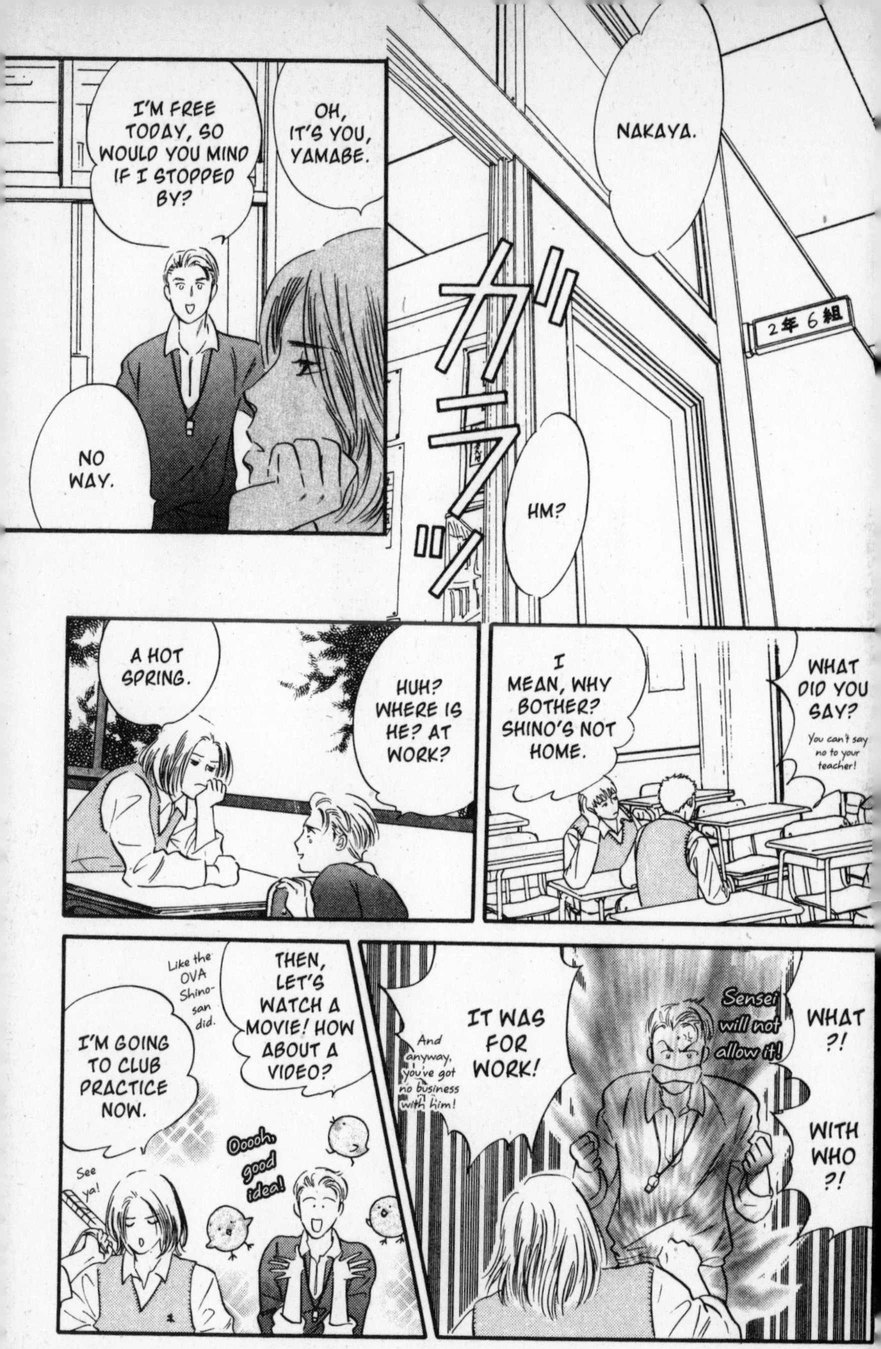
NAKAYA.
ガラッ
2年 6組
HM?
OH, IT'S YOU, YAMABE.
I'M FREE TODAY, SO WOULD YOU MIND IF I STOPPED BY?
NO WAY.
WHAT DID YOU SAY?
You can't say no to your teacher!
I MEAN, WHY BOTHER? SHINO'S NOT HOME.
HUH? WHERE IS HE? AT WORK?
A HOT SPRING.
WHAT?!
WITH WHO?!
Sensei will not allow it!
IT WAS FOR WORK!
And anyway, you've got no business with him!
THEN, LET'S WATCH A MOVIE! HOW ABOUT A VIDEO?
Like the OVA Shino-san did.
I'M GOING TO CLUB PRACTICE NOW.
Ooooh, good idea!
See ya!

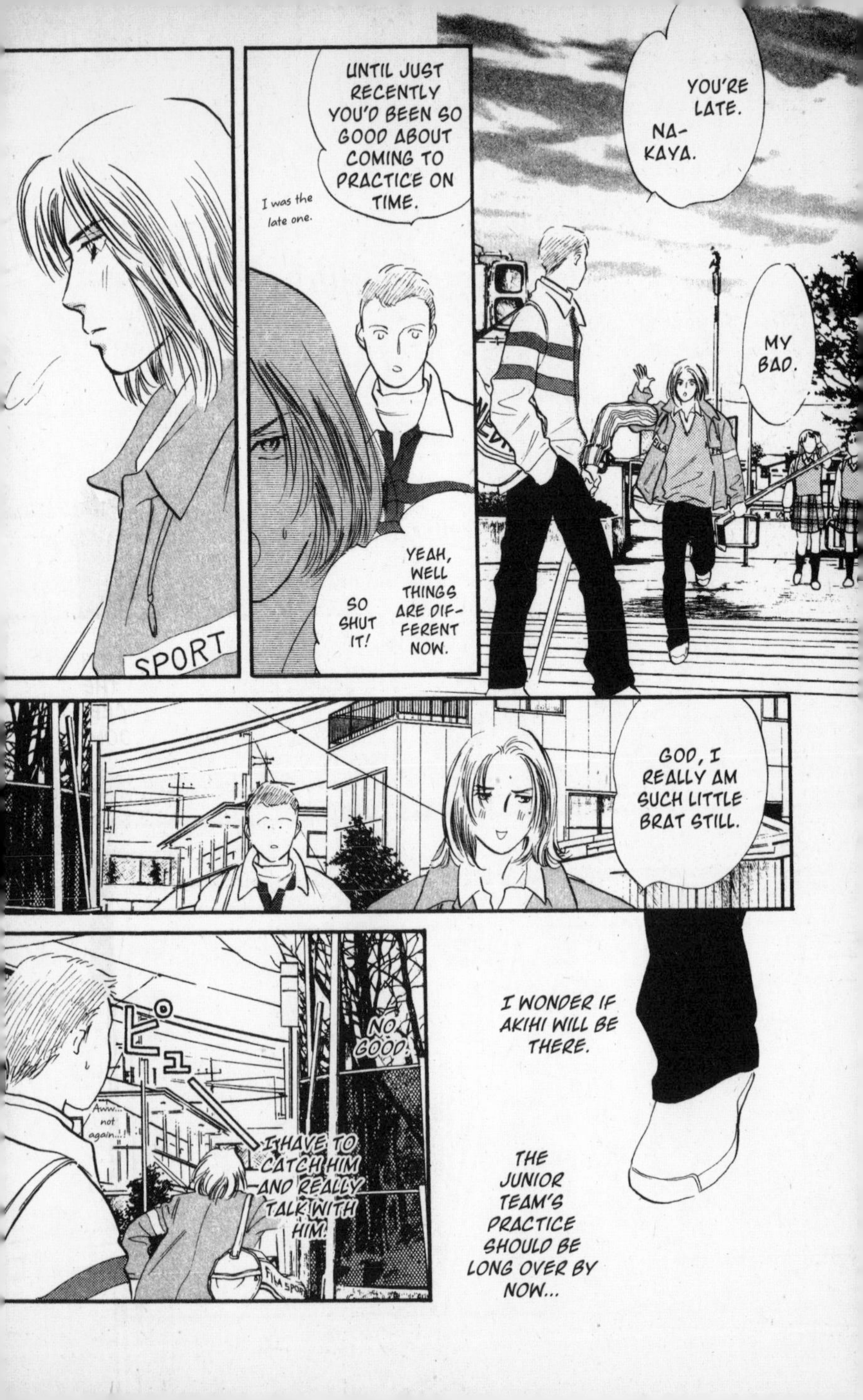
YOU'RE LATE. NA-KAYA.
MY BAD.
UNTIL JUST RECENTLY YOU'D BEEN SO GOOD ABOUT COMING TO PRACTICE ON TIME.
I was the late one.
YEAH, WELL THINGS ARE DIF-FERENT NOW.
SO SHUT IT!
SPORT
GOD, I REALLY AM SUCH LITTLE BRAT STILL.
I WONDER IF AKIHI WILL BE THERE.
THE JUNIOR TEAM'S PRACTICE SHOULD BE LONG OVER BY NOW...
ピュ
NO GOOD.
Aww... not again..!
I HAVE TO CATCH HIM AND REALLY TALK WITH HIM.

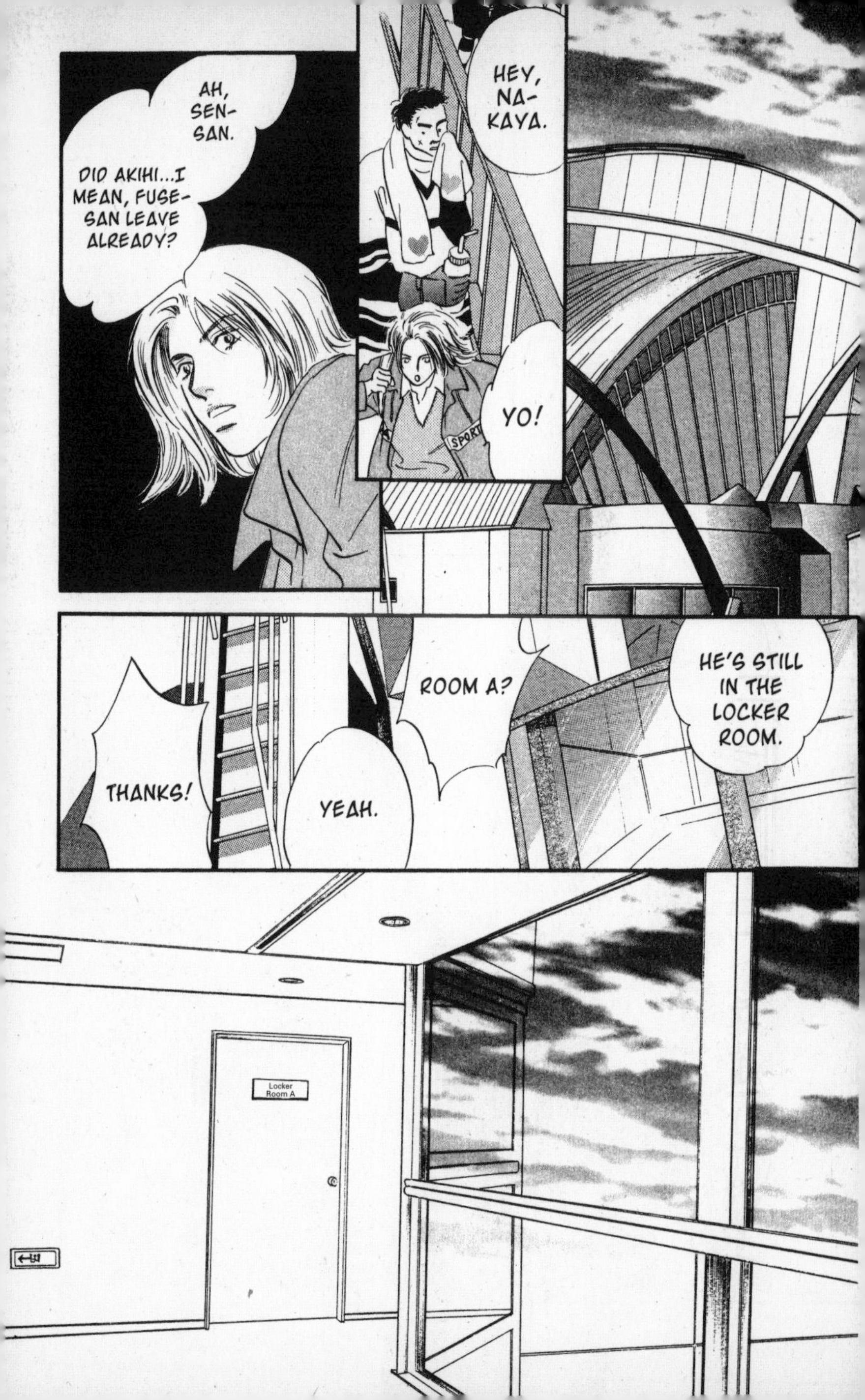
HEY, NAKAYA.
YO!
AH, SEN-SAN.
DID AKIHI...I MEAN, FUSE-SAN LEAVE ALREADY?
HE'S STILL IN THE LOCKER ROOM.
ROOM A?
YEAH.
THANKS!
Locker Room A

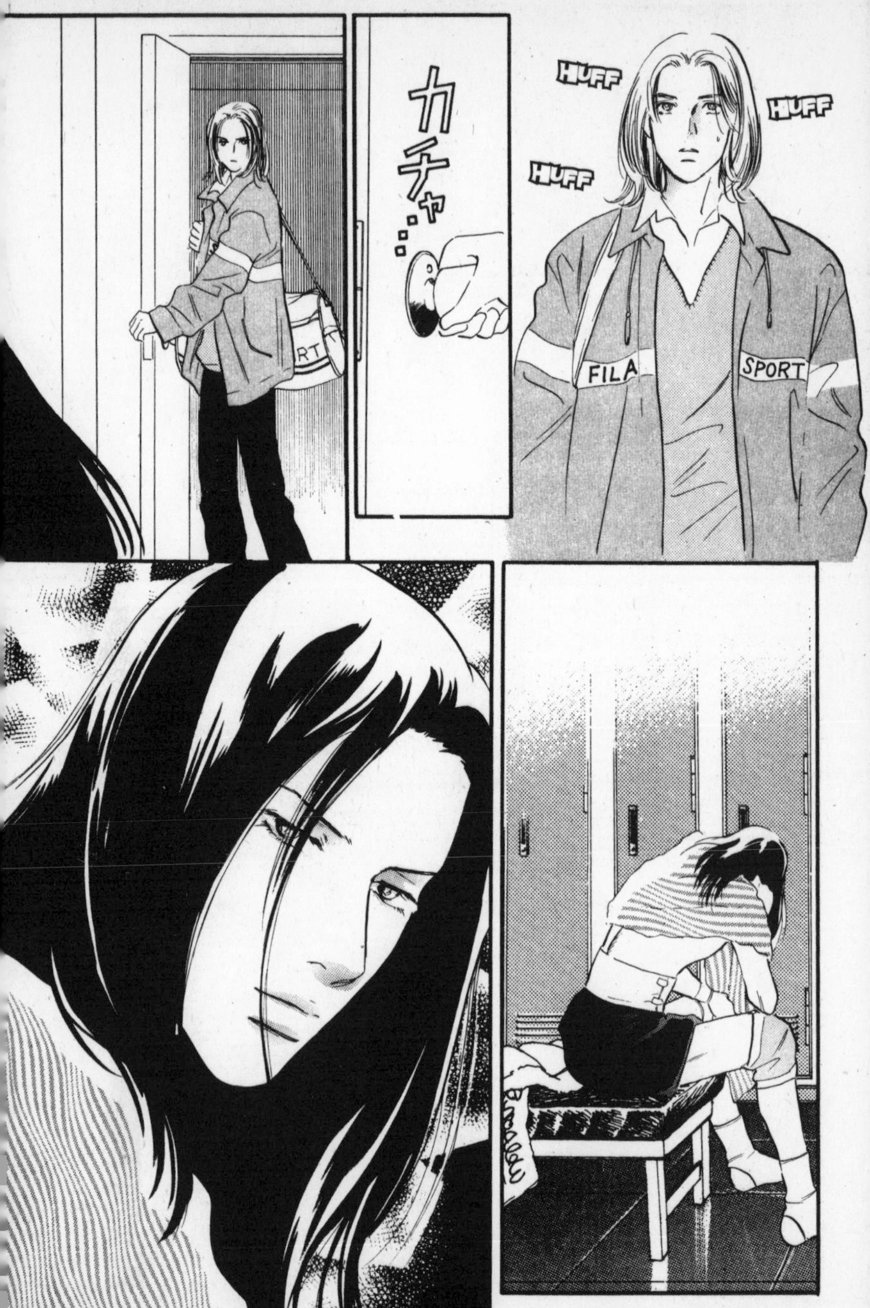
HUFF
HUFF
HUFF
FILA
SPORT
カチャ…

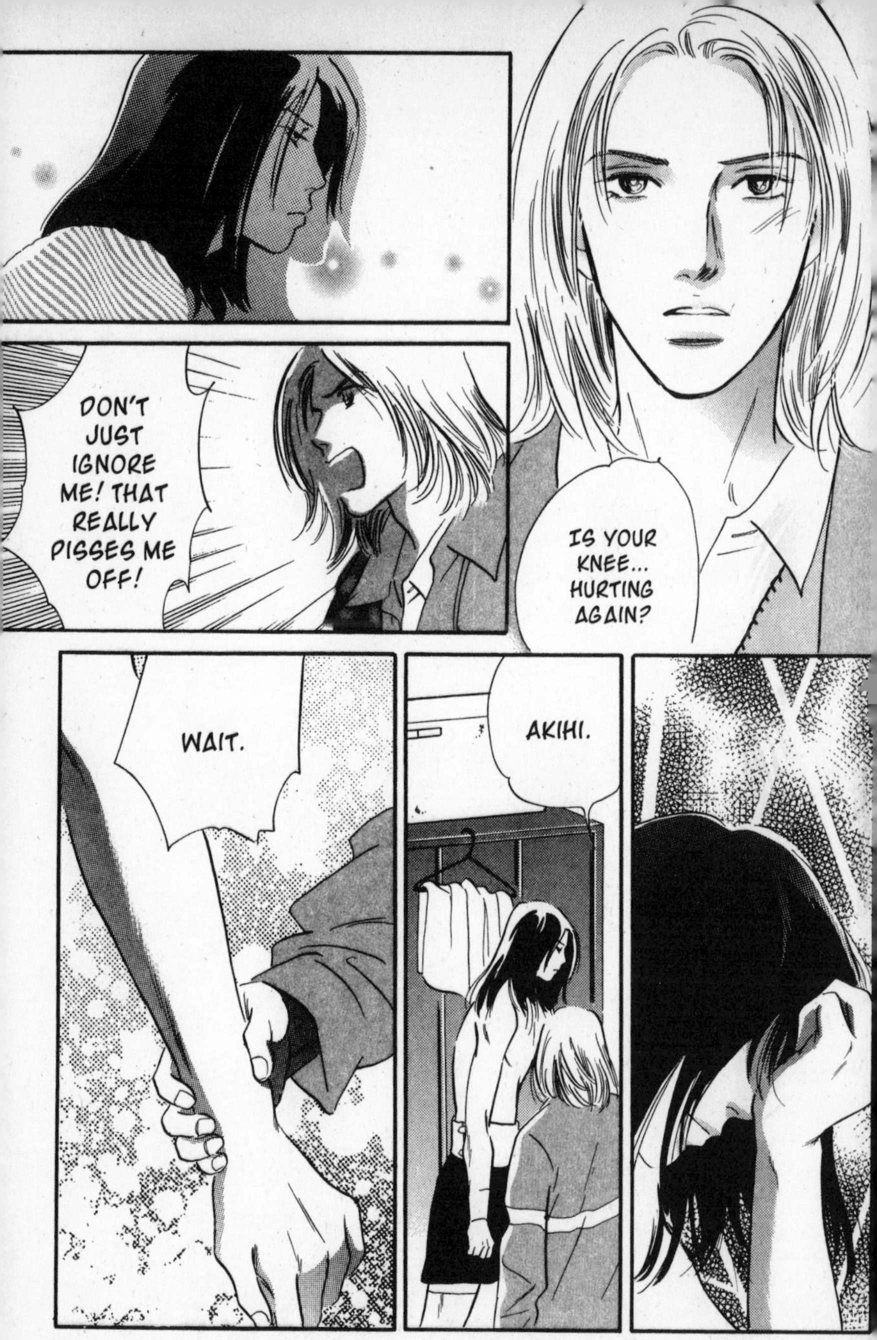
IS YOUR KNEE... HURTING AGAIN?
DON'T JUST IGNORE ME! THAT REALLY PISSES ME OFF!
AKIHI.
WAIT.

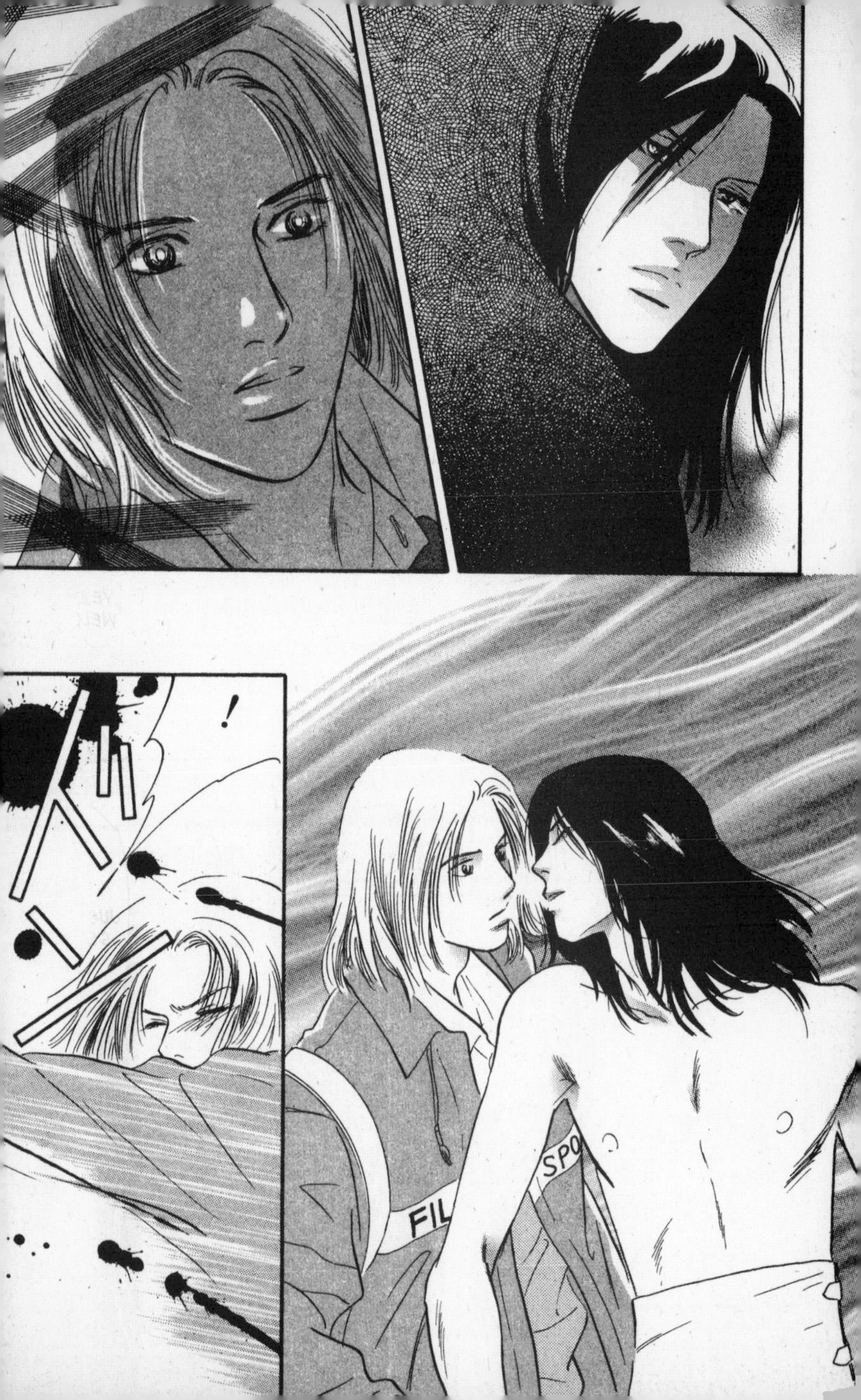
SPO
FIL
!

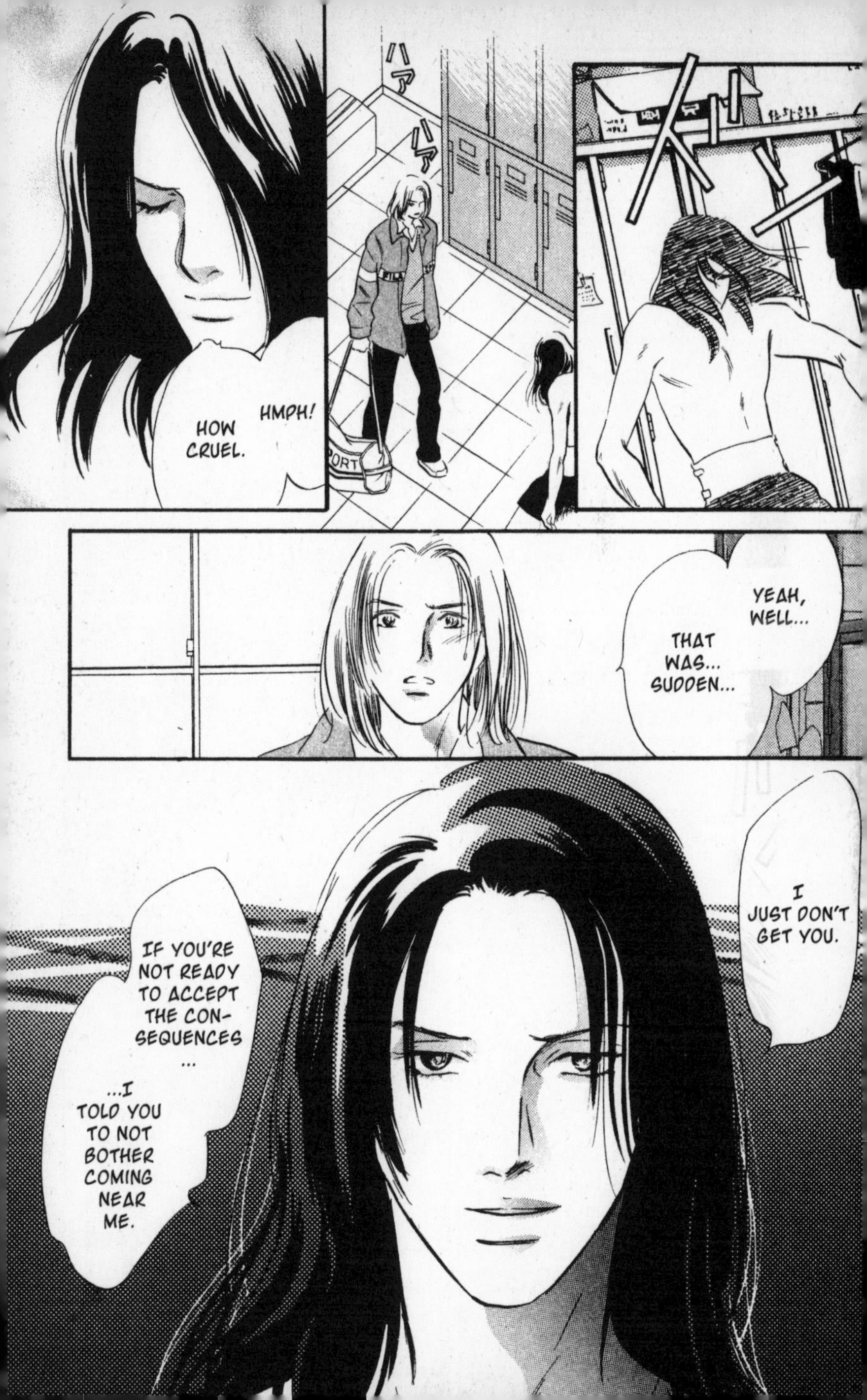
ハア
ハア
HMPH!
HOW CRUEL.
YEAH, WELL...
THAT WAS... SUDDEN...
I JUST DON'T GET YOU.
IF YOU'RE NOT READY TO ACCEPT THE CON-SEQUENCES...
...I TOLD YOU TO NOT BOTHER COMING NEAR ME.

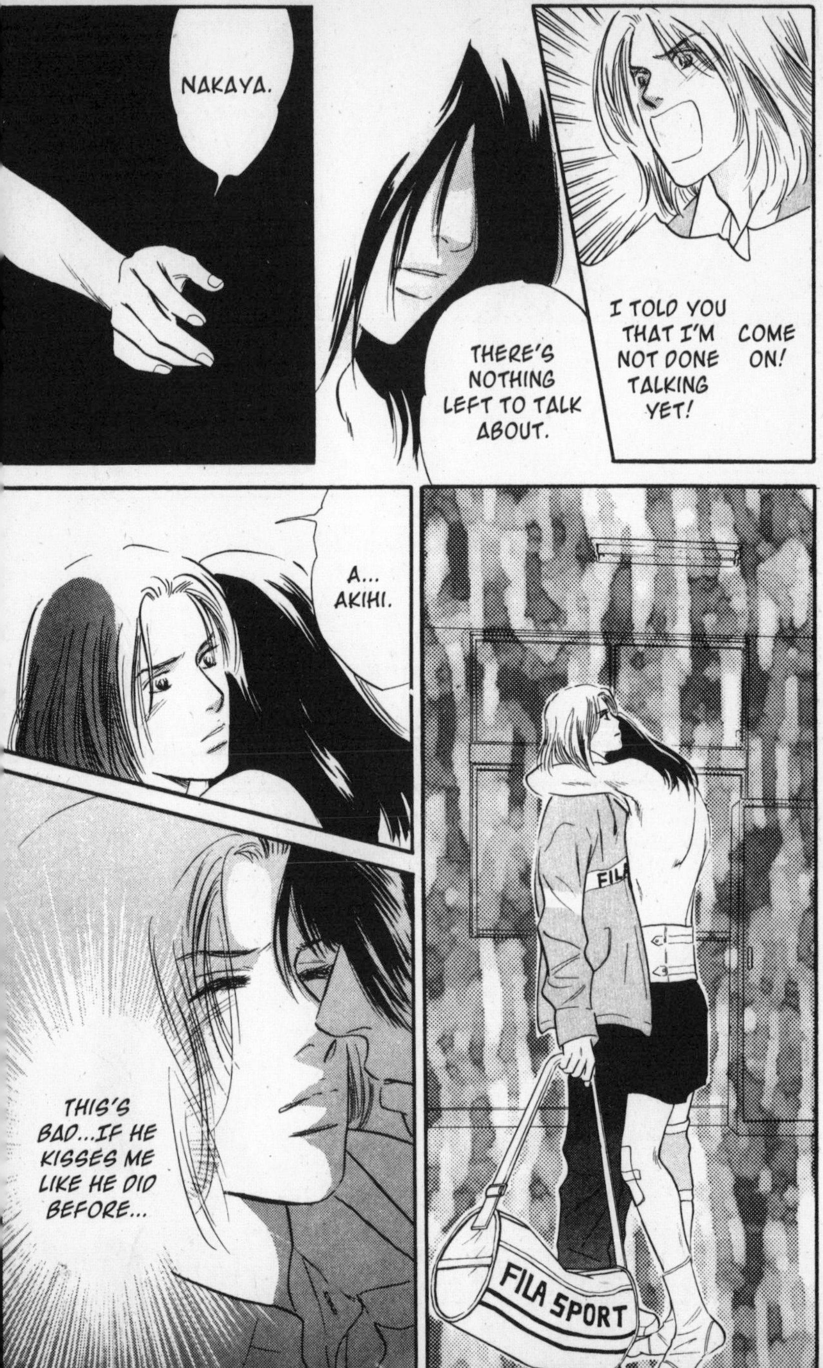
COME ON!
I TOLD YOU THAT I'M NOT DONE TALKING YET!
THERE'S NOTHING LEFT TO TALK ABOUT.
NAKAYA.
FILA
FILA SPORT
A... AKIHI.
THIS'S BAD...IF HE KISSES ME LIKE HE DID BEFORE...

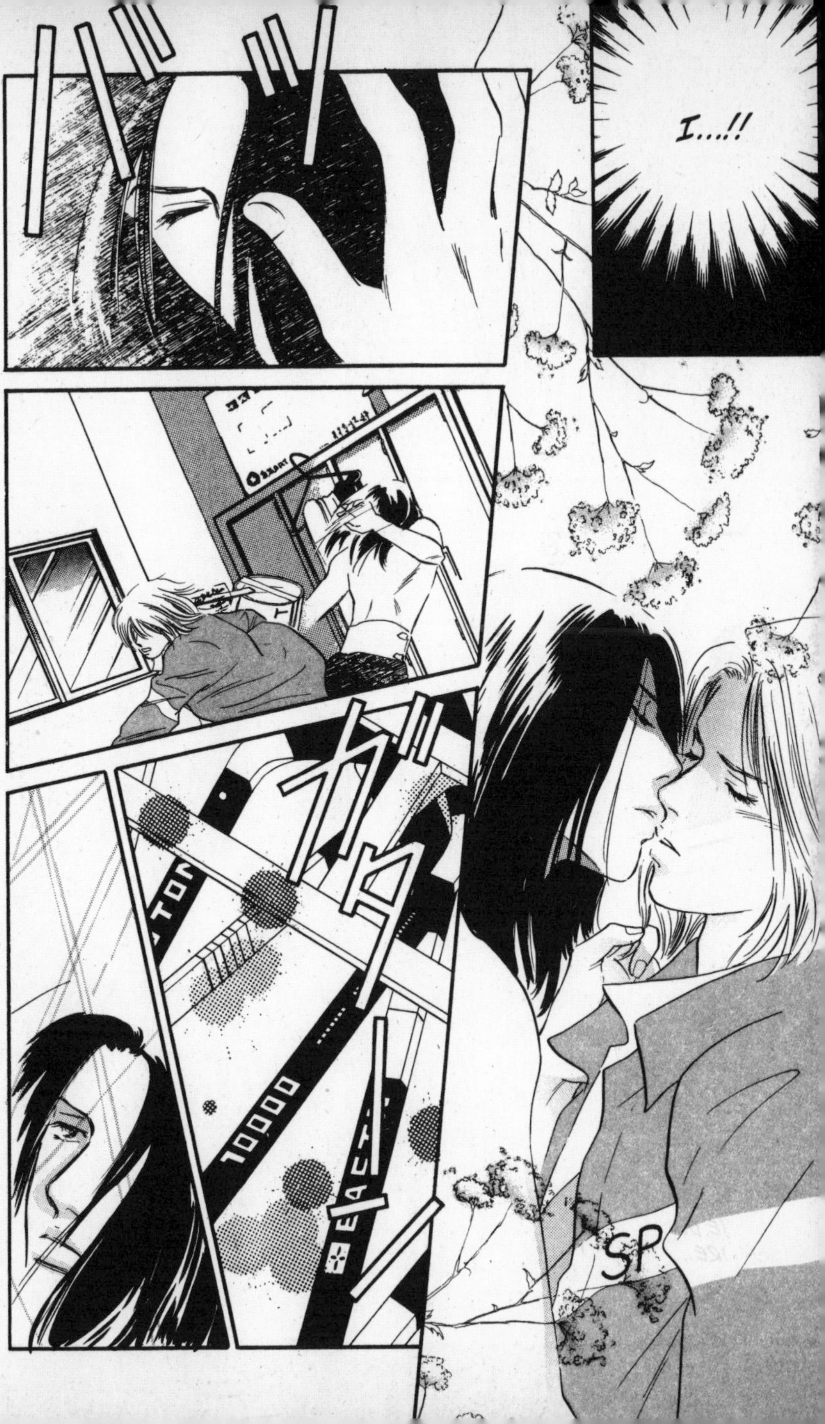
I...!!
SP

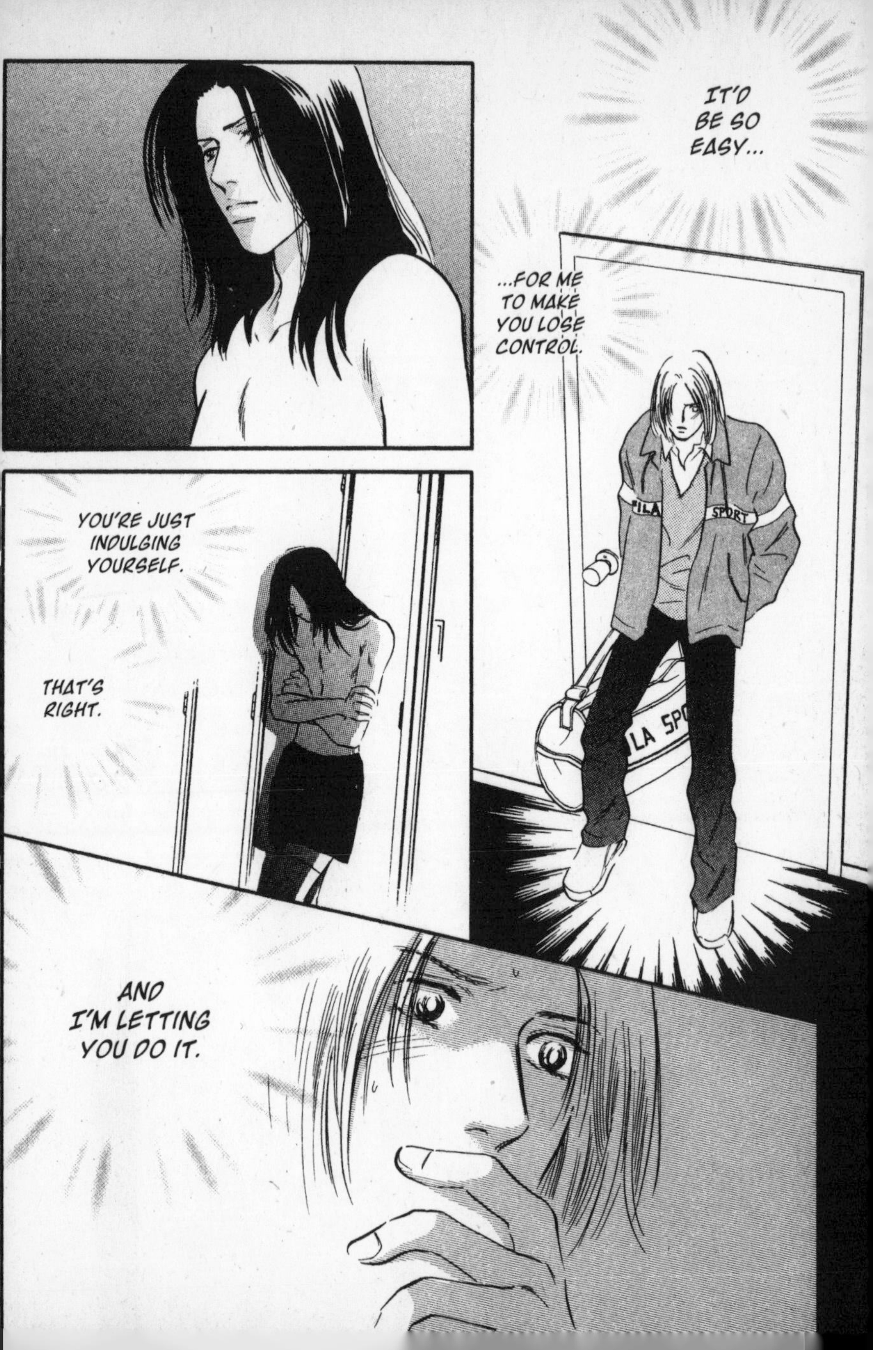
IT'D BE SO EASY...
...FOR ME TO MAKE YOU LOSE CONTROL.
YOU'RE JUST INDULGING YOURSELF.
THAT'S RIGHT.
AND I'M LETTING YOU DO IT.

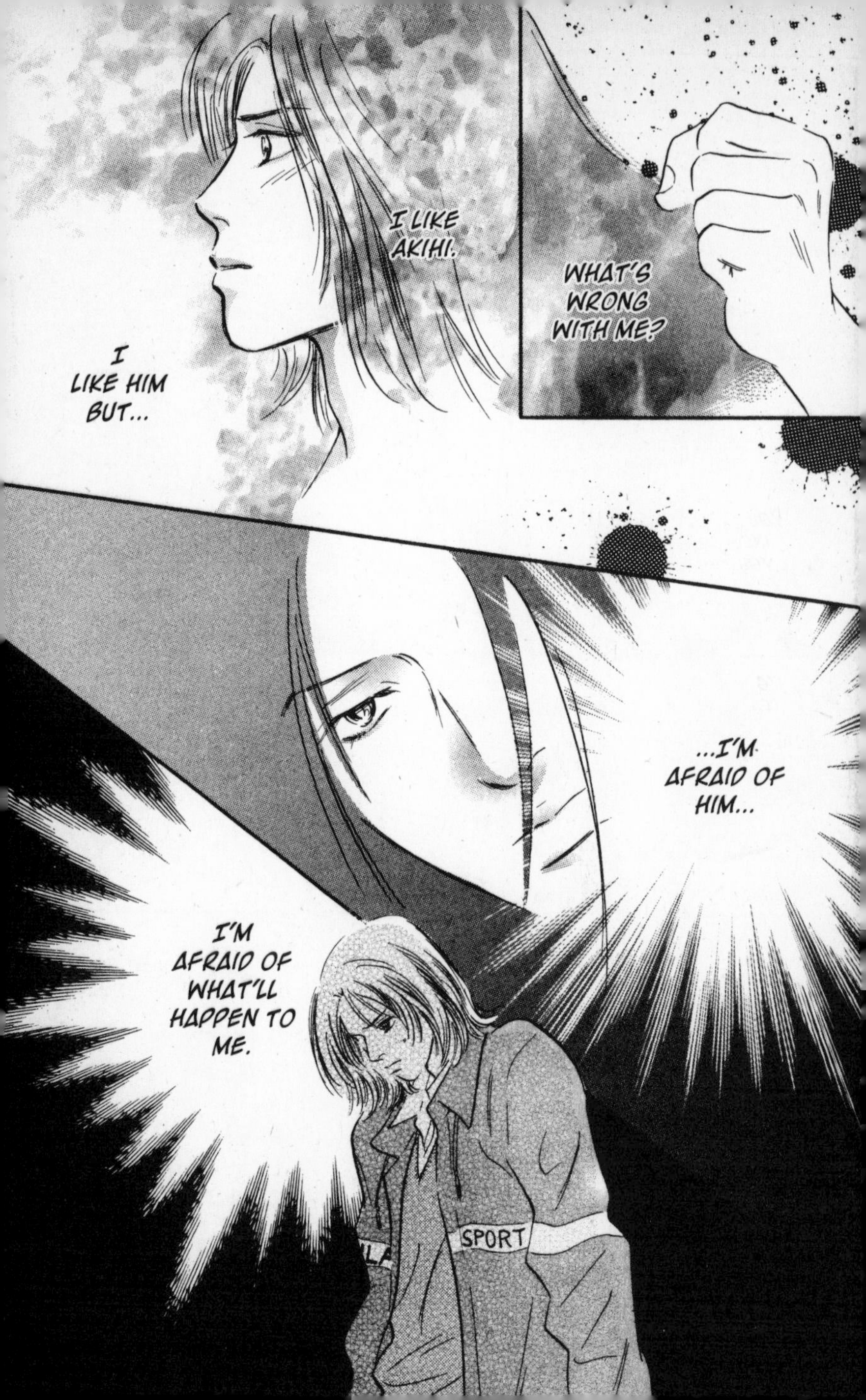
WHAT'S WRONG WITH ME?
I LIKE AKIHI.
I LIKE HIM BUT...
...I'M AFRAID OF HIM...
I'M AFRAID OF WHAT'LL HAPPEN TO ME.
SPORT

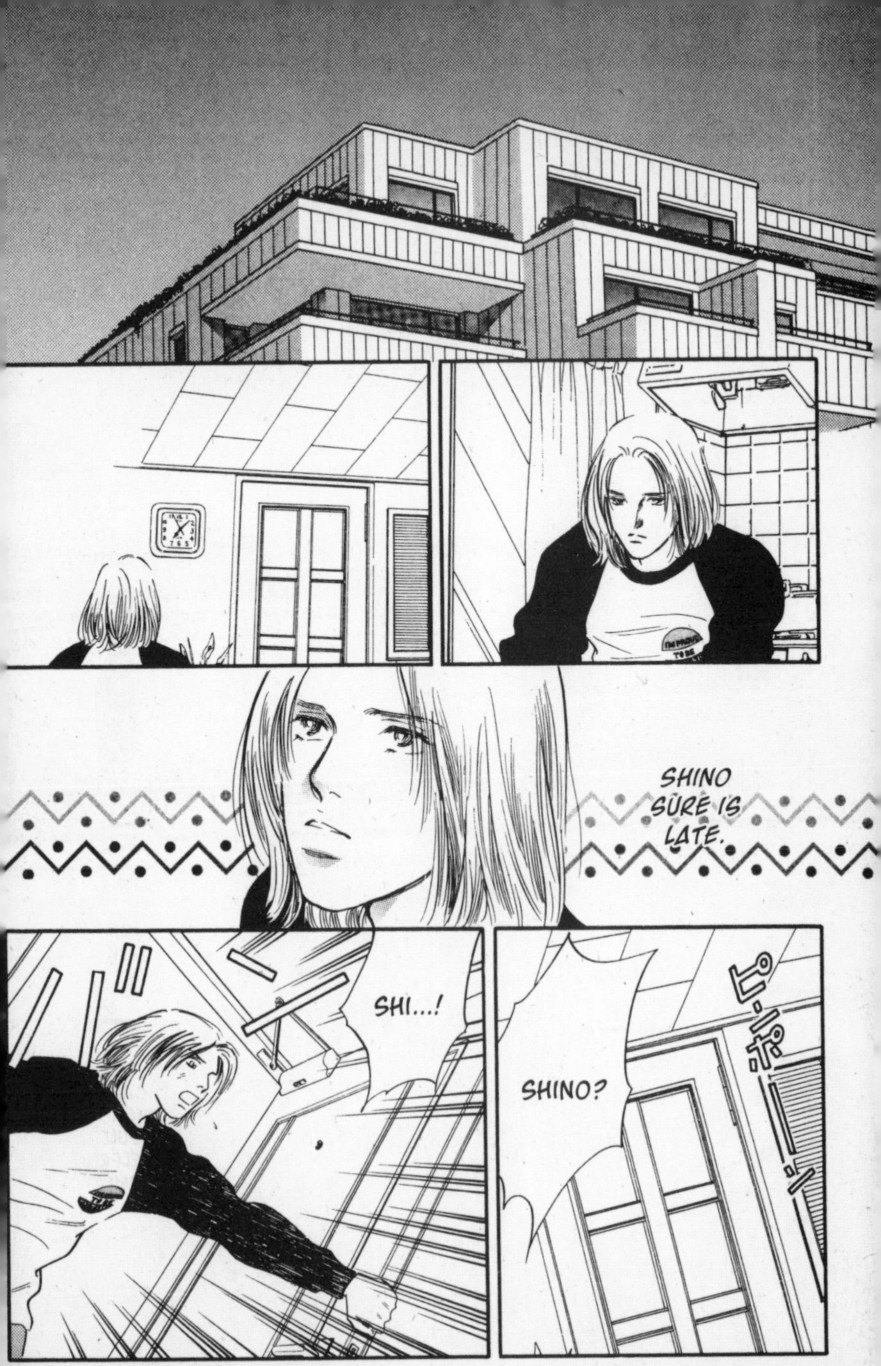
SHINO SURE IS LATE.
ピンポーン
SHINO?
SHI...!

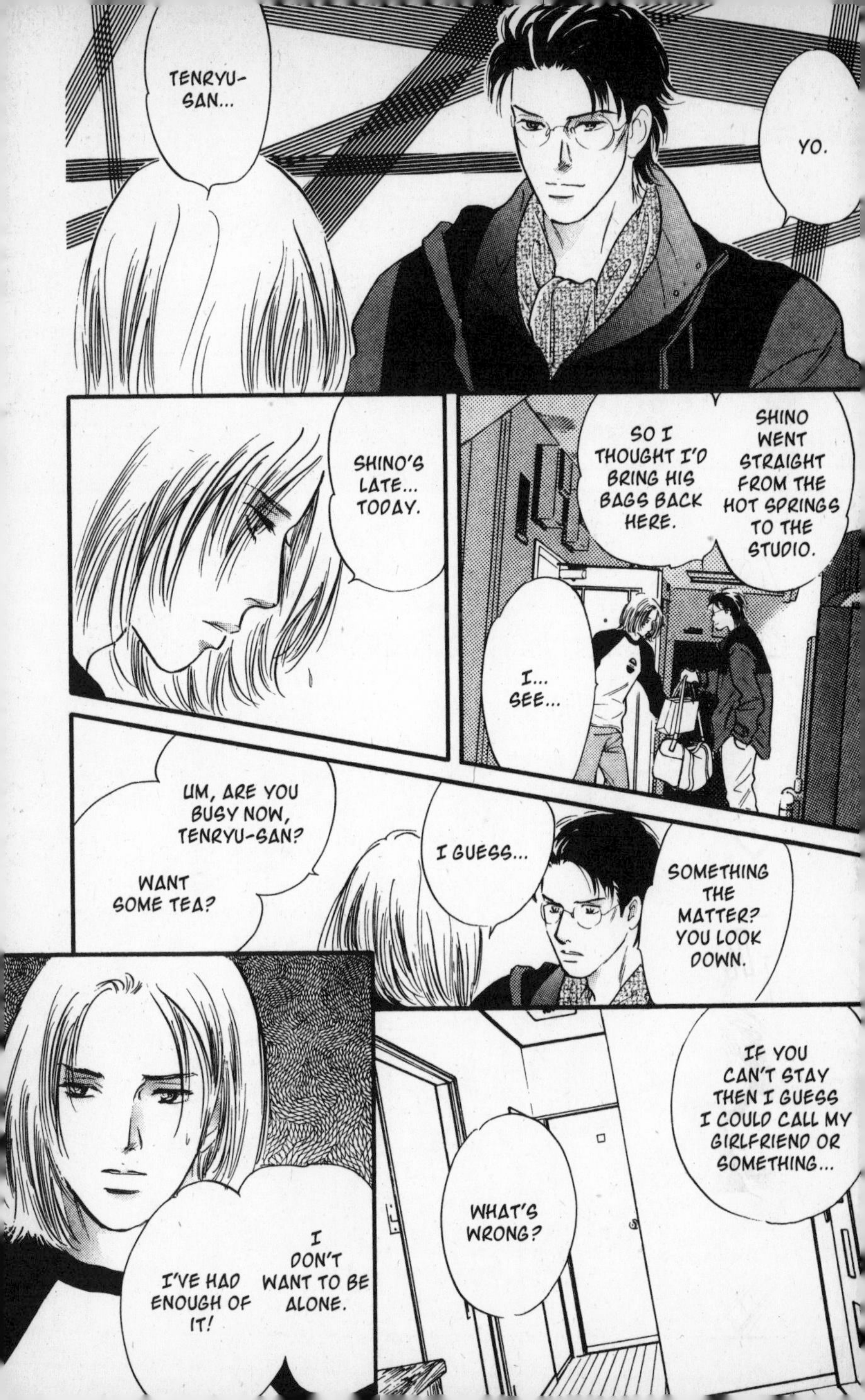
TENRYU-SAN...
YO.
SHINO WENT STRAIGHT FROM THE HOT SPRINGS TO THE STUDIO.
SO I THOUGHT I'D BRING HIS BAGS BACK HERE.
I... SEE...
SHINO'S LATE... TODAY.
SOMETHING THE MATTER? YOU LOOK DOWN.
I GUESS...
UM, ARE YOU BUSY NOW, TENRYU-SAN?
WANT SOME TEA?
IF YOU CAN'T STAY THEN I GUESS I COULD CALL MY GIRLFRIEND OR SOMETHING...
WHAT'S WRONG?
I DON'T WANT TO BE ALONE.
I'VE HAD ENOUGH OF IT!

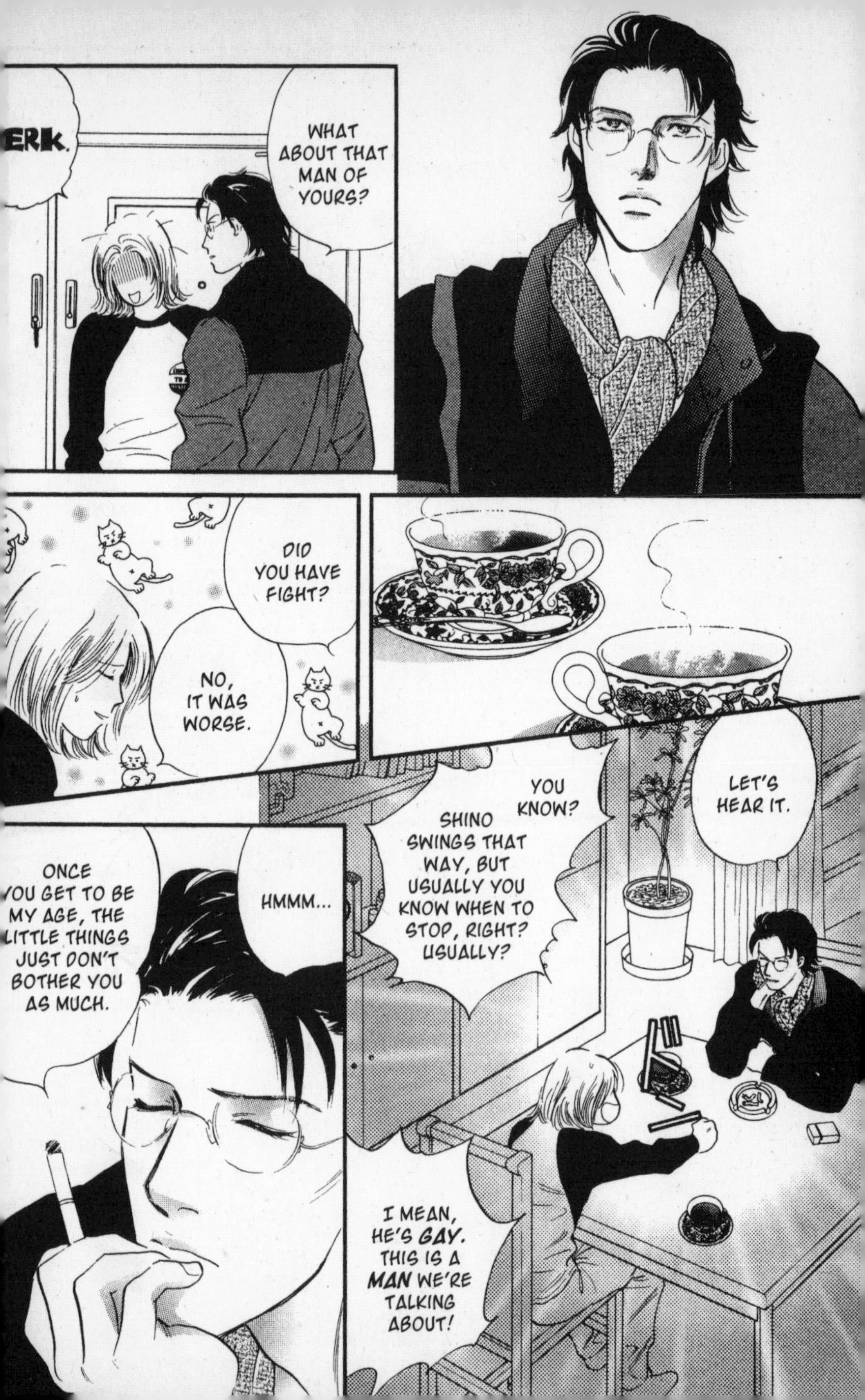
WHAT ABOUT THAT MAN OF YOURS?
ERK.
DID YOU HAVE FIGHT?
NO, IT WAS WORSE.
LET'S HEAR IT.
YOU KNOW?
SHINO SWINGS THAT WAY, BUT USUALLY YOU KNOW WHEN TO STOP, RIGHT? USUALLY?
I MEAN, HE'S GAY. THIS IS A MAN WE'RE TALKING ABOUT!
HMMM...
ONCE YOU GET TO BE MY AGE, THE LITTLE THINGS JUST DON'T BOTHER YOU AS MUCH.

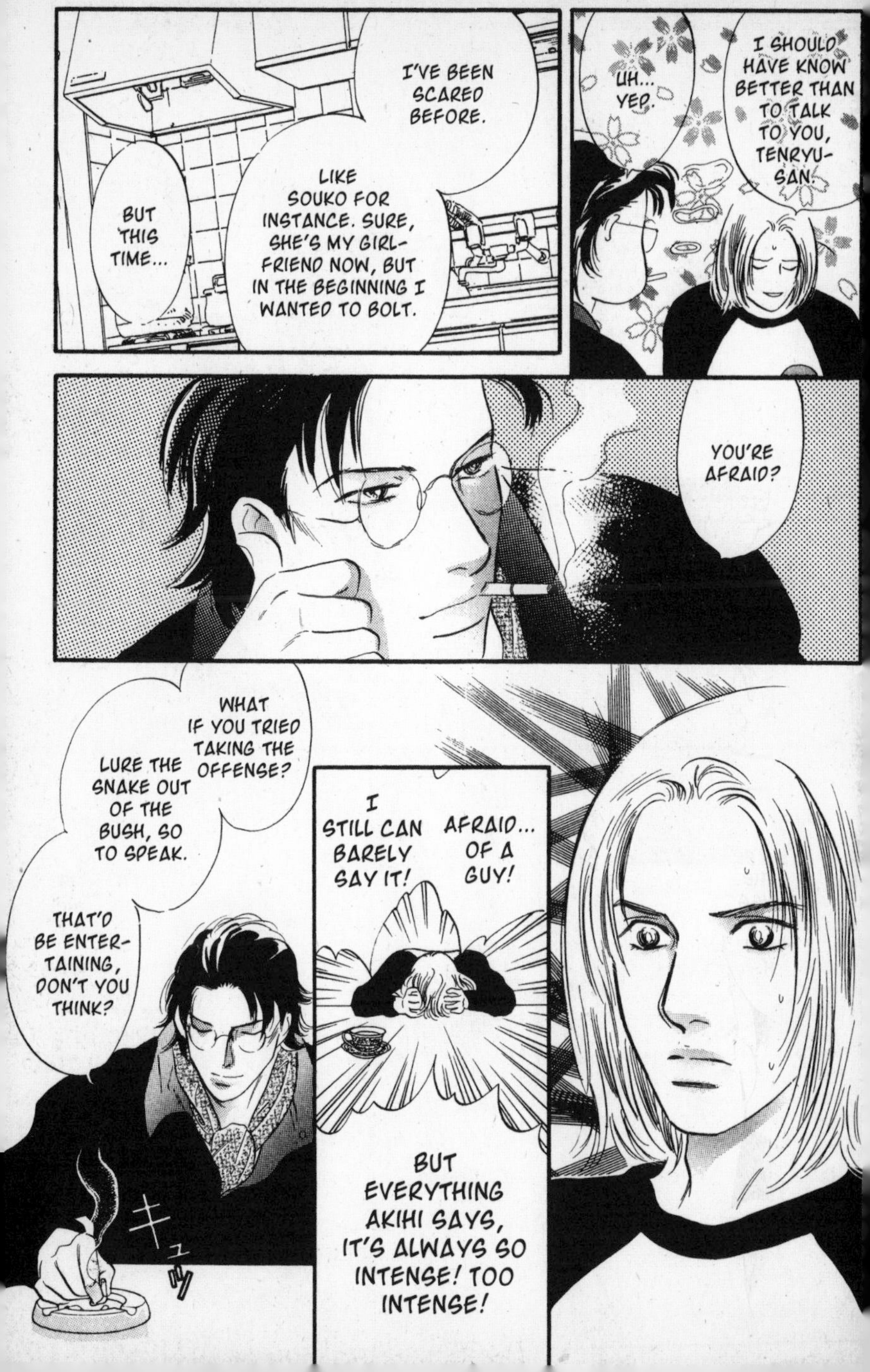
I SHOULD HAVE KNOW BETTER THAN TO TALK TO YOU, TENRYU-SAN.
UH... YEP.
I'VE BEEN SCARED BEFORE.
LIKE SOUKO FOR INSTANCE. SURE, SHE'S MY GIRL-FRIEND NOW, BUT IN THE BEGINNING I WANTED TO BOLT.
BUT THIS TIME...
YOU'RE AFRAID?
AFRAID... OF A GUY!
I STILL CAN BARELY SAY IT!
BUT EVERYTHING AKIHI SAYS, IT'S ALWAYS SO INTENSE! TOO INTENSE!
WHAT IF YOU TRIED TAKING THE OFFENSE?
LURE THE SNAKE OUT OF THE BUSH, SO TO SPEAK.
THAT'D BE ENTERTAINING, DON'T YOU THINK?
キュッ

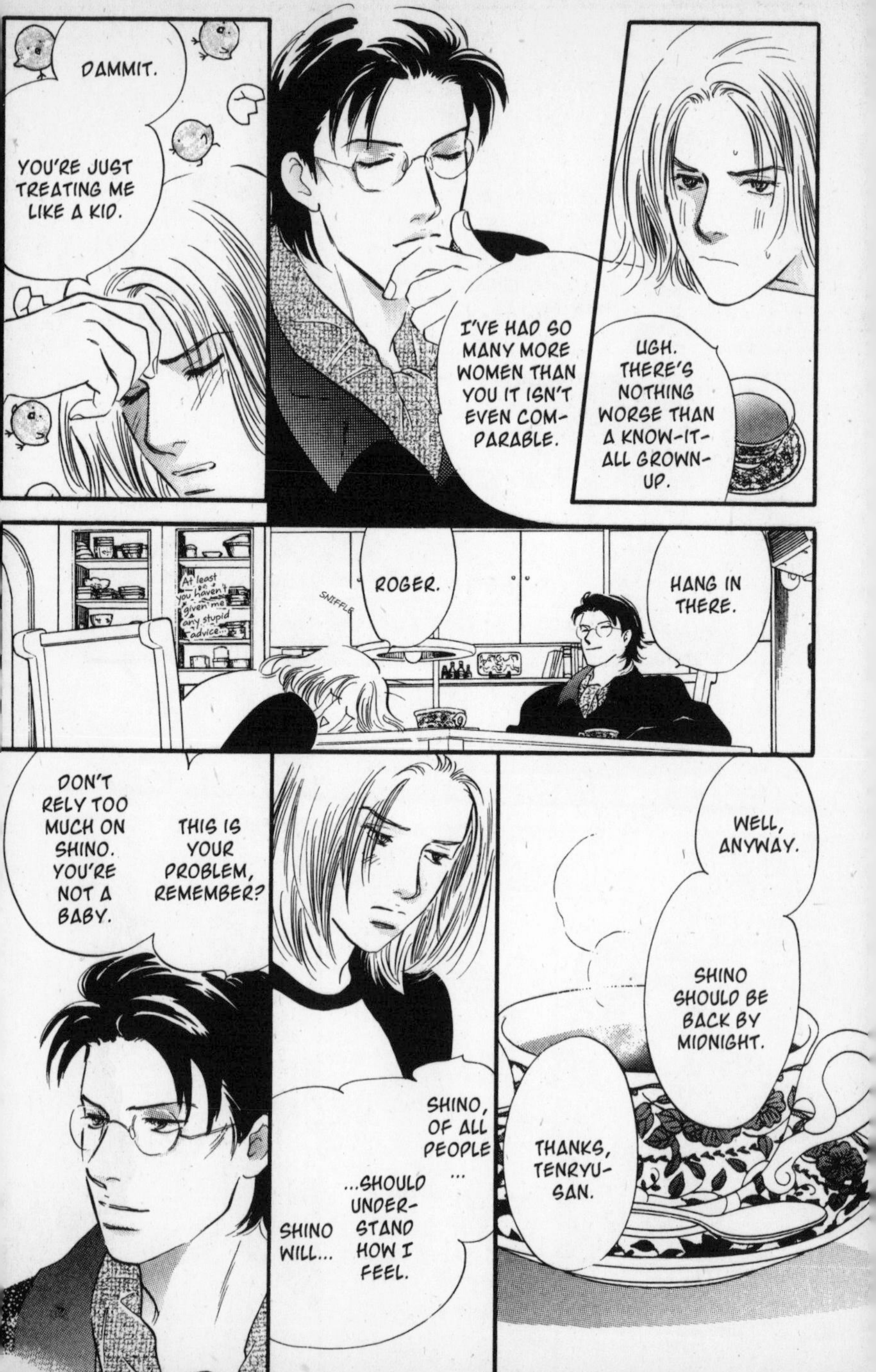
UGH. THERE'S NOTHING WORSE THAN A KNOW-IT-ALL GROWN-UP.
I'VE HAD SO MANY MORE WOMEN THAN YOU IT ISN'T EVEN COMPARABLE.
DAMMIT.
YOU'RE JUST TREATING ME LIKE A KID.
HANG IN THERE.
ROGER.
SNIFFLE
At least you haven't given me any stupid advice...
WELL, ANYWAY.
SHINO SHOULD BE BACK BY MIDNIGHT.
THANKS, TENRYU-SAN.
SHINO, OF ALL PEOPLE...
...SHOULD UNDERSTAND HOW I FEEL.
SHINO WILL...
THIS IS YOUR PROBLEM, REMEMBER?
DON'T RELY TOO MUCH ON SHINO. YOU'RE NOT A BABY.

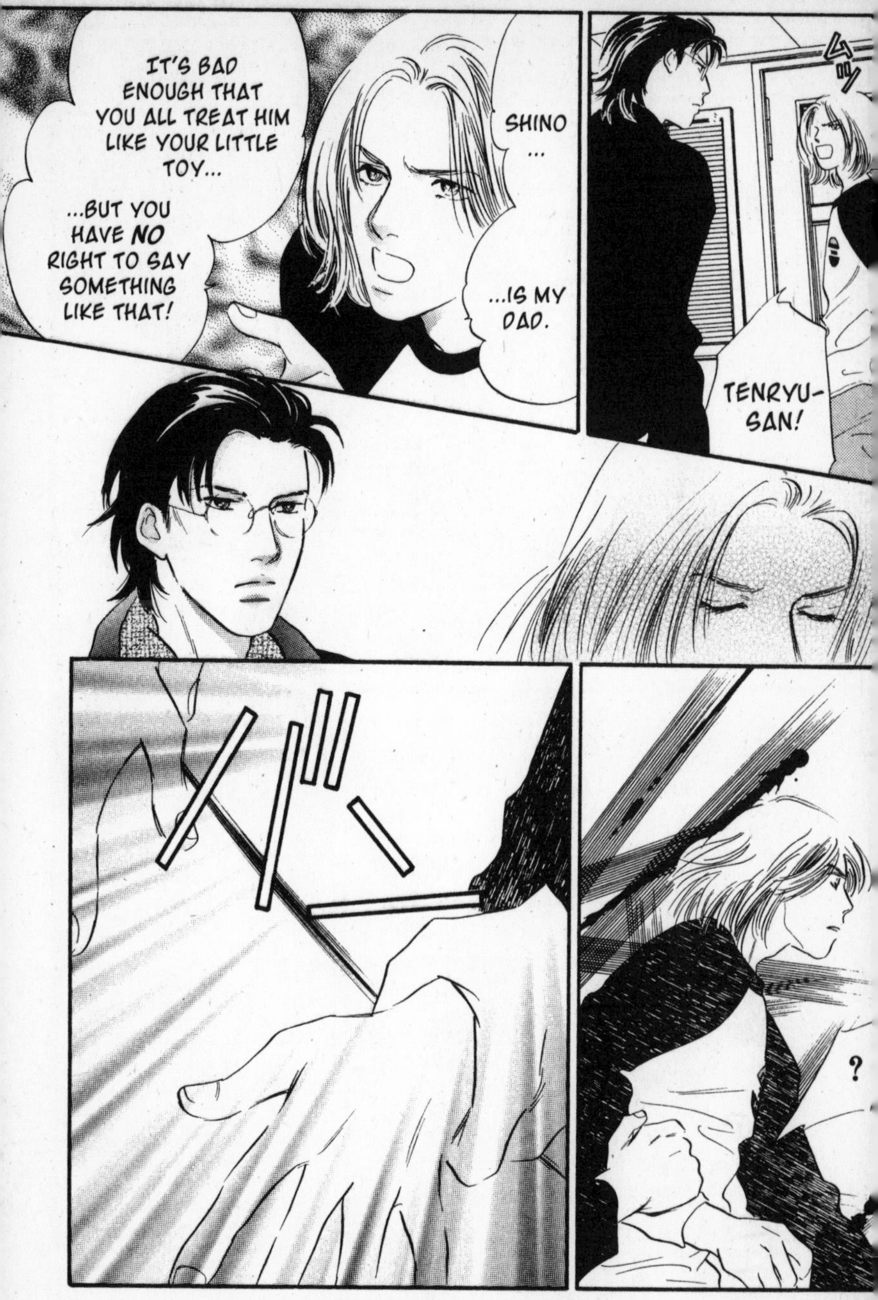
TENRYU-SAN!
SHINO ...
...IS MY DAD.
IT'S BAD ENOUGH THAT YOU ALL TREAT HIM LIKE YOUR LITTLE TOY...
...BUT YOU HAVE **NO** RIGHT TO SAY SOMETHING LIKE THAT!
?

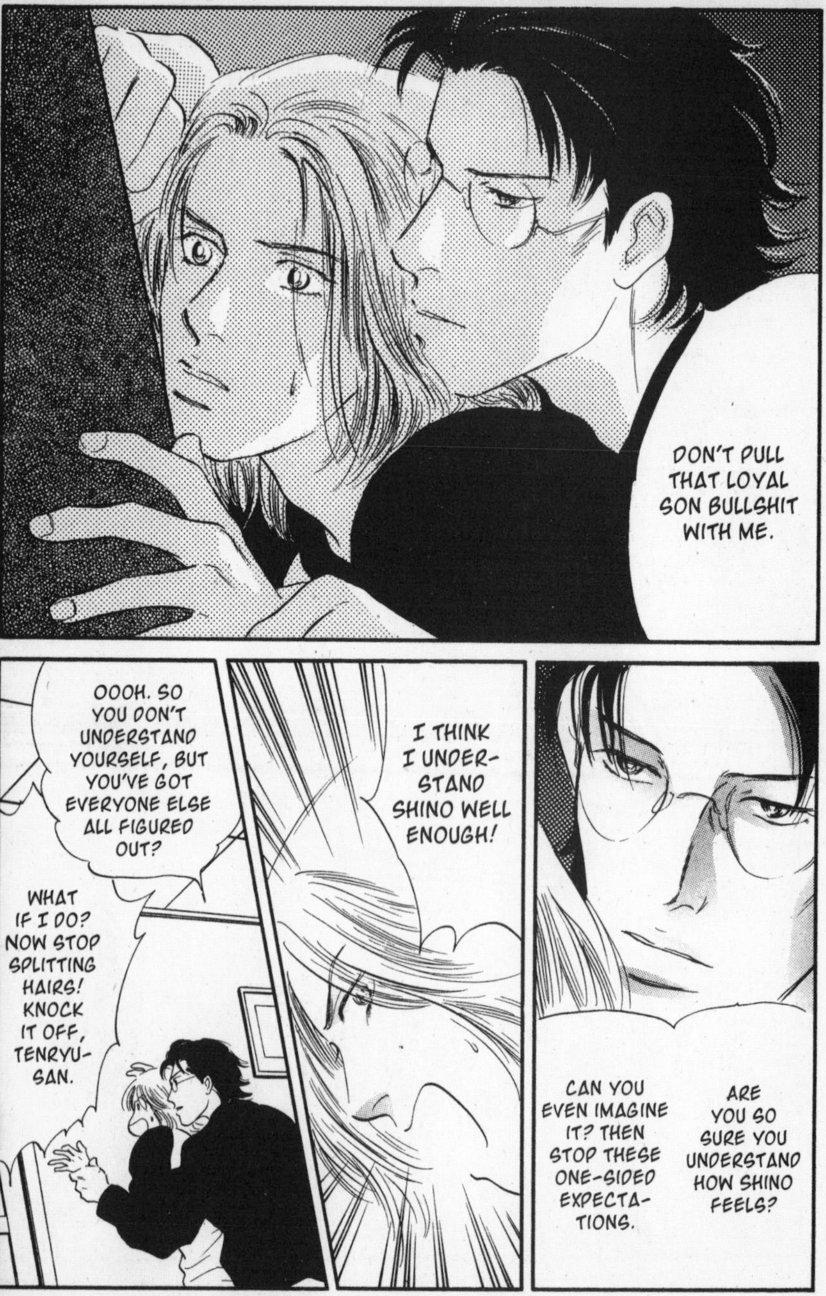
DON'T PULL THAT LOYAL SON BULLSHIT WITH ME.
ARE YOU SO SURE YOU UNDERSTAND HOW SHINO FEELS?
CAN YOU EVEN IMAGINE IT? THEN STOP THESE ONE-SIDED EXPECTA-TIONS.
I THINK I UNDER-STAND SHINO WELL ENOUGH!
OOOH. SO YOU DON'T UNDERSTAND YOURSELF, BUT YOU'VE GOT EVERYONE ELSE ALL FIGURED OUT?
WHAT IF I DO? NOW STOP SPLITTING HAIRS! KNOCK IT OFF, TENRYU-SAN.

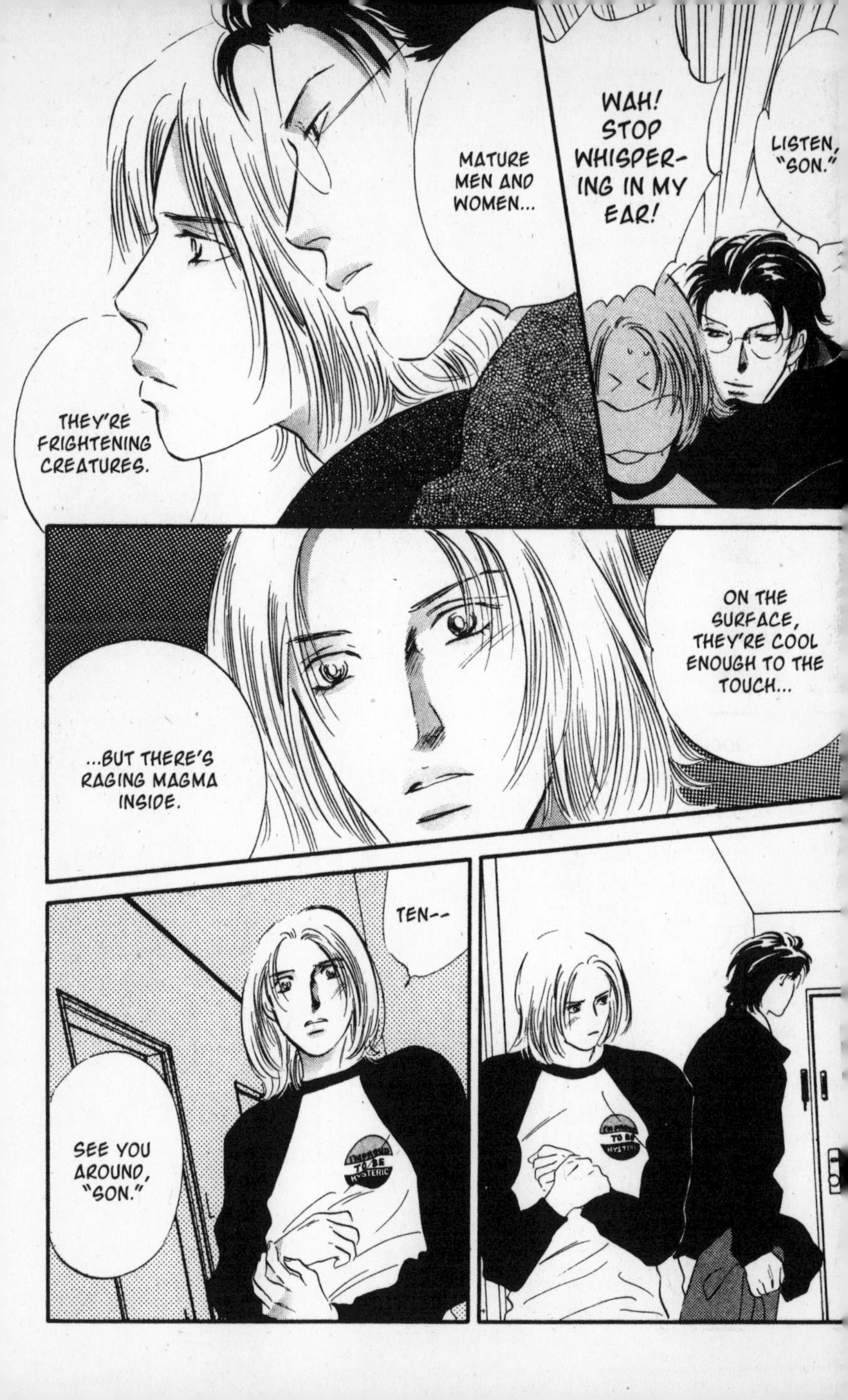
LISTEN, "SON."
WAH! STOP WHISPER-ING IN MY EAR!
MATURE MEN AND WOMEN...
THEY'RE FRIGHTENING CREATURES.
ON THE SURFACE, THEY'RE COOL ENOUGH TO THE TOUCH...
...BUT THERE'S RAGING MAGMA INSIDE.
TEN--
SEE YOU AROUND, "SON."

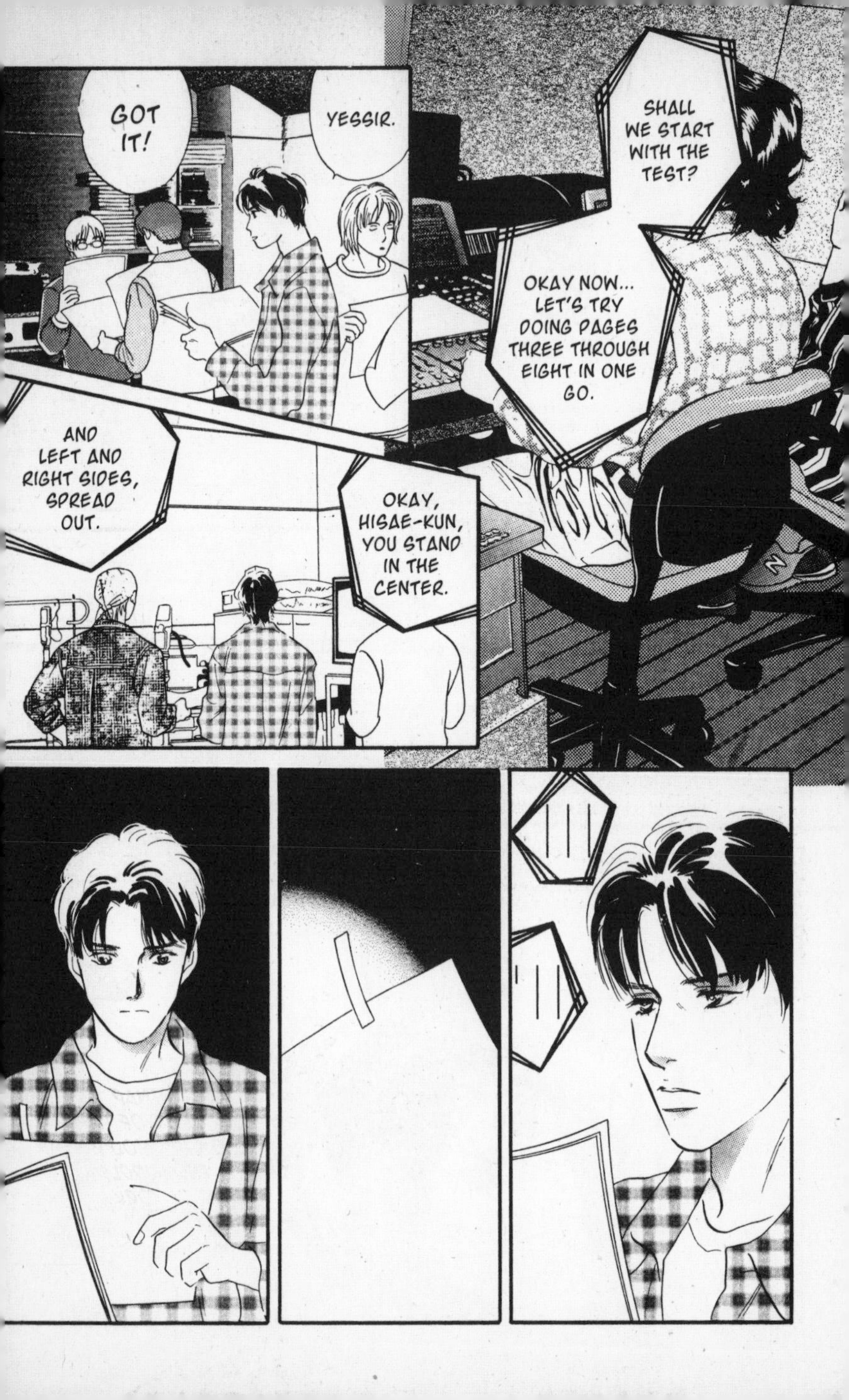
SHALL WE START WITH THE TEST?
OKAY NOW... LET'S TRY DOING PAGES THREE THROUGH EIGHT IN ONE GO.
YESSIR.
GOT IT!
OKAY, HISAE-KUN, YOU STAND IN THE CENTER.
AND LEFT AND RIGHT SIDES, SPREAD OUT.

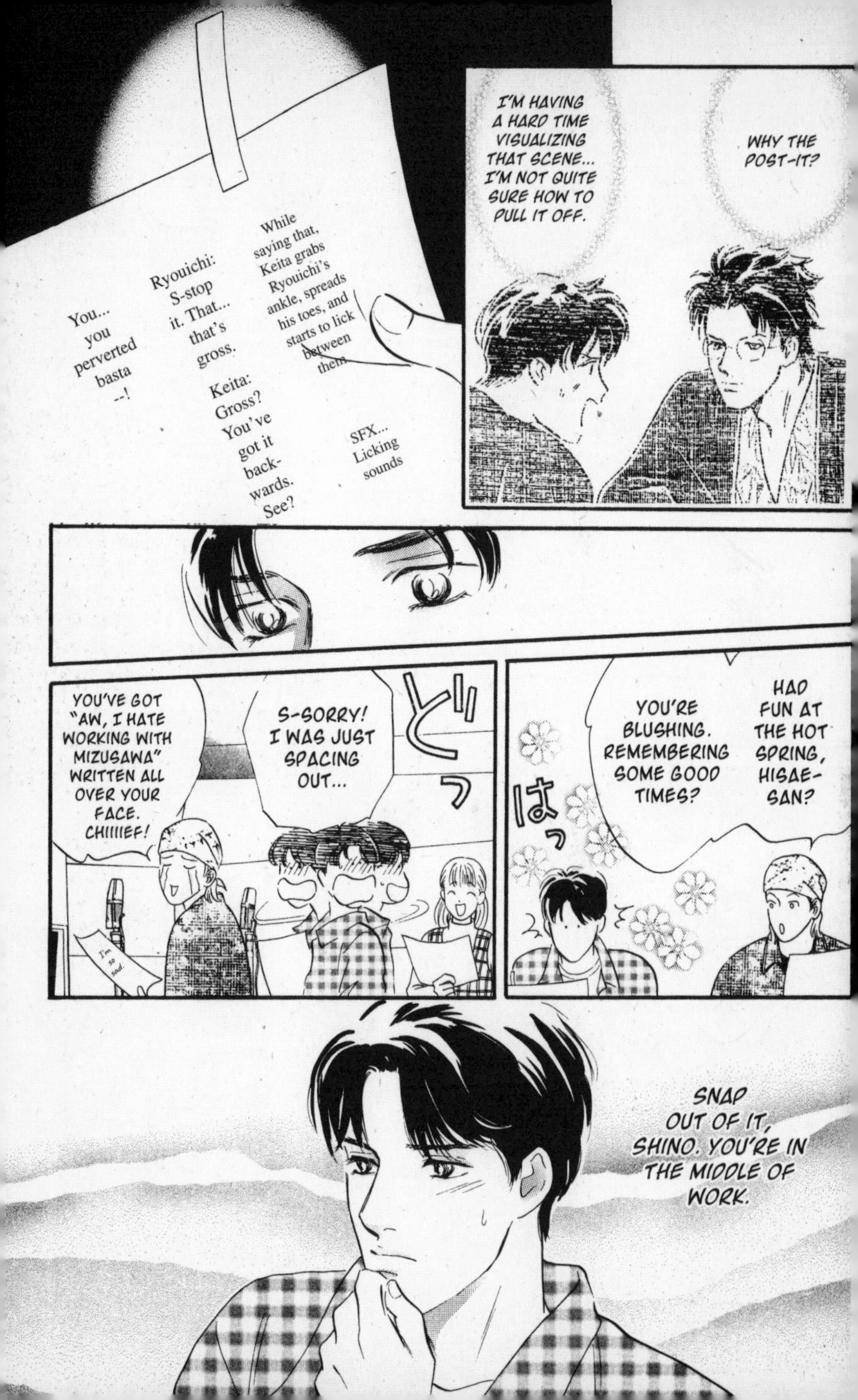
WHY THE POST-IT?
I'M HAVING A HARD TIME VISUALIZING THAT SCENE... I'M NOT QUITE SURE HOW TO PULL IT OFF.
While saying that, Keita grabs Ryouichi's ankle, spreads his toes, and starts to lick between them.
SFX... Licking sounds
Ryouichi: S-stop it. That... that's gross.
Keita: Gross? You've got it back-wards. See?
You... you perverted basta --!
HAD FUN AT THE HOT SPRING, HISAE-SAN?
YOU'RE BLUSHING. REMEMBERING SOME GOOD TIMES?
はっ
どッ
S-SORRY! I WAS JUST SPACING OUT...
YOU'VE GOT "AW, I HATE WORKING WITH MIZUSAWA" WRITTEN ALL OVER YOUR FACE. CHIIIIEF!
I'm so sad.
SNAP OUT OF IT, SHINO. YOU'RE IN THE MIDDLE OF WORK.

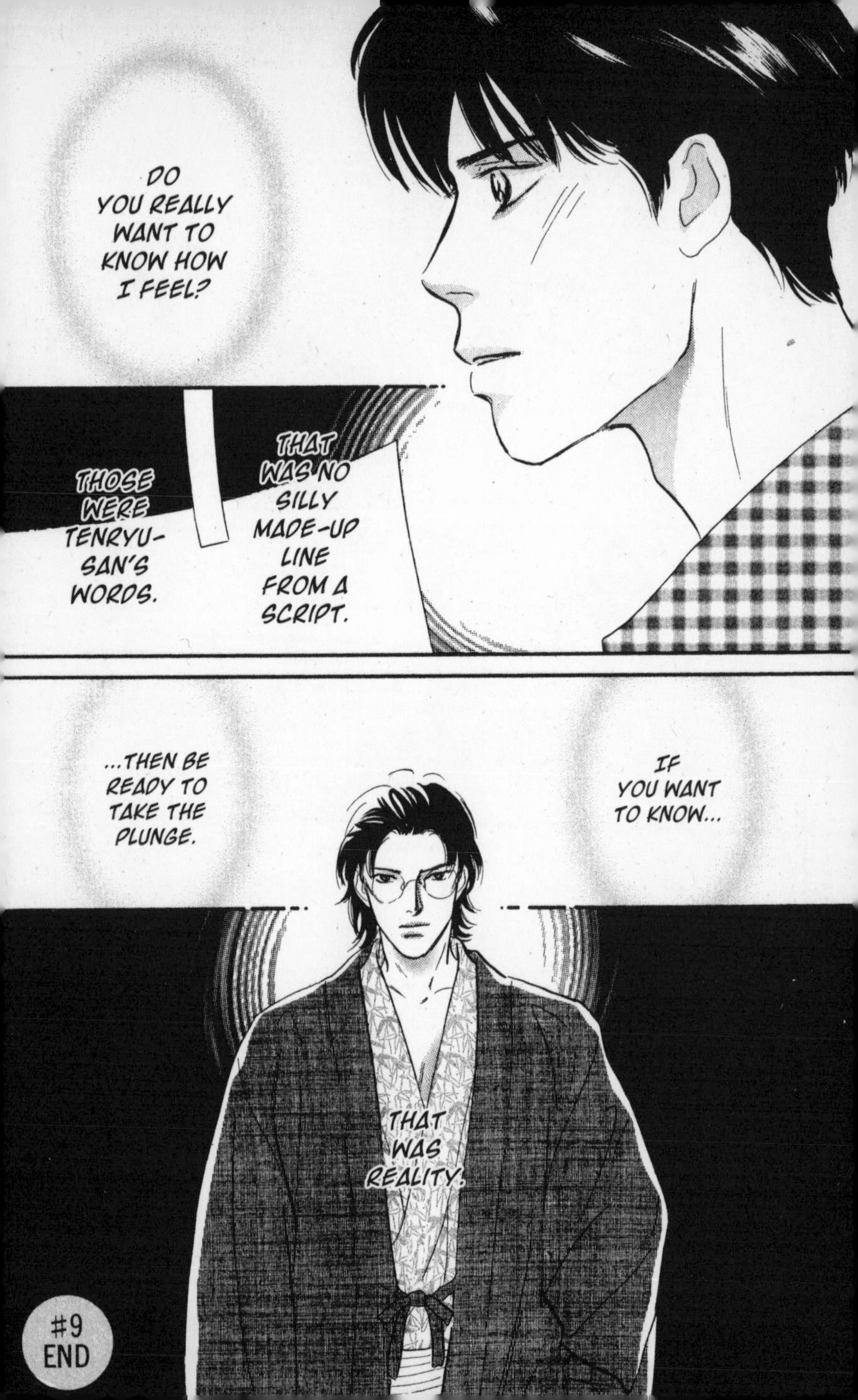
DO YOU REALLY WANT TO KNOW HOW I FEEL?
THAT WAS NO SILLY MADE-UP LINE FROM A SCRIPT.
THOSE WERE TENRYU-SAN'S WORDS.
IF YOU WANT TO KNOW...
...THEN BE READY TO TAKE THE PLUNGE.
THAT WAS REALITY.
#9 END

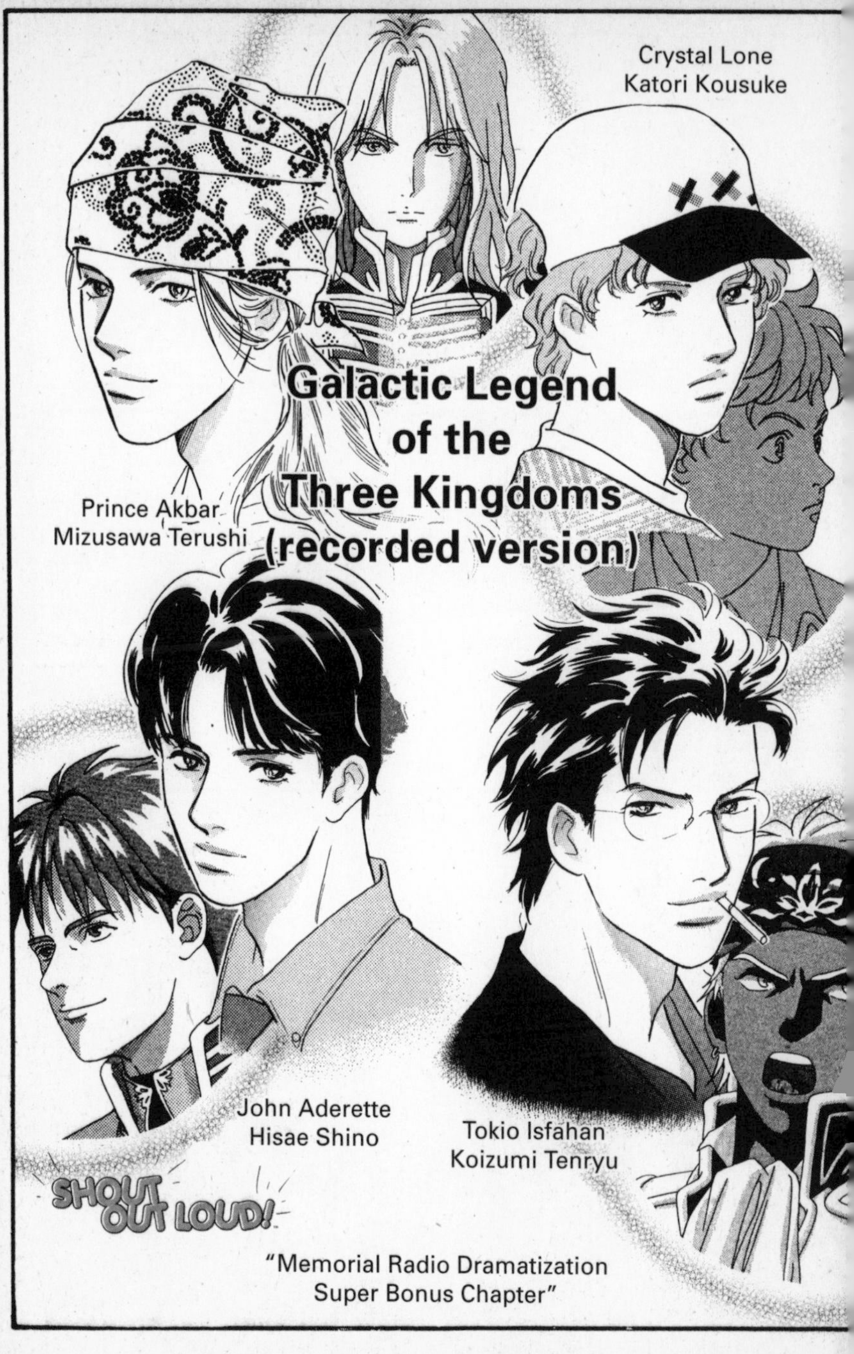
Crystal Lone
Katori Kousuke
Galactic Legend of the Three Kingdoms (recorded version)
Prince Akbar
Mizusawa Terushi
John Aderette
Hisae Shino
Tokio Isfahan
Koizumi Tenryu
SHOUT OUT LOUD!
"Memorial Radio Dramatization Super Bonus Chapter"

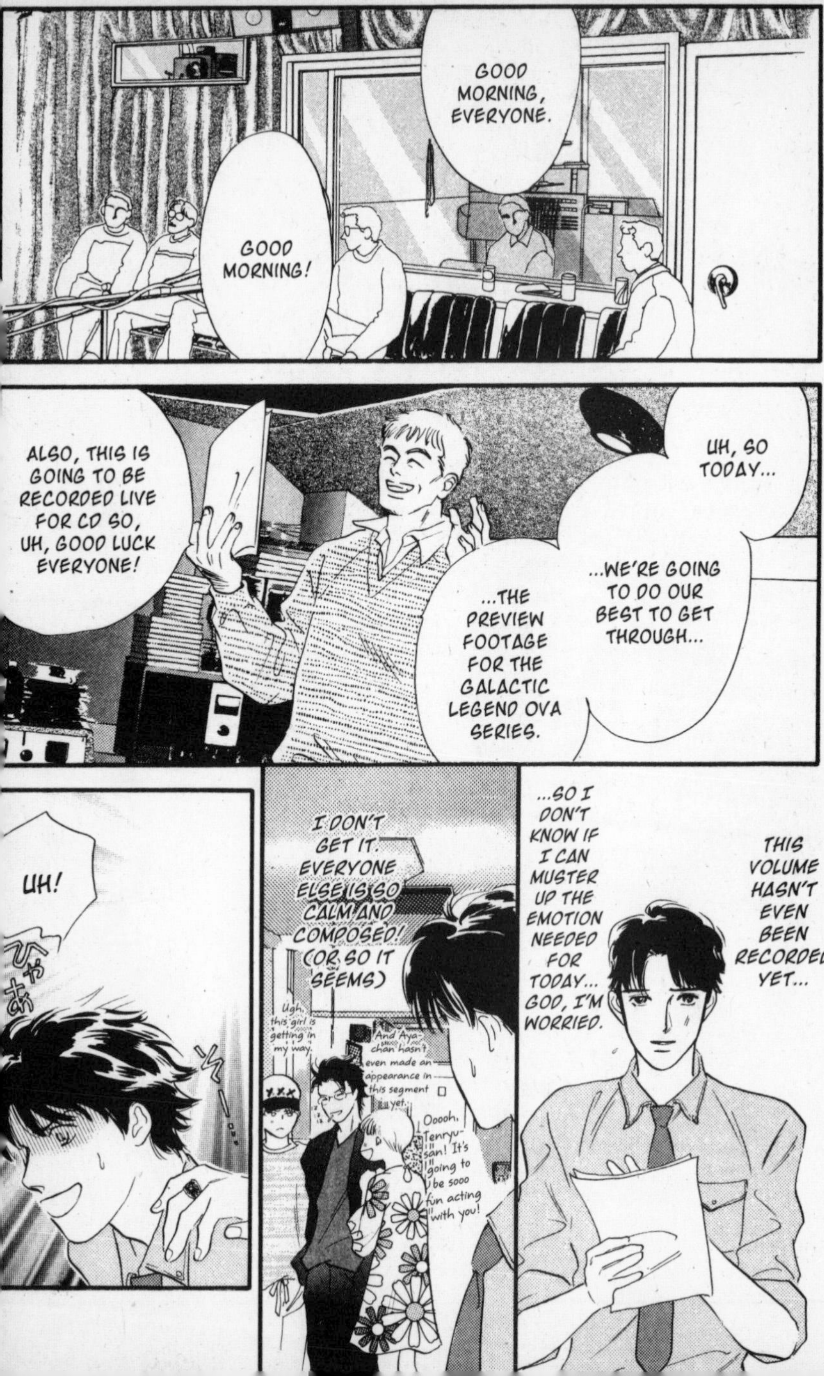
GOOD MORNING, EVERYONE.
GOOD MORNING!
UH, SO TODAY...
...WE'RE GOING TO DO OUR BEST TO GET THROUGH...
...THE PREVIEW FOOTAGE FOR THE GALACTIC LEGEND OVA SERIES.
ALSO, THIS IS GOING TO BE RECORDED LIVE FOR CD SO, UH, GOOD LUCK EVERYONE!
THIS VOLUME HASN'T EVEN BEEN RECORDED YET...
...SO I DON'T KNOW IF I CAN MUSTER UP THE EMOTION NEEDED FOR TODAY... GOD, I'M WORRIED.
I DON'T GET IT. EVERYONE ELSE IS SO CALM AND COMPOSED! (OR SO IT SEEMS)
And Aya-chan hasn't even made an appearance in this segment yet.
Ugh, this girl is getting in my way.
Ooooh, Tenryu-san! It's going to be sooo fun acting with you!
UH!

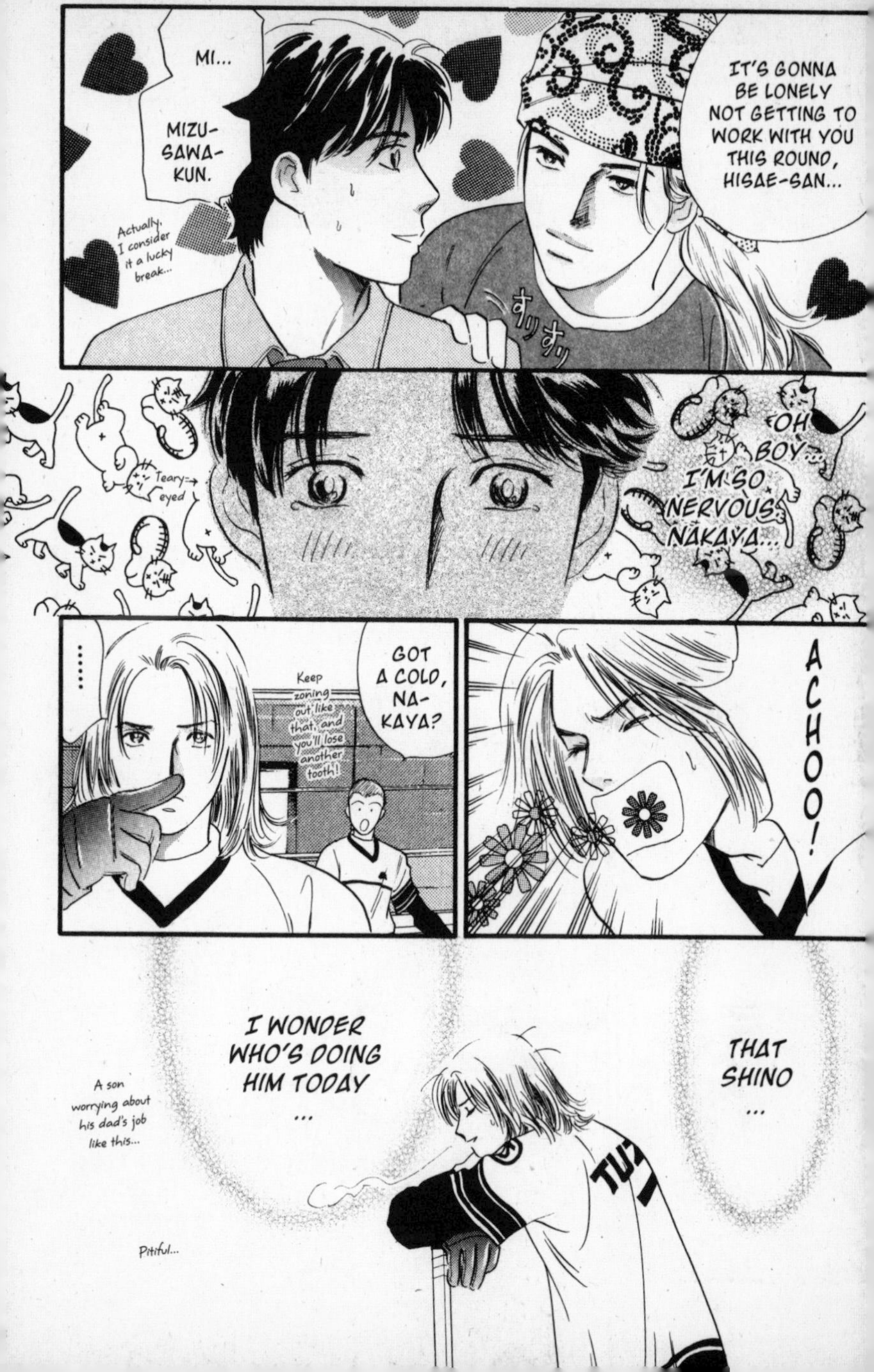
IT'S GONNA BE LONELY NOT GETTING TO WORK WITH YOU THIS ROUND, HISAE-SAN...
すりすり
MI...
MIZU-SAWA-KUN.
Actually, I consider it a lucky break...
OH BOY I'M SO NERVOUS NAKAYA...
Teary-eyed
ACHOO!
GOT A COLD, NA-KAYA?
Keep zoning out like that, and you'll lose another tooth!
......
THAT SHINO ...
I WONDER WHO'S DOING HIM TODAY ...
A son worrying about his dad's job like this...
Pitiful...

Was it the era that called to them?
Or did they draw the era to themselves?

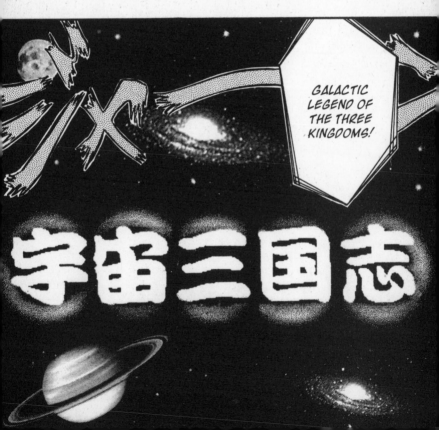

GALACTIC LEGEND OF THE THREE KINGDOMS!

宇宙三国志

The year is 156 in the Space calendar.
As the giant empire that ruled over the vast galaxy weakened, space was thrown into an age of upheaval.

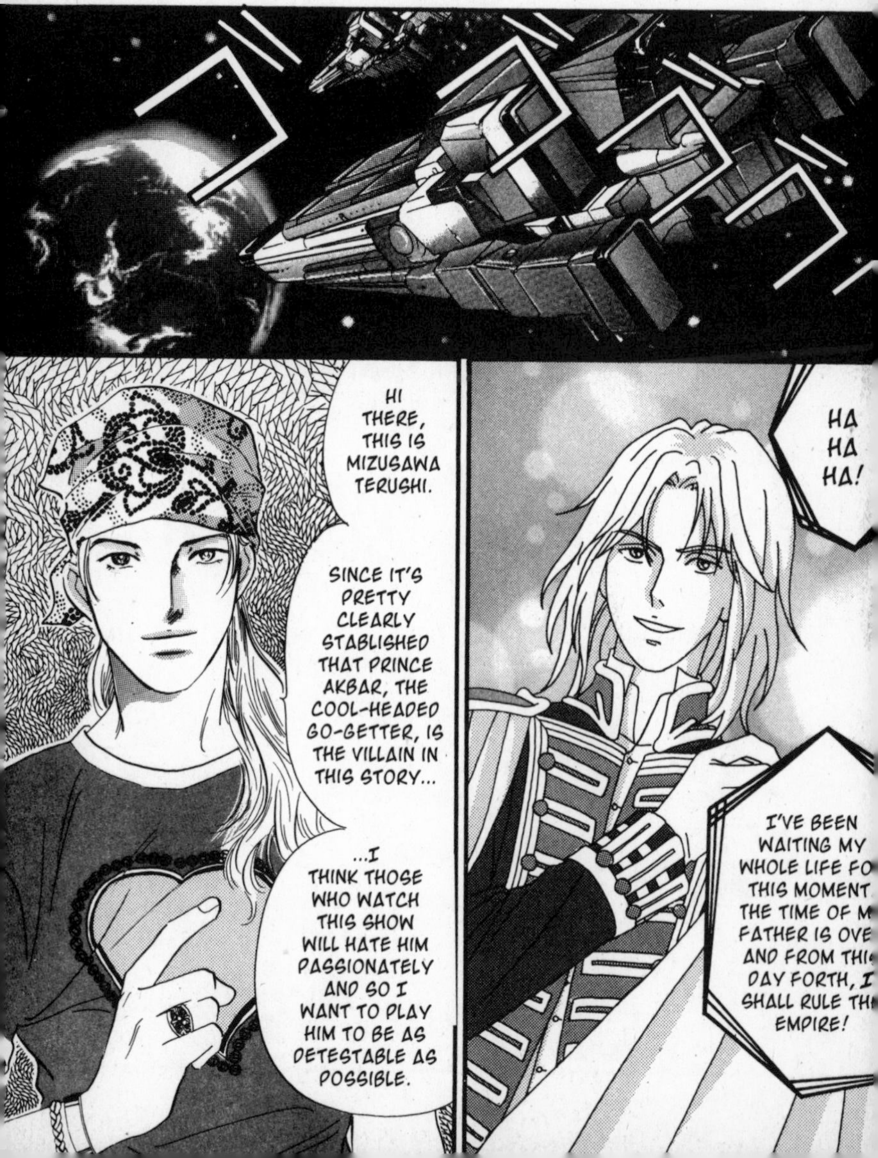
HA HA HA!
I'VE BEEN WAITING MY WHOLE LIFE FO THIS MOMENT THE TIME OF M FATHER IS OVE AND FROM THI DAY FORTH, I SHALL RULE TH EMPIRE!
HI THERE, THIS IS MIZUSAWA TERUSHI.
SINCE IT'S PRETTY CLEARLY STABLISHED THAT PRINCE AKBAR, THE COOL-HEADED GO-GETTER, IS THE VILLAIN IN THIS STORY...
...I THINK THOSE WHO WATCH THIS SHOW WILL HATE HIM PASSIONATELY AND SO I WANT TO PLAY HIM TO BE AS DETESTABLE AS POSSIBLE.

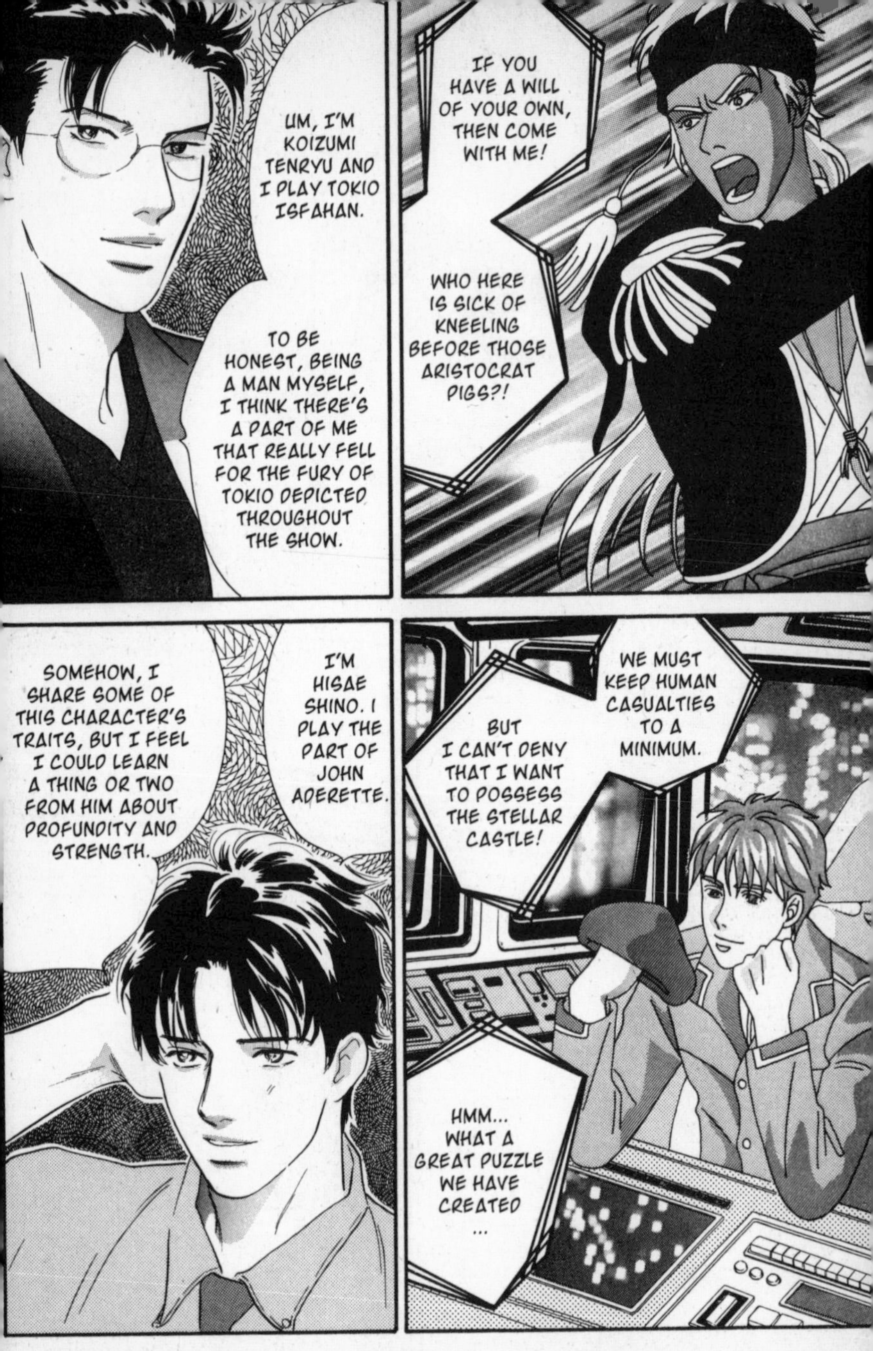
IF YOU HAVE A WILL OF YOUR OWN, THEN COME WITH ME!
WHO HERE IS SICK OF KNEELING BEFORE THOSE ARISTOCRAT PIGS?!
UM, I'M KOIZUMI TENRYU AND I PLAY TOKIO ISFAHAN.
TO BE HONEST, BEING A MAN MYSELF, I THINK THERE'S A PART OF ME THAT REALLY FELL FOR THE FURY OF TOKIO DEPICTED THROUGHOUT THE SHOW.
WE MUST KEEP HUMAN CASUALTIES TO A MINIMUM.
BUT I CAN'T DENY THAT I WANT TO POSSESS THE STELLAR CASTLE!
HMM... WHAT A GREAT PUZZLE WE HAVE CREATED ...
I'M HISAE SHINO. I PLAY THE PART OF JOHN ADERETTE.
SOMEHOW, I SHARE SOME OF THIS CHARACTER'S TRAITS, BUT I FEEL I COULD LEARN A THING OR TWO FROM HIM ABOUT PROFUNDITY AND STRENGTH.

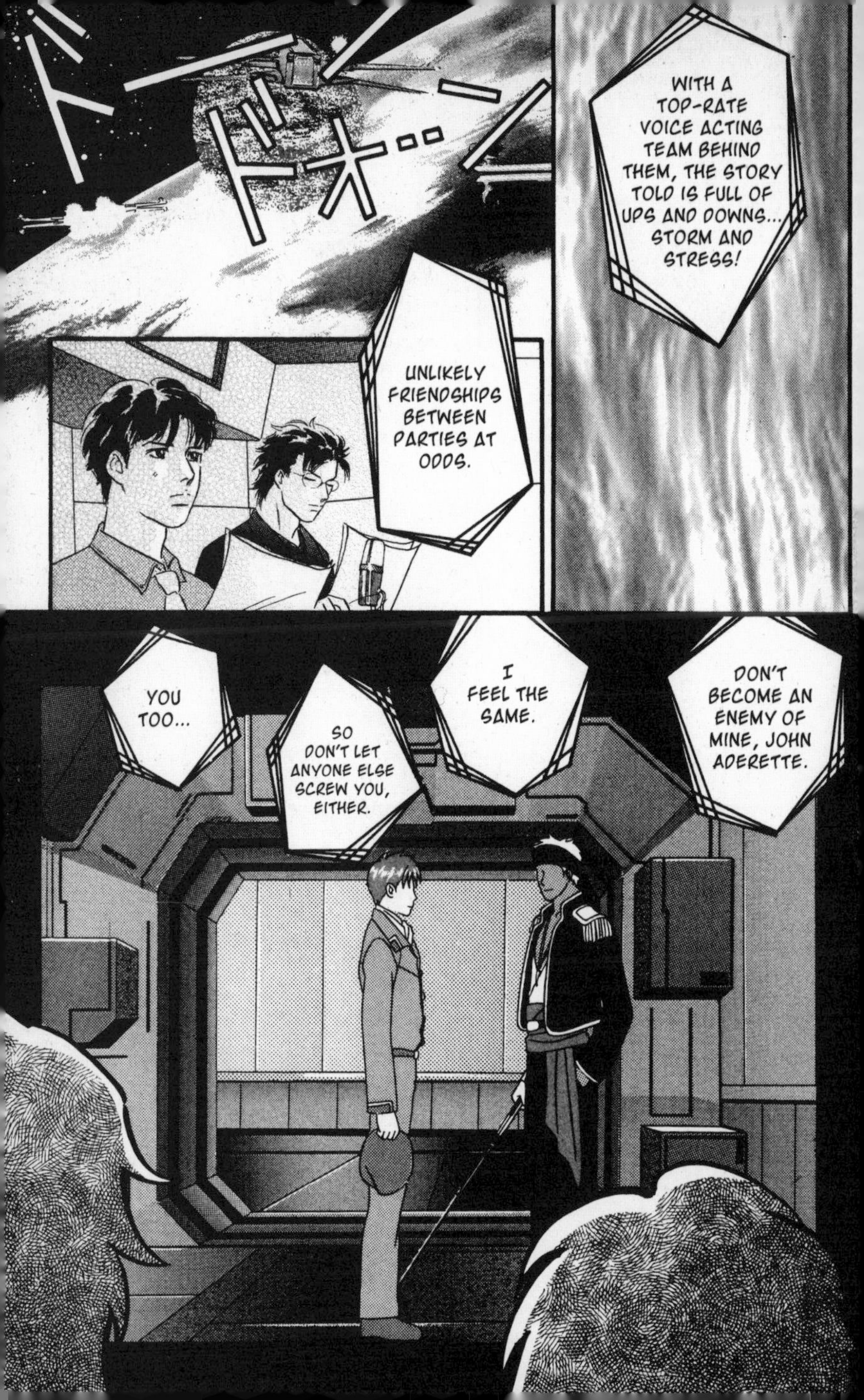
WITH A TOP-RATE VOICE ACTING TEAM BEHIND THEM, THE STORY TOLD IS FULL OF UPS AND DOWNS... STORM AND STRESS!
ドドオ‥
UNLIKELY FRIENDSHIPS BETWEEN PARTIES AT ODDS.
DON'T BECOME AN ENEMY OF MINE, JOHN ADERETTE.
I FEEL THE SAME.
SO DON'T LET ANYONE ELSE SCREW YOU, EITHER.
YOU TOO...

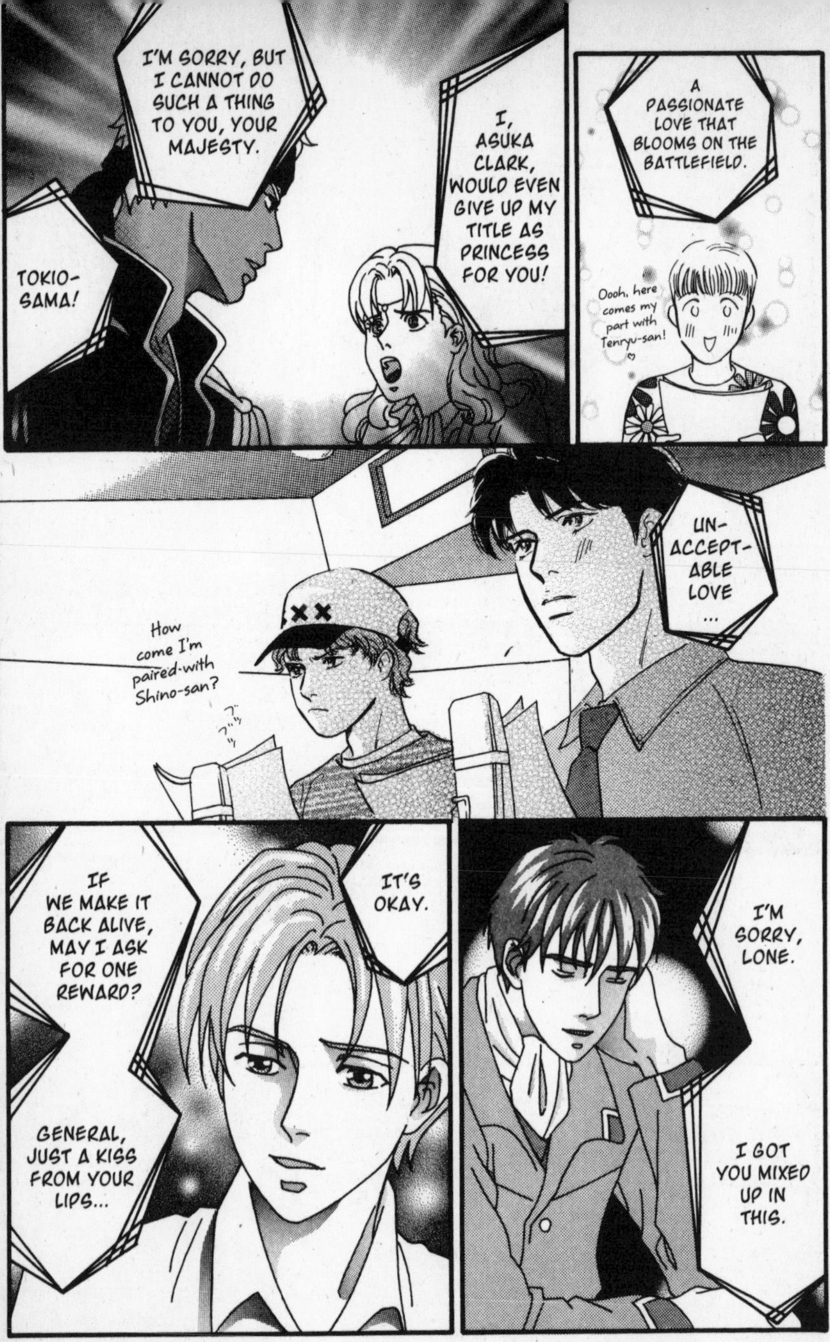
A PASSIONATE LOVE THAT BLOOMS ON THE BATTLEFIELD.
Oooh, here comes my part with Tenryu-san! ♡
I, ASUKA CLARK, WOULD EVEN GIVE UP MY TITLE AS PRINCESS FOR YOU!
I'M SORRY, BUT I CANNOT DO SUCH A THING TO YOU, YOUR MAJESTY.
TOKIO-SAMA!
UN-ACCEPT-ABLE LOVE ...
How come I'm paired with Shino-san?
I'M SORRY, LONE.
I GOT YOU MIXED UP IN THIS.
IT'S OKAY.
IF WE MAKE IT BACK ALIVE, MAY I ASK FOR ONE REWARD?
GENERAL, JUST A KISS FROM YOUR LIPS...

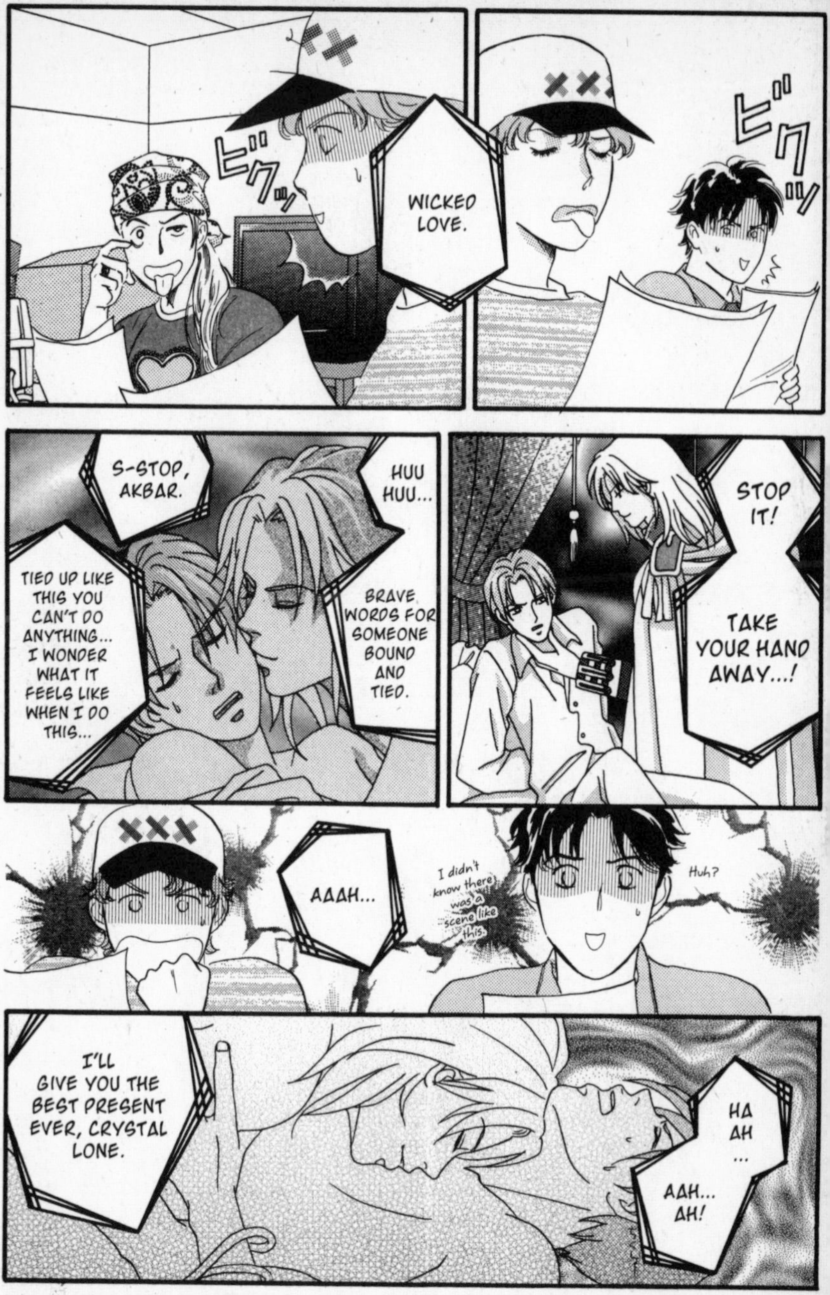
ビクッ
WICKED LOVE.
ビクッ
STOP IT!
TAKE YOUR HAND AWAY...!
HUU HUU...
S-STOP, AKBAR.
BRAVE WORDS FOR SOMEONE BOUND AND TIED.
TIED UP LIKE THIS YOU CAN'T DO ANYTHING... I WONDER WHAT IT FEELS LIKE WHEN I DO THIS...
Huh?
I didn't know there was a scene like this.
AAAH...
HA AH ...
AAH... AH!
I'LL GIVE YOU THE BEST PRESENT EVER, CRYSTAL LONE.

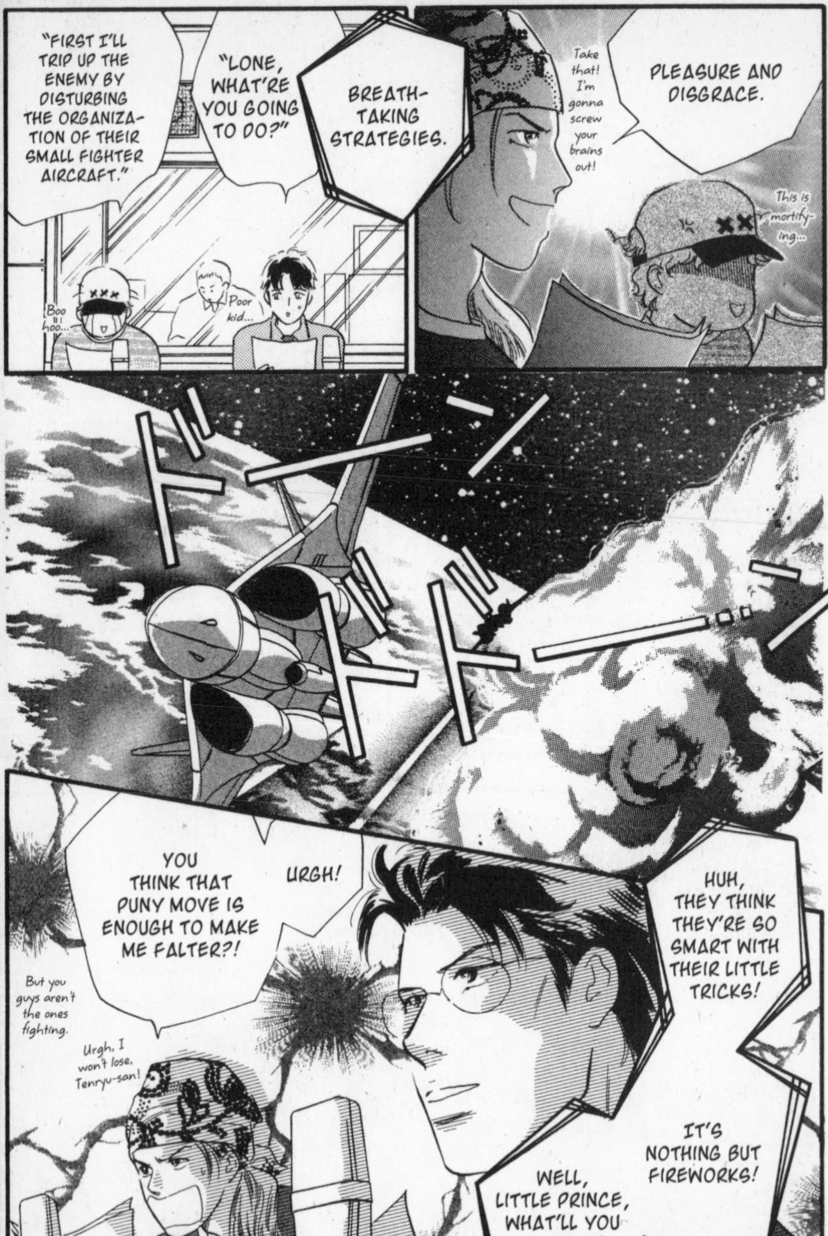
PLEASURE AND DISGRACE.
Take that! I'm gonna screw your brains out!
This is mortifying...
BREATH-TAKING STRATEGIES.
"LONE, WHAT'RE YOU GOING TO DO?"
"FIRST I'LL TRIP UP THE ENEMY BY DISTURBING THE ORGANIZATION OF THEIR SMALL FIGHTER AIRCRAFT."
Poor kid...
Boo hoo...
HUH, THEY THINK THEY'RE SO SMART WITH THEIR LITTLE TRICKS!
IT'S NOTHING BUT FIREWORKS!
WELL, LITTLE PRINCE, WHAT'LL YOU DO NOW?
URGH!
YOU THINK THAT PUNY MOVE IS ENOUGH TO MAKE ME FALTER?!
But you guys aren't the ones fighting.
Urgh, I won't lose, Tenryu-san!

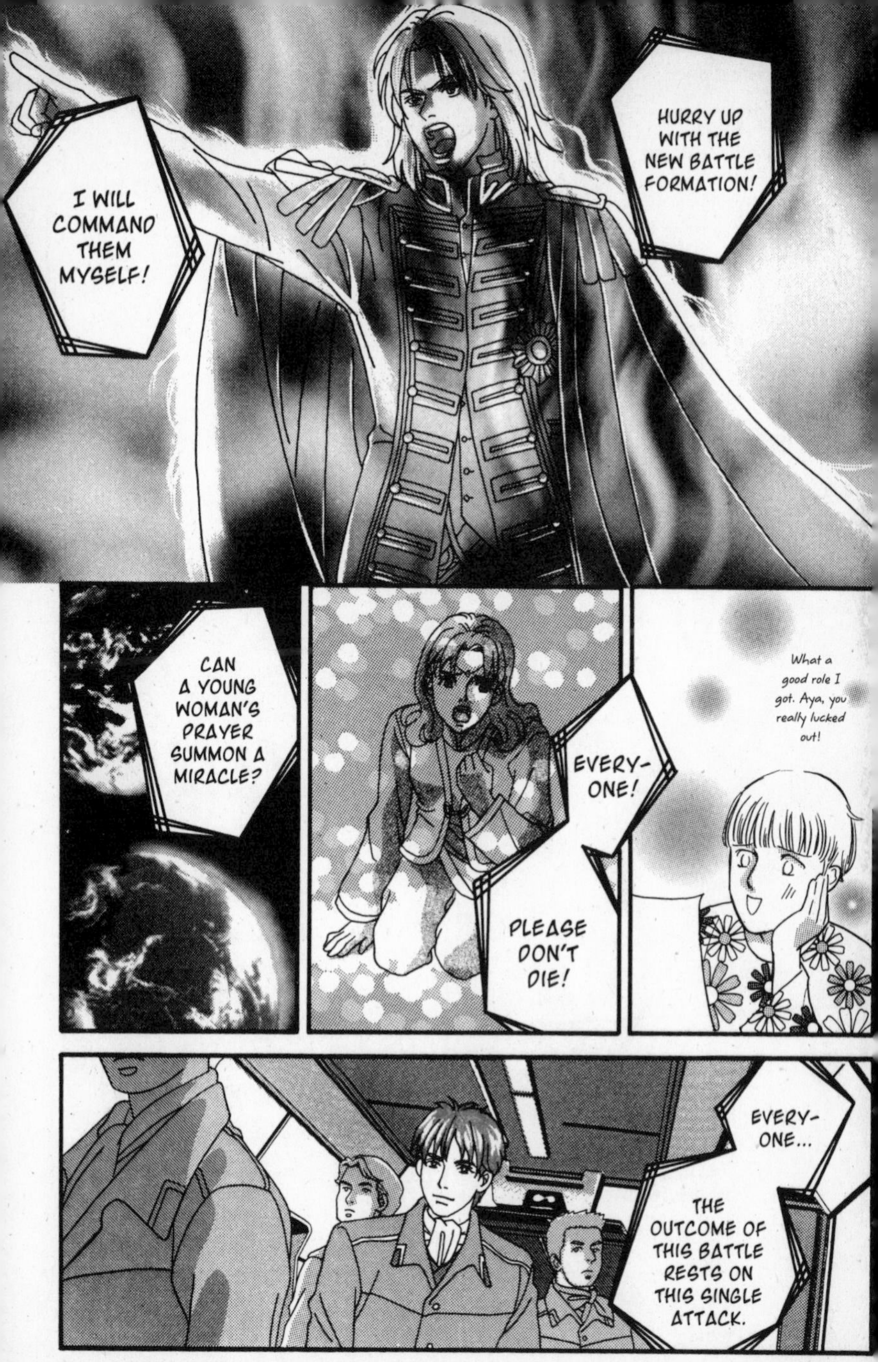
HURRY UP WITH THE NEW BATTLE FORMATION!
I WILL COMMAND THEM MYSELF!
What a good role I got. Aya, you really lucked out!
EVERY-ONE!
PLEASE DON'T DIE!
CAN A YOUNG WOMAN'S PRAYER SUMMON A MIRACLE?
EVERY-ONE...
THE OUTCOME OF THIS BATTLE RESTS ON THIS SINGLE ATTACK.

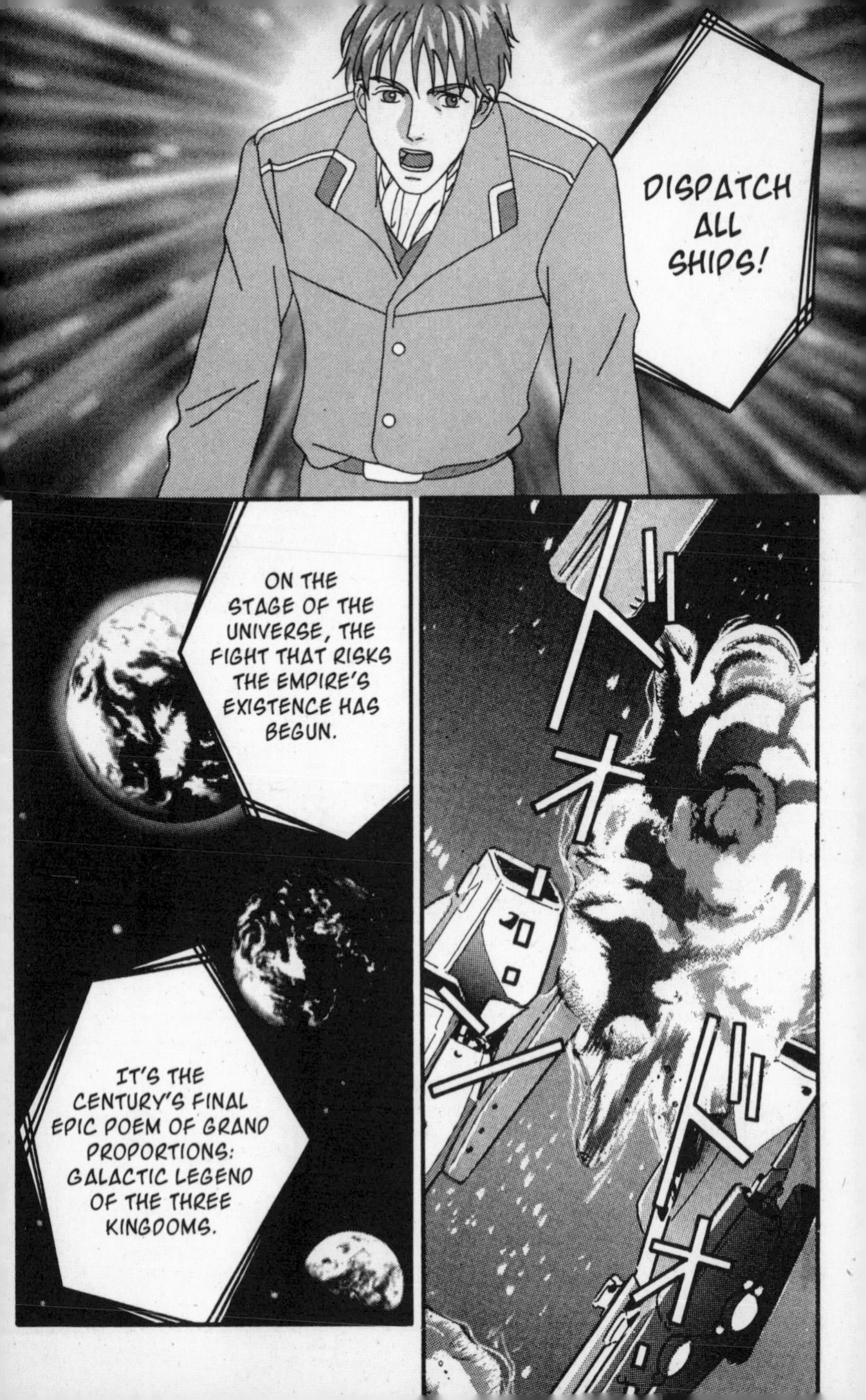
DISPATCH ALL SHIPS!
ON THE STAGE OF THE UNIVERSE, THE FIGHT THAT RISKS THE EMPIRE'S EXISTENCE HAS BEGUN.
IT'S THE CENTURY'S FINAL EPIC POEM OF GRAND PROPORTIONS: GALACTIC LEGEND OF THE THREE KINGDOMS.

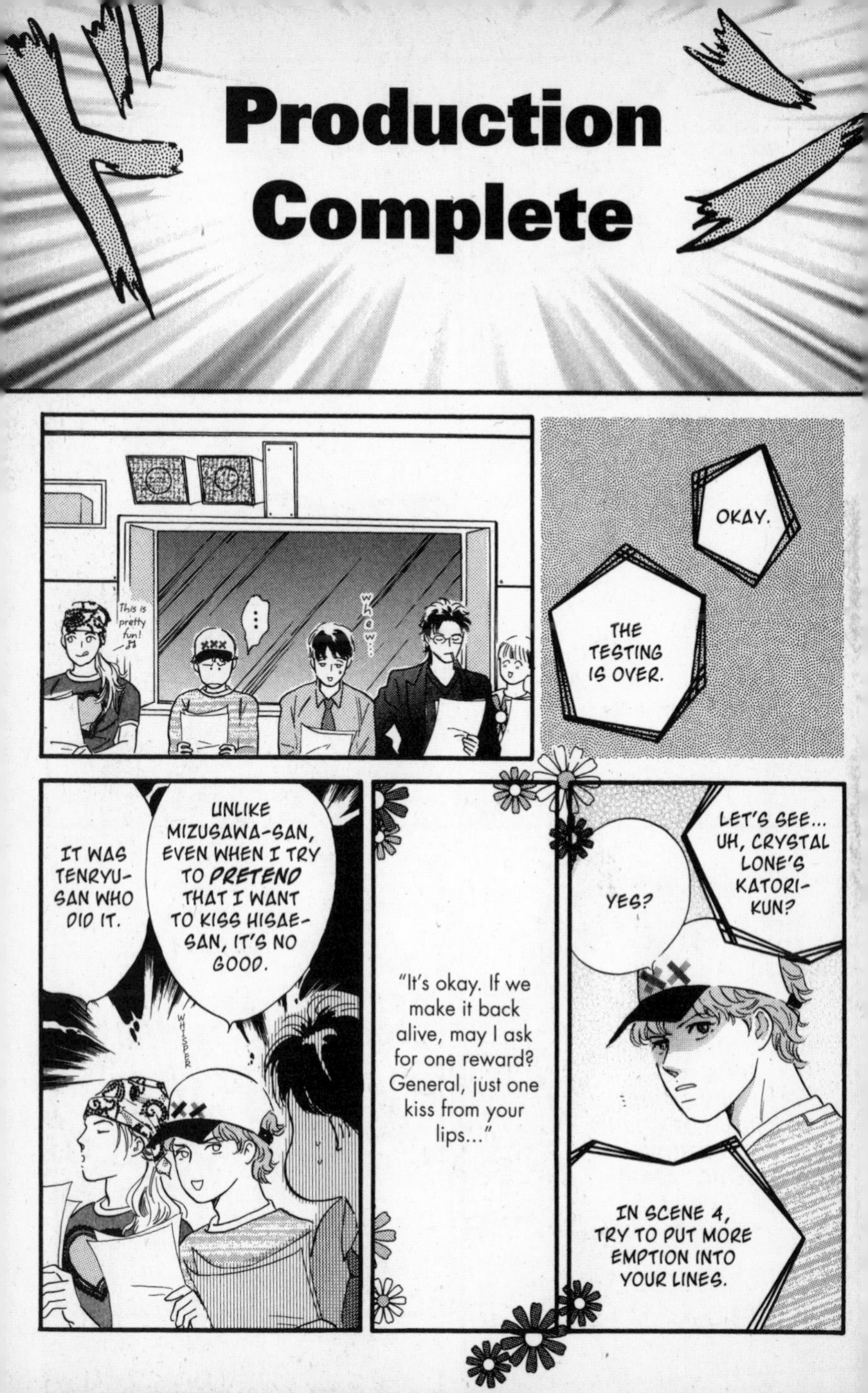

Production Complete
OKAY.
THE TESTING IS OVER.
This is pretty fun! ♫
...
whew...
LET'S SEE... UH, CRYSTAL LONE'S KATORI-KUN?
YES?
IN SCENE 4, TRY TO PUT MORE EMPTION INTO YOUR LINES.
"It's okay. If we make it back alive, may I ask for one reward? General, just one kiss from your lips..."
UNLIKE MIZUSAWA-SAN, EVEN WHEN I TRY TO PRETEND THAT I WANT TO KISS HISAE-SAN, IT'S NO GOOD.
IT WAS TENRYU-SAN WHO DID IT.
WHISPER

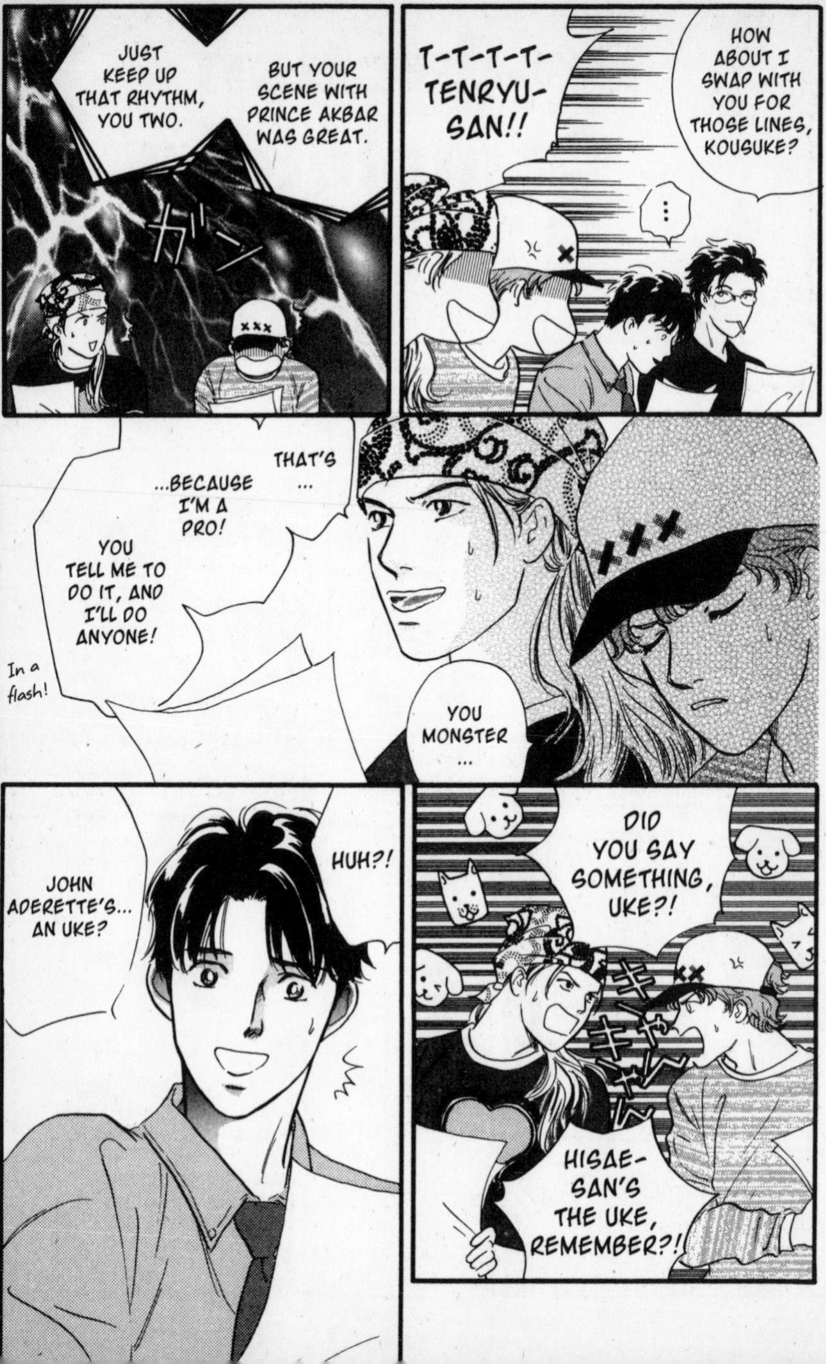
HOW ABOUT I SWAP WITH YOU FOR THOSE LINES, KOUSUKE?
T-T-T-T-TENRYU-SAN!!
...
BUT YOUR SCENE WITH PRINCE AKBAR WAS GREAT.
JUST KEEP UP THAT RHYTHM, YOU TWO.
ガーン
THAT'S ...
...BECAUSE I'M A PRO!
YOU TELL ME TO DO IT, AND I'LL DO ANYONE!
YOU MONSTER ...
In a flash!
DID YOU SAY SOMETHING, UKE?!
HISAE-SAN'S THE UKE, REMEMBER?!
HUH?!
JOHN ADERETTE'S... AN UKE?

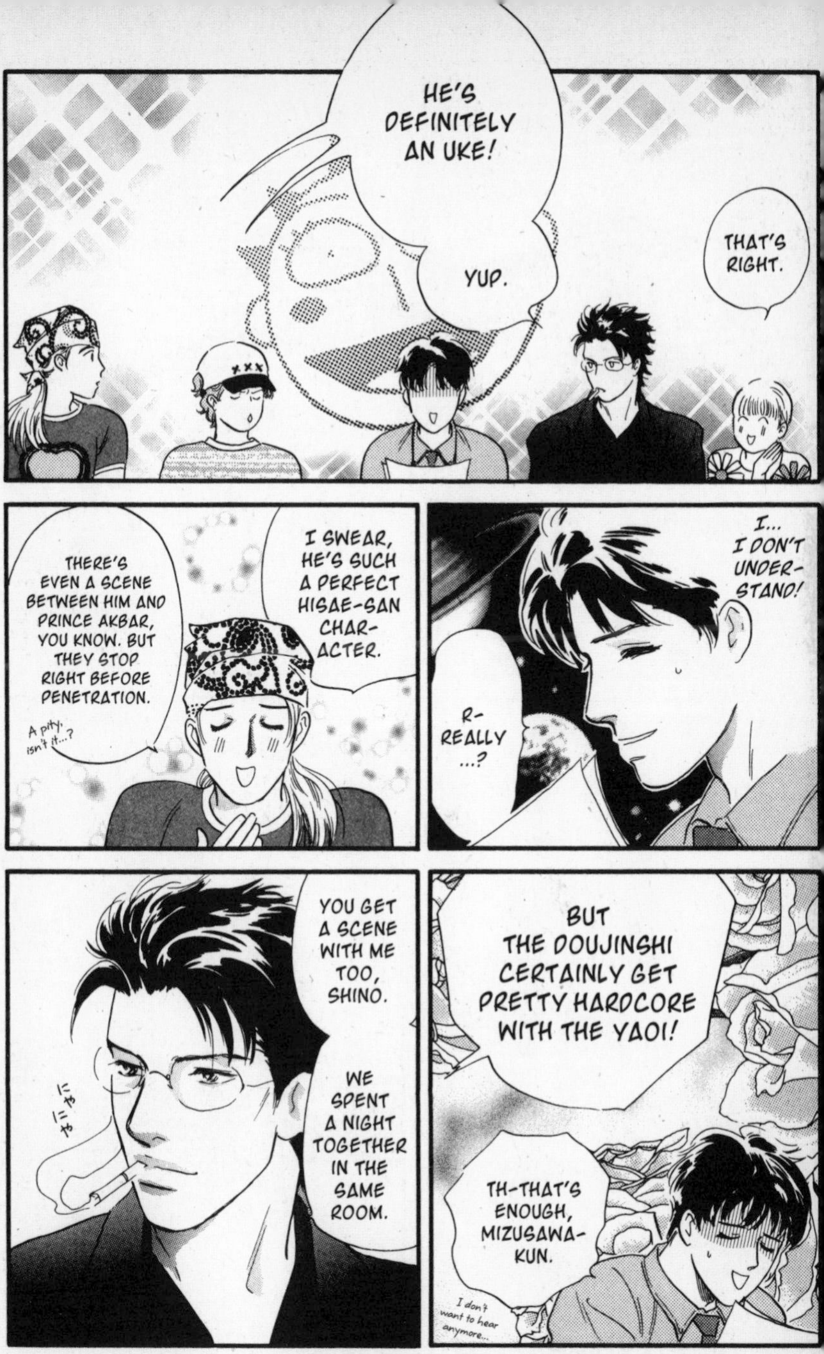
HE'S DEFINITELY AN UKE!
THAT'S RIGHT.
YUP.
I... I DON'T UNDER-STAND!
R-REALLY ...?
I SWEAR, HE'S SUCH A PERFECT HISAE-SAN CHAR-ACTER.
THERE'S EVEN A SCENE BETWEEN HIM AND PRINCE AKBAR, YOU KNOW. BUT THEY STOP RIGHT BEFORE PENETRATION.
A pity, isn't it...?
BUT THE DOUJINSHI CERTAINLY GET PRETTY HARDCORE WITH THE YAOI!
TH-THAT'S ENOUGH, MIZUSAWA-KUN.
I don't want to hear anymore...
YOU GET A SCENE WITH ME TOO, SHINO.
WE SPENT A NIGHT TOGETHER IN THE SAME ROOM.
にやにや

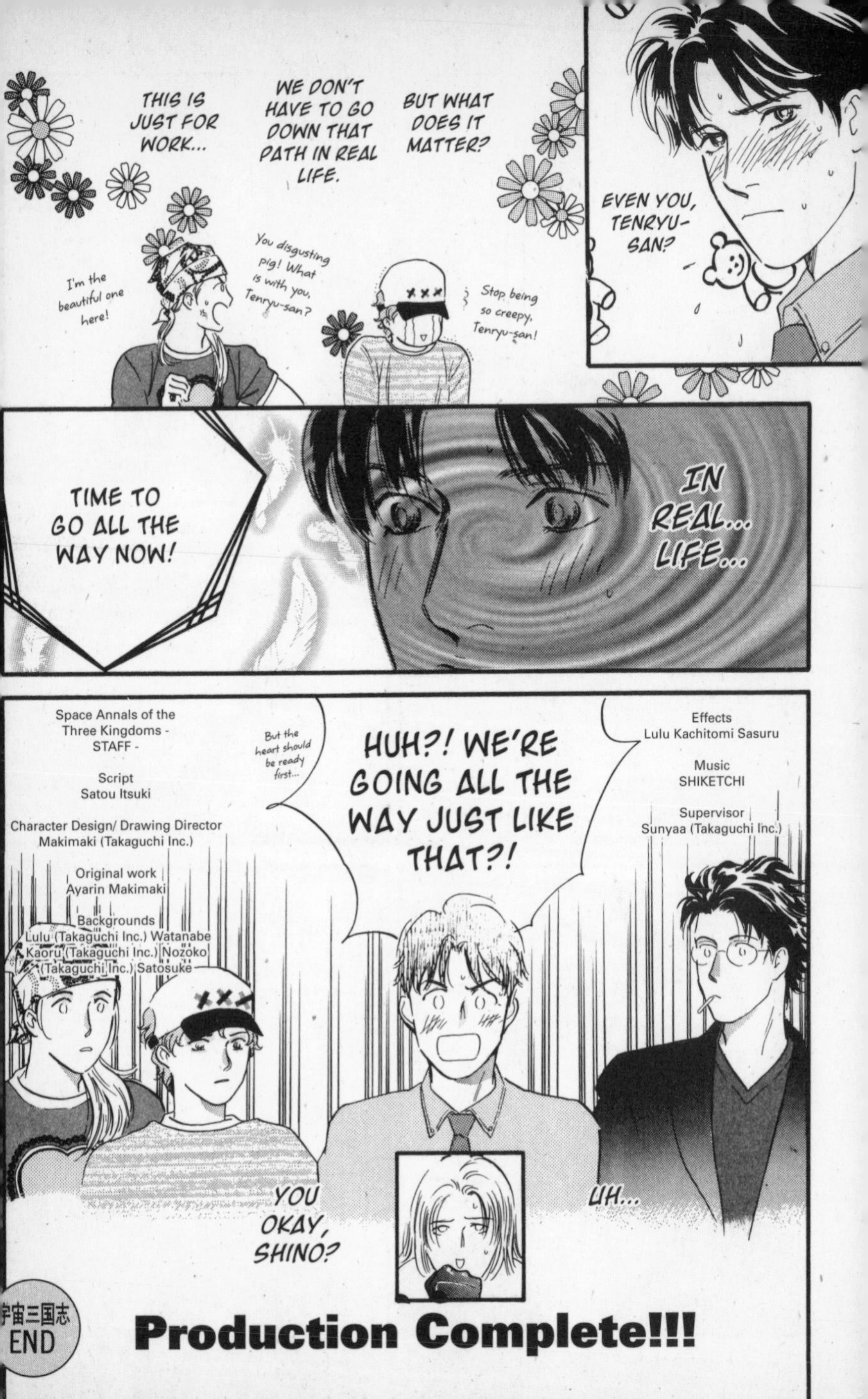
EVEN YOU, TENRYU-SAN?
BUT WHAT DOES IT MATTER?
WE DON'T HAVE TO GO DOWN THAT PATH IN REAL LIFE.
THIS IS JUST FOR WORK...
Stop being so creepy, Tenryu-san!
You disgusting pig! What is with you, Tenryu-san?
I'm the beautiful one here!
IN REAL... LIFE...
TIME TO GO ALL THE WAY NOW!
Space Annals of the Three Kingdoms - STAFF -
Script
Satou Itsuki
Character Design/ Drawing Director
Makimaki (Takaguchi Inc.)
Original work
Ayarin Makimaki
Backgrounds
Lulu (Takaguchi Inc.) Watanabe Kaoru (Takaguchi Inc.) Nozoko (Takaguchi Inc.) Satosuke
Effects
Lulu Kachitomi Sasuru
Music
SHIKETCHI
Supervisor
Sunyaa (Takaguchi Inc.)
HUH?! WE'RE GOING ALL THE WAY JUST LIKE THAT?!
But the heart should be ready first...
UH...
YOU OKAY, SHINO?
宇宙三国志
END
Production Complete!!!

MIZUSAWA-KUN...2

BY NOZOKO (DIRECTOR OF COMPLETELY UNRECOGNIZABLE DRAWINGS)

AFTER-WORD

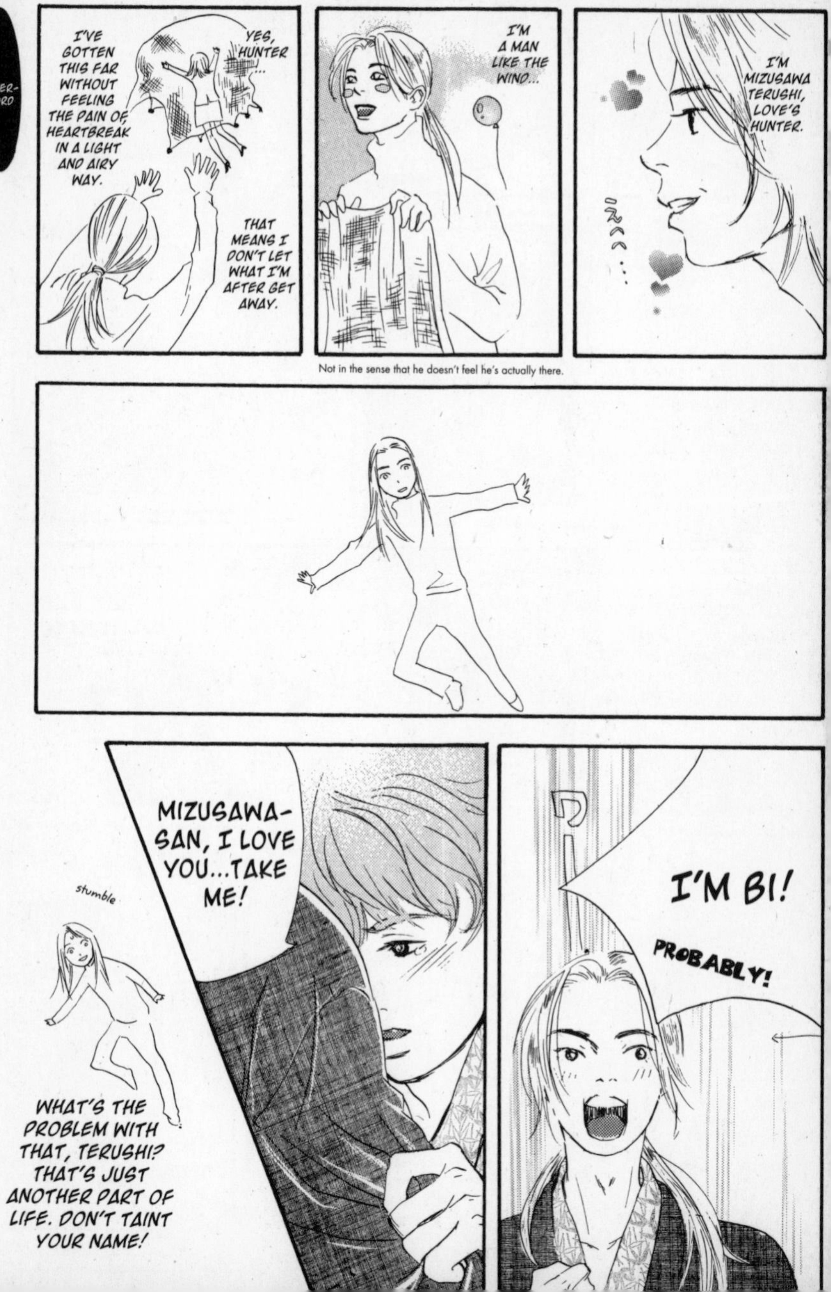
I'M MIZUSAWA TERUSHI, LOVE'S HUNTER.
えへへ...
I'M A MAN LIKE THE WIND...
YES, HUNTER...
I'VE GOTTEN THIS FAR WITHOUT FEELING THE PAIN OF HEARTBREAK IN A LIGHT AND AIRY WAY.
THAT MEANS I DON'T LET WHAT I'M AFTER GET AWAY.
Not in the sense that he doesn't feel he's actually there.
ワー
I'M BI!
PROBABLY!
MIZUSAWA-SAN, I LOVE YOU...TAKE ME!
stumble
WHAT'S THE PROBLEM WITH THAT, TERUSHI? THAT'S JUST ANOTHER PART OF LIFE. DON'T TAINT YOUR NAME!

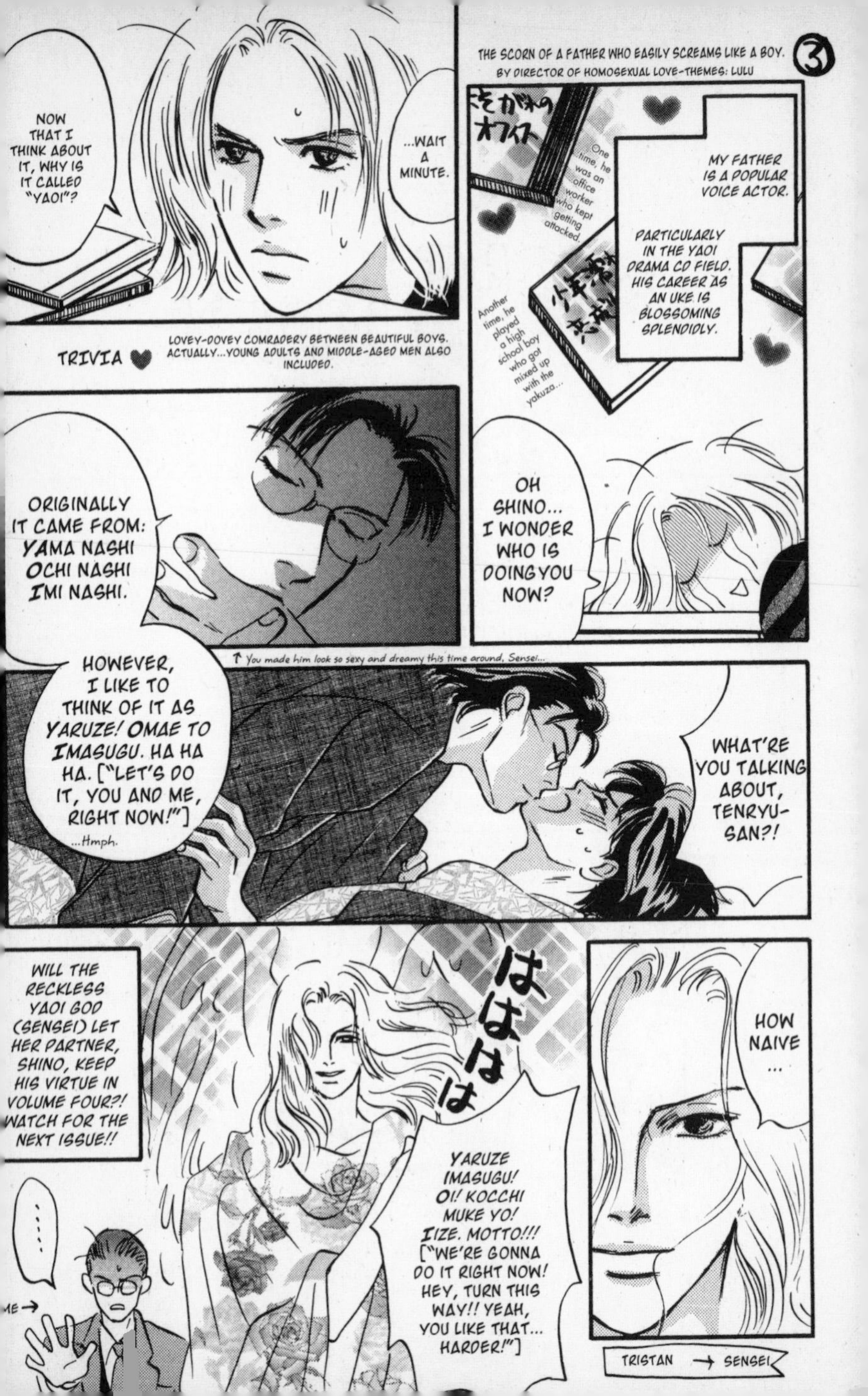

THE SCORN OF A FATHER WHO EASILY SCREAMS LIKE A BOY.
BY DIRECTOR OF HOMOSEXUAL LOVE-THEMES: LULU
3
そがれのオフィス
One time, he was an office worker who kept getting attacked.
MY FATHER IS A POPULAR VOICE ACTOR.
PARTICULARLY IN THE YAOI DRAMA CD FIELD. HIS CAREER AS AN UKE IS BLOSSOMING SPLENDIDLY.
Another time, he played a high school boy who got mixed up with the yakuza...
...WAIT A MINUTE.
NOW THAT I THINK ABOUT IT, WHY IS IT CALLED "YAOI"?
TRIVIA
LOVEY-DOVEY COMRADERY BETWEEN BEAUTIFUL BOYS. ACTUALLY...YOUNG ADULTS AND MIDDLE-AGED MEN ALSO INCLUDED.
OH SHINO... I WONDER WHO IS DOING YOU NOW?
ORIGINALLY IT CAME FROM: YAMA NASHI OCHI NASHI IMI NASHI.
↑ You made him look so sexy and dreamy this time around, Sensei...
WHAT'RE YOU TALKING ABOUT, TENRYU-SAN?!
HOWEVER, I LIKE TO THINK OF IT AS YARUZE! OMAE TO IMASUGU. HA HA HA. ["LET'S DO IT, YOU AND ME, RIGHT NOW!"]
...Hmph.
HOW NAIVE ...
TRISTAN → SENSEI
ははははは
YARUZE IMASUGU! OI! KOCCHI MUKE YO! IIZE. MOTTO!!! ["WE'RE GONNA DO IT RIGHT NOW! HEY, TURN THIS WAY!! YEAH, YOU LIKE THAT... HARDER!"]
WILL THE RECKLESS YAOI GOD (SENSEI) LET HER PARTNER, SHINO, KEEP HIS VIRTUE IN VOLUME FOUR?! WATCH FOR THE NEXT ISSUE!!
......
ME →

NEXT TIME IN

Grandmother Tsuzaka drops in on Shino and Nakaya to present them with a portfolio containing photos of a potential wife for Shino! She's set on hooking Shino up with a kind widow named Misato, but Nakaya is totally against the idea. He finally found his father, and he's not ready to give him up yet, so Shino faces the prospect growing old alone, or hiding his love for one person and satisfying the wishes of another. And Fuse has a surprise in store for Nakaya as well. When the unthinkable happens, Nakaya is torn between remaining a child in Shino's care, and beginning to become an adult and move forward.

IKENAI PERSONALITIES//COUNT. 1:1 PAGE "FERVOR! THE TALE OF A VOICE-ACTOR" ANECDOTE

WRONG PERSONALITIES

"So about Mizusawa-san..."

Met suddenly by a voice behind him, Midorikawa spun around in surprise.

"You think he really kissed Hisae-san or not?"

Always teased by Mizusawa for being his junior in the workplace, the speaker was supposed to be moping in the studio corner but instead had popped up beside the young voice actor without warning.

"Don't ask ME!"

His words came out harsh but how could he help it? *If you're standing right behind me, then say so, godammit!* Met by such a cold-stone stare from Kouichi's face, Shojumaru's already-quickened heart rate from the blunder was provoked even further.

"But I wanna know! I wanna knooow!"

Shojumaru was obviously completely unaware of Kouichi's bad mood as he balled up his fists in protest.

"Go ask him yourself. Why would I know about their little fling?"

He had just gotten dragged into a stupid conversation with Mizusawa earlier and recalling the 30 year-old man with the extremely charming voice and figure, Midorikawa sighed to himself. Having heard enough from his lascivious friends who had spread the rumor that conformed so well to his acting roles, he longed to close his eyes and never hear another word about the whole matter.

"But I don't like that guy. Come on, Senpai...I thought you two were buddies. Although I can't imagine how..."

For some reason, the young man was getting very riled up and finally fed up with his face, drawing ever closer, Midorikawa hit him over the head with the script he held tightly in his hand before his brain even calculated it.

"Ow!"

"Well, back off!"

The teary puppy-dog eyes looking up at him only spurred him on and with all emotions turned off, he repeatedly wopped the man on the head.

"Ow! Ow!!"

Usually, no one but himself was in charge of remonstrating the younger man, but this time he took the role of Mizusawa.

"Stop it...ow! Why're you hitting me?!" Shojumaru yelled out as he clutched at his head. *He just finished standing up for me, so how come he's the one smacking me around now?* His final outcry left Midorikawa speechless for a second and soon his cheeks were burning red with shame.

"Hmmmm. Now this is suspcious. Sticking up for him like this."

Those teasing words from Mizusawa resurfaced in his mind.

"You just can't leave him alone, the way you're always looking after him. He'll be moved by it if you're not careful. What can I say? There are plenty of instances. No matter. Watch out that he doesn't dominate you."

That jerk...he's been listening in on our conversations.

"W-who are you to decide who I'm buddies with? And anyway, why're you so interested in the guy when you don't even like him? Or is it Hisae-san you're after?!"

"It's not that at all!"

Usually quick to falter, the man retorted with unusually strong conviction.

"I just figured that if Mizusawa was following through so close to what the rumors said, then...I guess I thought...you might also...is all..."

Taken aback, Midorikawa was only in for more as Shojumaru opened his mouth again, "Well, I mean it's just there was that strange conversation that came up when those manga-ka came as guests... Since then, somehow you've been..."

Uh-oh, he realized it... He scratched his head.

In the midst of his confusion, Midorikawa suddenly came to and looked around him. He pulled Shojumaru into a less-frequented hallway and yelled at him, "I don't care if you're just joking; I don't want to hear you saying things like that! You're just seeing things...I mean, not about me..."

"Okay, I was wrong," Shojumaru blurted out, "I...I like you, Senpai."

His face fell into shadow as he hung his head, and his lowered eyelashes trembled in confusion.

"I...I never meant to dump this on you...but I started to think that maybe...you wouldn't mind so much if I DID."

Please stop. Midorikawa thought to himself. *Somebody, do something about him!*

"I don't like this."

Cut off suddenly by his refusal, Shojumaru looked up with a sorrow-stricken face. Guilt was written all over him.

"Do you hate me?"

No. That's not it...

"Or...do you like me back?"

Feeling suddenly unwanted, he stiffened his arm only to run into Midorikawa's chest. He was standing closer to him than he'd thought.

"...Idiot."

There are certainly plenty of difficult things to be tackled besides work so there's no denying that sometimes there are characters you can't help but tease. But for a junior, it's okay to say you personally favor him. I think he's cute. Actually, I adore him.

So it sucks getting awkward after saying that.

"...Hey, listen."

Oh god, but just what does that makes us?!

"Can I touch you?" Shojumaru asked softly.

"Wh-why would you do that...?!" Midorikawa retorted, grabbing his fingers before they could touch his lips.

His body shivered at the difference between the cold of the wall at his back and the heat of the body pressed against him.

"Just a kiss."

"Just...? What's THAT supposed to mean?"

If he granted him that, then there'd be no going back.

"Please, Senpai...General Daimyoujin...please."

He was begging, his face scrunched up as though he'd start crying any minute.

"...Look at you...make up your mind! Are you trying to make me laugh or make me cry?"

I can't bring myself to laugh at him at all. Midorikawa thought to himself. *After all, I'm the one who should be ashamed here.*

"Midorikawa-san."

The sound of his name, just like that, snapped his wandering mind back to reality and he let out a rough exhale. Listening to the ringing alarm bells going off in his body, he screamed out in his heart for someone to save him and do something about it.

"Shoju...maru."

The words were supposed to be tinged with resentment but instead ran with only the sweetest of compassion. *Now look what you've done to me.*

"I wish you would call me by my real name now."

Gimme a break. Midorikawa scowled at the man who had warmed up to him so.

"It's not like you don't know my name..."

"Oh, stop it!"

Midorikawa glared with all his might.

"B-but why...?" he asked, the corners of his mouth turning down in a pout.

"Because..."

Because then I'd be crossing the boundaries of fiction.

This story is nothing but the result of a wild whim and has absolutely not connection to any people and such from real life. I think...no, I mean, I swear to God.

"I LIGHT FIRES WHERE THERE ARE NONE." CREED OF DIRECTOR: K.W.

Am I gonna get stabbed?

SHOUT OUT LOUD! VOL. 3
Created by Satosumi Takaguchi

ISBN: 1-59816-318-3

First Printing: December 2006
10 9 8 7 6 5 4 3 2 1
Printed in the USA

A YOUNG PRINCE TRAINS FOR BATTLE
BUT INSTEAD LEARNS TO LOVE!

WHEN CHRIS AND ZEKE MEET IN MILITARY SCHOOL, THEY EMBARK ON A LIFE-LONG RELATIONSHIP FRAUGHT WITH DANGER, TREACHERY, AND ABOVE ALL, LOVE.

BLACK KNIGHT IS A SWEEPING ROMANTIC FANTASY EPIC ABOUT THE RELATIONSHIP BETWEEN A DASHING PRINCE AND HIS GUARDSMAN, WITH PLENTY OF SWORD ACTION TO KEEP BOYS' LOVE FANS ENTICED AND ENTHRALLED!

FOR MATURE AUDIENCES ONLY

Price: $9.99
Available in stores July 2006

For information about where to buy BLU MANGA titles, visit www.BLUMANGA.com   © 2003 KAI TSURUGI

Where schoolwork is the last thing you need to worry about...

When Keita is admitted to the prestigous all-boys school Bell Liberty Academy, his life gets turned upside down!

Filled with the hottest cast of male students ever put together, this highly anticipated boys' love series drawn by You Higuri (*Gorgeous Carat*) is finally here!

Liberté! Égalité! Fraternité!...and Love!

Become enraptured by a thrilling and erotic tale of an unlikely pair of lovers during the tumultuous times of the French Revolution. Freed from a high-class brothel, noble-born Jacques becomes a servant in Gerard's house. First seduced by his new master's library, Jacques begins to find himself falling for the man as well...but can their love last in the face of the chaos around them?

stop

blu manga are published in the original japanese format

go to the other side and begin reading